NORTH KOREA

ANONYMOUS COUNTRY

PHOTOGRAPHER | JULIA LEEB
TEXTS | JULIA LEEB, NIKO KARASEK & JR

teNeues

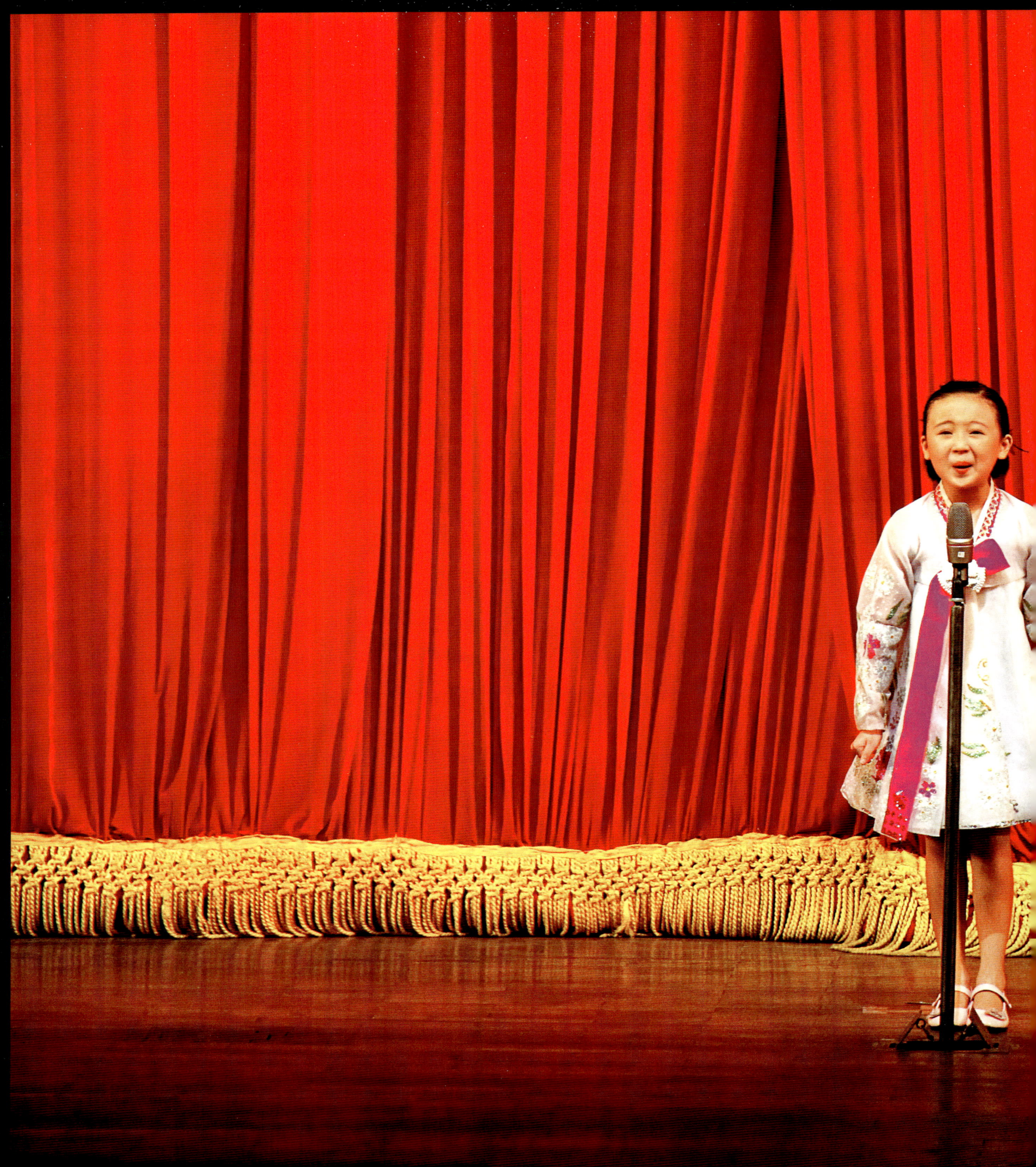

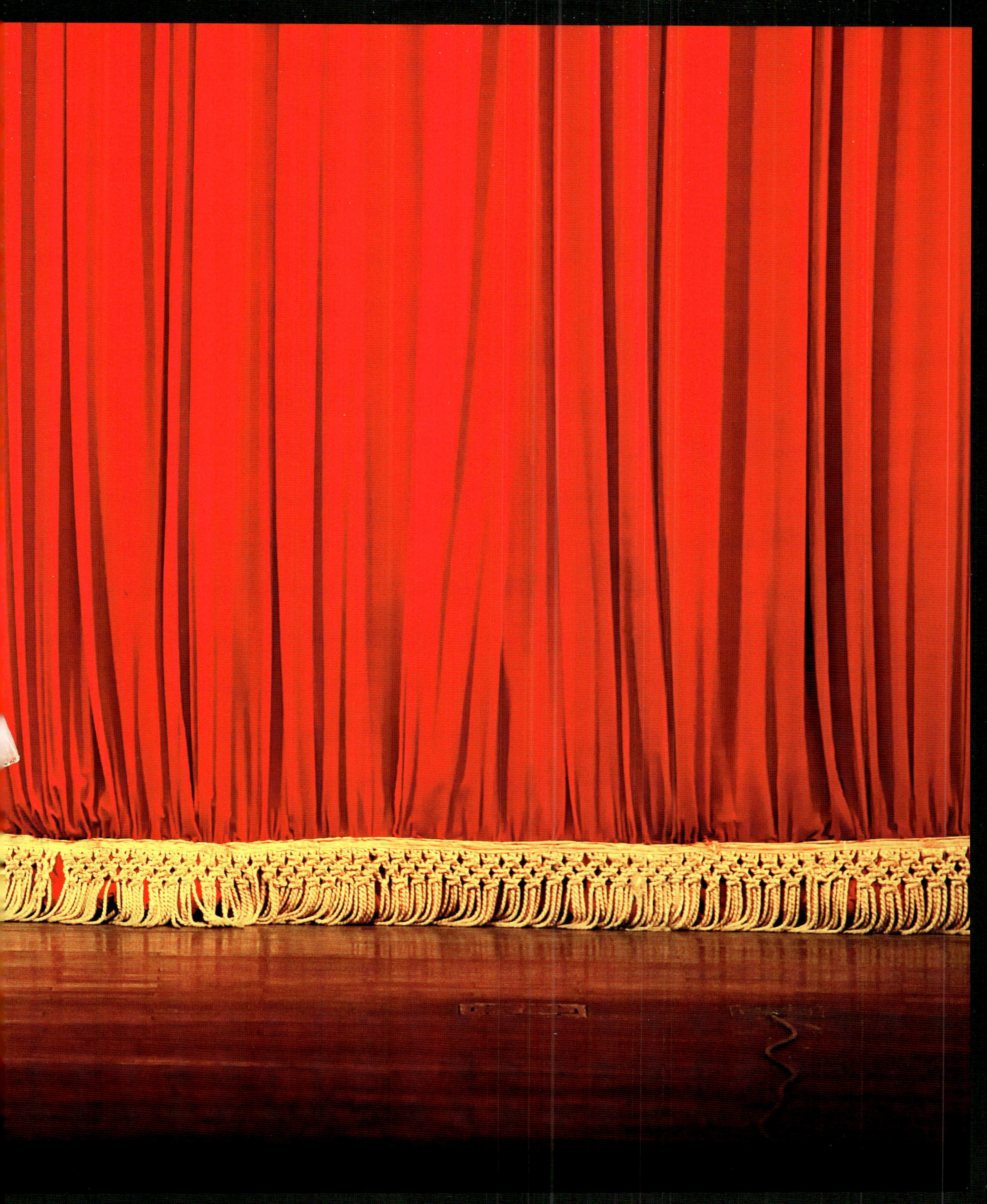

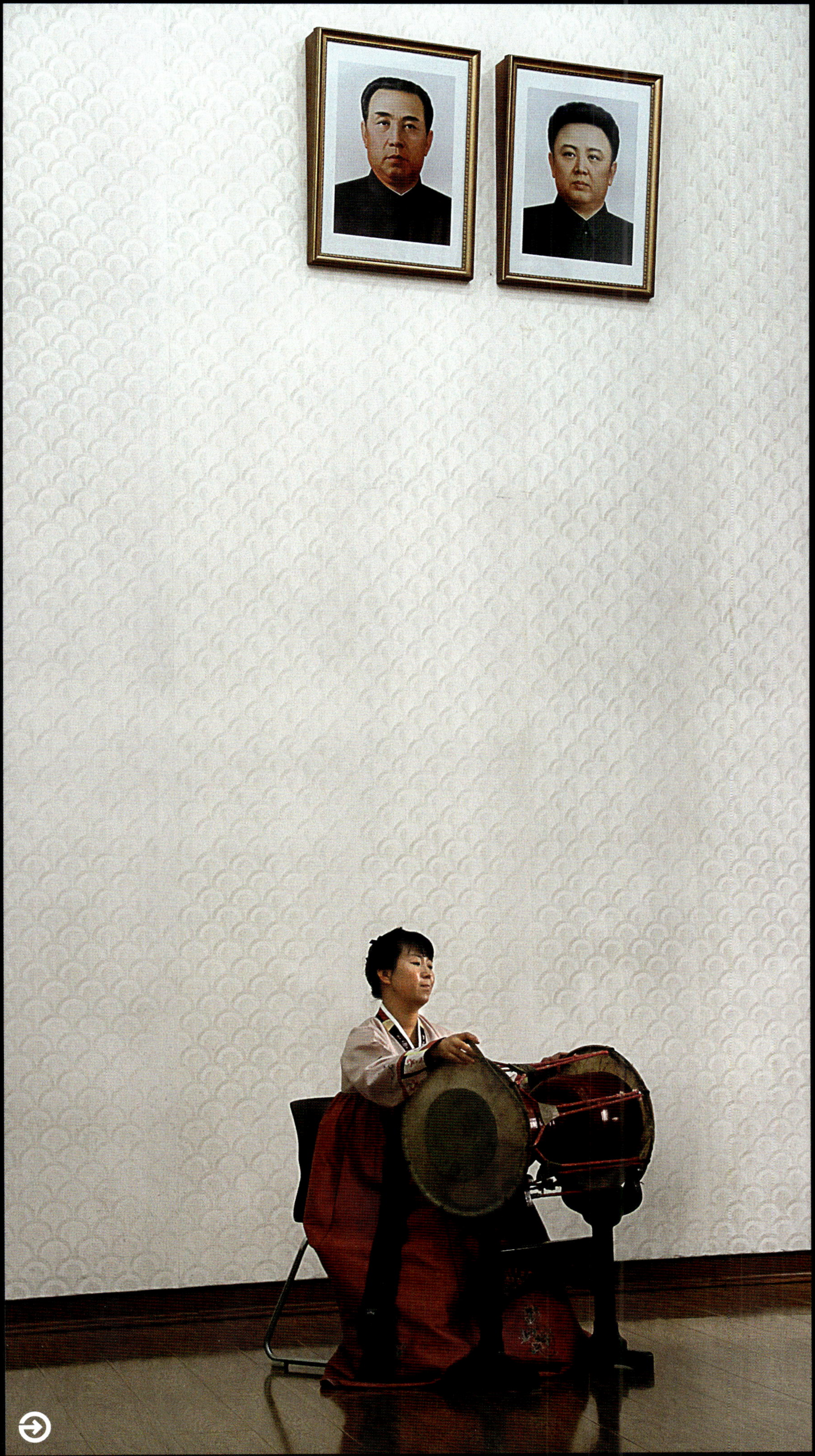

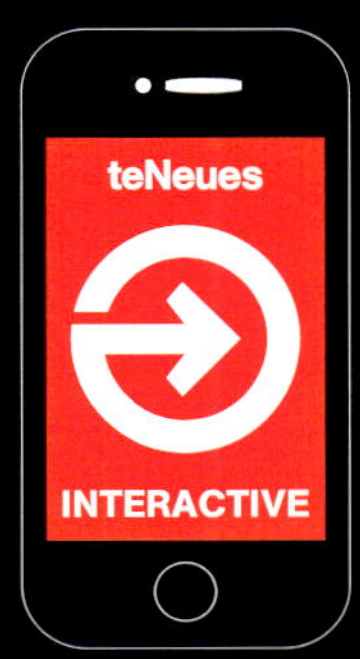

THIS BOOK IS **INTERACTIVE**

After downloading the teNeues Interactive App on your smartphone or tablet, surprising features will appear by scanning the photo on the pages where you find this icon: ➔

Sobald Sie die teNeues Interactive App auf Ihrem Smartphone oder Tablet-Computer installiert haben, starten Sie überraschende Anwendungen, wenn Sie Fotos mit diesem Symbol scannen: ➔

Téléchargez l'application interactive de teNeues sur votre Smartphone ou sur votre tablette. Vous pourrez ainsi accéder à des fonctionnalités surprenantes en flashant les photos accompagnées du symbole suivant : ➔

FOREWORD
VORWORT
PRÉFACE

Niko Karasek

North Korea. The name alone has come to signify a place more remote than Timbuktu or the Amazon Basin. Remote, elusive, shrouded in mystery. A trip to North Korea is like traveling back in time. It feels almost like visiting another planet, one that has no Internet, no contact with the outside world. A place cloaked entirely in darkness if you were to see it at night from outer space. It is the last spot on our digitally-connected planet that you cannot virtually discover on a whim. Not even the world's biggest intelligence organizations know of the happenings in North Korea. The only reports that make their way to the outside are filled with terrible news: threats of war, prison camps, crazy dictators. And yet one thing is clear: North Korea is an unfamiliar land in a world where everything else is connected.

Perhaps it is even the safest destination on earth, where a visitor's every move is tracked and monitored—by government minders and the curious glances of residents, for whom a tourist must seem almost like a visitor from another planet. It is a country where it is imperative not to attract attention; where standing out from the crowd is both unwise and undesirable. The capital of Pyongyang is the perfect model of a socialist city, whose architecture reflects the state ideology and both molds and guides its residents—along grand boulevards, culminating in monuments and sacred buildings that pay homage to the leader. It is a silent city. A metropolis of four million where you won't hear any cars honking, cell phones ringing, or even birds chirping. After decades of living under an iron-fisted dictatorship, even the animals seem to have fallen silent.

Nordkorea. Allein der Begriff wirkt mittlerweile fremder als Timbuktu oder das Amazonasbecken. Abgeschottet. Eigenartig. Unnahbar. Und so ist eine Reise nach Nordkorea auch eine Reise in eine andere Zeit, gefühlt fast schon auf einen anderen Planeten. Einen Planeten ohne Internet, ohne Kontakt zur Außenwelt, einen, der aus dem Weltall beobachtet nachts dunkel ist. Der letzte dunkle Fleck in unserer Welt, die man jederzeit digital bereisen und erkunden kann. Was in Nordkorea vor sich geht, wissen nicht einmal die großen Geheimdienste wirklich. Die einzigen Meldungen, die nach außen dringen, sind Schreckensnachrichten. Über Kriegsdrohungen, Straflager, verrückte Diktatoren. Fest steht: Nordkorea ist das unbekannte Land in einer vollkommen vernetzten Welt.

Vielleicht ist es das sicherste Reiseziel der Erde, wird man doch auf Schritt und Tritt begleitet und überwacht – von staatlichen Aufpassern und den neugierigen Blicken der Bewohner, auf die ein Tourist wohl fast wie ein Außerirdischer wirkt. Dabei besucht man ein Land, in dem man nicht auffallen soll. Nicht auffallen will. Nicht auffallen darf. Pjöngjang, die Hauptstadt, verkörpert eine sozialistische Musterstadt, deren Architektur die Staatsideologie widerspiegelt und ihre Bewohner prägt und lenkt – entlang von Achsen hin zu Monumental- und Sakralbauten zu Ehren der Führer. Es ist eine stille Stadt. Eine Vier-Millionen-Einwohner-Metropole ohne Verkehrshupen, ohne Handyklingeln, ja sogar ohne Vogelgezwitscher. Die Jahrzehnte der eisernen Diktatur scheinen selbst die Tiere mundtot gemacht zu haben.

La Corée du Nord. Le simple nom de ce pays coupé du reste du monde, singulier et inaccessible est devenu plus exotique que celui de Tombouctou ou d'Amazonie. Aussi un voyage en Corée du Nord emmène-t-il le visiteur également dans une autre époque, presque sur une autre planète, une planète sans Internet, ni contact avec le monde extérieur, une planète plongée dans l'obscurité quand on l'observe de l'espace la nuit. C'est la dernière tache sombre à la surface de la Terre, que l'on peut normalement parcourir et explorer à tout moment par les médias numériques. Ce qu'il se passe en Corée du Nord, même les services secrets des grandes puissances ne le savent pas vraiment. Les seules informations qui filtrent sont des nouvelles alarmantes, à savoir des menaces de guerre, des camps d'internement, des dictateurs fous. Une chose est sûre, la Corée du Nord est le dernier pays inconnu dans un monde parfaitement interconnecté.

Peut-être s'agit-il de la destination la plus sûre au monde, car on y est escorté dans ses moindres déplacements et tenu à l'œil par des agents de surveillance de l'État ainsi que par les habitants poussés par la curiosité, auxquels les touristes font l'effet d'extraterrestres. Et ce, alors que l'on visite un pays dans lequel nul ne doit, ne veut, ni n'a le droit de se faire remarquer. Pyongyang, la capitale, est la ville socialiste par excellence. Avec son architecture reflétant l'idéologie d'État, elle modèle les habitants et les conduit le long de grands axes jusqu'à des édifices sacrés monumentaux à la gloire du dirigeant. C'est une ville silencieuse, une métropole de quatre millions d'habitants sans bruits de klaxon, ni sonneries de portable, ni même de gazouillis d'oiseaux. Des décennies d'une dictature de fer semblent avoir frappé de mutisme jusqu'aux animaux.

Yet North Korea is hardly a lifeless land. Indeed, once you get past the unwavering uniformity, the practiced choreography, and the submissive adoration of a dictator, the people you meet are completely normal: anxious mothers, couples in love, young people who are wild about soccer. Life here involves far more than military parades and threats of war, more than totalitarian communism. During the making of this book, photographer Julia Leeb and her travel companions documented contemporary life in this hidden society. The photos paint a portrait of an unknown people. Of course, there are the inevitable misunderstandings. Miscommunication. Things that cannot be expressed. On both sides. And yet the inhabitants of this strange land and their foreign guests find a common basis for understanding. In North Korea, visitors can expect to encounter surprises at every turn. Even if it's that the people living under this uniform military regime can laugh about the same things that we do.

On the surface, North Korea is a functioning country. Everything seems to run smoothly even though very little has actually worked for a long time. After all, North Korea lost the ability to keep pace with its southern neighbor and the world beyond long ago. For more than sixty years, the country has deluded itself with what can sometimes be a rather absurd self-image, so that the nearly infinite amount of deceptions and fables have ultimately become an accepted reality for the nation's twenty-four million inhabitants. Yet this reality does not persist outside the national borders.

With this book, readers are given the rare opportunity to glimpse behind the veil of a place so enigmatic that it seems to exist in a different thread of the space-time continuum. It records moments in the lives of a people in an isolated microcosm. A people who will someday be overtaken by the reality that prevails in the rest of the world. After all, the status quo in this isolated parallel universe cannot last forever. But until that day arrives, travel reports and photographs taken by outsiders are the only way to put a face on the people of North Korea. Not the ever-present portrait of a dictator but the face of a worker, a mother and child, an excited bride. Through these images, North Korea, with all its eccentricities, recreates a moment of normality, if only for an instant.

Dennoch ist Nordkorea kein lebloses Land. Denn hinter der perfekten Uniformität, hinter den einstudierten Choreografien und der demütigen Diktatorenliebe stehen eben doch ganz normale Menschen: fußballvernarrte Jugendliche, sorgenvolle Mütter, verliebte Pärchen. Mehr als nur Militärparaden und Kriegsdrohungen, mehr als Steinzeit-Kommunismus. Während der Entstehungsreise zu diesem Bildband haben die Fotografin Julia Leeb und ihre Begleiterinnen Zeitdokumente einer unsichtbaren Gesellschaft angefertigt. Die Bilder vermitteln einen Eindruck von einem uns unbekannten Volk. Natürlich gibt es Missverständnisse, Unverständnis, Unaussprechliches. Auf beiden Seiten. Und doch entdeckt man auf einer Reise durch dieses fremde Land eine Basis des gegenseitigen Verstehens. In Nordkorea erwartet Besucher minütlich eine Überraschung: Und sei es, dass die Menschen in diesem uniformierten Militärregime über die gleichen Dinge lachen können wie wir.

An der Oberfläche funktioniert Nordkorea. Und zwar angeblich perfekt, obwohl im Land schon lange kaum noch etwas wirklich läuft, denn Nordkorea hat den Anschluss an den südlichen Nachbarn und den Rest der Welt längst verpasst. Man täuscht sich selbst seit mehr als 60 Jahren mit teilweise absurden Illusionen, sodass aus den schier endlosen Täuschungen, Fabeln und Märchen schließlich eine Wahrheit für die 24 Millionen Einwohner geworden ist. Doch diese Wahrheit existiert nicht außerhalb der Landesgrenzen.

Der vorliegende Bildband bietet eine Gelegenheit, die Einzigartigkeit eines Landes kennenzulernen, das in seiner eigenen Zeit- und Raumvorstellung zu leben scheint. Es sind Momentaufnahmen eines Volkes in einem abgeschotteten Mikrokosmos. Eines Volkes, das irgendwann von der weltweit geltenden Realität eingeholt werden wird. Denn der Status Quo dieser isolierten Simultan-Welt kann nicht für die Ewigkeit sein. Doch bis dahin bleiben Reiseberichte und Aufnahmen von Außenstehenden die einzige Möglichkeit, den Menschen im Land ein Gesicht zu geben. Und zwar nicht das allgegenwärtige Portrait eines Diktatoren, sondern das Gesicht eines Arbeiters, einer Mutter mit ihrem Kind, einer aufgeregten Braut. Und dann schafft es selbst Nordkorea in seiner ganzen Skurrilität, für einen Augenblick von dieser Welt zu sein.

La Corée du Nord n'est cependant pas un pays sans vie. Derrière l'uniformité parfaite, derrière les chorégraphies bien rodées et derrière la dévotion qu'ils vouent à leur dictateur, il y a des gens comme vous et moi : des jeunes passionnés de foot, des mères attentionnées, des couples d'amoureux. Il y a davantage que de simples parades militaires et menaces de guerre, plus qu'un communisme sclérosé. Au cours du voyage ayant donné naissance à ce beau livre, la photographe Julia Leeb et ses compagnes de route ont consigné des témoignages historiques d'une société invisible. Leurs photographies nous ouvrent une fenêtre sur ce peuple qui nous est inconnu. Bien sûr, il y a des malentendus, de l'incompréhension et ces choses indicibles, et ce, dans les deux sens. Cependant, à la faveur d'un voyage dans ce pays singulier, on découvre ce qui peut constituer le fondement d'une compréhension mutuelle. En Corée du Nord, une surprise attend le visiteur à chaque minute, ne serait-ce que de constater que, sous ce régime militaire (en) uniforme, les habitants peuvent rire des mêmes choses que nous.

En surface, la Corée du Nord fonctionne, et ce à la perfection, à ce que l'on y prétend. Or depuis longtemps, pratiquement plus rien ne fonctionne vraiment dans ce pays coupé depuis des décennies de ses voisins et du reste du monde. À force de se bercer d'illusions parfois absurdes depuis plus de 60 ans, ses 24 millions d'habitants ont fini par accepter comme étant la vérité un flot quasi intarissable de leurres, de fables et de contes. Mais cette vérité n'a cours qu'à l'intérieur des frontières de ce pays.

Ce beau livre nous emmène à la découverte d'un pays pas comme les autres, qui semble vivre dans sa propre bulle spatiotemporelle. Il présente des instantanés d'un peuple habitant un microcosme coupé du reste du monde et qui sera tôt ou tard rattrapé par la réalité qui existe partout ailleurs, car le statu quo régnant dans ce monde parallèle isolé ne peut pas être éternel. Pour l'heure, les récits de voyage et les photographies émanant de visiteurs étrangers sont la seule possibilité de donner un visage à ce pays, non pas le portrait omniprésent d'un dictateur, mais le visage d'un ouvrier, d'une mère avec son enfant, d'une mariée ivre de joie. Et c'est en cela que même la Corée du Nord réussit, dans toute sa bizarrerie, à être de ce monde pour un instant.

FOREWORD
VORWORT
PRÉFACE

JR

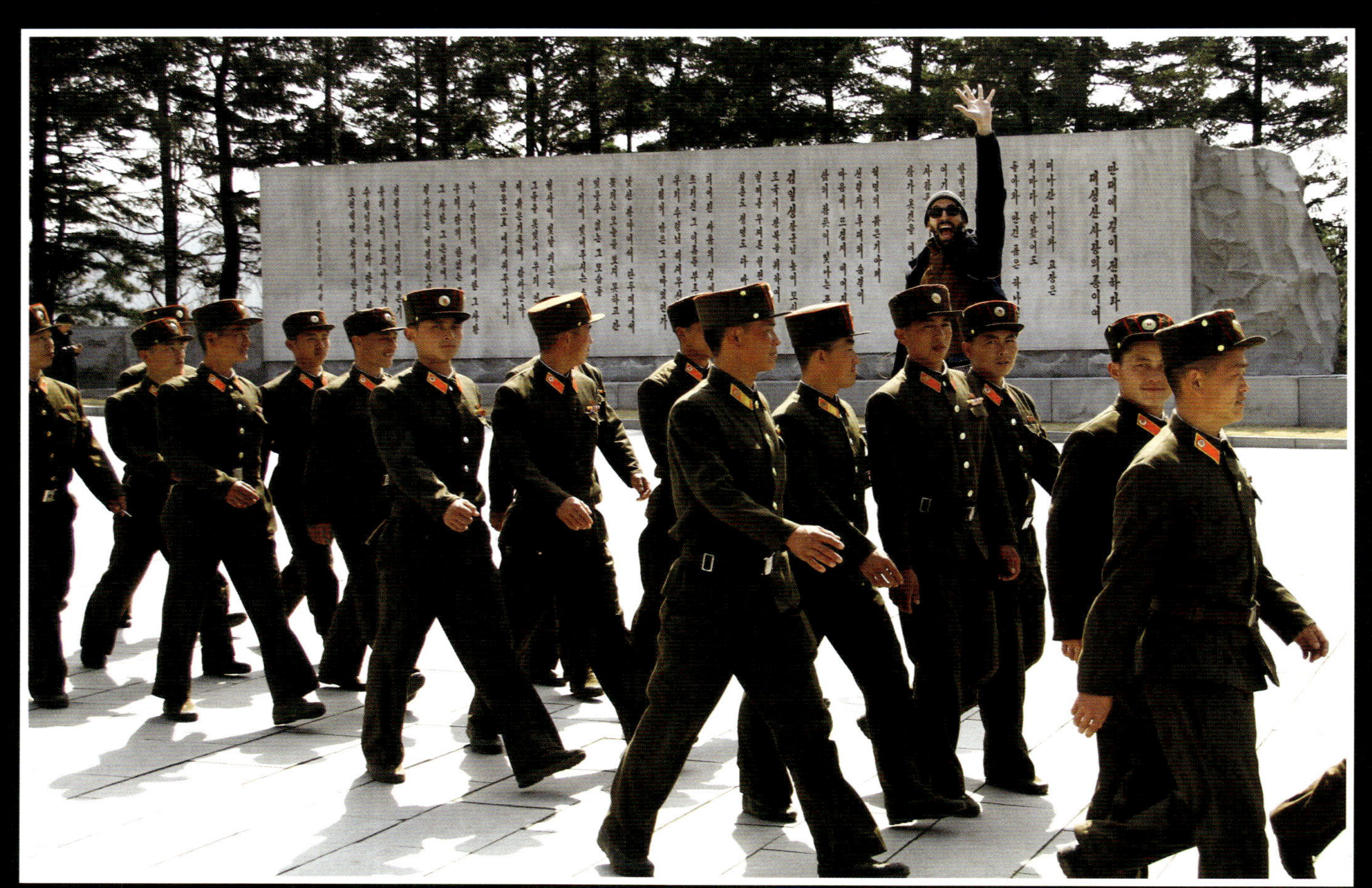

April 2012. It all started out as a joke. In North Korea, they were preparing for the big thing: the commemoration of the Eternal President Kim Il-sung's 100th birthday. For the occasion, they wanted to launch a satellite of some sort.
It was so intriguing. We hear so much about North Korea that I decided I had to see it with my own eyes. I travel around the globe to do massive paintings and exhibitions, but there was no way I would have been able to organize a participative art project in North Korea. So, I took off my sunglasses and my hat and used my real name. I was an anonymous French tourist in an organized tour; the only way to visit the country.
Grey. No art, very few cars, no advertising: The streets of Pyongyang are empty and bleak. No billboards with smiling babies, no attractive women and athletic men, no burgers with tomatoes, cheese, and meat; just propaganda. There are posters, often hand-painted, depicting the people: the soldiers, the leaders, and their favorite flowers. This is when you realize that everywhere else, we are constantly subjected to intense advertising: images trying to sell something.
The whole tourist experience in North Korea is a campaign to the glory of the regime: The guides show you how modern the country is, how their courageous people defeated the "U.S. imperialists" in 1953, and how great the leaders have been for the country. But everything looks fake, be it the two subway stations tourists are authorized to see or the obsolete medical equipment in the hospitals.
Sometimes, in the bus, or whenever I could escape from the group, I would snap images of the streets, of the life of North Koreans, even if we had to play hide-and-seek with the guides in order to take photos. After all, they don't want you to take pictures that wouldn't be "appropriate for the rest of the world to see."
I really understood the significance of the images I took when I shared them on social networks after I left North Korea. The reactions were spectacular: People are very curious about this country, which probably remains the most secretive in the world.
Although I usually work on large-scale installations, the only thing I was able to put up in North Korea was a little sticker with the big eyes of a woman in the lobby of my hotel. She is probably wondering what the future has in store for this country…

April 2012. Alles begann als Spaß. In Nordkorea liefen die Vorbereitungen für das große Ereignis: die Feier zum Gedenken an den 100. Geburtstag des „Ewigen Präsidenten" Kim Il-sung. Es sollte sogar ein Satellit ins All geschossen werden.
Mich hat das einfach fasziniert. Ich musste dieses Land mit eigenen Augen sehen! Ich reise durch die ganze Welt, um riesige Bilder zu malen und Ausstellungen zu planen, aber ein Kunstprojekt in Nordkorea zu organisieren war unmöglich. Deshalb nahm ich Sonnenbrille und Hut ab und verwendete meinen echten Namen. Ich war jetzt ein anonymer französischer Tourist auf einer organisierten Tour; die einzige Möglichkeit, das Land zu besuchen.
Grau. Keine Kunst, sehr wenige Autos, keine Werbung: Die Straßen von Pjöngjang sind leer und düster. Keine Werbeplakate mit lächelnden Babys, attraktiven Frauen, athletischen Männern, keine Burger mit Tomaten, Käse, Fleisch. Nur Propaganda. Auf einigen Postern – oft handgemalt – sind Menschen: Soldaten, die politischen Führer und ihre Lieblingsblumen. Mir wird bewusst, dass wir sonst permanent einer Werbeflut ausgesetzt sind: Bildern, die uns etwas verkaufen wollen.
Alles, was ein geführter Tourist in Nordkorea erlebt, ist eine einzige Propaganda-Kampagne zum Ruhme des Regimes. Die Reiseleiter zeigen dir, wie modern das Land ist, wie die mutigen Bürger die „US-Imperialisten" 1953 besiegt haben und wie viel Gutes die Führer für das Volk getan haben. Aber alles scheint künstlich, seien es die beiden U-Bahn-Stationen, die wir Touristen besichtigen dürfen, oder die veralteten medizinischen Geräte in den Krankenhäusern.
Manchmal, wenn ich mich von der Gruppe entfernen konnte, habe ich Schnappschüsse von den Straßen gemacht, vom Leben der Nordkoreaner, auch wenn ich mich dafür auf ein Versteckspiel mit den Reiseleitern einlassen musste. Schließlich wollten sie nicht, dass man Bilder machte, die „nicht angemessen für die übrige Welt" seien.
Die Bedeutung solcher Fotos wurde mir erst klar, als ich sie, zurück in Frankreich, in sozialen Netzwerken teilte. Die Reaktionen waren spektakulär: Die Menschen sind sehr neugierig auf dieses Land, das für uns vorerst das geheimnisvollste der Welt bleiben wird.
Statt großen Installationen war das Einzige, womit ich mich in Nordkorea verewigen konnte (und zwar in der Lobby meines Hotels), ein kleiner Aufkleber mit den großen Augen einer Frau. Sie fragt sich wahrscheinlich, was die Zukunft diesem Land bringen wird …

Avril 2012. Tout a commencé sur le mode de la plaisanterie. La Corée du Nord se préparait à un grand événement : le centième anniversaire de la naissance du président éternel Kim Il-sung. Pour l'occasion, elle voulait mettre en orbite un satellite.
Cela m'intriguait beaucoup. Comme on entend dire tant de choses sur ce pays, j'ai jugé préférable de m'en rendre compte par moi-même. Je réalise à tour de bras des peintures et des expositions dans le monde entier, mais je ne voyais pas comment organiser une action artistique participative en Corée du Nord. J'ai donc rangé lunettes de soleil et chapeau, et j'ai voyagé sous mon vrai nom. J'étais devenu un touriste français lambda en voyage organisé, la seule manière de visiter ce pays.
Grisaille. Pas d'art, très peu de voitures, pas de publicités : les rues de Pyongyang sont désertes et froides. Pas d'affiches publicitaires montrant des bébés souriants, de jolies femmes et des hommes musclés, ou encore des hamburgers garnis de tomate, de fromage et de viande ; rien que de la propagande. On voit des affiches, souvent peintes à la main, qui représentent les gens : en fait, des militaires et les leaders du pays. Vous réalisez alors que dans tous les autres pays, vous êtes exposés en permanence au matraquage publicitaire.
Le vécu touristique en Corée du Nord se résume à une campagne à la gloire du régime : les guides vous montrent combien leur pays est moderne, comment leur peuple courageux a vaincu les « impérialistes américains » en 1953, et à quel point leurs dirigeants ont œuvré pour le bien du pays. Mais tout semble factice, comme les deux stations de métro ouvertes aux touristes ou le matériel médical obsolète des hôpitaux.
Par la fenêtre de l'autocar ou quand j'arrivais à m'échapper du groupe, déjouant la vigilance des guides, j'ai photographié sur le vif les rues, la vie des Nord-Coréens. En fait, les guides ne veulent pas que vous preniez des photos qu'ils estimeraient « ne pas être bonnes à montrer au reste du monde. »
J'ai véritablement saisi l'importance des images que j'ai prises quand je les ai diffusées sur les réseaux sociaux à mon retour de Corée du Nord. Elles ont trouvé un écho spectaculaire : la curiosité des gens est grande à l'égard de ce pays, qui reste probablement le plus secret au monde.
Moi qui réalise d'habitude des installations monumentales, j'ai dû en Corée du Nord me contenter de coller dans le hall de mon hôtel un petit sticker représentant les grands yeux d'une femme. Celle-ci se demande sans doute ce que l'avenir réserve à ce pays…

ON THE ROAD TO NORTH KOREA

BEHIND THE VEIL OF A HIDDEN SOCIETY

Julia Leeb

The Air Koryo flight lands in North Korea just as a typhoon touches down. We will be spending several equally turbulent weeks in a country that so often makes headlines and yet remains virtually unknown. The nuclear weapon tests conducted by North Korea not only sent out seismic waves to all measuring stations around the globe; they also triggered a political earthquake, and since then, the world has lived in fear of the Democratic People's Republic of Korea. At the end of a long flight, we have finally arrived in North Korea, a nation that has become the latest threat to world peace.

Very few tourists visit this country. And even fewer journalists. Since reporters are very rarely granted permission to enter North Korea, I am touring this isolated nation on a tourist visa. Soldiers who look as though they belong in a long forgotten era stand before the arrivals hall of the international airport, which is about the same size as the gymnasium at my former elementary school. They take a good hard look at me and my two companions before letting us pass. Our trio—architecture student Hemma, sound designer Xenia, and myself, a photojournalist—are the first women's tour group to visit North Korea. It was clear even before we set out on our journey that nothing in this country is anything like the rest of the world. The German Foreign Office advised me to take cash along, since there is no way to draw cash in North Korea and no one accepts credit cards. The entry regulations include an advisory that cell phones, radios, binoculars, TVs, and wireless equipment may not be brought into the country. It is forbidden to import publications that "are hostile toward the North Korean socialist system or damaging to the country's political and cultural development."

Therefore, we will spend the coming days without cell phones or Internet access. We are cut off from the outside world. Our two obligatory minders greet us in excellent German and never leave our side from that point on. Once our tour is over, Yeong-su, the older minder, Joon, the younger one, and even Seung-hyung, our driver, will have to file a report. The three men not only spy on us, they also monitor each other. Before we get out of the car, they tell us not to fold any newspapers, since by doing so we could unwittingly crease a picture of the "Beloved Leader." It is important, they say, to pay one's respects to Kim Il-sung and Kim Jong-il, which means bowing before their statues at the Mansudae Grand Monument and placing flowers at their feet. Will we shed this sense of an unbridgeable gulf between us during the course of our stay? As though Joon can read my mind, he says, "I know that many things here are different than in your country."

First impressions: Pyongyang is clean and there is almost no traffic. The residents are well dressed. No animals are to be seen anywhere. Xenia opens the window of our bus in disbelief to verify that she did indeed hear music playing. It is windy out, but the rain has stopped. The houses seem to be more colorful now. The North Koreans have invested a lot of money in their capital; not only in the Potemkin village-like façades, but also in the colossal architecture of this city of millions. The country was razed to the ground during the Korean War—also known as the Forgotten War—which ended in 1953. Financial aid from other communist states helped rebuild the city according to an idiosyncratic, symmetrical master plan. The large-scale layout of the public spaces and the question of whether architecture has the ability to raise awareness were the reasons why Hemma decided to undertake this journey. Indeed, the huge proportions, the uniform cityscape and the way lines of sight are used leave the architecture student speechless.

Shortly before we set out on our trip, North and South Korea dissolved the armistice agreement between the two countries. North Korea advised the German Embassy to evacuate, since the authorities could no longer guarantee its safety. The country is officially at war. However, without access to the news or the Internet, I keep forgetting about the supposedly imminent nuclear strike over the course of the day. The city's inhabitants goose-step in orchestrated formations in honor of their "Beloved Leader," Kim Jong-il. He was promoted posthumously to "Eternal General Secretary," just as his father, Kim Il-sung—the founder of Juche ideology—has remained the "Eternal President." Therefore, North Korea is de jure governed by two dead statesmen and one living leader—Kim Jong-un.

The sun also shines in North Korea. I look out the bus window where hundreds of people are trekking to their rice paddies for the spring planting. Situated on an island in the Taedong River, our hotel is deserted, even though the official word is that its forty-seven floors are overbooked. I sit in the restaurant, the only patron. In the background, Kim Jong-un is visiting a school on the television. The anchorwoman reports the comrade's wondrous deeds in theatrical tones. The restaurant's daily specials are snake wine and raw fish. What I don't realize is that, instead of killing the fish before consumption, it is merely anesthetized with alcohol. After I've eaten nearly half of its body, and the creature—or whatever is left of it—begins to emerge from its state of comatose intoxication, it begins to thrash about frantically. After this experience, I leave the dog soup untouched. Who knows what surprises lurk in the tureen? In the elevator, I glance at the control panel and quickly figure out where the secret service do their eavesdropping. There is no evidence of a fifth floor. During the night, I seek out this level by way of the employee staircase but have to abort my mission when I run into some security guards.

In the morning, Yeong-su is in a good mood when he greets us. Our tour guides proudly show us North Korea's most prized trophy: the U.S. spy ship USS Pueblo. The North Korean navy captured the enemy reconnaissance vessel in 1968. Its American crew tried to destroy all the classified information but were unable to get rid of everything before their arrest. To secure the prisoners' release, the "U.S. imperialists" (as the Americans are called here) were required to issue an official apology and promise to cease all espionage activities. To date, the USS Pueblo remains the only American naval vessel in foreign hands.

"Always exercise prudence when photographing even the most benign of subjects," warns the German Foreign Office. "It is forbidden to take photos from a moving bus." No one tries to stop me, so I take pictures continuously. And yet the secret service is watching me. The mood in our vehicle shifts. Our minders are phoning around frantically. They whisper unnecessarily. I am a journalist who has entered the country on a tourist visa, a circumstance that can have extremely unpleasant consequences.

As we visit the technology museum, our passports are finally taken away. Later, I learn that the travel agency in Germany is in danger of losing its license. Yeong-su is unable to look me in the eye. Our tour guides back off only when we reach a room with pre-installed microphones. Once again, there is that unbridgeable gulf between us. Both parties put on a brave face and act as though nothing happened. We continue the tour without our passports.
Named after an old Korean folk song, Arirang is a festival involving masses of performers that takes place in the Rungnado May Day Stadium. Thousands of people march in strict formation before the stadium, then abruptly change directions, guided by a signal that no outsider can see. It's as though we are standing on an oversized galley. Close to 100,000 people participate in the spectacle. They form an enormous human mosaic and move in meticulously calculated waves, both of which are like no other anywhere in the world. Mass dances, choreographed with precision, portray the history of North Korea: liberation from Japanese colonialism, the Korean War, and the socialist period. Over and over again, the performances express a yearning for the imminent reunification between North and South Korea. The Arirang Festival is a surreal highlight of everyday life in North Korea, which already has plenty of bizarre moments.

Slightly dazed by the sensory overload, we make our way south. Few cars are to be seen on the enormously wide highway. I grow sleepy from the monotonous sound of tires on asphalt. Our itinerary is relentless. Yeong-su is asleep. What could he be dreaming about? Do North Koreans dream about the same things as people elsewhere? Laborers stand by the roadside in the middle of nowhere and clear away the weeds. No one is watching me for the moment, so I seize the opportunity to take pictures of workers who seem to have missed the industrial age. They use the simplest of tools to patch the deserted roads. North Korea is the last outpost of a once vast communist empire. The world has changed everywhere, just not in this country or for its people. We are in the midst of it all, in our very own "Lives of Others."

The personality cult that exists in the last Stalinist state on earth has banished religion from daily life almost entirely. Although the constitution guarantees freedom of religion, only very few people choose to practice their faith. Kim Jong-il claimed: "Anyone who wants to can go to church, as the constitution protects the freedom of religion. However, the people never attend services because they are free of all cares and worries. They have no need to confess their sins." We stand in the Buddhist Pohyon Temple. A monk is explaining how North Koreans experience religious freedom, but to be on the safe side, he refers to the Buddha by the name of Kim Jong-il. "Our great Leader must prepare the world for peace and friendship."

On the underground—Pyongyang's metro system—the passengers seem to look right through us. It is almost impossible to strike up casual conversations with the locals. Once again, I sense that cultural gulf opening between us. Each of us has formed unsurmountable preconceptions about the other. We pass through palatial subterranean halls with their chandeliers and frescos to the accompaniment of classical music. The stations have grand names such as "Shining Light," "Resurrection," and "Golden Field." Unfortunately, we have to get off the train before we reach "Reunification."

In the evening, we take a side trip to an amusement park, where we mingle with the locals. As they focus on the games and take great pleasure in the cutting-edge carnival rides, they lose the sense that they are being watched. For the moment, I forget that I'm in North Korea. Yeong-su and Joon roar with laughter and behave like children.

On the drive to an agricultural collective, Yeong-su asks me what Westerners think of North Korea. I wonder: What do we even know about these people? Most of us assume that Kim is a first name. We pass a sign saying, "Glory be our excellent party and the leader of our nation, Comrade Kim Jong-un." I try to be diplomatic as I tell him that North Korea doesn't exactly have the best reputation in the West. That it is often depicted as an aggressor. "That's just Western propaganda," he scoffs. "What have we ever done to you? The Americans have stationed 30,000 soldiers in South Korea. Which of us is the one imposing sanctions? Why is it so hard to believe that we are people too?"

"What about the human rights violations, all your political prisoners?" I blurt out. "Is that just propaganda as well?"

The silence stretches until we reach the farming collective. 300 families work together growing produce and raising livestock in this model cooperative. We are told about the time that the "Beloved Leader" visited the farm and inspected a pair of yellow rubber boots, which now occupies a place of honor. They also describe his generosity: a gift of forty TVs and ten tractors for the farmers. The laborers plow the fields to the accompaniment of Korean-style motivational music. Our guides want to give us a tour of a farmhouse. The first three are empty, since all hands are needed in the fields—including the dog's paws, as we learn from a Korean proverb. Finally, we enter a house whose residents are at home. I can tell from the owner's expression that we make him uneasy. Quickly, we inspect the kitchen and tour the nearly unfurnished living room and bedrooms, after which we leave. Still groggy with sleep, the farmer must have found our visit something like the sudden appearance of extraterrestrials.

We spend the night in Sariwŏn, the only guests in the city. Men wearing oversized army hats sit behind the hotel reception desk and look right through us. All the lights in Sariwŏn go out before we've finished eating dinner. Joon is exhausted. He's not supposed to leave us alone, so he stumbles down the dark hallway like a zombie. We feel sorry for him. On the way to our room, he tells us about the mountains and his girlfriend. It's too dark to see his face. Is he smiling?
The water has been turned off. The city is completely cloaked in darkness. A short time later, we hear a crackling noise that at first sounds like radio static. But it turns out to be megaphones broadcasting the Juche ideology, which the inhabitants are supposed to internalize. Propaganda in the dark. The day's indoctrination session begins at five in the morning. A group run early in the morning is the first item on the agenda.

Signs along the way to the border in the Demilitarized Zone depict the tragedy of a divided country from the North Korean point of view. We are the only foreigners.

The situation is extremely tense. "Don't make any trouble," Joon calls out to us in the bus. His dark eyes bore into me for several seconds. Our bus approaches South Korea through a trench many feet deep. Enormous, concrete cylinders are positioned in the way so that enemy tanks can't reach Pyongyang should an emergency situation arise. They are constant reminders of the war, like gaping wounds, in Korean minds. Concrete slabs that resemble sidewalks mark the border. Ever since a fatality occurred here, no one is allowed to cross the military demarcation line. Three blue buildings in Panmunjom straddle the border, half in South Korea and half in North Korea, where the two sides can meet for talks. Each of these barracks contains a brown table and chairs, with a black microphone cable marking the boundary between the two countries. When the delegates meet for negotiations, they can sit at the same table and never leave their own country. Two doors are located behind the rows of seats, one opening to the south and the other to the north. I stand for a few minutes in South Korea, officially a hostile nation. "You once had a border too, isn't that right?" Joon whispers. "Your country was also divided." I nod.

This thin cable divides the last Stalinist stronghold, the world's most isolated nation, from its prosperous, capitalist neighbor. After 1945, the 38th parallel marked the border between the U.S.-occupied South Korea and the Soviet zone in the north. The occupation forces are gone now, but in 1950, the tensions between the divided republics culminated in one of the most brutal wars in military history. Three years and three million casualties later, the proxy war ended without a winner, and the old border was restored. Nearly all of the cities in the north had been reduced to rubble and ashes. North Korea no longer existed. Starving children numbering in the hundreds of thousands wandered through the skeletons of bombed-out houses. For an instant, I grasp the enormity of this catastrophic war. "We are prepared to defend ourselves if they attack," Yeong-su asserts, sounding as though he's trying to convince himself.

A 20-minute drive takes us to our meeting with Major Hwang. He is wearing a uniform cap that is much too big for him, a symbol of power. He looks like a caricature of himself. It seems that he receives few visitors. Big busses never come up here. The Major compliments us on our courage.

"The 38th parallel is the most dangerous border in the world," he says. "Our countries are still at war." Vast minefields serve as buffers between capitalism and communism, between north and south, between brother and sister. Both sides disseminate propaganda. South Korea, for instance, long refused to acknowledge the existence of the wall, even though it is clearly visible through the telescope. Like all other walls in the world, it is far more than its physical structure but has taken root in the minds of the people on both sides. It divides a people of shared heritage into "us" and "them."

For the first time, the TV in our hotel room gets Chinese broadcasts. The Americans are preparing for war with North Korea. The aircraft carriers of the world's mightiest country advance toward the border. Missiles are fired as part of military maneuvers. For me, war is no longer an abstract concept. The wailing of sirens wakes us up in the morning. We have no way to make a phone call. My travel companions are afraid that war has broken out. We eat breakfast in a kind of banquet hall. Yeong-su talks about self-defense. The city's best restaurant serves only powdered milk and individual portions of Austrian jam, which were obviously taken from an airplane. The neatly creased napkin turns out to be a tissue folded in half. Everything is in short supply these days, thanks to the sanctions. As long as they can, the people will continue to improvise and pretend that everything is normal. There are different ways to wage war, I tell myself. War is the answer, I've come to realize. But what then was the question?

While hiking in the Myohyang Mountains, we see North Korea's magnificent natural landscape. Although it's a beautiful day, I'm racked by nerves. I've lied about my profession on the visa application, and the thought is unsettling. By chance, our tour guide Yeong-su and I find ourselves alone; away from the watchful gazes of his comrades, he opens up. He tells me about his children. He is worried that his son is not doing well in school. We stray from the path and discover a bunker in the forest. Frantically, we dash back to the paved track. When Joon rejoins us, we break off our conversation. Joon smiles at me. He has loosened up over the past few days. I think he would like to be friends with us.

Back in the capital, we visit the Children's Palace, an enormous, gray building. A girl declares her love for Kim Jong-il. She leads us down the long corridors of this training ground for the next generation of young cadres. So this is Kim Jong-il's idea of an appropriate building for children, I think. Extracurricular activities include dancing, calligraphy, embroidery, and singing. The boys and girls surprise us with their achievements and precision. "Children are the future," explains the eight-year-old girl, pointing to a picture of flowers. They are magnolias, the Koreans' favorite blossoms, grown specifically for the "Eternal Leaders," and are appropriately named Kim Il Sungia and Kim Jong Ilia.

We go out for an evening of bowling. The North Koreans know how to brew excellent beer. The barriers between us slowly crumble. I'm developing affection for my tour guides—despite their unwavering need to keep a close eye on us. We sit barefoot around a stone table in the balmy summer evening. Our driver has bought some mussels and arranges the black shellfish in a circle on the table. He drenches them in gasoline and sets them on fire. We sit in the beams of the headlights and relish the unexpected delicacy. Even in North Korea, men are in charge of the barbecue. We laugh a lot. Later, Joon enjoys a game of table tennis with Xenia. Seung-hyung, our driver, grins broadly. He gives Hemma a friendly hug. At long last, he is in snake wine heaven.

At dinner, they return our passports without us having to ask for them. What a relief. We can leave the country now. We return to our room and talk even though we know there are hidden microphones. Korea remains a mystery. One people, two countries—one of which has long been forgotten. A people divided by two systems and a vast minefield. What direction will North Korea choose? Will it give in to the market economy or go to war? How long can an entire country live in an isolated time capsule, in a parallel universe? No matter which path the north takes in the end, the country as we know it today will disappear. North Korea, in its present form, has come to the end of the road. Later, I go through my pictures. I think of them as valuable snapshots of a shadow people. The photographs open a window into a society that we cannot begin to imagine. They are like a conversation between the North Korean people and ourselves.

QUO VADIS NORDKOREA?

EINBLICK IN EINE VERBORGENE WELT

Julia Leeb

Zeitgleich mit einem Taifun erreicht die Air Koryo Maschine Nordkorea. Turbulent wird auch unser mehrwöchiger Aufenthalt in einem Land werden, über das man viel redet, aber wenig weiß. Seitdem nordkoreanische Atomtests nicht nur seismische Wellen in sämtlichen Messstationen rund um den Globus auslösten, sondern auch ein politisches Erdbeben verursachten, zittert die Welt vor der Demokratischen Volksrepublik. Nach einer langen Reise sind wir in Nordkorea, dem neuen Ruhestörer des Weltfriedens, gelandet.

Nur sehr wenige Touristen finden den Weg hierher. Noch weniger Journalisten. Da es beinahe unmöglich ist als Journalist eine Einreisegenehmigung zu bekommen, reise ich mit einem Touristenvisum in das abgeschottete Land. Vor der Halle des internationalen Flughafens – sie ist ungefähr so groß wie die Turnhalle meiner ehemaligen Grundschule – stehen Soldaten, die wie aus einer längst vergangenen Zeit wirken. Sie mustern mich und meine zwei Begleiterinnen streng, dann dürfen wir passieren. Wir, das sind die Architekturstudentin Hemma, die Tondesignerin Xenia und ich, die Fotojournalistin: die erste Frauen-Reisegruppe in Nordkorea. Dass in diesem Land so ziemlich alles anders ist als im Rest der Welt, ahnt man schon vor Reiseantritt. Vom Auswärtigen Amt werde ich darauf hingewiesen Bargeld mitzunehmen, da es in Nordkorea weder Möglichkeiten zum Geldabheben noch zur Kreditkartennutzung gibt. Zu den Einreisebestimmungen gehört unter anderem, dass Mobiltelefone, Radio, Ferngläser, Fernseh- und Funkgeräte nicht eingeführt werden dürfen. Es ist verboten Publikationen mitzunehmen, „die dem nordkoreanischen sozialistischen System feindlich gesinnt oder für die politische und kulturelle Entwicklung schädlich sind".

Die nächsten Tage werden wir also ohne Handy und ohne Internet verbringen. Wir sind von der Außenwelt abgeschnitten. In perfektem Deutsch begrüßen uns die zwei obligatorischen Begleiter und weichen von nun an nicht mehr von unserer Seite. Nach der Reise werden Yeong-su, der Ältere, Joon, der Jüngere, und auch der Fahrer Seunghyung Bericht erstatten müssen. Die drei bespitzeln nicht nur uns, sondern überwachen sich auch gegenseitig. Noch im Auto wird uns geraten, keine Zeitungen zu knicken, da ungewollt ein Bild vom „Geliebten Führer" zerknittert werden könnte. Es sei wichtig, Kim Il-sung und Kim Jong-il Ehre zu erweisen, wozu auch das Ablegen eines Blumenstraußes und eine Verbeugung vor den Mansudae-Statuen gehöre. Ob wir dieses Wir-Ihr-Gefühl im Laufe des Aufenthalts ablegen? Als ob Joon Gedanken lesen kann, sagt er: „Ich weiß, bei uns ist vieles anders als bei euch."

Der erste Eindruck: Pjöngjang ist sauber, es gibt kaum Verkehr. Die Einwohner sind sehr ordentlich gekleidet. Wir sehen keine Tiere. Ungläubig öffnet Xenia das Busfenster, um sich zu vergewissern, dass sie in der Tat Musik hört. Draußen ist es windig, aber es regnet nicht mehr. Die Farben der Häuser wirken jetzt noch bunter. In die Hauptstadt wurde viel Geld investiert; nicht nur in die potemkinschen Häuserfassaden, sondern auch in die kolossale Architektur der Millionenstadt. Im Koreakrieg – dem sogenannten Vergessenen Krieg – wurde das Land bis 1953 dem Erdboden gleichgemacht. Mit finanzieller Hilfe der kommunistischen Partner erfolgte dann eine Neugründung der Stadt nach einem eigenwillig symmetrischen Gesamtplan. Die großmaßstäbliche Anlage des öffentlichen Raums und die Frage nach der bewusstseinsbildenden Wirkung von Architektur hatten Hemma dazu bewegt, die Reise anzutreten. Und in der Tat machen die enormen Proportionen, das einheitliche Stadtbild und die Nutzung der Blickachsen die angehende Architektin sprachlos.

Kurz vor unserem Reiseantritt wurde das Waffenstillstandsabkommen zwischen Nord- und Südkorea aufgehoben. Nordkorea hatte der deutschen Botschaft die Evakuierung angeraten, da man nicht mehr für ihre Sicherheit garantieren könne. Offiziell befindet sich das Land im Kriegszustand. Doch ohne Nachrichtenzugang und Internet gerät der angeblich drohende Atomschlag im Laufe des Tages immer wieder in Vergessenheit. Orchestriert marschieren die Stadtbewohner im Stechschritt, um dem „Geliebten Führer" Kim Jong-il zu huldigen. Posthum wurde er zum „Ewigen Generalsekretär" erhoben, so wie sein Vater Kim Il-sung – Erfinder der Juche-Ideologie – der „Ewige Präsident" bleibt. De jure wird Nordkorea also von zwei toten Staatsmännern und einem lebendigen – Kim Jong-un – regiert.

Die Sonne scheint auch in Nordkorea. Ich schaue aus dem Busfenster. Hunderte Menschen marschieren zur Reissaat. Im Hotel, auf einer Insel im Taedong-Fluss, herrscht trotz offizieller Überbuchung der 47 Stockwerke gähnende Leere. Im Restaurant bin ich der einzige Gast. Der Fernseher läuft im Hintergrund. Kim Jong-un besucht gerade eine Schule. Theatralisch verkündet die Ansagerin neue Wundertaten des Genossen. Spezialität des Tages sind Schlangenschnaps und roher Fisch. Was ich nicht weiß, ist, dass der Fisch vor dem Verzehr nicht getötet, sondern lediglich mit Alkohol betäubt wurde. Nach dem die Hälfte seines Körpers verspeist und das Tier – oder was von ihm übrig blieb – aus seinem komatösen Rausch erwacht ist, beginnt es hektisch zu zappeln. Die Hundesuppe bleibt daraufhin unberührt. Wer weiß, was für Überraschungen in diesem Topf warten. Im Lift reicht ein Blick auf die Aufzugtafel und man begreift, wo das Abhörgeschoss liegt. Die Anzeige für den fünften Stock fehlt. Ein nächtlicher Versuch, diese Etage über die Angestelltentreppe zu erreichen, scheitert an dem plötzlich auftauchenden Sicherheitspersonal.

Am nächsten Morgen begrüßt uns Yeong-su gut gelaunt. Stolz wird meine Reisegruppe zur Prestigetrophäe der Nordkoreaner gefahren, dem US-Spionageschiff USS-Pueblo. 1968 kaperte die nordkoreanische Marine das feindliche Aufklärungsschiff. Die amerikanische Besatzung versuchte noch geheime Informationen zu vernichten, konnte aber nicht alles zerstören, bevor sie verhaftet wurde. Um die Gefangenen frei zu bekommen, mussten sich die „US-Imperialisten" (so werden Amerikaner hier genannt) offiziell entschuldigen und zusichern keine weitere Spionage zu betreiben. Bis heute ist die USS-Pueblo das einzige Schiff der US-Marine, das sich in fremden Händen befindet.

„Beim Fotografieren auch harmloser Motive sollte stets umsichtig vorgegangen werden. Fotos aus dem fahrenden Bus sind verboten", warnt das Auswärtige Amt. Da mich niemand hindert, fotografiere ich unaufhörlich. Doch ich werde vom Geheimdienst beobachtet. Die Stimmung in unserem Fahrzeug kippt. Hektisch telefonieren unsere Begleiter hin und her. Überflüssigerweise flüstern sie. Dass ich als Journalistin mit einem Touristenvisum eingereist bin, kann sehr unangenehme Konsequenzen haben. Im Technikmuseum werden uns schließlich die Pässe abgenommen. Später erfahre ich, dass dem Reisebüro in Deutschland der Lizenzentzug droht. Yeong-su kann mir nicht mehr in die Augen schauen. Nur wenn Mikrofone in der Einrichtung installiert sind, lassen unsere Reiseleiter von uns ab. Sie und Wir. Beide Parteien machen gute Miene zum bösen Spiel und schweigen die Situation tot. Das Programm geht auch ohne Pass weiter.

Im Rungnado May Day Stadion findet das Massenspektakel Arirang statt, benannt nach einem alten koreanischen Volkslied. Vor dem Stadion marschieren Tausende von Menschen. Schlagartig ändern die Kohorten ihre Richtung, gelenkt durch für Außenstehende unsichtbare Signale. Wir fühlen uns wie auf einer überdimensionalen Galeere. An der Veranstaltung wirken etwa 100 000 Personen mit. Das voluminöse Menschenmosaik und die minutiös kalkulierten Wellenbewegungen sind weltweit einzigartig. In präzise choreografierten Massentänzen wird die Geschichte Nordkoreas dargestellt: die Befreiung vom japanischen Kolonialismus, der Koreakrieg und die Zeit des Sozialismus. Immer wieder wird die Sehnsucht nach der baldigen Wiedervereinigung von Nord und Süd ausgedrückt. Die Gigashow Arirang ist surrealer Höhepunkt der ohnehin bizarren Realität Nordkoreas.

Etwas benommen von dieser Reizüberflutung machen wir uns auf den Weg Richtung Süden. Auf einer immens breiten Autobahn sehen wir kaum Fahrzeuge. Das monotone Geräusch der Reifen macht schläfrig. Überhaupt ist unser Programm sehr anstrengend. Yeong-su schläft. Was er wohl träumt? Träumen Nordkoreaner anders als der Rest der Welt? An den Straßenrändern stehen Menschen, die mitten im Nichts Unkraut jäten. In einem unbeobachteten Augenblick gelingt es mir, Arbeiter zu fotografieren, an denen die Industrialisierung unbemerkt vorbeigezogen ist. Mit einfachsten Mitteln flicken sie die verwaisten Straßen. Der große Kommunismus ist bis auf Nordkorea geschrumpft. Die ganze Welt hat sich verändert, dieses Land und sein Volk nicht. Und wir sind mittendrin, im Leben der Anderen.

Im letzten stalinistischen Staat hat der Personenkult die Religion fast ganz aus dem Alltag vertrieben. Laut Verfassung herrscht Religionsfreiheit, doch das fehlende Interesse an deren Ausübung erklärte Kim Jong-il so: „Jeder kann zwar nach Belieben die Kirche besuchen, weil wir Religionsfreiheit haben, wie es in der Verfassung festgelegt ist; aber die Menschen suchen sie nicht auf, weil sie von jeder Art Kummer und Sorgen frei sind und auch nichts zu beichten haben." Wir sind im buddhistischen Pohyon-Tempel. Ein Mönch erzählt von gelebter Religionsfreiheit. Vorsichtshalber hat er den Buddha jedoch Kim Jong-il getauft. „Der große Führer muss die Welt auf Frieden und Freundschaft vorbereiten."

Im Untergrund – der U-Bahn Pjöngjangs – scheinen die Passanten durch uns hindurchzusehen. Einen ungezwungenen Kontakt zu Einheimischen aufzubauen ist schier unmöglich. Da empfinde ich es wieder, dieses Wir-Ihr-Gefühl. Die Vorurteile auf beiden Seiten sind wohl grenzenlos. Zu klassischer Musik durchschreiten wir die mit Kronleuchtern und Fresken ausgestatteten unterirdischen Paläste. Die Stationen tragen große Namen wie „Blühendes Licht", „Wiederauferstehung" und „Goldenes Feld". Bevor wir die „Vereinigung" erreichen, müssen wir leider aussteigen.
Abends unternehmen wir einen Abstecher in den Vergnügungspark. Hier kommt man den Einheimischen ganz nah. Während sie sich auf die Spiele konzentrieren und die hypermodernen Fahrgeschäfte in vollen Zügen genießen, fühlen sie sich unbeobachtet. Für einen Moment vergesse ich, dass ich in Nordkorea bin. Yeong-su und Joon lachen lauthals. Sie benehmen sich wie Kinder.

Auf der Fahrt zu einer landwirtschaftlichen Produktionsgenossenschaft fragt mich Yeong-su, was man im Westen über Nordkorea denkt. Was wissen wir schon über dieses Volk, denke ich mir. Die meisten glauben ja auch, dass Kim ein Vorname ist. Wir passieren einen Schriftzug, auf dem steht: „Gepriesen sei unsere allerbeste Partei und der Volksführer, Genosse Kim Jong-un". Mit viel Schönmalerei gebe ich Yeong-su zu erkennen, dass Nordkorea nicht den besten Ruf hat und oft als Aggressor dargestellt wird. „Alles westliche Propaganda", antwortet er bestürzt. „Was tun wir euch? In Südkorea sind 30 000 amerikanische Soldaten stationiert. Wer verhängt denn die Sanktionen? Warum ist es so schwer zu akzeptieren, dass auch wir Menschen sind?" „Und was ist mit den Menschenrechtsverletzungen, mit all den politischen Gefangenen? Ist das auch nur Propaganda?", rutscht es mir heraus.

Nach längerem Schweigen erreichen wir die bäuerliche Einrichtung. In der Vorzeigekooperative betreiben 300 Haushalte zusammen Ackerbau und Viehzucht. Wir erfahren, wann der „Geliebte Führer" zu Besuch war, und dass er sich die gelben Gummistiefel ansah, die nun einen Ehrenplatz haben. Außerdem hört man von seiner Großzügigkeit: 40 Fernseher und zehn Traktoren für die Bauern. Zu koreanischer Motivationsmusik pflügen die Arbeiter die Felder. Unsere Begleiter wollen uns ein Bauernhaus von innen zeigen. Die ersten drei sind leer, da jede Hand auf dem Feld gebraucht wird; sogar die Pfoten der Hunde, wie uns ein koreanisches Sprichwort lehrt. Endlich betreten wir ein belebtes Haus. Dem Gesichtsausdruck des Hausherrn nach zu schließen sind wir ihm nicht ganz geheuer. Schnell begutachten wir die Küche, das möbelfreie Wohn- und Schlafzimmer; dann sind wir wieder weg. Für den aus dem Schlaf gerissenen Bauern muss es wie eine Stippvisite von Außerirdischen gewirkt haben.

Die Nacht verbringen wir in Sariwŏn. Außer uns sind keine Gäste in der Stadt. Männer mit übergroßen Militärmützen sitzen an der Rezeption des Hotels und schauen durch uns hindurch. Noch während wir zu Abend essen, verlöscht das Licht in ganz Sariwŏn. Joon ist sehr müde. Da er uns nicht alleine lassen darf, läuft er wie ein Untoter durch den finsteren Gang. Wir geben nach. Auf dem Weg ins Zimmer erzählt er uns von den Bergen und von seiner Freundin. Im Dunkeln kann ich sein Gesicht nicht sehen. Lächelt er?
Das Wasser wurde abgestellt. Die Stadt liegt in absoluter Finsternis. Kurz darauf hören wir ein Rauschen, das anfangs wie ein kaputtes Radio klingt. Schließlich wird den Einwohnern mit Megafonen die Juche-Ideologie verinnerlicht. Propaganda im Dunkeln. Ab fünf Uhr morgens beginnt die Indoktrination des Tages. Kollektives Früh-Joggen ist der erste Tagesordnungspunkt.

Auf dem Weg zur Grenze in der demilitarisierten Zone wird die Tragödie der Teilung aus nordkoreanischer Sicht geschildert. Wir sind die einzigen Ausländer. Die Lage ist extrem angespannt. „Macht keinen Ärger!", ruft Joon in den Bus. Für einige Sekunden durchbohren mich seine dunklen Augen. Durch einen meterhohen Graben fahren wir Richtung Südkorea. Große Betonwalzen sollen im Ernstfall feindlichen Panzern den Weg nach Pjöngjang versperren. Wie ein klaffender Riss schmerzen die Kriegserinnerungen im Gedächtnis der Koreaner. Bürgersteigähnliche Betoneinlassungen markieren die Grenze. Seit einem tödlichen Vorfall ist es nicht mehr gestattet, die Demarkationslinie zu überschreiten. Um sich für Gespräche zu treffen, wurden in Panmunjeom drei blaue Grenzhäuschen je zur Hälfte auf nord- und südkoreanischem Boden gebaut. Im Inneren einer solchen Baracke steht ein brauner Tisch mit Stühlen.

Ein schwarzes Mikrofonkabel markiert den Grenzverlauf. Bei Verhandlungen können sich so die Fraktionen an einen Tisch setzen und trotzdem in ihrem eigenen Land bleiben. Hinter den Sitzreihen öffnet sich je eine Tür nach Süd- und eine nach Nordkorea. Für ein paar Minuten betrete ich das offizielle Feindesland Südkorea. Joon flüstert: „Ihr hattet auch eine Grenze, nicht wahr? Euer Land war auch entzweit." Ich nicke.

Dieses dünne Kabel trennt den letzten stalinistischen, den isoliertesten Staat der Welt vom kapitalistisch boomenden Nachbarland. Der 38. Breitengrad markierte ab 1945 den Grenzverlauf zwischen dem von Amerikanern besetzten Südkorea und der sowjetischen Zone im Norden. Die Besatzungstruppen zogen ab. Doch die Spannungen zwischen den beiden Teilrepubliken mündeten 1950 in einem der brutalsten Kriege der Militärgeschichte. Drei Jahre und drei Millionen Tote später endete der Stellvertreterkrieg ergebnislos. Die alte Grenze wurde die neue. Fast alle nordkoreanischen Städte lagen in Schutt und Asche. Nordkorea existierte nicht mehr. Hunderttausend hungernde Waisenkinder zogen durch die Skelette der ausgebombten Häuser. Für einen kurzen Moment ist das Ausmaß dieses alles vernichtenden Krieges zu ahnen. „Wenn wir angegriffen werden, sind wir bereit, uns zu verteidigen", sagt Yeong-su so laut, als wolle er sich selbst Mut machen.

Nach einer zwanzigminütigen Fahrt treffen wir Major Hwang. Als Insigne der Macht trägt er eine viel zu große Generalsmütze. Er sieht aus wie seine eigene Karikatur. Oft scheint er nicht Besuch zu empfangen, denn große Busse kommen hier nicht herauf. Er gratuliert uns zu unserem Mut. „Der 38. Breitengrad ist die gefährlichste Grenze der Welt; die Länder sind immer noch im Krieg", sagt er. Riesige Minenfelder dienen als Pufferzone zwischen Kapitalismus und Kommunismus, zwischen Nord und Süd, zwischen Bruder und Schwester. Beide Seiten betreiben Propaganda. Südkorea zum Beispiel negierte jahrelang die Existenz der Mauer, doch ein Blick durch das Fernrohr genügt. Wir sehen sie. Und wie alle Mauern dieser Welt endet sie nicht mit dem Mauerwerk. Sie hat sich in den Köpfen der Menschen auf beiden Seiten manifestiert, teilt das Brudervolk in Wir und Ihr.

Im Hotelzimmer gibt es zum ersten Mal chinesisches Fernsehen. Kriegsvorbereitungen Amerikas gegen Nordkorea werden gezeigt. Die Flugzeugträger des mächtigsten Landes der Welt rücken vor. Im Rahmen der Militärmanöver werden Raketen abgefeuert. Das Wort Krieg verliert an Abstraktheit. Morgens werden wir durch Sirenengeheul geweckt. Es gibt keine Möglichkeit zu telefonieren. Meine Begleiterinnen fürchten, der Krieg sei ausgebrochen. In einer Art Ballsaal sitzen wir beim Frühstück. Yeong-su spricht von Selbstverteidigung. Im besten Restaurant der Stadt gibt es statt Milch nur Milchpulver; Einzelportionen von österreichischer Marmelade wurden offensichtlich aus dem Flugzeug mitgenommen und die akkurat gefaltete Serviette entpuppt sich als halbiertes Papiertaschentuch. Durch die Sanktionen fehlt es in der Zwischenzeit an allem. Improvisieren und Normalität vorspielen, solange es geht, heißt die Devise. Es gibt verschiedene Arten Kriege zu führen, denke ich mir. Krieg ist die Antwort, das habe ich nun verstanden, doch wie war eigentlich die Frage?

Bei einer Wanderung im Myohyang-Gebirge sehen wir die grandiose Natur Nordkoreas. Es ist ein wunderschöner Tag, doch ich bin nervös. Auf dem Visumsbogen habe ich einen falschen Beruf angegeben. Der Gedanke daran macht mich unruhig. In einem unbeobachteten Moment – durch einen Zufall sind wir nur zu zweit – öffnet sich Reiseleiter Yeong-su. Er erzählt mir von seinen Kindern. Die schulischen Leistungen seines Sohnes bereiten ihm Sorgen. Von der Route abgekommen, stehen wir vor einem Bunker im Wald. Hektisch traben wir wieder zum asphaltierten Weg zurück.
Als Joon wiederkommt, reißt das Gespräch abrupt ab. Joon lacht mich an. In den letzten Tagen ist er immer offener geworden. Ich glaube, er wäre auch gerne unser Freund.

Zurück in der Hauptstadt besuchen wir den Kinderpalast, einen grauen Kolossalbau. Ein Mädchen beteuert ihre Liebe zu Kim Jong-il. Über lange Gänge führt sie uns durch die Kaderschmiede der Nachwuchstalente. So stellte sich Kim Jong-il also ein kindgerechtes Gebäude vor, denke ich. Die außerschulischen Aktivitäten beinhalten Tanz, Kalligrafie, Sticken und Singen. Die Leistung und Präzision der Mädchen und Jungen überrascht uns. „Kinder sind die Zukunft", erklärt mir die Achtjährige, während sie auf ein Blumenbild zeigt. Es sind die Lieblingsblumen der Koreaner: Magnolien, eigens für die „Ewigen Führer" gezüchtet. Sie heißen – wie könnte es auch anders sein – Kim Il Sungia und Kim Jong Ilia.

Am Abend gehen wir kegeln. Nordkoreanisches Bier schmeckt gut. Die Barrikaden fallen langsam. Ich beginne, meine Reiseleiter – trotz ihres ausgeprägten Kontrollzwangs – zu mögen. Barfuß setzen wir uns an dem lauen Sommerabend um eine Steinplatte. Unser Fahrer hat Muscheln besorgt. Kreisförmig ordnet er die schwarzen Meeresfrüchte auf der Platte, übergießt sie mit Benzin und zündet sie an. In den Lichtkegeln der Autoscheinwerfer genießen wir die unerwartete Köstlichkeit. Grillen ist auch in Nordkorea Männersache. Wir lachen viel. Später spielt Joon amüsiert Tischtennis mit Xenia. Seung-hyung, der Fahrer, strahlt über das ganze Gesicht. Freundschaftlich umarmt er Hemma. Jetzt befindet er sich endgültig im Schlangenschnapshimmel.

Beim Abendessen bekommen wir unaufgefordert unsere Pässe zurück. Erleichterung: Wir können ausreisen. Auf unseren Zimmern diskutieren wir trotz der versteckten Mikrofone. Korea bleibt ein Mysterium. Ein Volk mit zwei Ländern, von denen eines lange vergessen war. Ein Volk, das durch zwei Systeme und ein endloses Minenfeld getrennt ist.
Wohin wird sich Nordkorea bewegen? Wird es vor der Marktwirtschaft kapitulieren oder in den Krieg ziehen? Wie lange kann ein Land in einer isolierten Zeitkapsel, in einem Paralleluniversum leben? Welche Richtung der Norden auch einschlagen wird – so wie wir ihn jetzt kennen, wird er verschwinden. Die Zeit für Nordkorea in dieser Form ist abgelaufen. Später schaue ich meine Bilder an. Sie erscheinen mir wie wertvolle Momentaufnahmen eines Schattenvolkes. Die Fotografien öffnen ein Fenster zu einer Gesellschaft, die wir uns nicht vorstellen können; sie sind eine Art Konversation zwischen den Nordkoreanern und uns.

QUO VADIS CORÉE DU NORD ?

FENÊTRE OUVERTE SUR UN MONDE DISSIMULÉ AUX REGARDS

Julia Leeb

L'avion d'Air Koryo arrive en Corée du Nord en même temps qu'un typhon. Des turbulences marqueront aussi notre séjour de plusieurs semaines dans un pays dont on parle beaucoup mais dont on sait peu de choses. Depuis que des essais nucléaires nord-coréens ont déclenché des ondes sismiques enregistrées dans toutes les stations sismologiques du globe mais aussi un séisme politique, le monde tremble devant cette République populaire démocratique. Au terme d'un long voyage, nous atterrissons en Corée du Nord, le nouveau perturbateur de la paix mondiale.

Si les touristes qui s'aventurent jusqu'ici sont rares, les journalistes le sont encore plus, car il leur est presque impossible d'entrer dans ce pays coupé du monde. Devant les bâtiments de l'aéroport international – qui sont à peu près de la taille du gymnase de mon ancienne école primaire – des soldats semblant appartenir à une époque révolue montent la garde. Après un contrôle approfondi, ils nous laissent passer. Nous, c'est-à-dire Hemma, étudiante en architecture, Xenia, ingénieure du son, et moi-même, qui suis photojournaliste. Nous sommes le premier groupe de touristes féminin en Corée du Nord. Avant même de partir, nous nous doutions que presque rien dans ce pays n'est comme ailleurs. Le ministère allemand des Affaires étrangères nous a signalé qu'il faut emporter suffisamment de devises en liquide, parce que la Corée du Nord n'est pas équipée de distributeurs automatiques de billets et que les cartes de crédit ne sont pas utilisables dans le pays. Il est par ailleurs interdit d'introduire des téléphones cellulaires, des postes de radio, des jumelles, des téléviseurs et des postes émetteurs-récepteurs, de même que des publications « hostiles au système socialiste ou nuisibles au développement politique et culturel. »

Nous vivrons donc pendant les jours à venir sans téléphone portable, ni Internet. Dans un allemand impeccable, les deux guides obligatoires nous accueillent. Ils ne nous quitteront plus d'une semelle de tout le séjour. Une fois le voyage terminé, Yeong-su, le plus âgé, et Joon, le plus jeune, ainsi que Seung-hyung, le chauffeur, feront un compte-rendu. Les trois hommes ont pour mission de nous espionner, mais aussi de se surveiller mutuellement. D'emblée, on nous conseille de ne pas plier les journaux pour éviter de froisser par inadvertance une photo du « cher dirigeant ». Il est en effet important de rendre hommage à Kim Il-sung, mais aussi à Kim Jong-il, notamment en déposant des fleurs au pied des statues de Mansudae et en s'inclinant devant elles. Surmonterons-nous cette impression d'opposition entre eux et nous ? Comme s'il pouvait lire dans nos pensées, Joon dit : « Je sais que chez nous il y a beaucoup de choses qui ne sont pas comme chez vous. »

Notre première impression de Pyongyang est celle d'une ville propre, pratiquement sans circulation, aux habitants en tenues soignées et où l'on n'aperçoit aucun animal. Incrédule, Xenia fait coulisser la vitre du minibus pour s'assurer qu'elle a bien entendu de la musique. Dehors, le vent souffle mais la pluie a cessé. Et les maisons semblent d'autant plus colorées. Beaucoup d'argent a été investi dans la capitale, et ce pas uniquement dans les façades Potemkine, mais aussi dans l'architecture colossale de cette métropole de plusieurs millions d'habitants. Pendant la guerre de Corée, qui a duré jusqu'en 1953, le pays a été rasé. Avec le soutien financier des pays communistes alliés, la ville a été reconstruite de zéro, selon un plan d'une symétrie très particulière. Hemma voulait se rendre compte par elle-même de la structuration des espaces publics sur une grande échelle et du rôle de l'architecture dans la formation des consciences. Et une fois sur place, la future architecte reste sans voix à la vue des proportions énormes, du paysage urbain uniforme et de l'exploitation qui est faite des perspectives urbanistiques.

Peu avant notre voyage, l'accord d'armistice intercoréen avait été rompu. Aussi la Corée du Nord avait-elle conseillé à l'ambassade d'Allemagne de procéder à son évacuation car sa sécurité ne pouvait plus été garantie. Officiellement, le pays est en état de guerre. Cependant, sans accès à l'information ni possibilité de communiquer par Internet, la frappe nucléaire prétendument imminente tombe toujours dans l'oubli au fil de la journée. De manière parfaitement orchestrée, les habitants de Pyongyang défilent au pas de l'oie pour rendre hommage à leur « cher dirigeant » Kim Jong-il, proclamé à titre posthume « secrétaire général éternel » du parti du Travail, tout comme son père Kim Il-sung – père de la doctrine du Juche –, qui demeure « président éternel ». D'un point de vue juridique, la Corée du Nord est gouvernée par trois chefs d'État, deux défunts et un vivant, Kim Jong-un.

Le soleil brille également en Corée du Nord. Des centaines de gens se rendent aux rizières à pied pour les semis. L'hôtel, dont les 47 étages sont officiellement surbookés, est absolument désert. Je suis d'ailleurs la seule cliente du restaurant. À la télévision, on voit Kim Jong-un en visite dans une école. La présentatrice annonce de nouveaux miracles du camarade. La spécialité du jour est du poisson cru à l'alcool de serpent. Le poisson n'a pas été tué avant d'être apprêté, mais simplement anesthésié avec l'alcool. Une fois la moitié de son corps dégustée, la moitié restante sort de son coma éthylique et se met à frétiller vigoureusement. Du coup, je ne touche pas au plat suivant, la soupe de chien. Qui sait ce que cette marmite réserve comme surprises. Dans l'ascenseur, un bouton manquant, celui du cinquième, trahit l'étage des tables d'écoute. Une tentative nocturne pour gagner cet étage par l'escalier de service est déjouée par l'irruption d'agents de sécurité.

Le lendemain matin, Yeong-su nous salue d'un air jovial et nous conduit fièrement au trophée de prestige des Coréens du Nord, le bateau espion américain Pueblo. En 1968, la marine nord-coréenne avait arraisonné ce navire de reconnaissance ennemi. Pour obtenir la libération des prisonniers, les « impérialistes américains » (comme on appelle les Américains dans ce pays) ont dû présenter des excuses officielles et s'engager à arrêter leurs activités d'espionnage.

Selon les mises en garde du ministère des Affaires étrangères allemand, les voyageurs qui photographient, même des sujets non sensibles, doivent constamment faire preuve de prudence. Il est par ailleurs interdit de photographier d'un véhicule en train de rouler. Comme personne ne m'en empêche, je photographie à tout-va. Or les services secrets m'ont à l'œil. Dans notre véhicule, l'ambiance se gâte : nos guides téléphonent à droite et à gauche en prenant l'inutile précaution de parler tout bas. Je suis entrée dans le pays avec un visa de tourisme, ce qui peut avoir des conséquences très désagréables. Au musée des Techniques, on nous confisque nos passeports. J'apprendrai par la suite que l'agence de voyage par laquelle nous sommes passées en Allemagne risque de perdre son accréditation. Yeong-su n'arrive plus à me regarder en face. Seulement une fois des micros installés dans le musée, nos guides lâchent du lest. Faisant contre mauvaise fortune bon cœur, les deux parties étouffent l'affaire, et le programme continue.

Dans le stade du Premier-Mai, sur l'île de Rungnado, nous assistons au festival Arirang, qui tient son nom d'une vieille chanson populaire coréenne. Des milliers de personnes se rendent à pied au stade. Les cohortes changent brusquement de direction, en réponse à des signaux invisibles aux personnes extérieures. Nous avons l'impression d'être dans une galère surdimensionnée. Quelque 100 000 personnes contribuent en effet au spectacle. L'immense mosaïque humaine et les mouvements ondoyants minutieusement calculés sont uniques au monde. Des danses de masse à la chorégraphie précise évoquent l'histoire de la Corée du Nord, la libération du colonialisme japonais, la guerre de Corée et l'ère du socialisme, avec pour leitmotiv le souhait d'une prochaine réunification du Nord et du Sud. Le mégaspectacle d'Arirang est le point d'orgue surréel de la réalité de toute façon singulière de la Corée du Nord.

En état de légère surcharge sensorielle, nous prenons la route pour le sud du pays. L'autoroute démesurément large est pratiquement déserte. Le bruit monotone du frottement des pneus nous endort. Du reste, notre programme est très fatigant. Yeong-su dort. À quoi peut-il bien rêver ? Les Coréens du Nord rêvent-ils différemment du reste du monde ? Des personnes désherbent les bas-côtés en rase campagne. Profitant d'un instant d'inattention, je photographie des ouvriers à côté desquels l'industrialisation est passée sans un bruit. Avec des moyens très rudimentaires, ils rafistolent les routes laissées à l'abandon. Le grand communisme de jadis se résume désormais à la Corée du Nord. Le monde entier a évolué, sauf ce pays et ses habitants. Et il se trouve que nous sommes au cœur de cette contrée, plongées dans la vie des autres.

Sous le dernier régime stalinien, le culte de la personnalité a presque complètement éradiqué la religion de la vie quotidienne. Bien que la Constitution garantisse la liberté religieuse, on observe une désaffection des fidèles, que Kim Jong-il a expliquée en substance : « Chacun peut aller à l'église à sa guise car la liberté de religion est inscrite dans notre Constitution. Cependant, les gens n'y vont pas parce qu'ils n'ont ni chagrins ni soucis de quelque sorte que ce soit et qu'ils n'ont pas non plus quoi que ce soit à confesser. » Dans le temple bouddhiste de Pohyon, un moine nous parle de la liberté de religion dans la pratique. Par mesure de précaution, il a tout de même baptisé le bouddha Kim Jong-il. « Le grand dirigeant doit préparer le monde à la paix et à l'amitié. »

Sous terre, c'est-à-dire dans le métro de Pyongyang, les voyageurs semblent nous regarder sans nous voir. Face à la quasi-impossibilité d'établir un contact avec les habitants, je ressens de nouveau cette opposition entre eux et nous. Les préjugés sont bel et bien sans bornes des deux côtés. Sur fond de musique classique, nous traversons à pied les palais souterrains ornés de lustres et de fresques. Les stations portent des noms grandiloquents, comme « Lumière florissante », « Renouveau » et « Champ d'or ». Nous devons hélas descendre avant la station « Réunification ».

Le soir venu, nous faisons un crochet par le parc d'attractions, où nous côtoyons des autochtones de très près. Pendant qu'ils se concentrent sur les jeux et s'en donnent à cœur joie sur les manèges hypermodernes, ils ne se sentent pas observés. Pendant un instant, j'oublie que je suis en Corée du Nord. Se comportant comme des enfants, Yeong-su et Joon rient à gorge déployée.

Sur le trajet qui mène à une coopérative de production agricole, Yeong-su me demande ce que les Occidentaux pensent de la Corée du Nord. Je réfléchis à ce que nous en savons. Il faut dire que la plupart d'entre nous croient que Kim est un prénom. Nous passons devant l'inscription suivante : « Loués soient notre parti, le meilleur d'entre tous, et le dirigeant du peuple, le camarade Kim Jong-un. Avec force euphémismes, je fais comprendre à Yeong-su que la Corée du Nord n'a pas très bonne réputation et qu'elle est souvent présentée comme un agresseur. « Tout cela n'est que de la propagande occidentale, réplique-t-il consterné. Qu'est-ce qu'on vous a fait ? Il y a 30 000 soldats américains stationnés en Corée du Sud. Et y a-t-il quelqu'un pour prononcer des sanctions ? Pourquoi avez-vous autant de mal à accepter que nous soyons des êtres humains nous aussi ? » Et moi de demander : « Et qu'en est-il des violations des droits de l'Homme, de tous les prisonniers politiques ? S'agit-il là aussi de simple propagande ? » La question m'a échappé.

Après un bon bout de chemin sans échanger une parole, nous arrivons à destination. Les 300 ménages réunis dans cette coopérative vitrine pratiquent l'agriculture et l'élevage communautaires. Nous apprenons quand le « cher dirigeant » est venu en visite et qu'il a examiné à cette occasion les bottes en caoutchouc jaunes qui ont maintenant une place d'honneur. On nous dit aussi que, dans sa générosité, il a offert 40 téléviseurs et 10 tracteurs aux paysans. Ceux-ci labourent les champs au son de musiques coréennes censées leur donner du cœur à l'ouvrage. Nos guides décident de nous montrer des maisons de paysans. Il n'y a personne dans les trois premières, car on a besoin aux champs de tous les bras, et jusqu'aux pattes des chiens, comme nous l'enseigne un proverbe coréen. Nous finissons par entrer dans une maison où il y a de la vie. On voit à l'expression du maître des lieux que cela ne lui plaît pas vraiment. Nous examinons en vitesse la cuisine et le salon-chambre à coucher dépourvu de meubles, puis nous quittons les lieux. Ce paysan arraché à son sommeil a dû croire à une visite éclair d'extraterrestres.

Nous passons la nuit à Sariwŏn, où nous sommes les seuls visiteurs. Assis derrière la réception de l'hôtel, des hommes portant des casquettes militaires démesurées nous transpercent du regard. Nous n'avons pas fini de dîner que Sariwŏn est plongée dans l'obscurité. Épuisé, Joon se traîne comme un mort-vivant dans le couloir sombre car il n'a pas le droit de nous laisser seules. En nous escortant jusqu'à notre chambre, il nous parle de la montagne et de son amie. Dans le noir, je ne peux pas voir son visage. Sourit-il ? L'eau a été coupée, et la ville est dans l'obscurité totale. Peu après, nous entendons un grésillement qui semble au début être celui d'un poste de radio défectueux. C'est la doctrine du Juche diffusée par mégaphones que l'on fait entrer dans la tête des habitants. De la propagande dans la nuit. Précisons que l'endoctrinement quotidien débute à cinq heures du matin par un jogging collectif.

Tandis que nous faisons route vers la frontière dans la zone démilitarisée, on nous dépeint la tragédie de la partition du point de vue nord-coréen. Nous sommes les seules étrangères. L'ambiance est très tendue. « Ne faites pas d'histoires », nous lance Joon dans le minibus, en me transperçant de son regard sombre. Roulant dans un fossé d'un mètre de profondeur, nous faisons route vers la Corée du Sud. D'énormes cylindres en béton sont censés, en cas de coup dur, barrer la route de Pyongyang aux blindés ennemis. Comme une plaie béante, les souvenirs de guerre sont douloureux dans les mémoires des Coréens. Des blocs de béton encastrés dans le sol marquent la frontière.

Depuis un incident mortel, il est interdit de franchir la ligne de démarcation. Pour rendre possibles les entretiens de visu, on a construit à Panmunjon trois postes-frontières peints en bleu, à cheval sur les territoires nord-coréen et sud-coréen. Dans une de ces baraques, il y a une table marron et des chaises. Un câble de microphone noir marque la frontière, si bien que des négociateurs du Nord et du Sud peuvent s'asseoir à une même table tout en restant dans leurs pays respectifs. Derrière les rangées de chaises, des portes donnent, qui en Corée du Sud, qui en Corée du Nord. Tandis que je foule pendant quelques minutes le sol du pays ennemi officiel, Joon murmure : « Vous aviez bien vous aussi une frontière ? Votre pays était aussi coupé en deux. » J'acquiesce d'un signe de tête.

Le mince câble de microphone noir sépare le dernier État stalinien, le pays le plus isolé du monde, de son voisin en plein essor capitaliste. En 1945, le 38e parallèle est adopté comme ligne de démarcation entre la Corée du Sud occupée par les États-Unis et la zone soviétique au nord. Après le retrait des troupes d'occupation, les tensions entre les deux Républiques issues de la partition débouchent en 1950 sur le conflit le plus meurtrier de toute l'histoire militaire. Trois ans et trois millions de morts plus tard, cette guerre par procuration s'achève sans résultat. L'ancienne ligne de démarcation devient la nouvelle frontière. Ses villes ayant été réduites en cendres, la Corée du Nord n'existe plus. Des centaines de milliers d'orphelins affamés errent dans les décombres des maisons bombardées. L'espace d'un instant, nous devinons l'étendue de cette guerre impitoyable. En effet, Yeong-su dit très fort comme pour se donner du courage : « Si l'on nous attaque, nous sommes prêts à nous défendre. »

Au bout de vingt minutes de route, nous rencontrons le chef d'escadron Hwang. Caricature de lui-même, il porte une casquette de général bien trop grande. On dirait qu'il n'a pas souvent de la visite, car les autocars ne montent pas jusque-là. L'officier nous félicite pour notre courage : « Le 38e parallèle est la frontière la plus dangereuse du monde, car elle sépare deux pays qui sont encore en guerre », explique-t-il. De vastes champs de mines tiennent lieu de zone tampon entre capitalisme et communisme, entre Nord et Sud, entre deux pays frères. L'un comme l'autre font de la propagande. La Corée du Sud, par exemple, a nié pendant des années l'existence du Mur, alors qu'il suffit de regarder dans une longue-vue pour le voir. Et comme tous les murs de ce monde, il ne s'arrête pas à l'ouvrage de maçonnerie, il se manifeste dans les mentalités des deux côtés, partageant un même peuple en « nous » et « vous ».

Dans la chambre d'hôtel, nous avons droit pour la première fois à la télévision chinoise. On y montre les préparatifs de guerre des États-Unis contre la Corée du Nord : les porte-avions de la première puissance mondiale progressent, et des missiles sont lancés dans le cadre de manœuvres militaires. Le mot guerre devient moins abstrait. Le lendemain matin, nous sommes réveillées par les hurlements des sirènes. Les lignes téléphoniques sont coupées. Mes compagnes de voyage craignent que la guerre n'ait éclaté. Tandis que nous prenons le petit-déjeuner dans une sorte de salle de bal, Yeong-su parle d'autodéfense. Dans le meilleur restaurant de la ville, il n'y a plus que du lait en poudre et des coupelles individuelles de confiture manifestement empochées à la descente de l'avion de la compagnie autrichienne, tandis que la serviette pliée au cordeau se révèle être une moitié de mouchoir en papier. Les sanctions sont à l'origine d'une pénurie générale. Improviser et entretenir un simulacre de normalité aussi longtemps que possible sont les maîtres mots. Il y a, j'imagine, différentes manières de faire la guerre. Si la guerre est la réponse, comme je l'ai maintenant compris, quelle était au fait la question ?

Lors d'une randonnée dans les monts Myohyang, nous découvrons une nature grandiose. En cette splendide journée, je suis cependant nerveuse : j'ai menti sur ma profession dans ma demande de visa, et je suis inquiète en y repensant. Profitant d'un moment où personne ne nous observe – le hasard veut que nous nous retrouvions seuls –, notre guide Yeong-su se confie : il me parle de ses enfants, notamment de son fils, dont les résultats scolaires le préoccupent. Le retour de Joon met brusquement fin à la conversation. Devenu plus communicatif au cours de ces derniers jours, Joon me sourit. Je crois qu'il aimerait bien être lui aussi notre ami.

De retour dans la capitale, nous visitons le Palais des enfants, un colossal édifice gris. Affirmant son amour pour Kim Jong-il, une fillette nous guide tout au long des interminables couloirs de la pépinière de jeunes talents. Je me dis que c'est ainsi que Kim Jong-il se représentait un immeuble fait pour les enfants. Les activités extrascolaires comprennent la danse, la calligraphie, la broderie et le chant. La force et la précision des filles et des garçons nous surprennent. « Les enfants sont l'avenir », nous explique la fillette du haut de ses huit ans tandis qu'elle nous montre un ouvrage de broderie représentant les fleurs préférées des Coréens. Cette orchidée et ce bégonia créés spécialement pour les « présidents éternels » s'appellent – et comment aurait-il pu en être autrement ? – kimilsungia et kimjongilia.

Le soir, nous allons au bowling. L'excellente bière de Corée du Nord fait lentement tomber les barrières. Je commence à apprécier mes guides, en dépit de leur besoin irrépressible de nous surveiller. Nous nous déchaussons avant de nous asseoir autour d'une dalle de pierre par cette chaude soirée d'été. Notre chauffeur s'est procuré des moules, qu'il dispose en cercles sur la dalle avant de les arroser d'essence et d'y mettre le feu. À la lumière des phares de la voiture, nous savourons ce délice inattendu. En Corée du Nord, le barbecue est aussi un art masculin. Nous rions beaucoup. Plus tard, c'est un Joon guilleret qui joue au tennis de table avec Xenia. Arborant un large sourire, Seung-hyung, le chauffeur, donne une accolade amicale à Hemma : il est définitivement dans les limbes de l'alcool de serpent.

Au dîner, nous récupérons nos passeports sans avoir à le demander. Nous sommes soulagées : nous pouvons quitter le pays. Dans nos chambres, nous bavardons malgré les micros cachés. La Corée demeure un mystère : un peuple avec deux pays, dont un longtemps oublié. Un peuple divisé par deux systèmes et un immense champ de mines.
Dans quelle voie la Corée du Nord va-t-elle s'engager ? Va-t-elle s'incliner devant l'économie de marché ou entrer en guerre ? Combien de temps un pays peut-il vivre dans une bulle temporelle coupée de tout, dans un univers parallèle ? Quelle que soit la direction que le Nord prendra, le pays tel que nous le connaissons disparaîtra. La Corée du Nord sous sa forme actuelle a fait son temps. Plus tard, je regarde mes photos. Elles me font l'effet de précieux instantanés d'un peuple fantôme : elles ouvrent une fenêtre sur une société que nous ne pouvons nous imaginer, elles ouvrent une sorte de dialogue entre le peuple nord-coréen et nous.

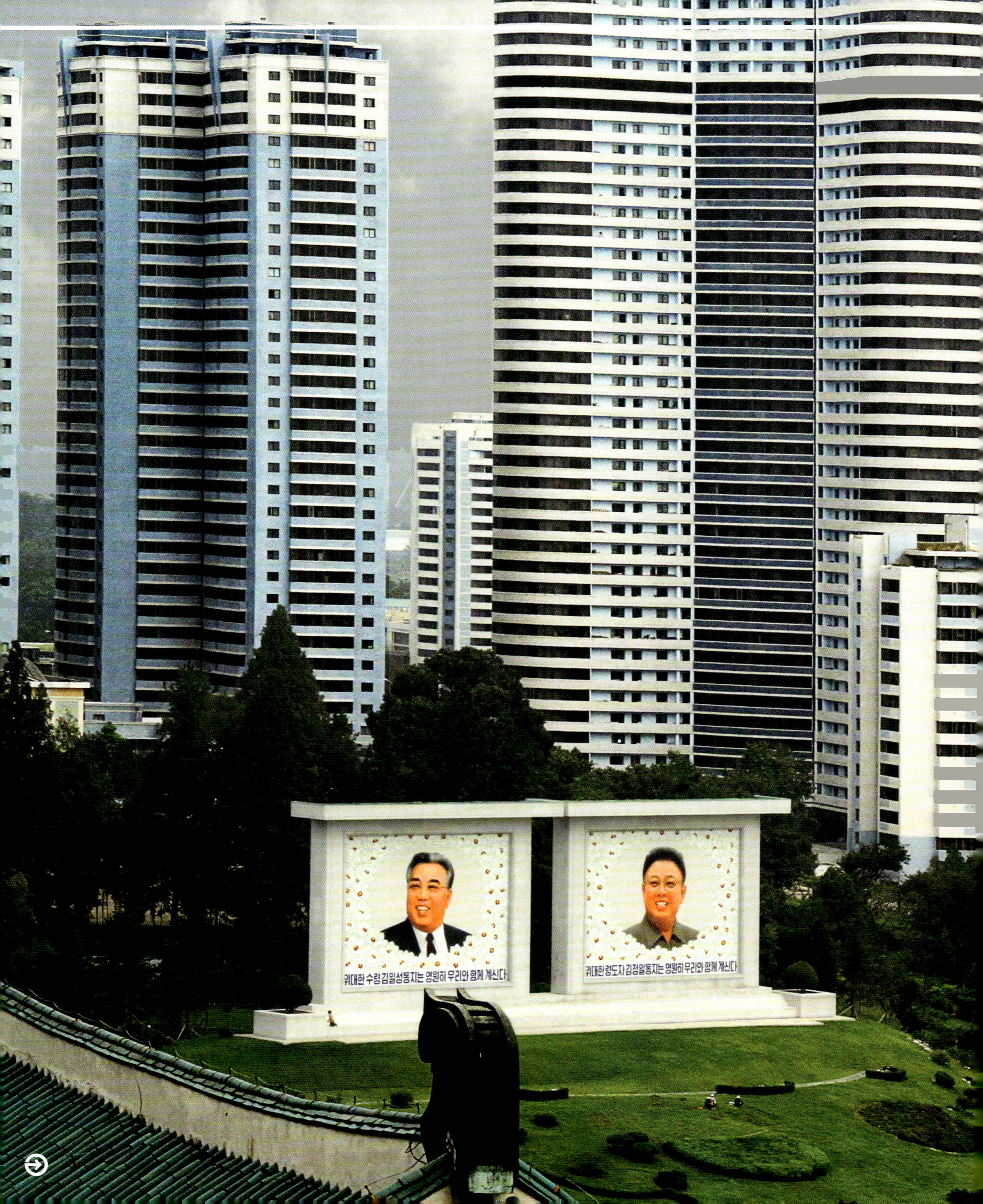
위대한 수령 김일성동지는 영원히 우리와 함께 계신다
위대한 령도자 김정일동지는 영원히 우리와 함께 계신다

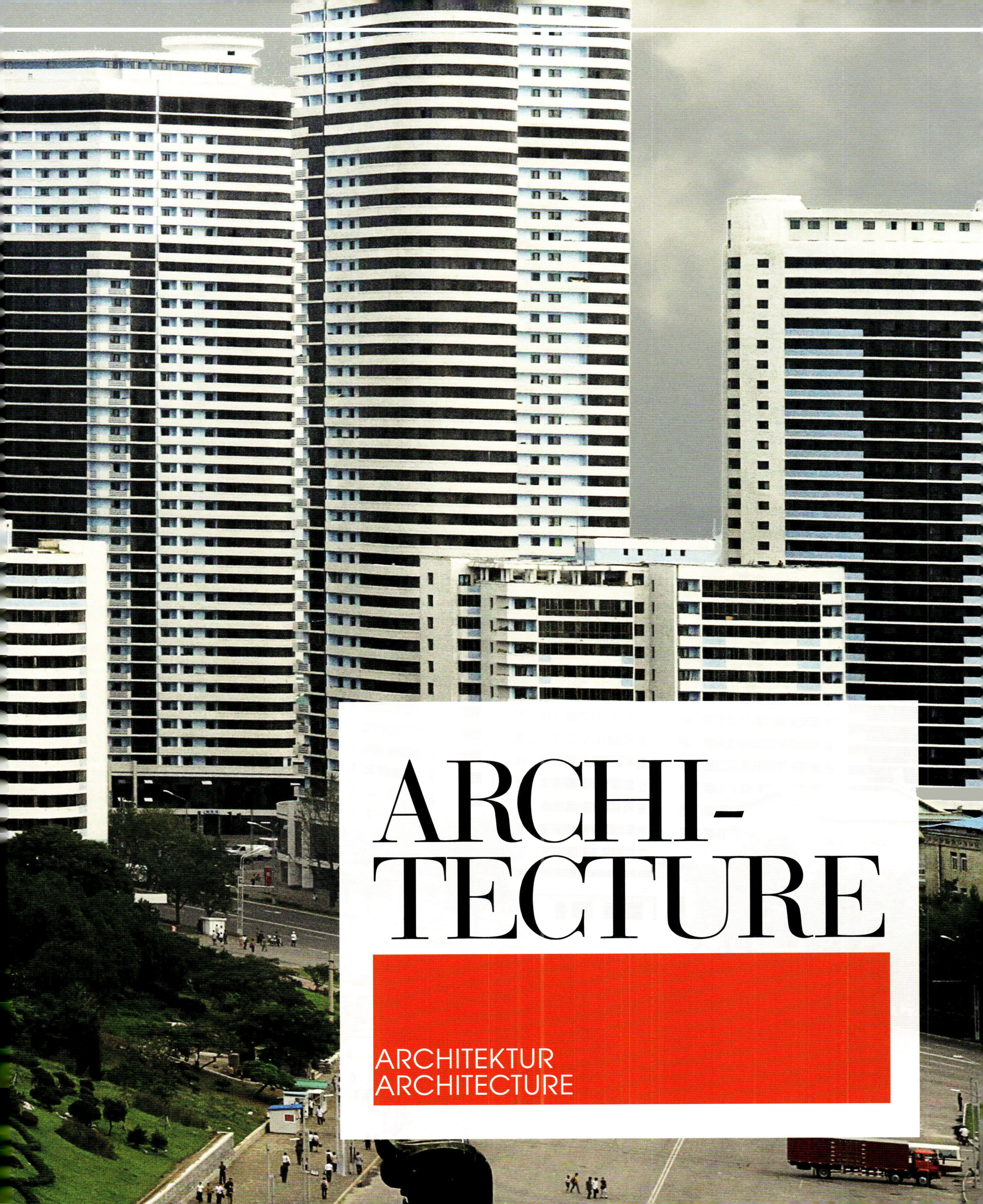

ARCHI-TECTURE

ARCHITEKTUR
ARCHITECTURE

Nearly all of the cities in North Korea were destroyed during the war. Reconstruction entered the history books as the pinnacle of solidarity between socialist nations. Since the new planning authority left nothing up to chance, the model city of Pyongyang took shape on the drawing board. All-pervasive symmetry, deliberate use of lines of sight and colossal design vocabulary are intended to affect people's perceptions and thereby build a new society. Symbols such as torches, magnolia blossoms, hammers, sickles, and paintbrushes are everywhere, representing the state ideology and acting as propaganda. North Koreans are accustomed to the overarching importance of public space and the monumentality of architecture, like in the days of the pharaohs. What would they think of the cityscapes of Western metropolises, with their chaotic layouts and individualism?

Fast alle Städte Nordkoreas wurden im Krieg zerstört. Der Wiederaufbau ging als Höhepunkt internationaler sozialistischer Solidarität in die Geschichte ein. Da die neue Planungshoheit nichts dem Zufall überließ, wurde die Musterstadt Pjöngjang am Reißbrett entworfen: Konsequente Symmetrie, durchdachte Nutzung der Blickachsen und überdimensionierte Formensprache sollen auf das Bewusstsein der Menschen wirken und so eine neue Gesellschaft kreieren. Symbole wie Fackel, Magnolie, Hammer, Sichel und Pinsel sind allgegenwärtig, stehen sinnbildlich für die Staatsideologie und dienen der Propaganda. Nordkoreaner sind die übergeordnete Bedeutung des öffentlichen Raumes und pharaonenhafte Monumentalität gewohnt. Was sie wohl über das individualistisch-chaotische Stadtbild westlicher Metropolen denken würden?

Presque toutes les villes de Corée du Nord ont été détruites pendant la guerre. Leur reconstruction est entrée dans l'Histoire comme un grand moment de solidarité socialiste internationale. Les nouvelles instances de planification ne laissant rien au hasard, la ville modèle a été conçue sur une planche à dessin : symétrie rigoureuse, exploitation ciblée des perspectives urbanistiques et langage formel caractérisé par la démesure sont censés former les consciences, et créer ainsi une nouvelle société. Symboles omniprésents de la doctrine d'État, la torche, le magnolia, le marteau, la faucille et le pinceau sont des outils de propagande. Les Coréens du Nord sont habitués à la suprématie de l'espace public et à une monumentalité digne des pharaons. Que peuvent-ils bien penser du paysage urbain désordonné et individualiste des métropoles occidentales ?

PUBLIC BUILDINGS & MONUMENTS

ÖFFENTLICHE GEBÄUDE & MONUMENTE
ÉDIFICES PUBLICS & MONUMENTS

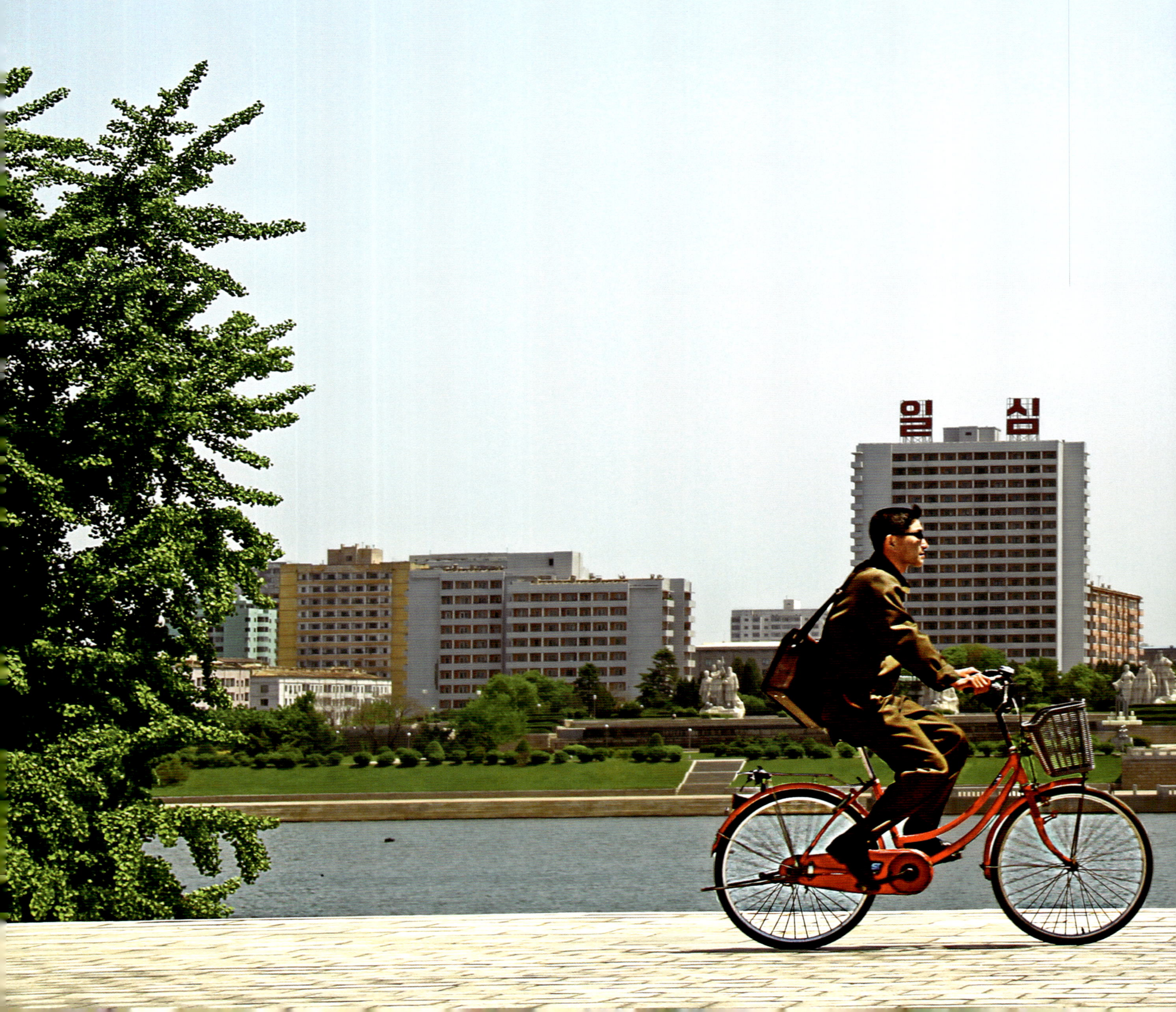

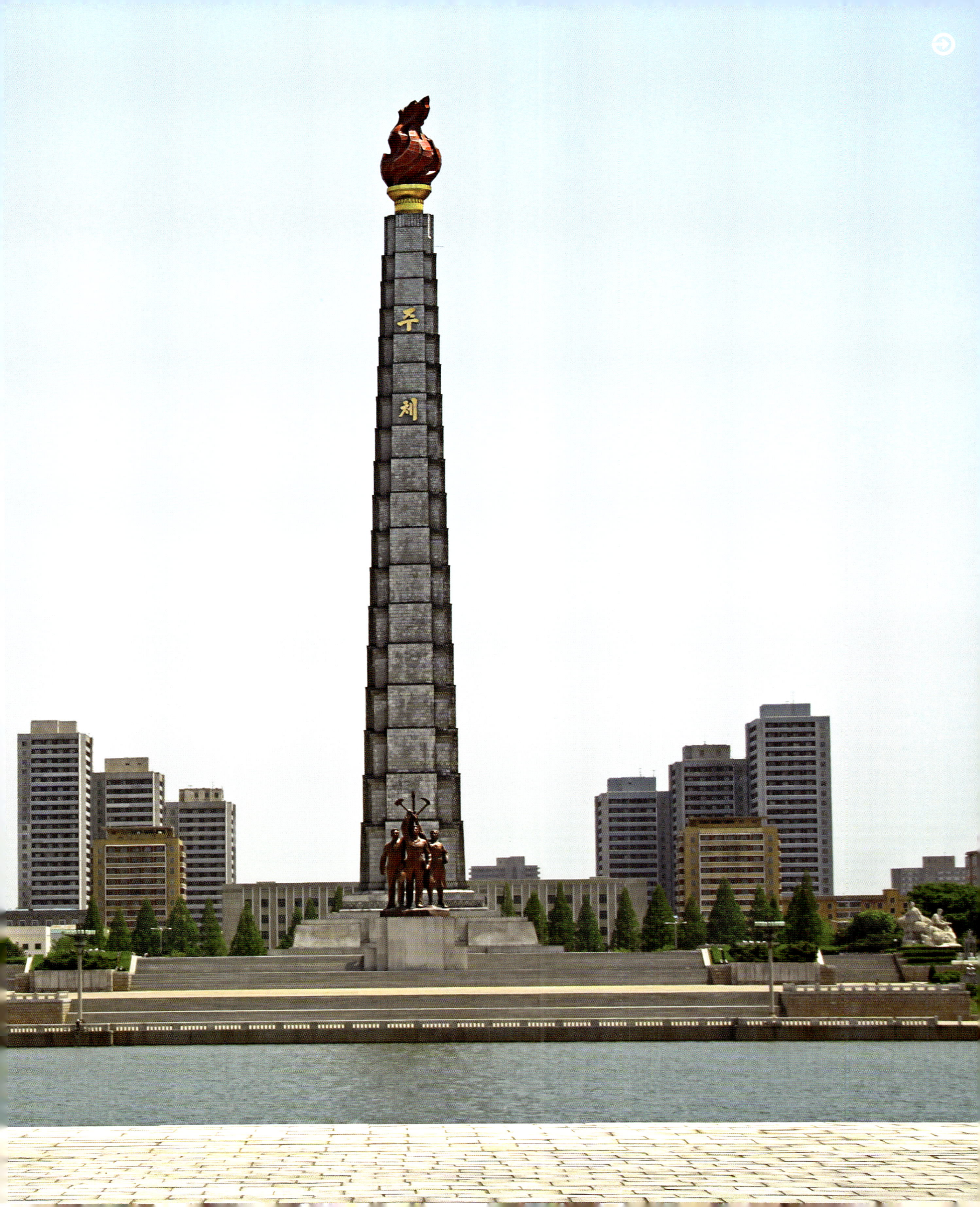
주체

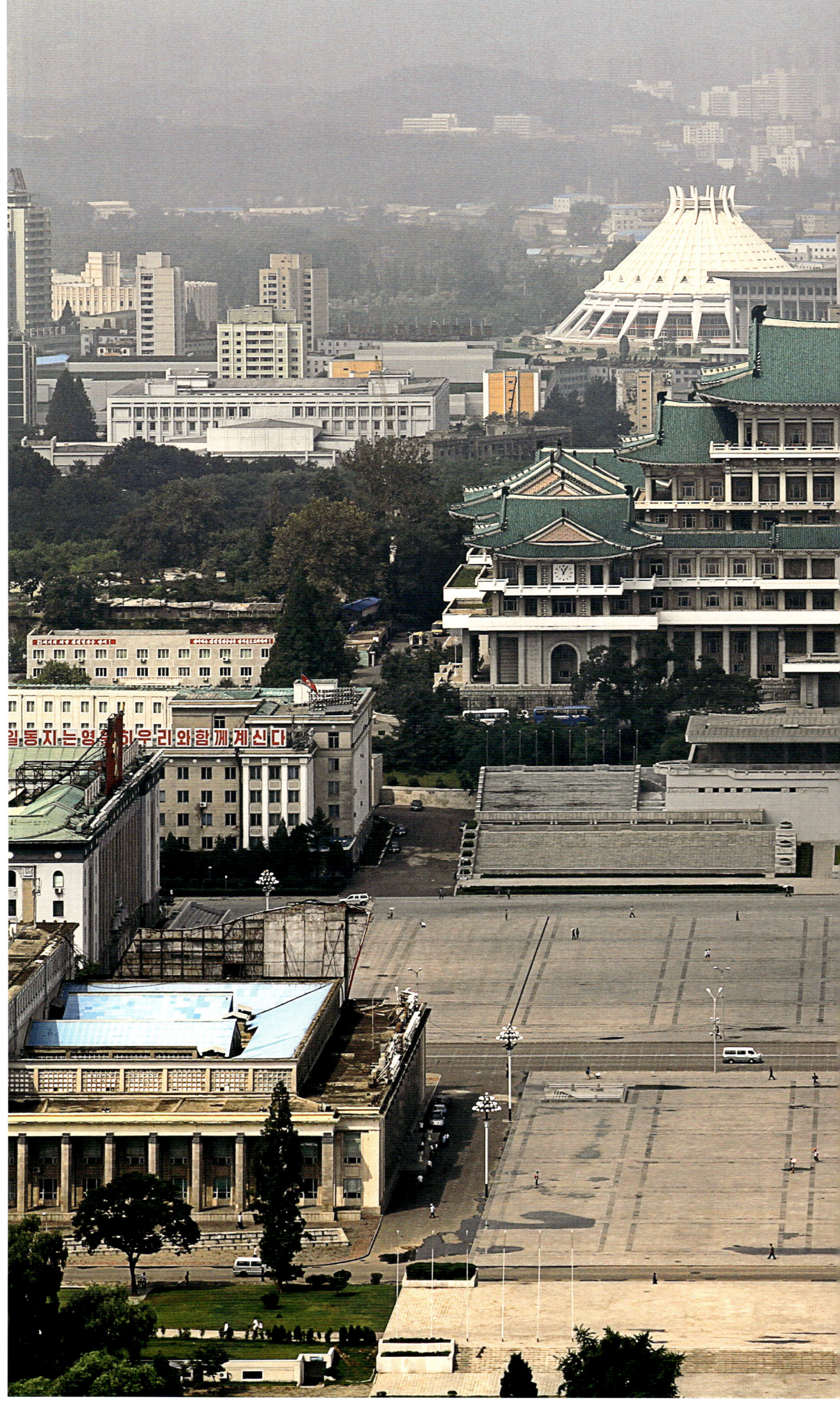

The Grand People's Study House in Pyongyang is said to provide space for 30 million books.
Große Studienhalle des Volkes, Pjöngjang: Sie bietet offiziell Platz für 30 Millionen Bücher.
La Grande Maison des études du peuple, à Pyongyang : cette bibliothèque peut accueillir 30 millions de livres.

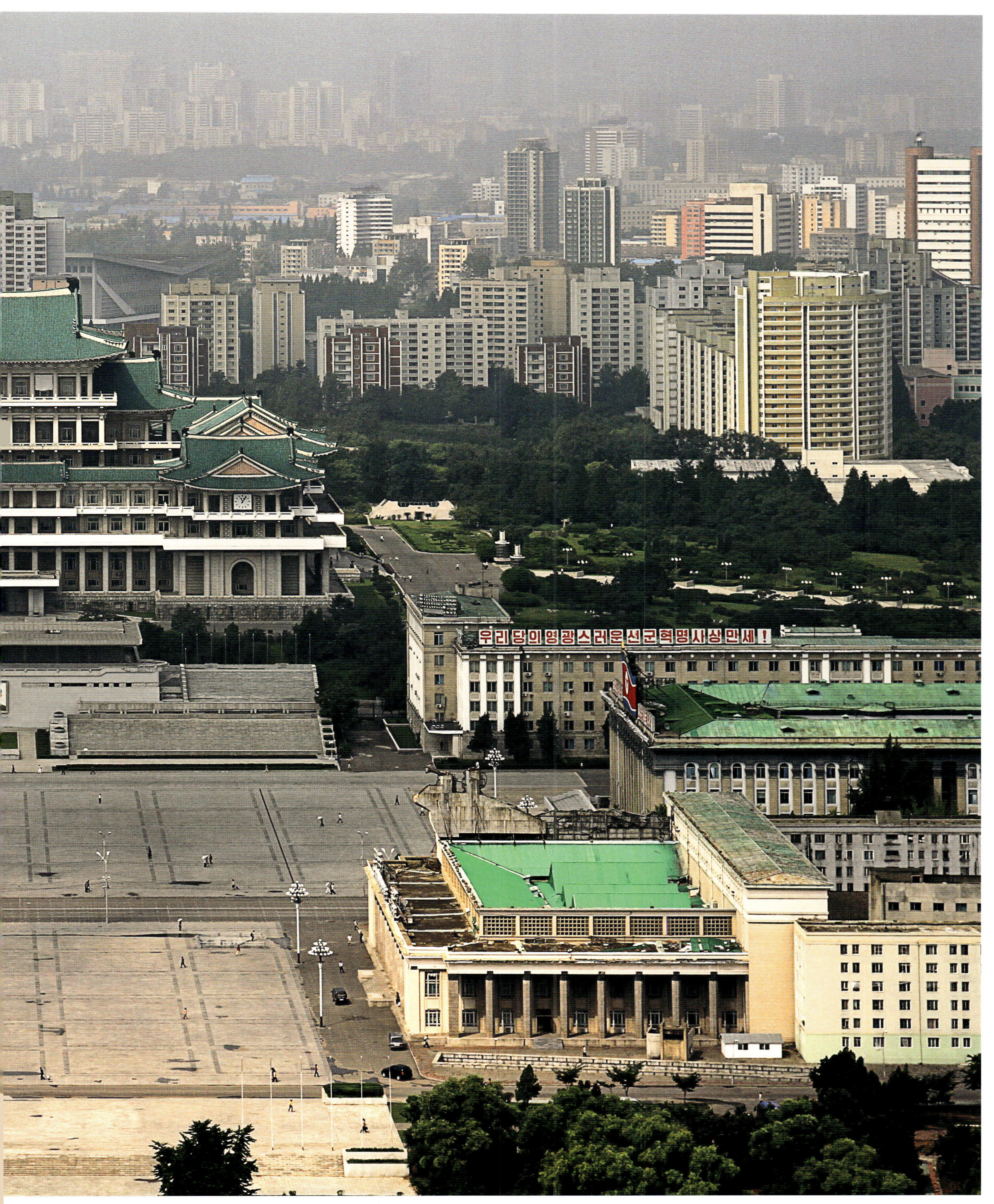
우리당의영광스러운선군혁명사상만세!

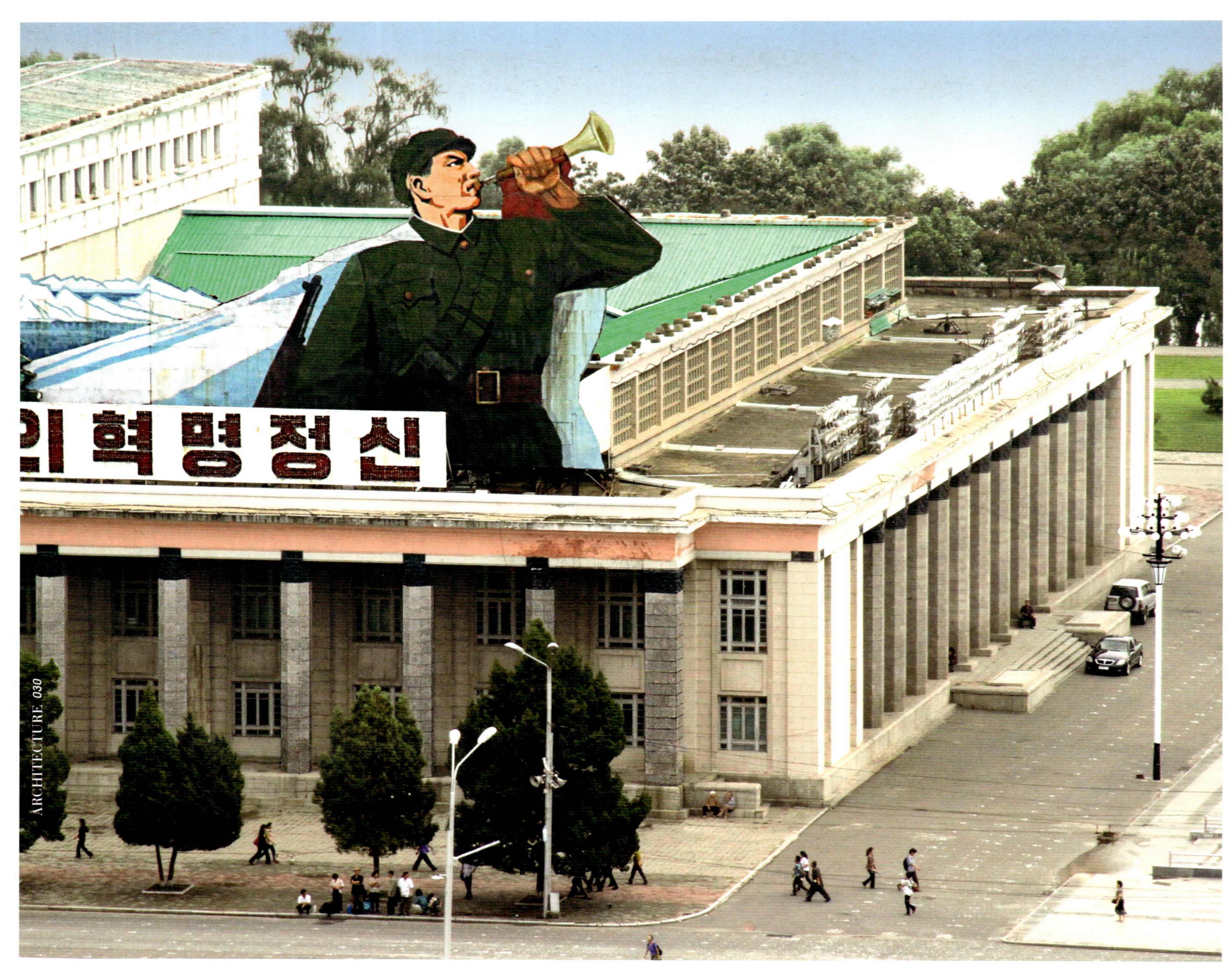

The Korean Central History Museum in Pyongyang covers the country's history from the Stone Age to the Japanese occupation. A highlight of its collection is a metal letter type. Koreans used those letter types to print books long before Johannes Gutenberg invented the printing press.

Historisches Museum, Pjöngjang: von der Steinzeit bis zur japanischen Besetzung. Besonderer Stolz ist eine Metallletter. Damit druckte man in Korea schon einige Zeit vor der Erfindung des Buchdrucks durch Johannes Gutenberg.

À Pyongyang, le musée central de l'Histoire de Corée – de l'âge de pierre à l'occupation japonaise. Un caractère d'imprimerie en métal bien antérieur à l'invention de l'imprimerie par Gutenberg fait la fierté du musée.

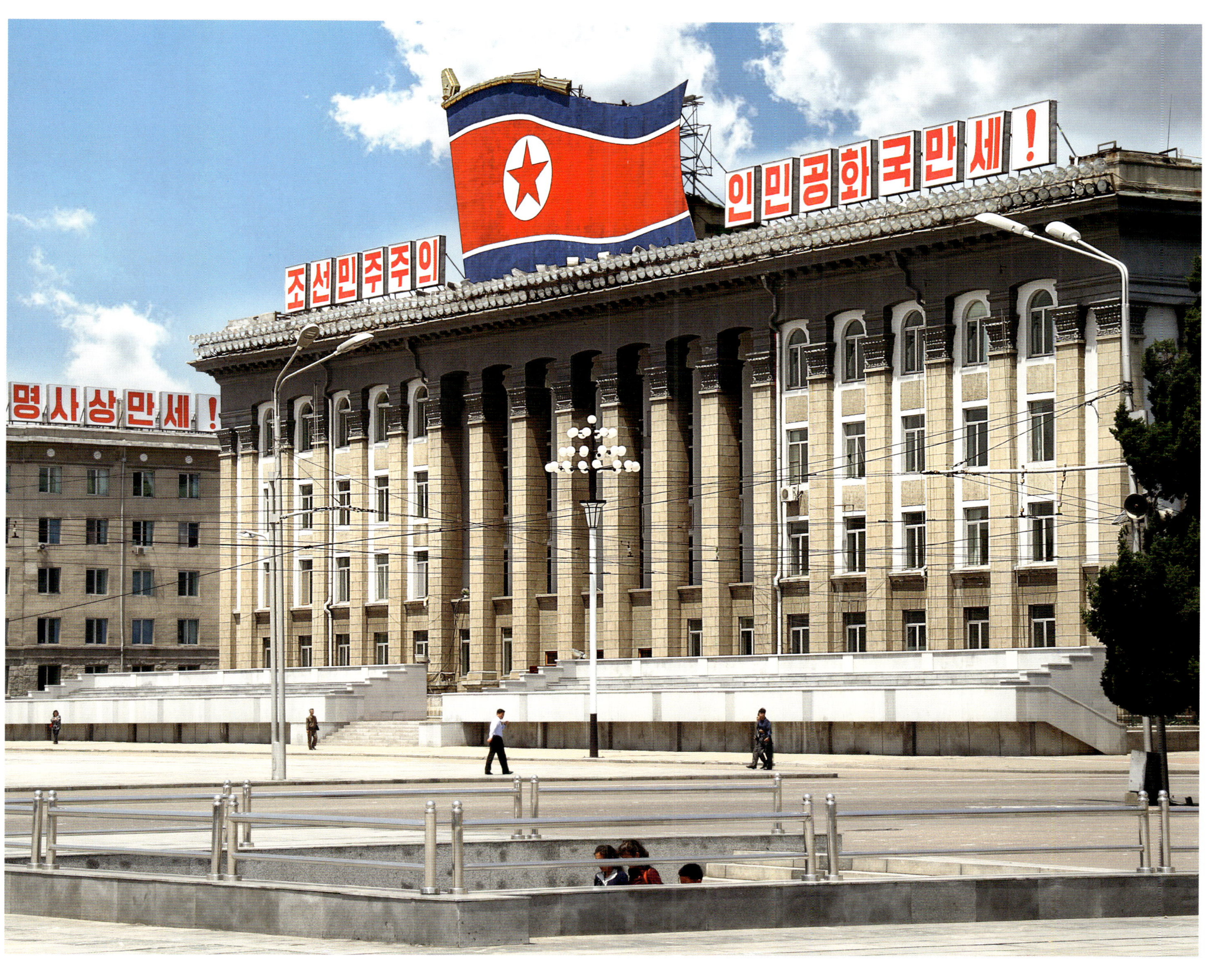

Propaganda at the Ministry of Foreign Trade in Pyongyang: "Long live the Democratic Republic of Korea!" Kim Jong-un ordered the portraits of Marx and Lenin to be removed.

Propaganda am Außenhandelsministerium von Pjöngjang: „Koreanische Demokratische Republik. Hurra!". Die Portraits von Marx und Lenin ließ Kim Jong-un abhängen.

Propagande sur le bâtiment du ministère du Commerce extérieur, à Pyongyang : « Vive la République populaire démocratique de Corée ! » Les portraits de Marx et de Lénine ont été décrochés sur ordre de Kim Jong-un.

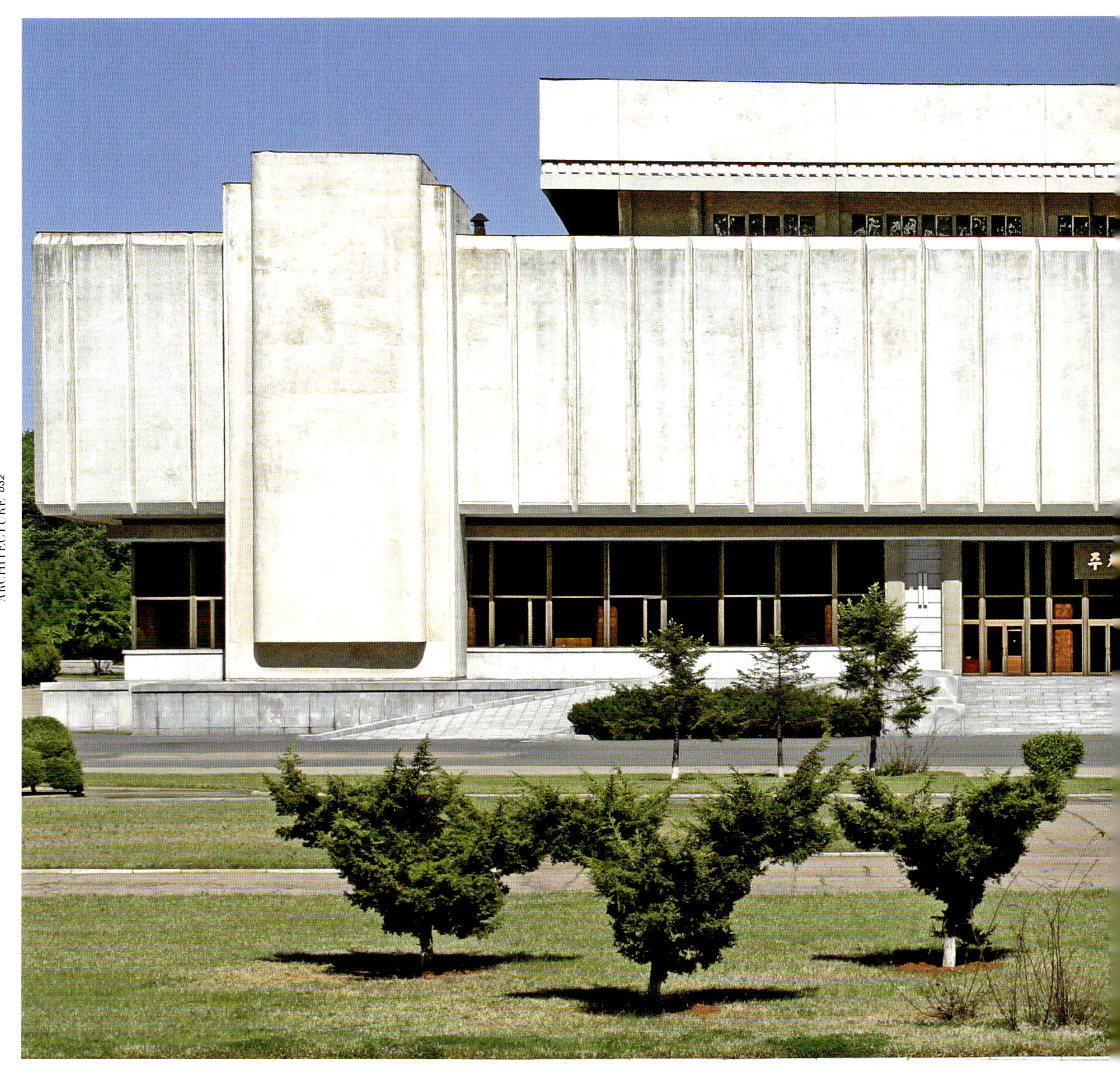

A family outing to the Three Revolutions Exhibition in Pyongyang. The complex's various buildings are dedicated to the ideological, technological, and cultural revolution.

Familienausflug zur Drei-Revolutionen-Ausstellung, Pjöngjang: Die verschiedenen Gebäude des Komplexes sind der ideologischen, technischen und kulturellen Revolution gewidmet.

Sortie en famille à l'Exposition sur les trois révolutions, à Pyongyang. Chacun des bâtiments du complexe est consacré à l'une des révolutions : idéologique, technique et culturelle.

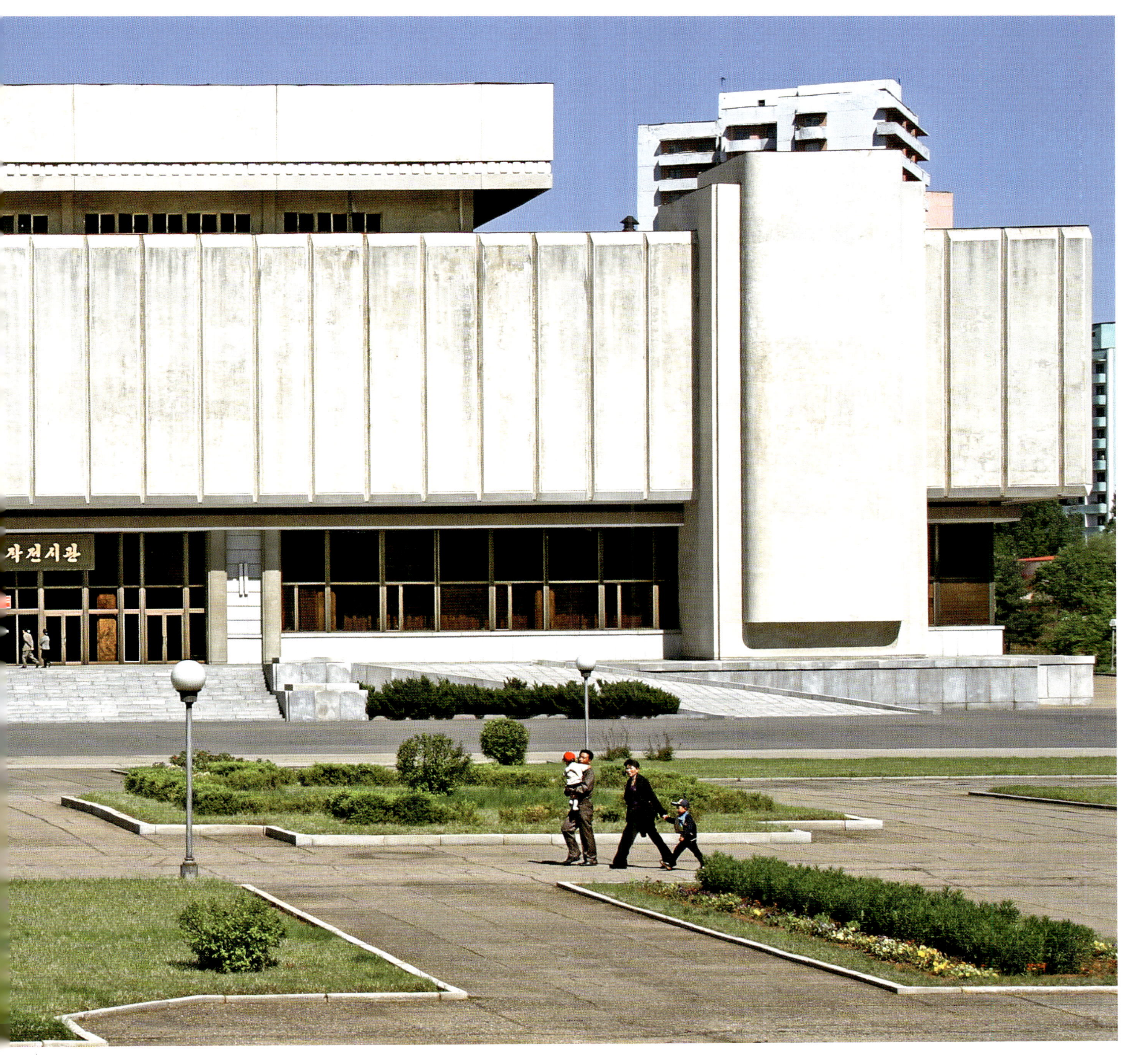
작전시관

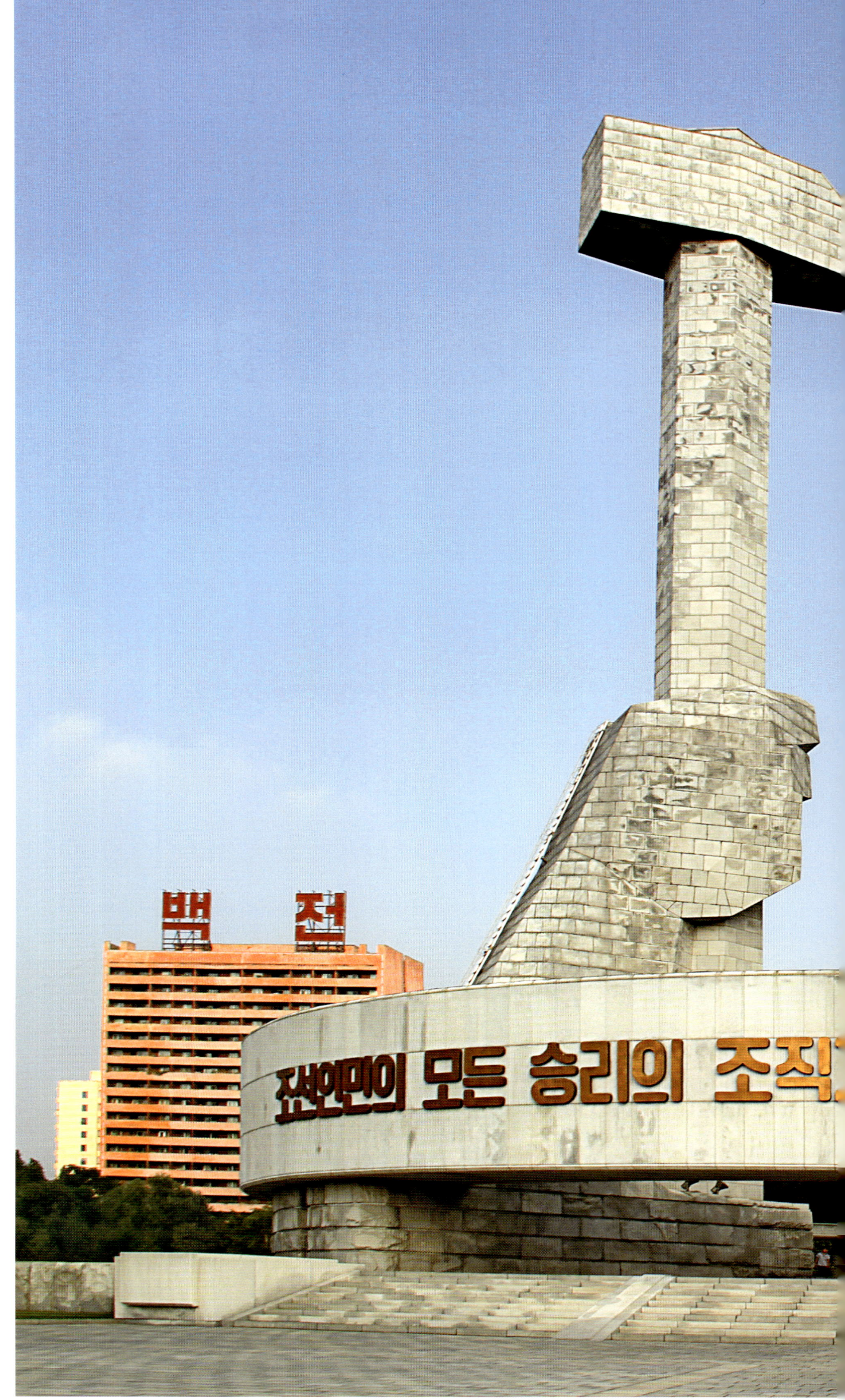

Monument to the Founding of the Workers' Party of Korea in Pyongyang. The hammer and sickle represent the workers and peasants, while the paintbrush stands for the intellectuals. The stone circle symbolizes the unity of the leader, people, and party.

Monument zur Gründung der Partei der Arbeit Koreas, Pjöngjang: Hammer und Sichel stehen für Arbeiterklasse und Bauernschaft. Der Pinsel repräsentiert die Intellektuellen. Als Symbol der Einheit von Führer, Volk und Partei ist der Steinring zu interpretieren.

Monument commémoratif de la création du parti du Travail de Corée, à Pyongyang : le marteau et la faucille symbolisent les classes ouvrière et paysanne. Le pinceau représente les intellectuels. Il faut voir dans l'anneau de pierre le symbole de l'unité du dirigeant, du peuple et du parti.

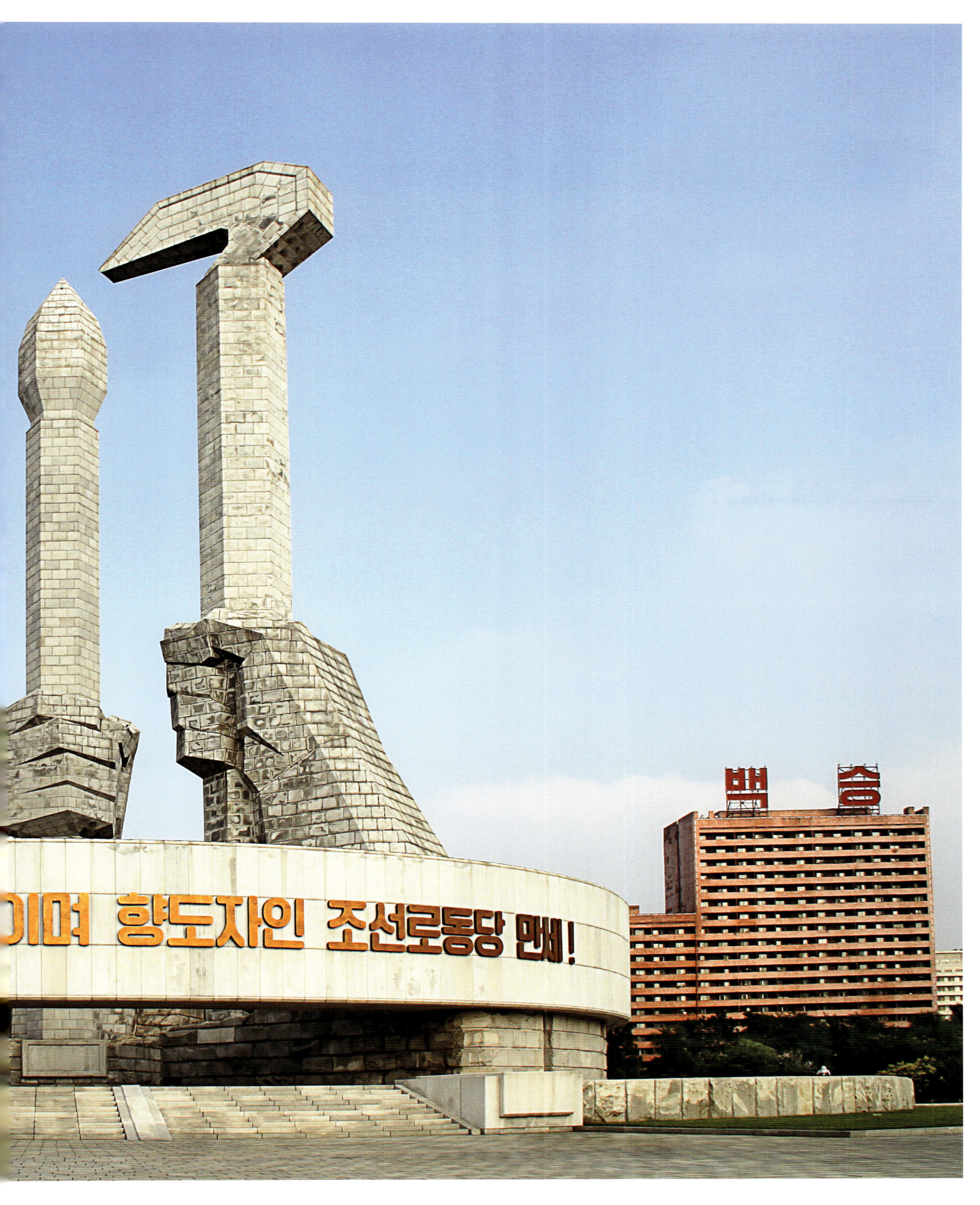

이며 향도자인 조선로동당 만세!
백
승

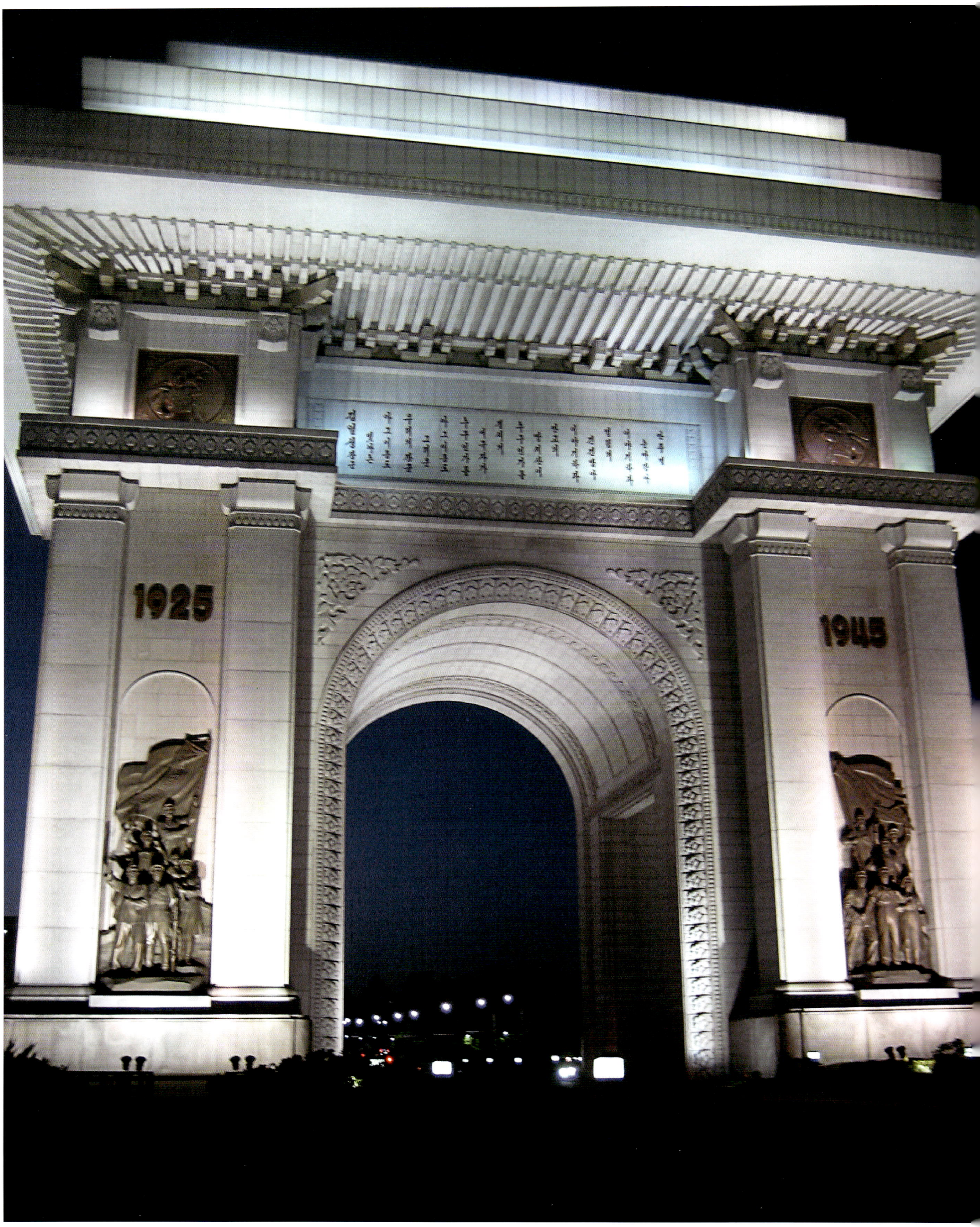

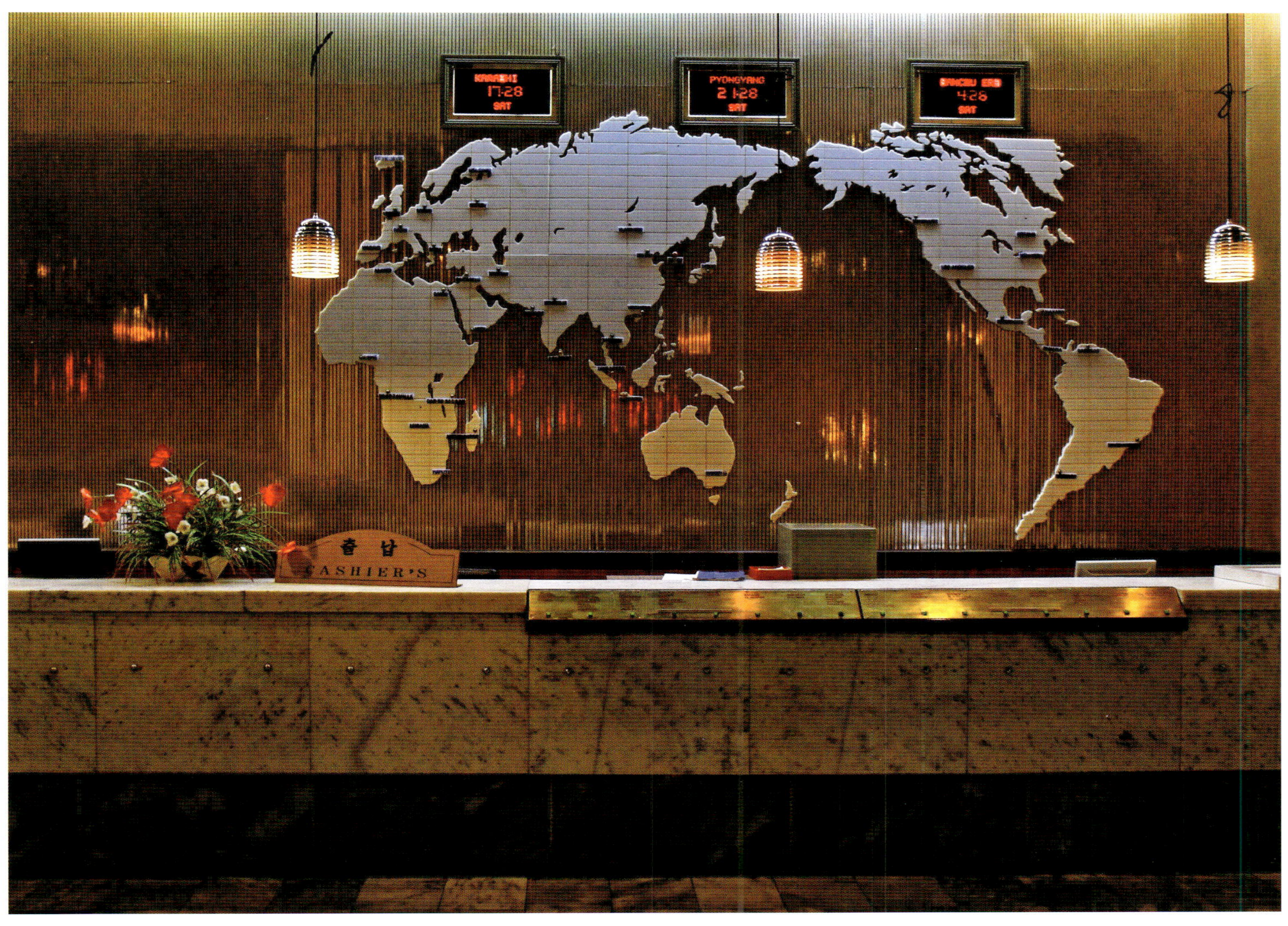

Left: The Triumphal Arch at the foot of Moran Hill in Pyongyang is ten feet taller than its counterpart in Paris.
Right: Lobby of the Koryo Hotel, Pyongyang

Links: Der Triumphbogen am Fuße des Moran-Hügels in Pjöngjang überragt sein französisches Pendant um drei Meter.
Rechts: Lobby des Koryo Hotels, Pjöngjang

À gauche : L'arc de triomphe situé au pied de la colline de Moran, à Pyongyang, dépasse de trois mètres son modèle français.
À droite : Le hall d'entrée de l'hôtel Koryo, à Pyongyang

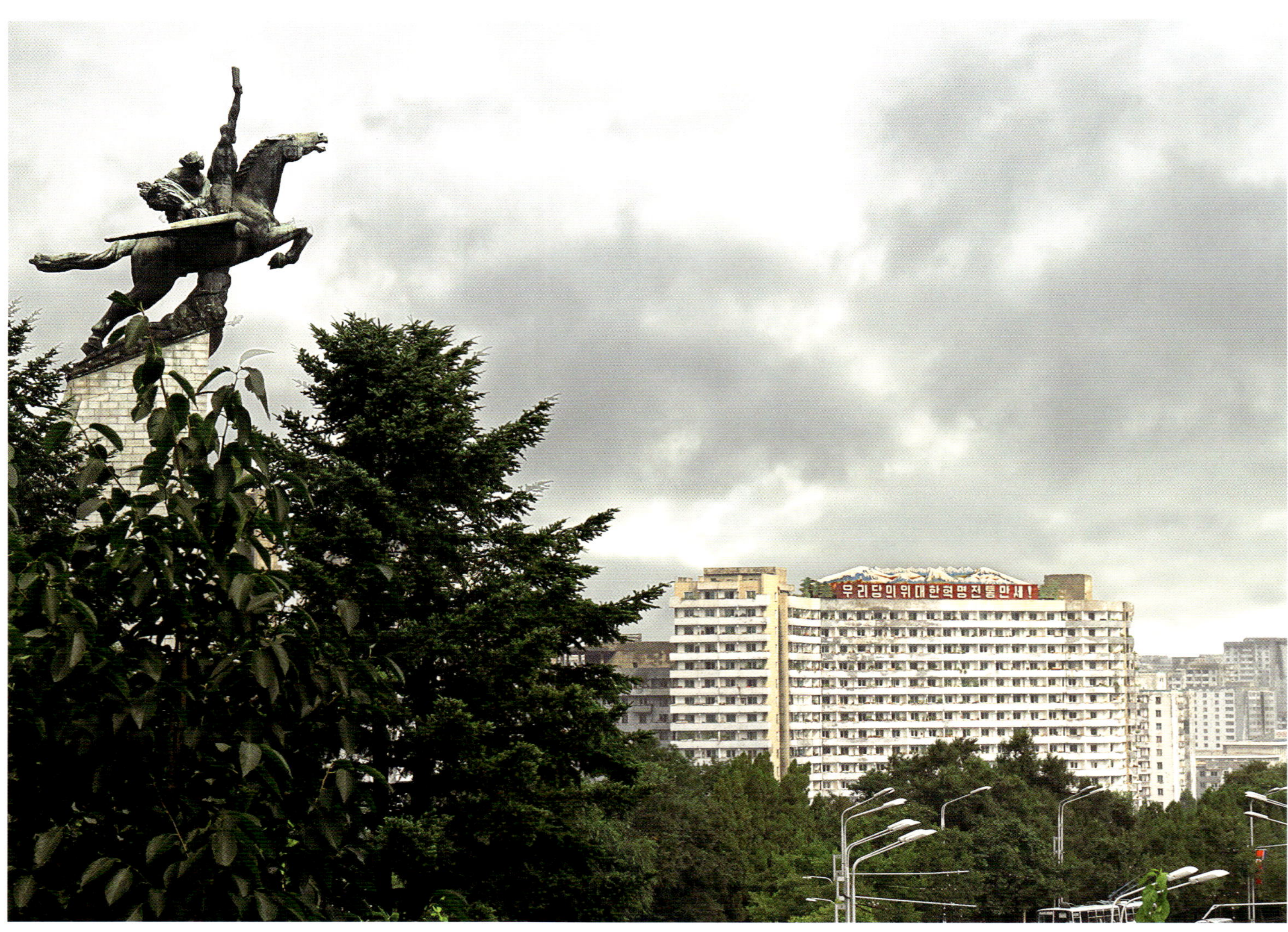

Chollima, Korea's mythological winged horse, came to symbolize reconstruction and industrialization in the aftermath of the Korean War.
Das geflügelte Pferd Ch'ŏllima aus der koreanischen Mythologie wurde nach dem Koreakrieg zum Symbol des Wiederaufbaus und der Industrialisierung.
Après la guerre de Corée, Tcheullima, le cheval ailé de la mythologie coréenne, est devenu le symbole de la reconstruction et de l'industrialisation.

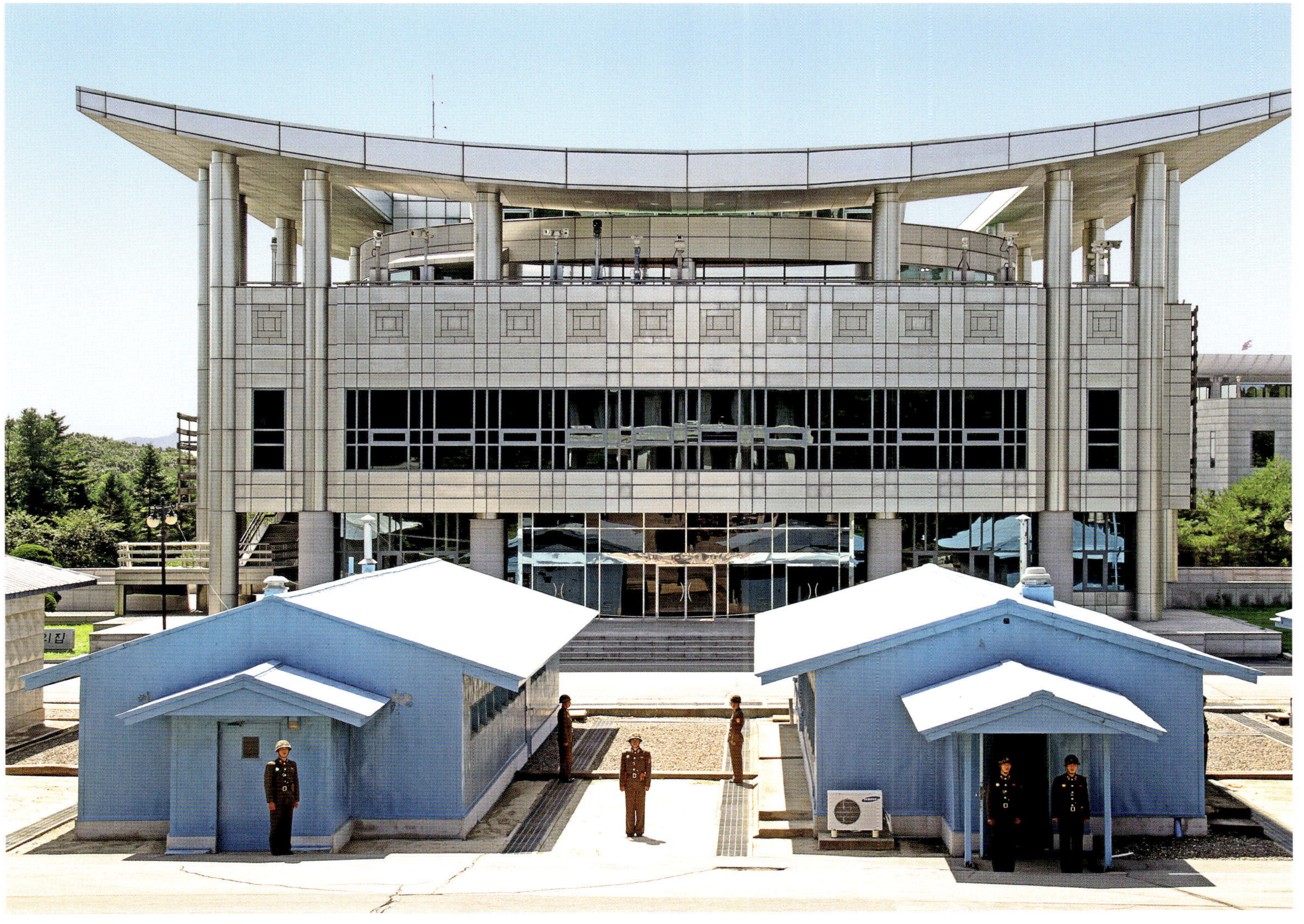

The blue barracks straddle the border, half in South Korea and half in North Korea. Inside, political adversaries can sit at the same table during negotiations without ever leaving their respective countries.
An der Grenze: Die blauen Baracken stehen jeweils zur Hälfte auf südkoreanischem und zur Hälfte auf nordkoreanischem Boden. Für Verhandlungen können sich die verfeindeten Fraktionen an den Tisch im Inneren setzen und trotzdem in ihrem eigenen Land bleiben.
À la frontière : Les baraques bleues sont à cheval sur les sols nord-coréen et sud-coréen. Les délégations ennemies peuvent s'asseoir à une même table tout en restant chacune dans son pays.

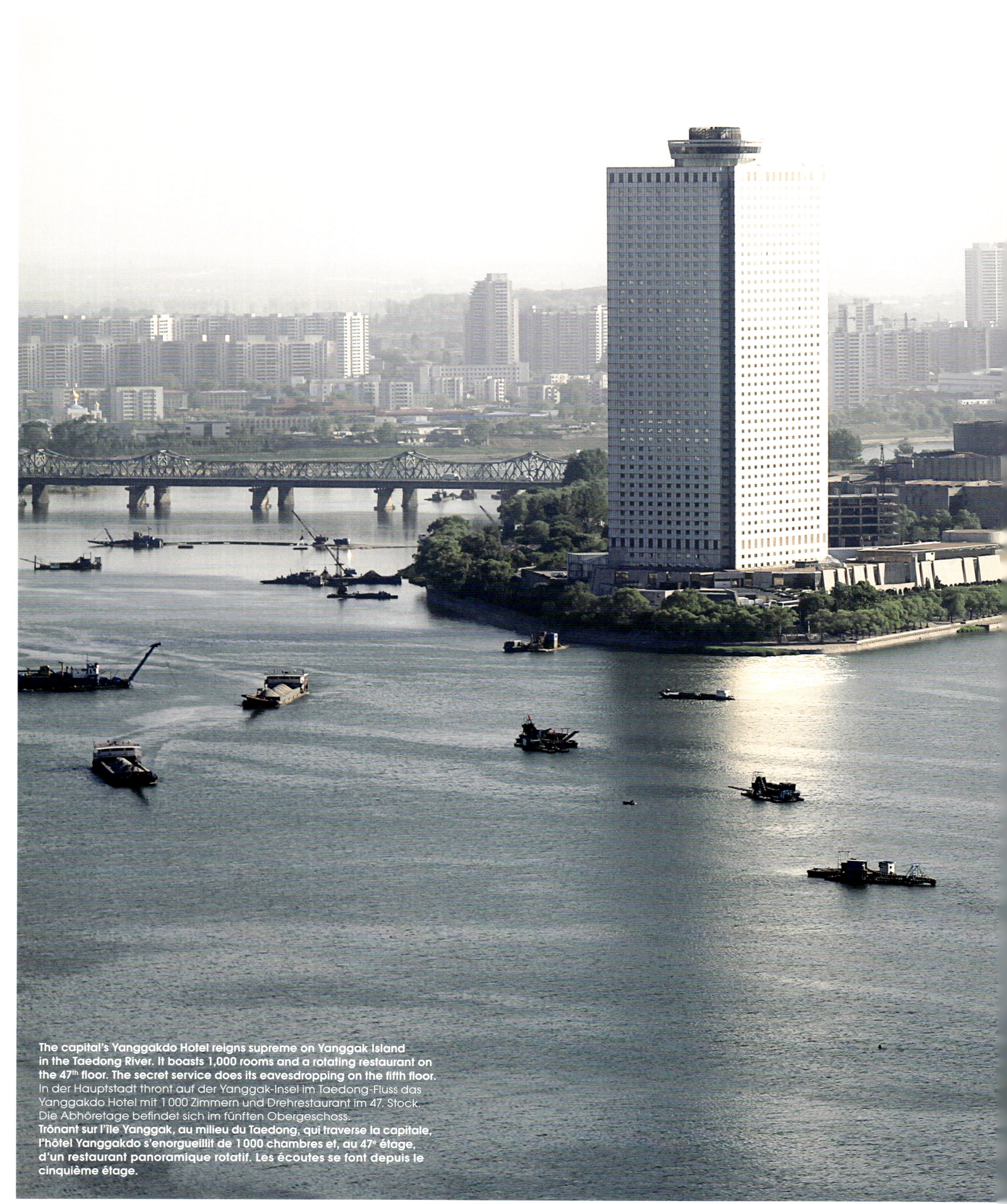

The capital's Yanggakdo Hotel reigns supreme on Yanggak Island in the Taedong River. It boasts 1,000 rooms and a rotating restaurant on the 47th floor. The secret service does its eavesdropping on the fifth floor.
In der Hauptstadt thront auf der Yanggak-Insel im Taedong-Fluss das Yanggakdo Hotel mit 1 000 Zimmern und Drehrestaurant im 47. Stock. Die Abhöretage befindet sich im fünften Obergeschoss.
Trônant sur l'île Yanggak, au milieu du Taedong, qui traverse la capitale, l'hôtel Yanggakdo s'enorgueillit de 1 000 chambres et, au 47e étage, d'un restaurant panoramique rotatif. Les écoutes se font depuis le cinquième étage.

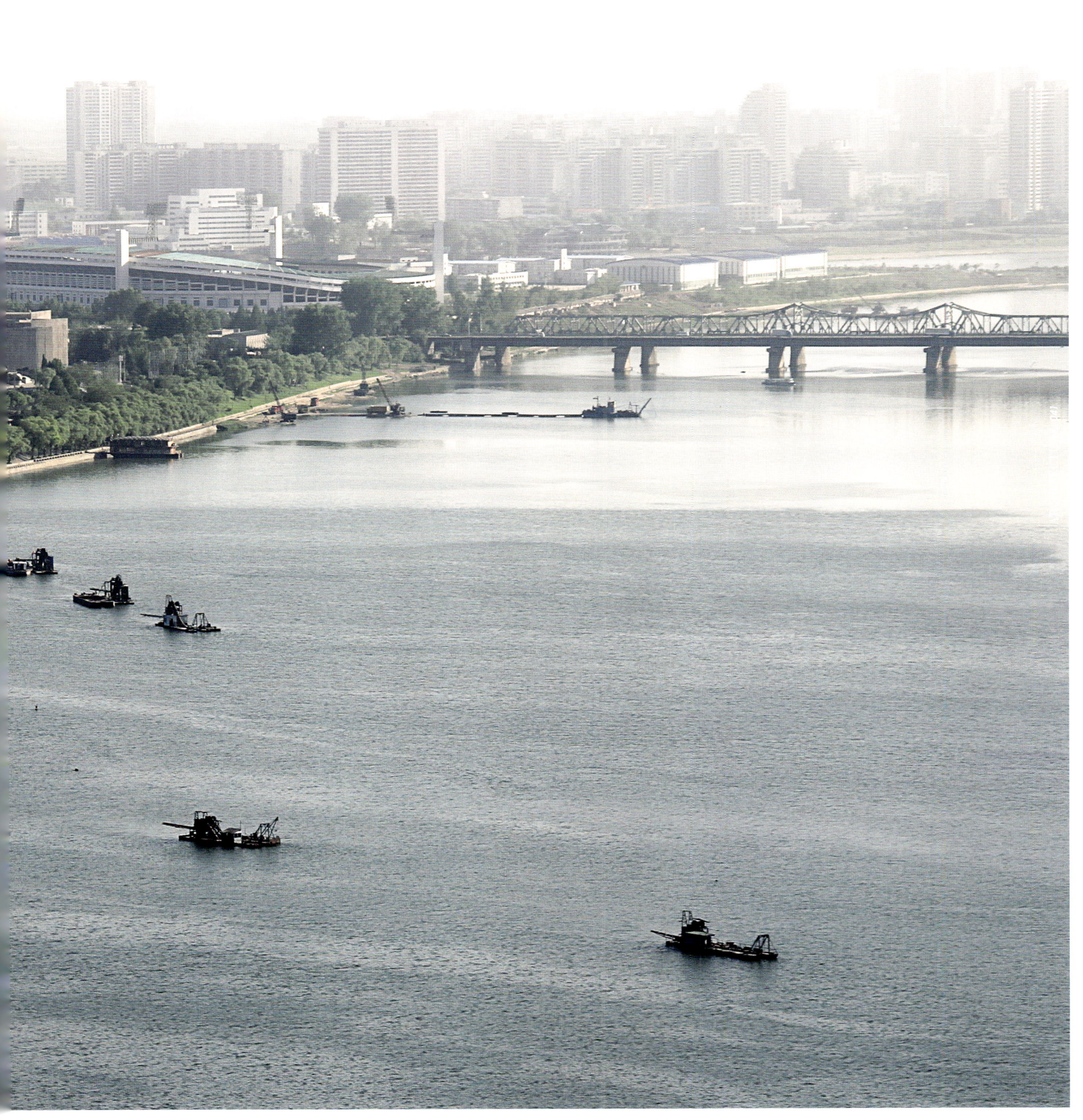

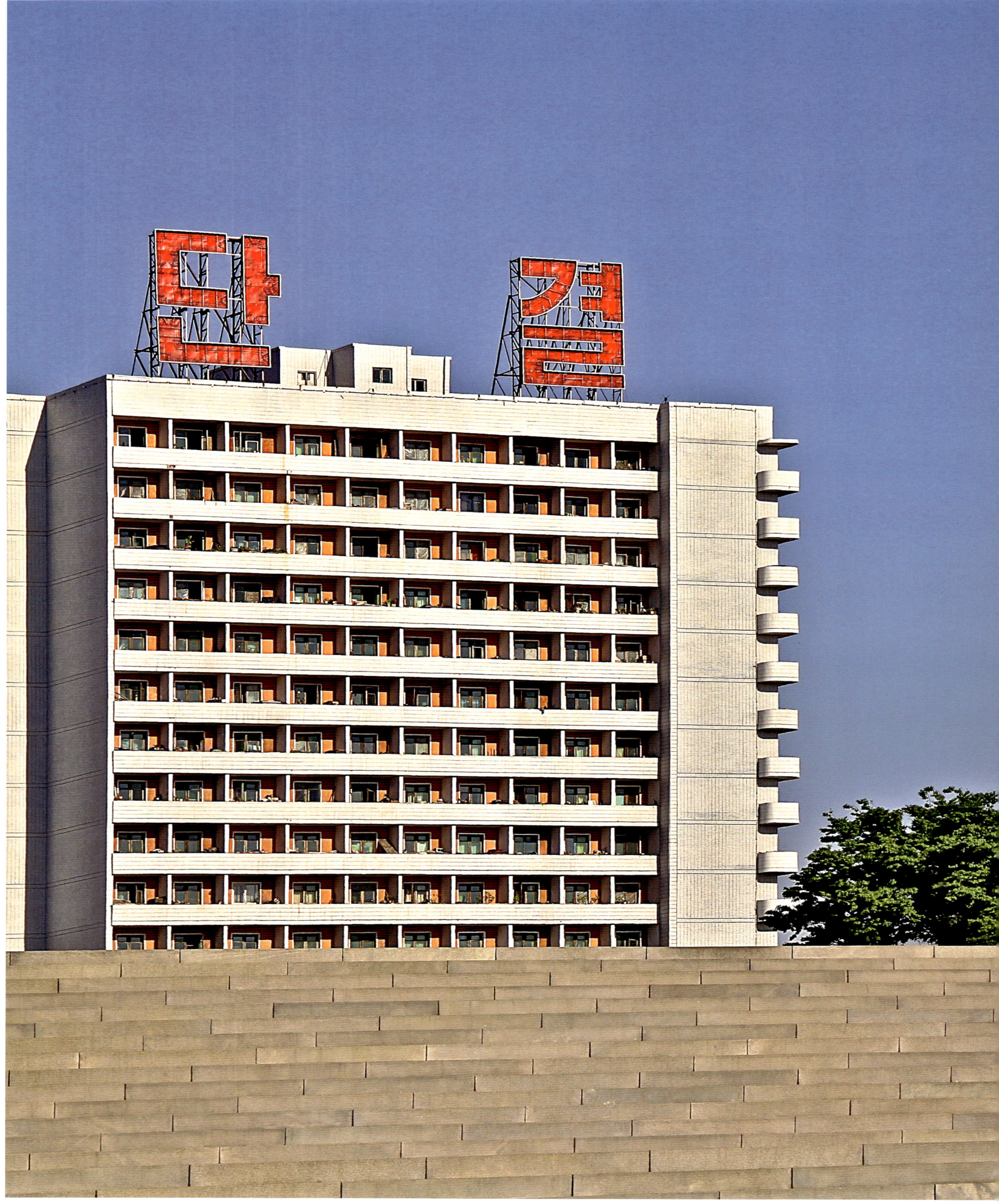
단결

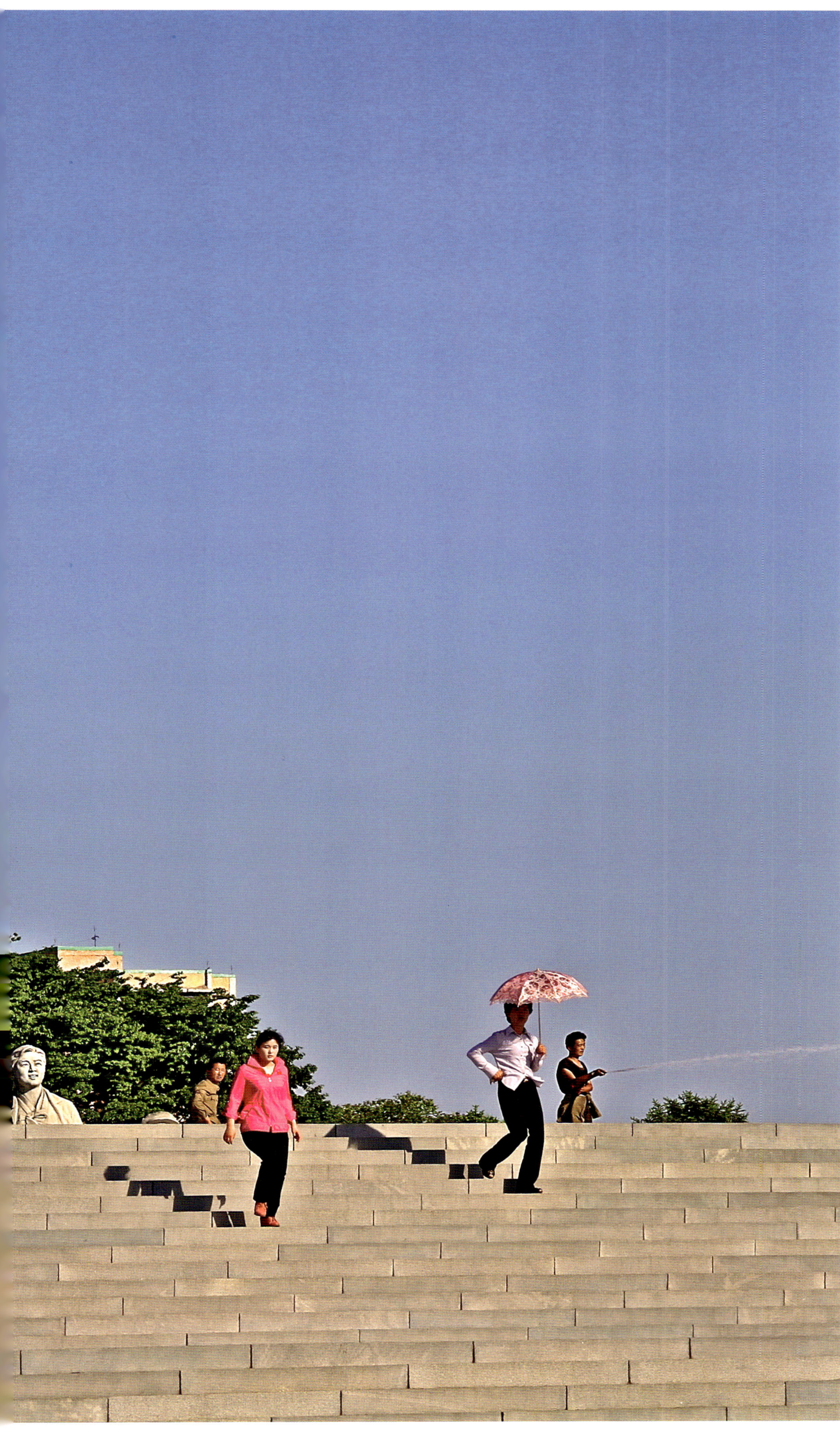

The characters on the roof stand for "solidarity."
Auf dem Gebäude prangen die Zeichen für „Solidarität".
Les caractères couronnant le bâtiment signifient « solidarité ».

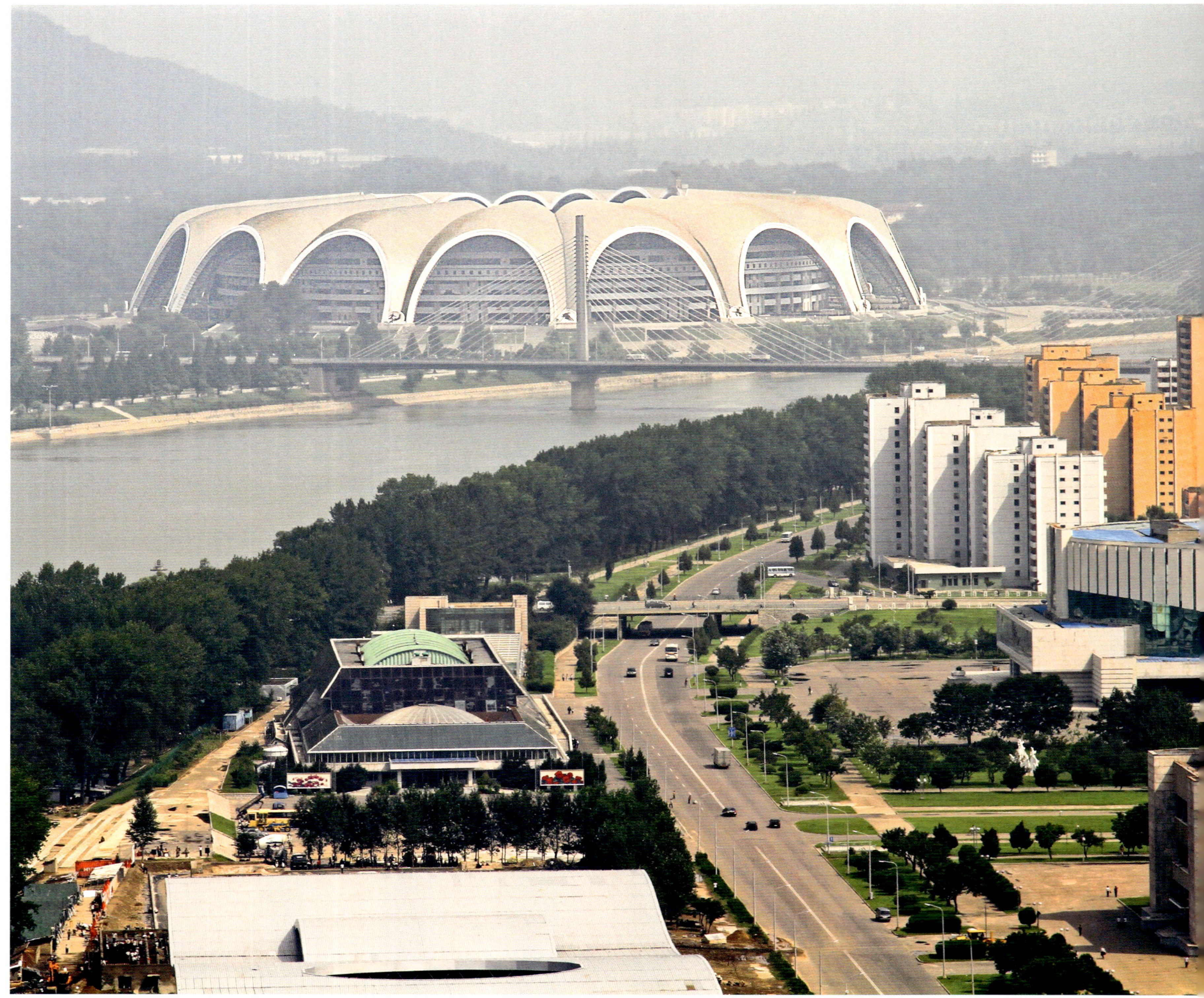

Left: May Day Stadium in Pyongyang, which is named for the day commemorating the worker's movement. The stadium can seat 150,000 people.
Right: View from Independence Tower, Pyongyang
Links: Stadion „Erster Mai", Pjöngjang. Der Name leitet sich vom Tag der Arbeiterbewegung ab. 150 000 Menschen finden hier Platz.
Rechts: Ausblick vom Unabhängigkeitsturm, Pjöngjang
À gauche : Le stade du Premier-Mai, à Pyongyang, ainsi nommé en hommage à la Journée internationale des travailleurs, peut accueillir jusqu'à 150 000 personnes.
À droite : Vue de la tour de l'Indépendance, à Pyongyang

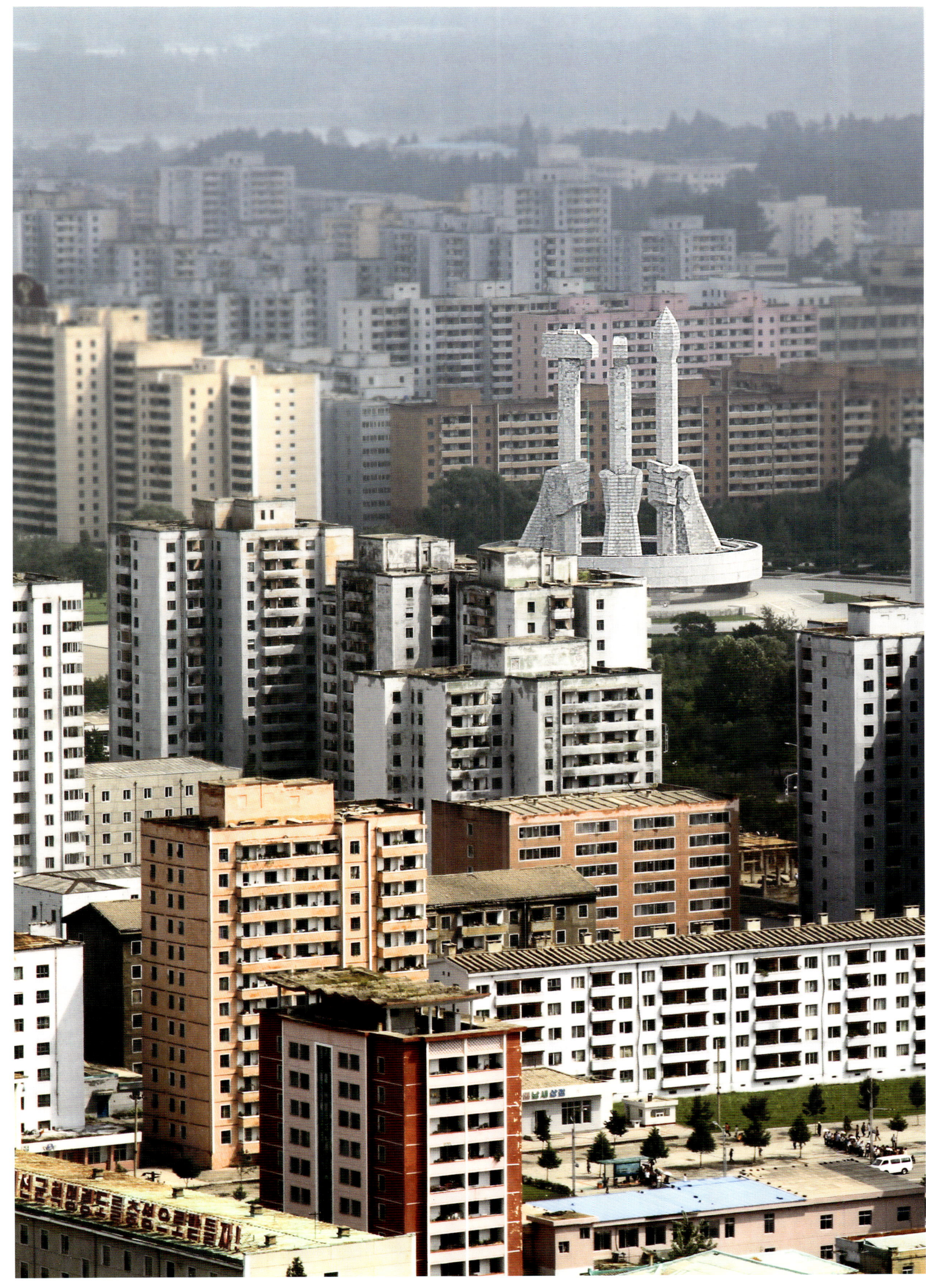

Left: Bust of Kim Jong-il's mother, Kim Jong-suk.
As a young girl, she joined the guerrillas in the struggle against the Japanese occupation forces.
Right: Revolutionary Martyrs' Cemetery, Pyongyang

Links: Büste der Kim Jong-suk, Mutter von Kim Jong-il.
Als junges Mädchen schloss sie sich den Guerillakriegern im Kampf gegen die japanischen Besatzer an.
Rechts: Friedhof der Revolutionshelden, Pjöngjang

À gauche : Buste de Kim Jong-suk, la mère de Kim Jong-il.
À l'adolescence, elle s'est engagée dans le mouvement de résistance à l'occupant japonais.
À droite : Le cimetière des héros de la Révolution, à Pyongyang

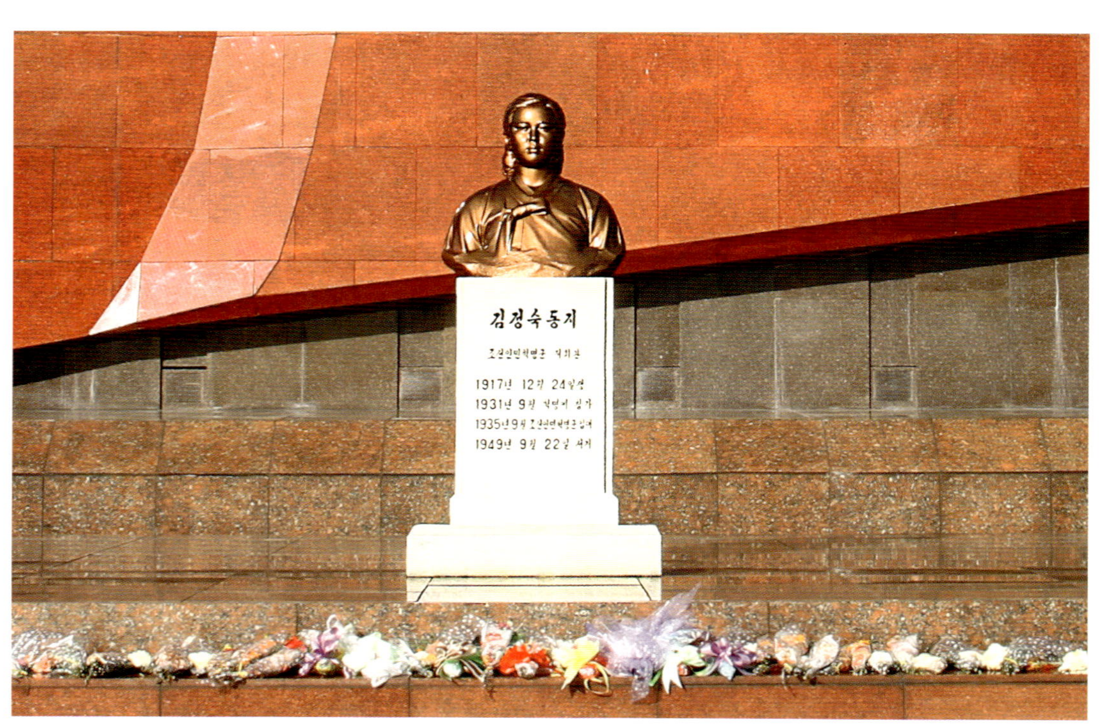

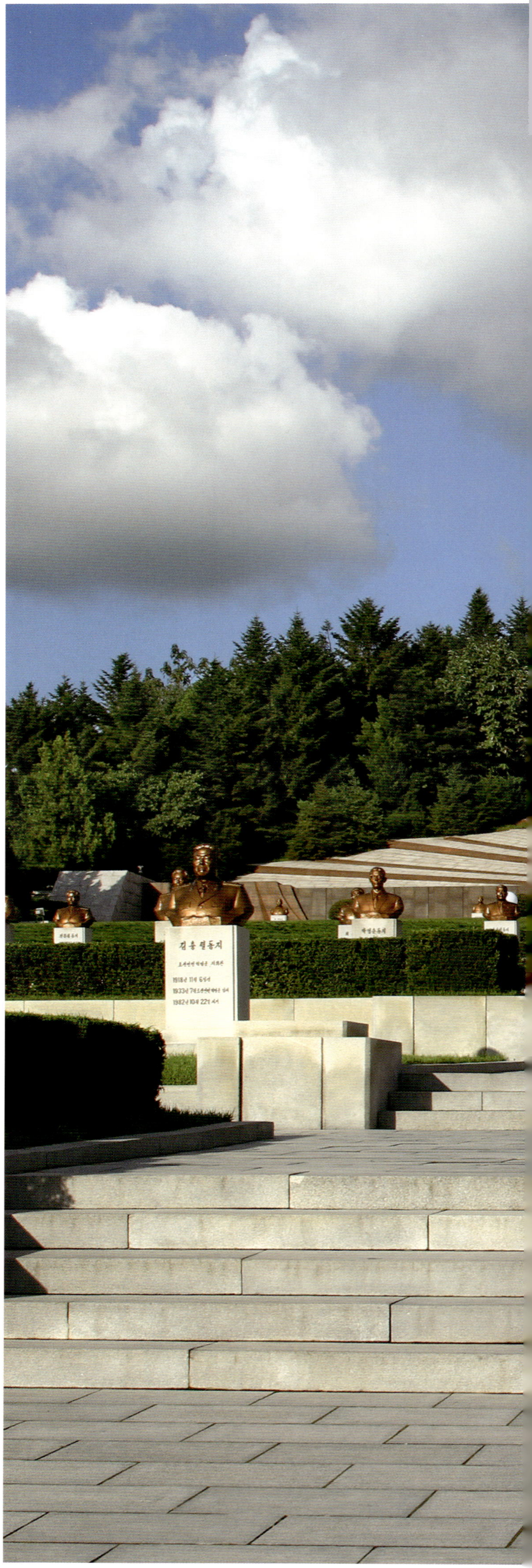

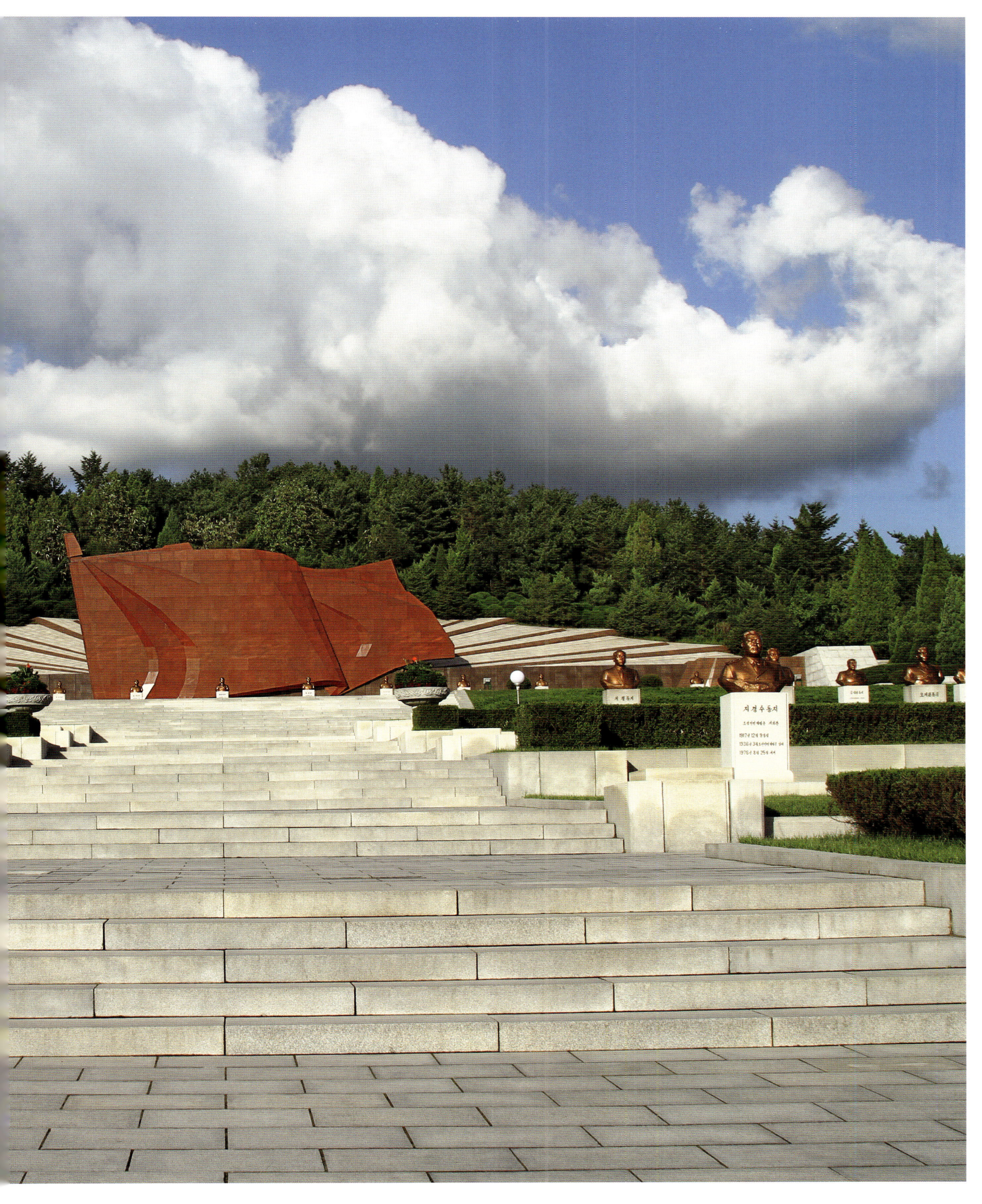
지경수동지

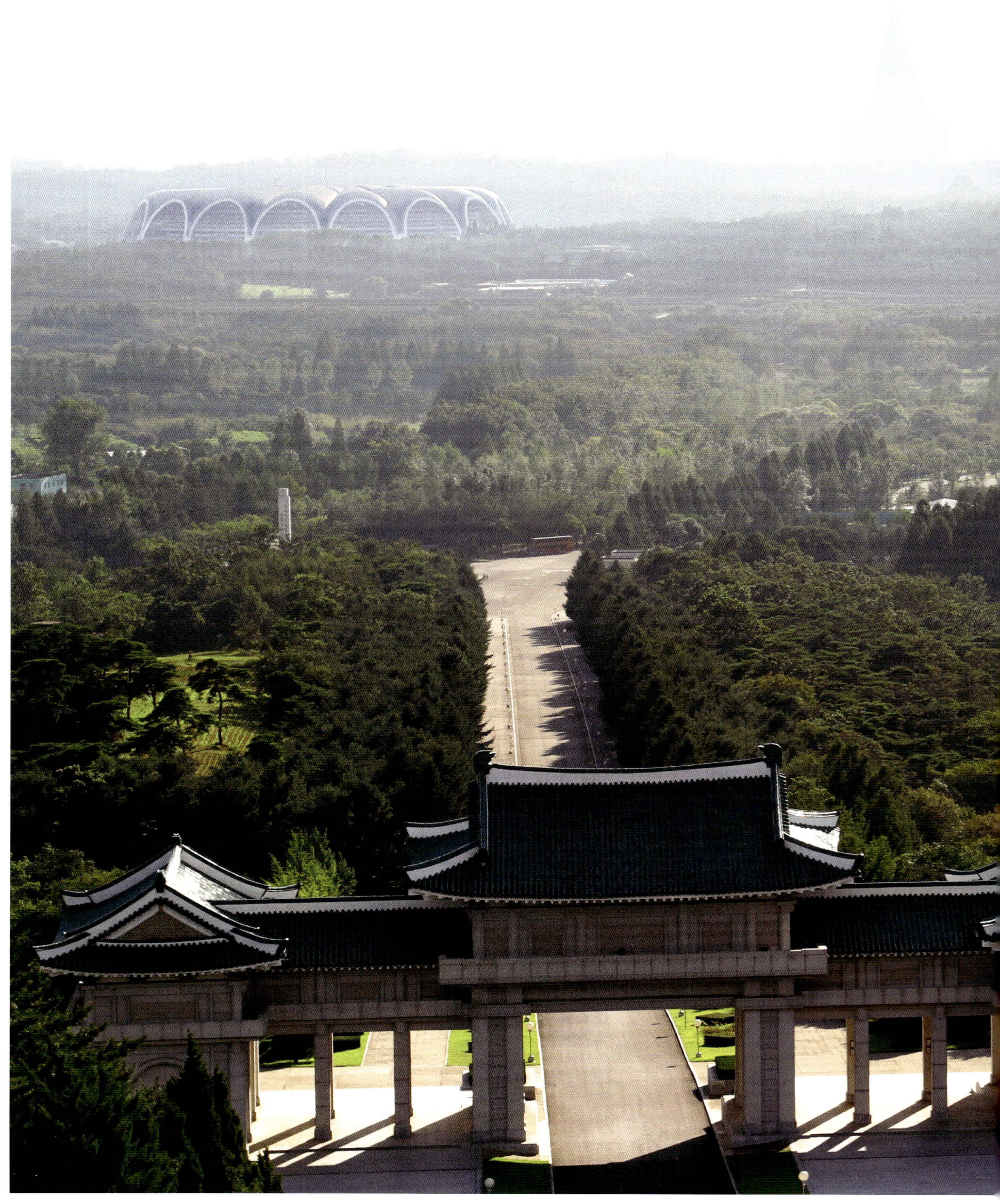

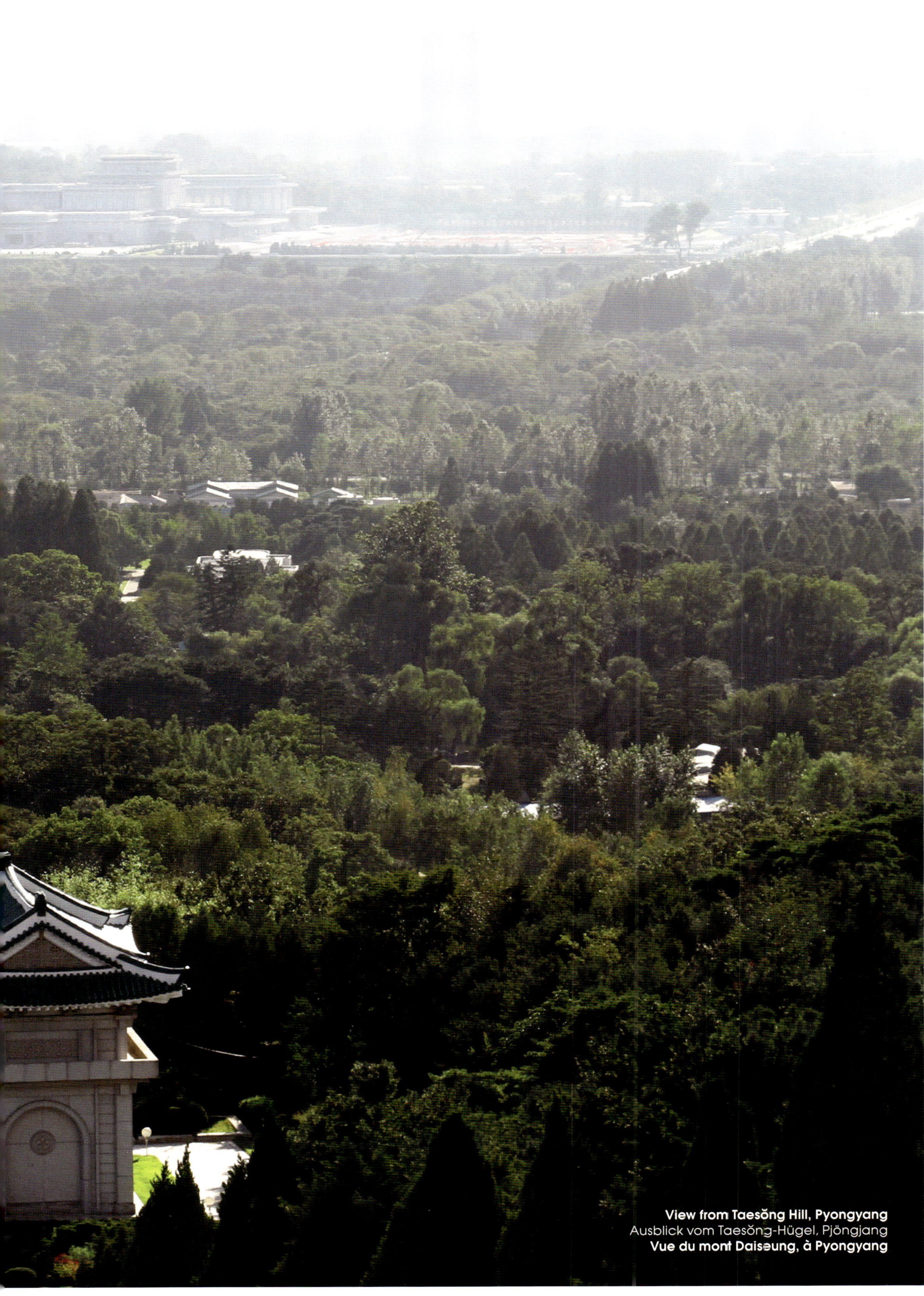

View from Taesŏng Hill, Pyongyang
Ausblick vom Taesŏng-Hügel, Pjöngjang
Vue du mont Daiseung, à Pyongyang

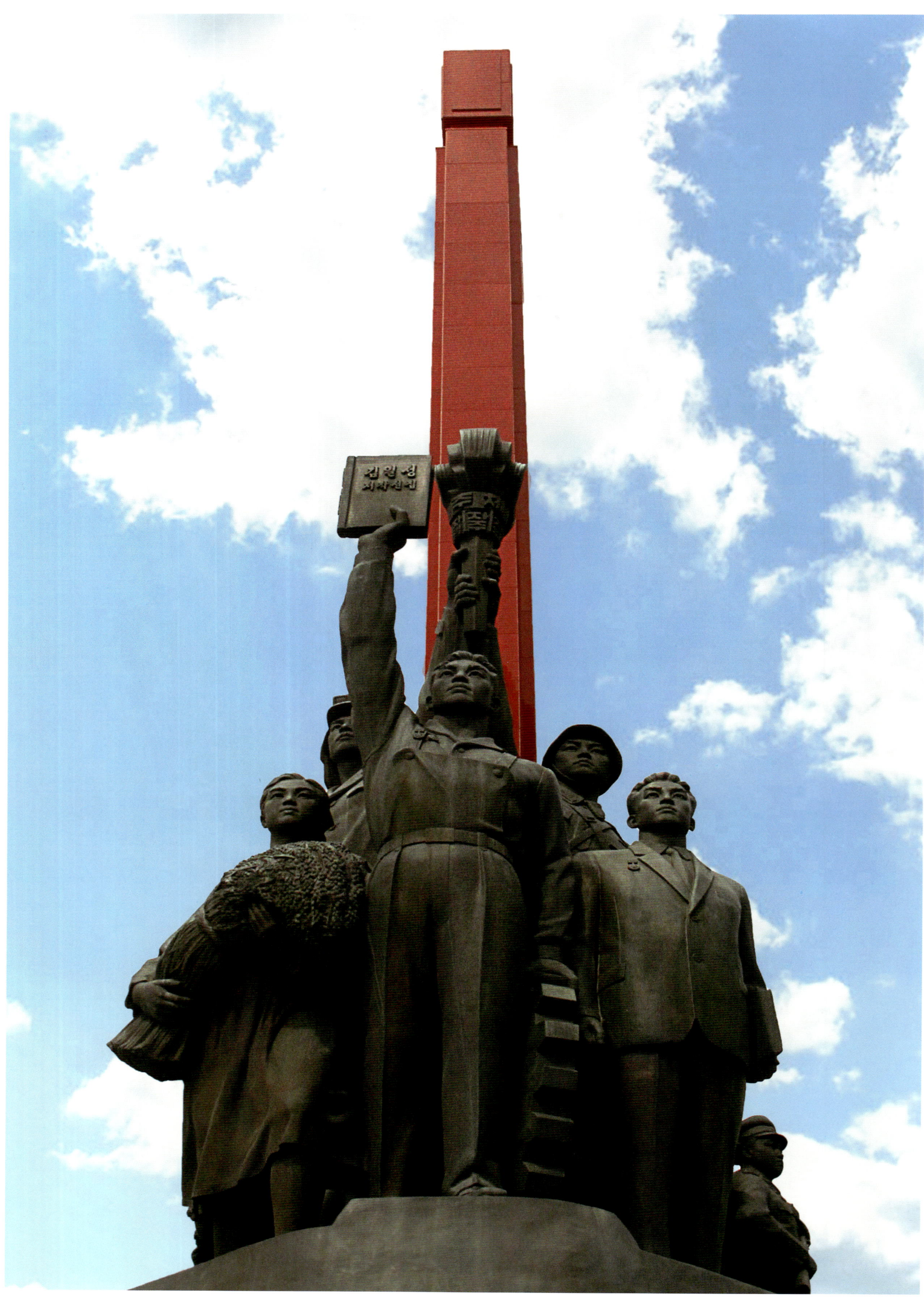
김일성

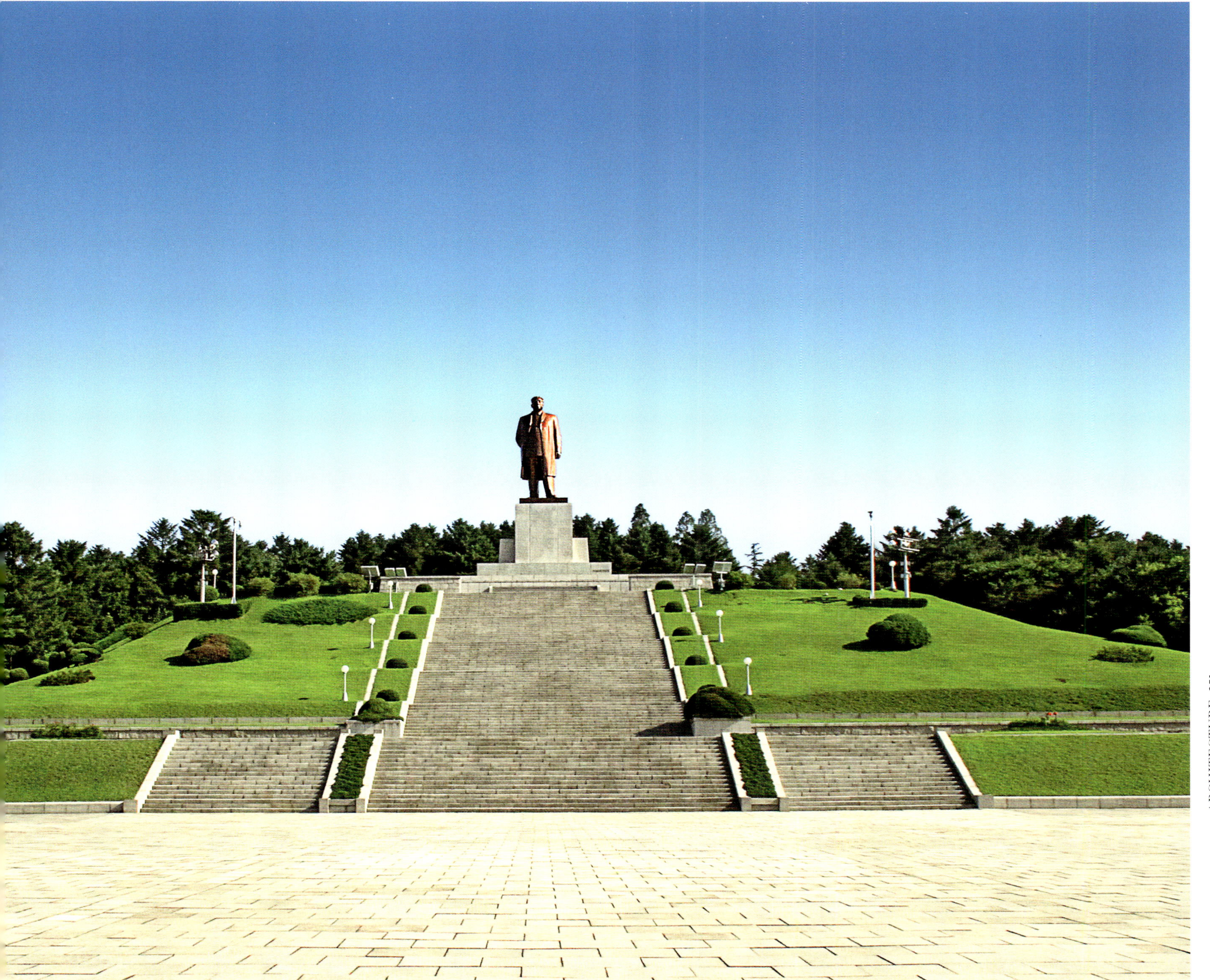

Left: Pulling together in the spirit of Juche: Industrial workers, farmers, soldiers, and intellectuals hold up the Juche flame.
Right: Statue of Kim Il-sung in Kaesŏng. North Korea is the only country that mass-produces giant statues cast in bronze. Although African rulers are the main customers for these exports, a number of figures decorating fountains in Frankfurt were also made in North Korea.
Links: Gemeinsam für Juche: Industriearbeiter, Bauern, Soldaten und Akademiker halten die Juche-Flamme hoch.
Rechts: Statue von Kim Il-sung in Kaesŏng. Nordkorea ist das einzige Land, das den Bronzeguss von Riesenstatuen in großer Zahl betreibt. Die Exportgüter stehen hoch im Kurs bei afrikanischen Herrschern, aber auch in Frankfurt am Main gibt es einige Brunnenfiguren, die aus Nordkorea stammen.
À gauche : Unis pour le Juche : des ouvriers, des paysans, des soldats et des universitaires portent haut la flamme du Juche.
À droite : La statue de Kim Il-sung à Kaesŏng. La Corée du Nord est le seul pays au monde qui fabrique en grand nombre des statues colossales en bronze. Si ces produits d'exportation ont surtout la faveur des souverains africains, on trouve aussi à Francfort-sur-le-Main des statues de fontaine « made in North Korea ».

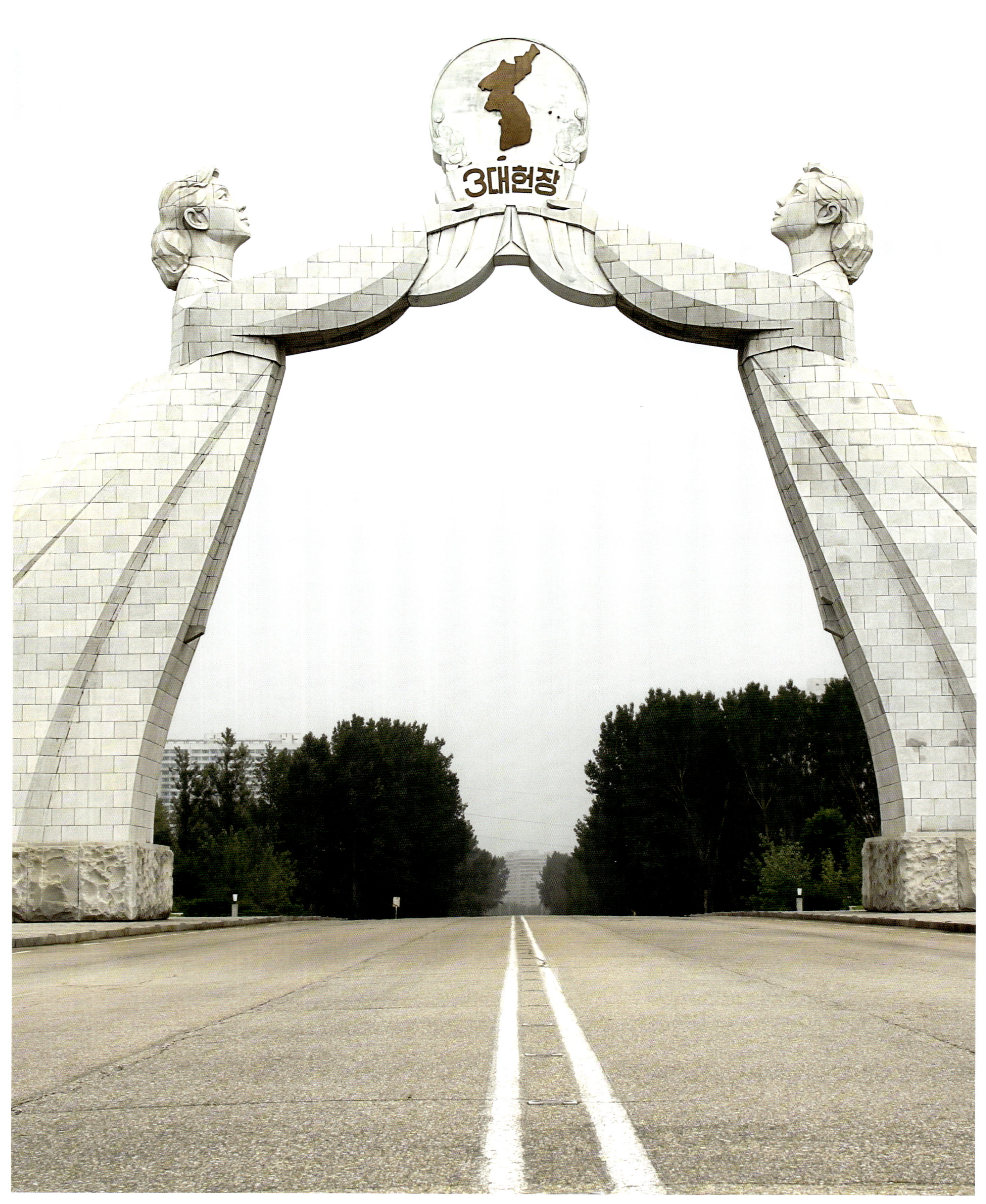
3대헌장

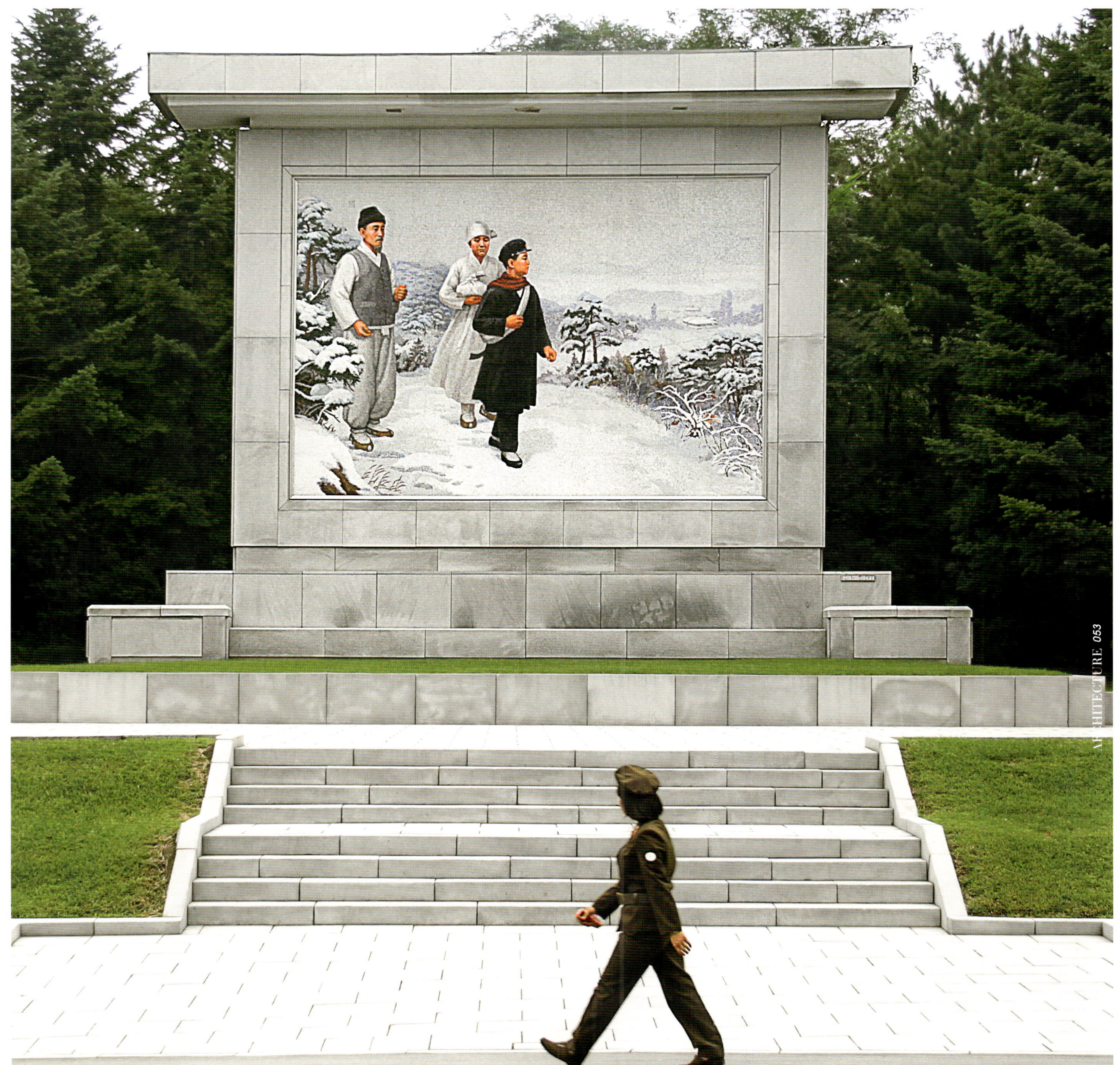

Left: The Korean sisters, South and North, reach out toward a unified country.
This monument symbolizes the idea of peaceful reunification, without any foreign meddling.
Right: In North Korea, the bloody, 100-day military campaign led by Kim Il-sung against the Japanese occupation forces is known as the first "Painful March." The monument shows a young Kim Il-sung as a guerrilla fighter.

Links: Die koreanischen Schwestern, Süden und Norden, reichen dem vereinten Korea die Hände. Das Denkmal symbolisiert die friedliche Wiedervereinigung frei von fremder Einmischung.
Rechts: Als ersten „anstrengenden Marsch" bezeichnet man in Nordkorea den blutigen, 100 Tage währenden Marsch, den Kim Il-sung gegen die japanischen Besatzer anführte. Das Monument zeigt ihn in seiner Jugend als Guerillakämpfer.

À gauche : Les sœurs coréennes, le Sud et le Nord, tendent les mains vers le pays réunifié. Ce mémorial symbolise la réunification pacifique, sans ingérence étrangère.
À droite : En Corée du Nord, on appelle « première Marche exténuante » la campagne de 100 jours menée par Kim Il-sung contre l'occupant nippon.
Ce monument le représente en jeune combattant indépendant.

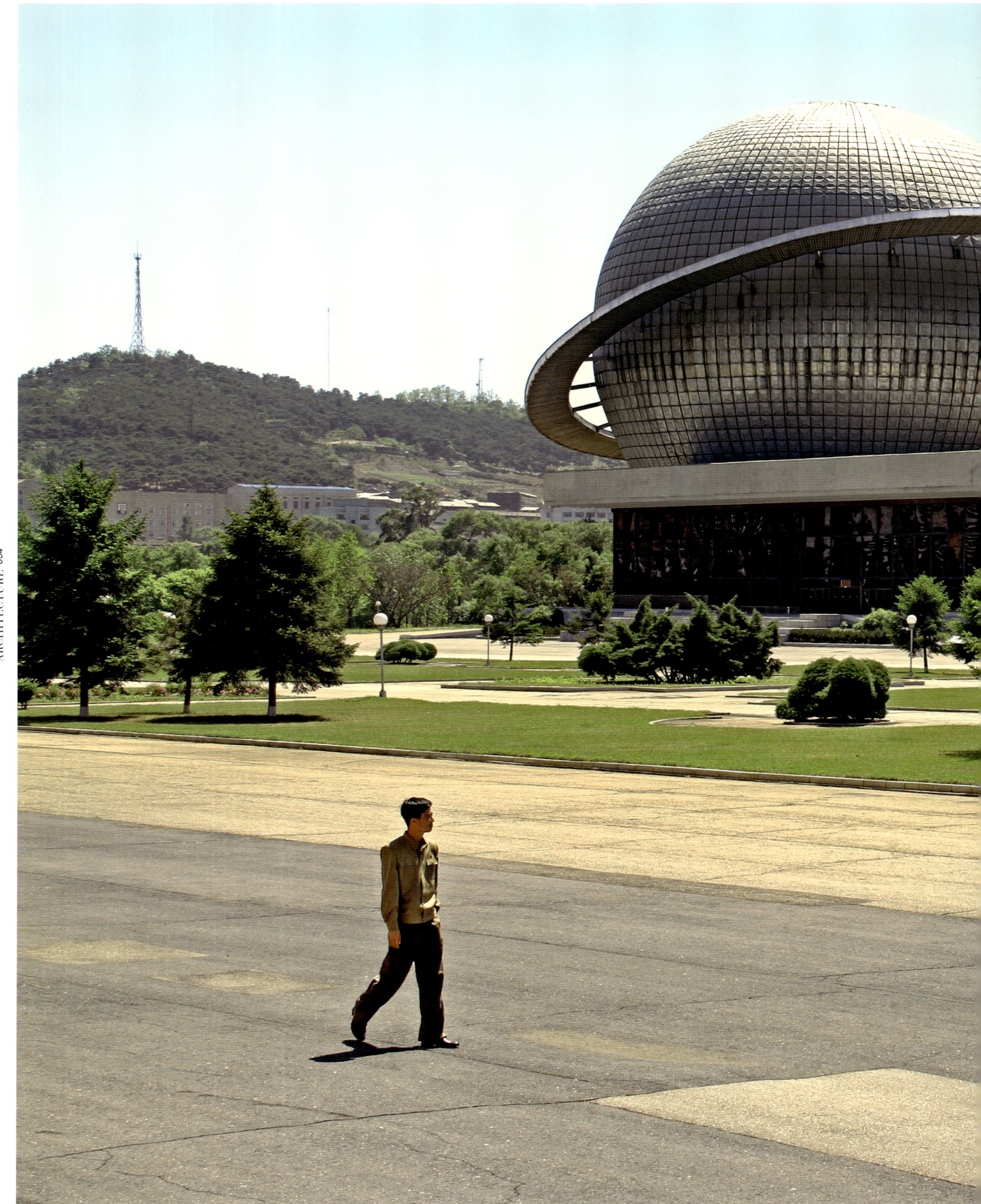

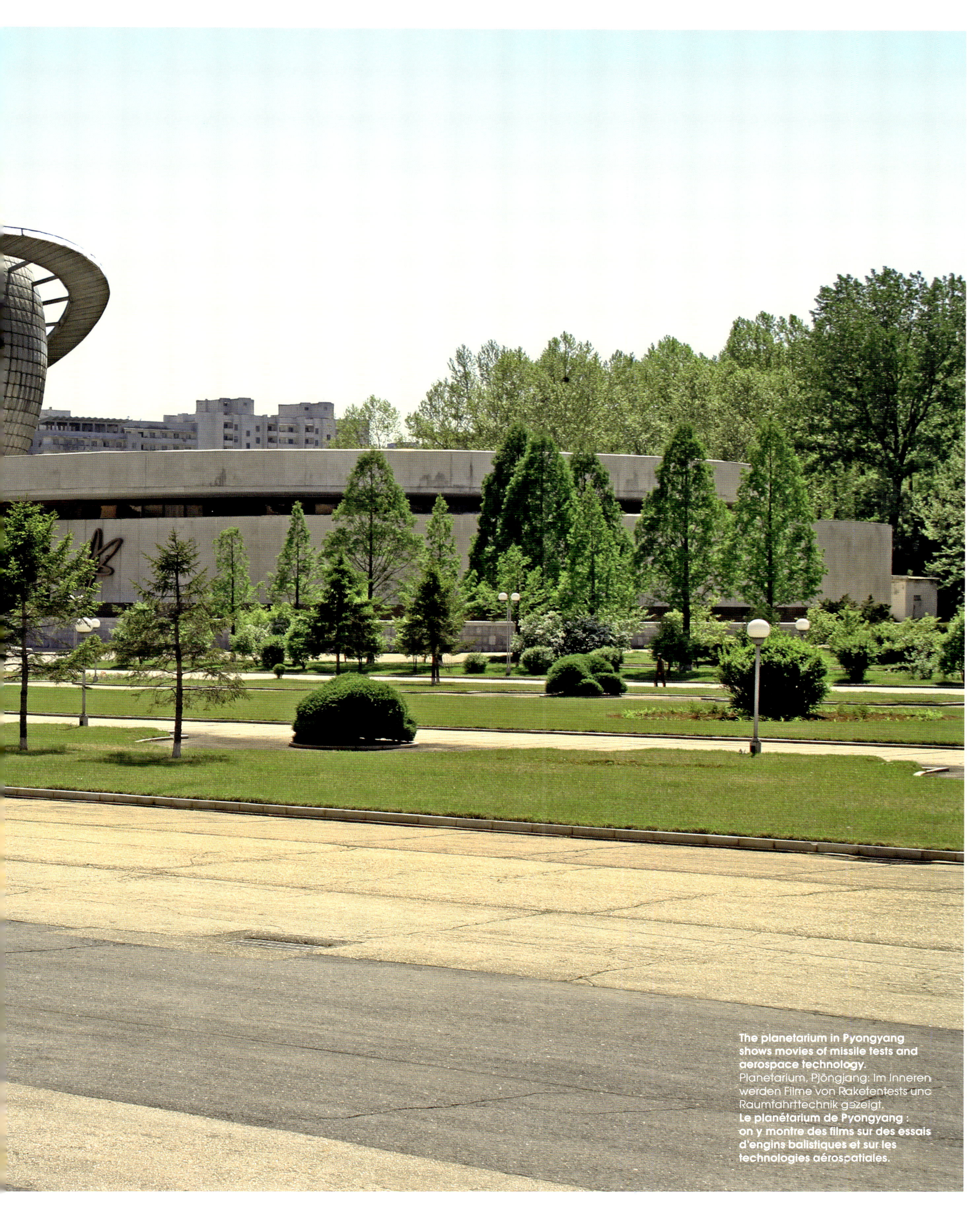

The planetarium in Pyongyang shows movies of missile tests and aerospace technology.
Planetarium, Pjöngjang: Im Inneren werden Filme von Raketentests und Raumfahrttechnik gezeigt.
Le planétarium de Pyongyang : on y montre des films sur des essais d'engins balistiques et sur les technologies aérospatiales.

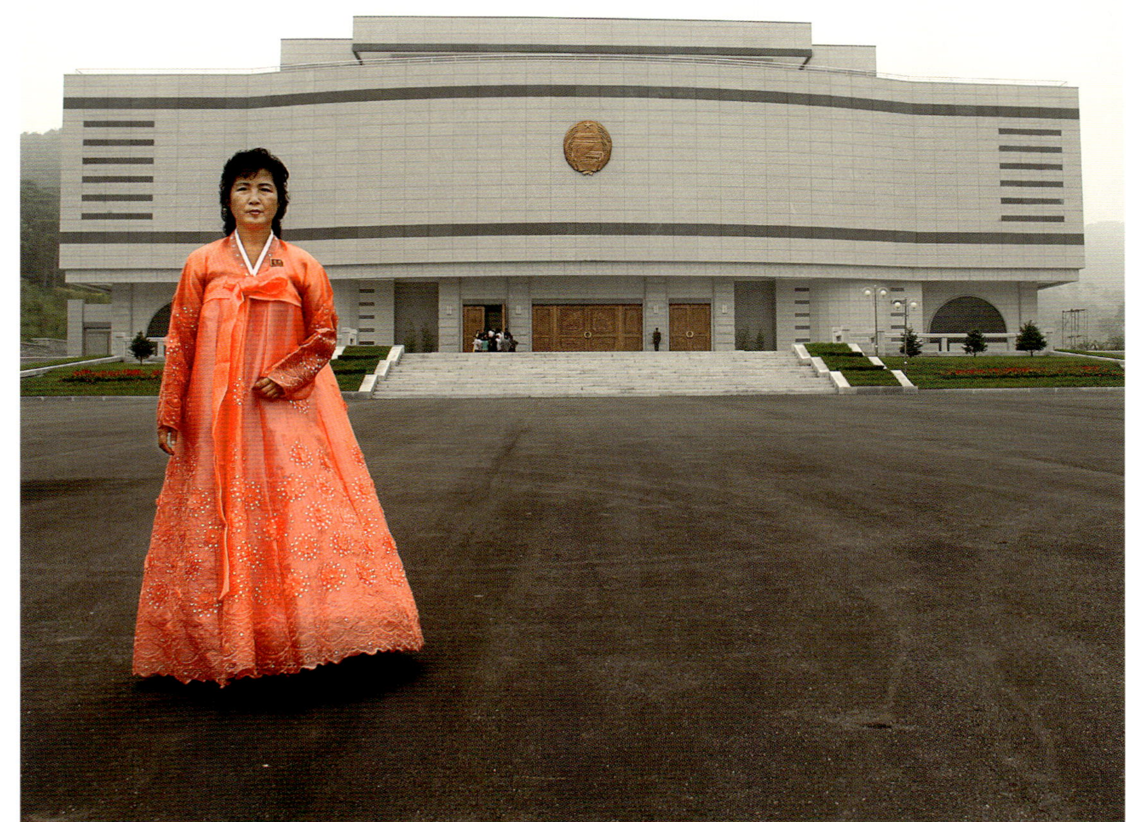

Left: Friendship exhibition in the Myohyang Mountains; the "Eternal Leader" in front of a painting of Paektusan, North Korea's highest mountain
Right: Reproduction of a missile in the Children's Palace. In 2012, the North Koreans fired a real-life missile into space, calling it the "Satellite of Love."
Links: Freundschaftsausstellung im Myohyang-Gebirge; der „Ewige Führer" vor dem gemalten Paektusan, dem höchsten Berg Nordkoreas
Rechts: Raketenattrappe im Kinderpalast. 2012 schoss eine echte nordkoreanische Rakete den „Satelliten der Liebe" ins Weltall.
À gauche : Exposition de l'Amitié internationale dans les monts Myohyang; « Le président éternel » devant une fresque représentant le mont Paektu
À droite : Fusée factice dans le Palais des enfants. En 2012, une vraie fusée nord-coréenne a placé en orbite le « satellite de l'amour ».

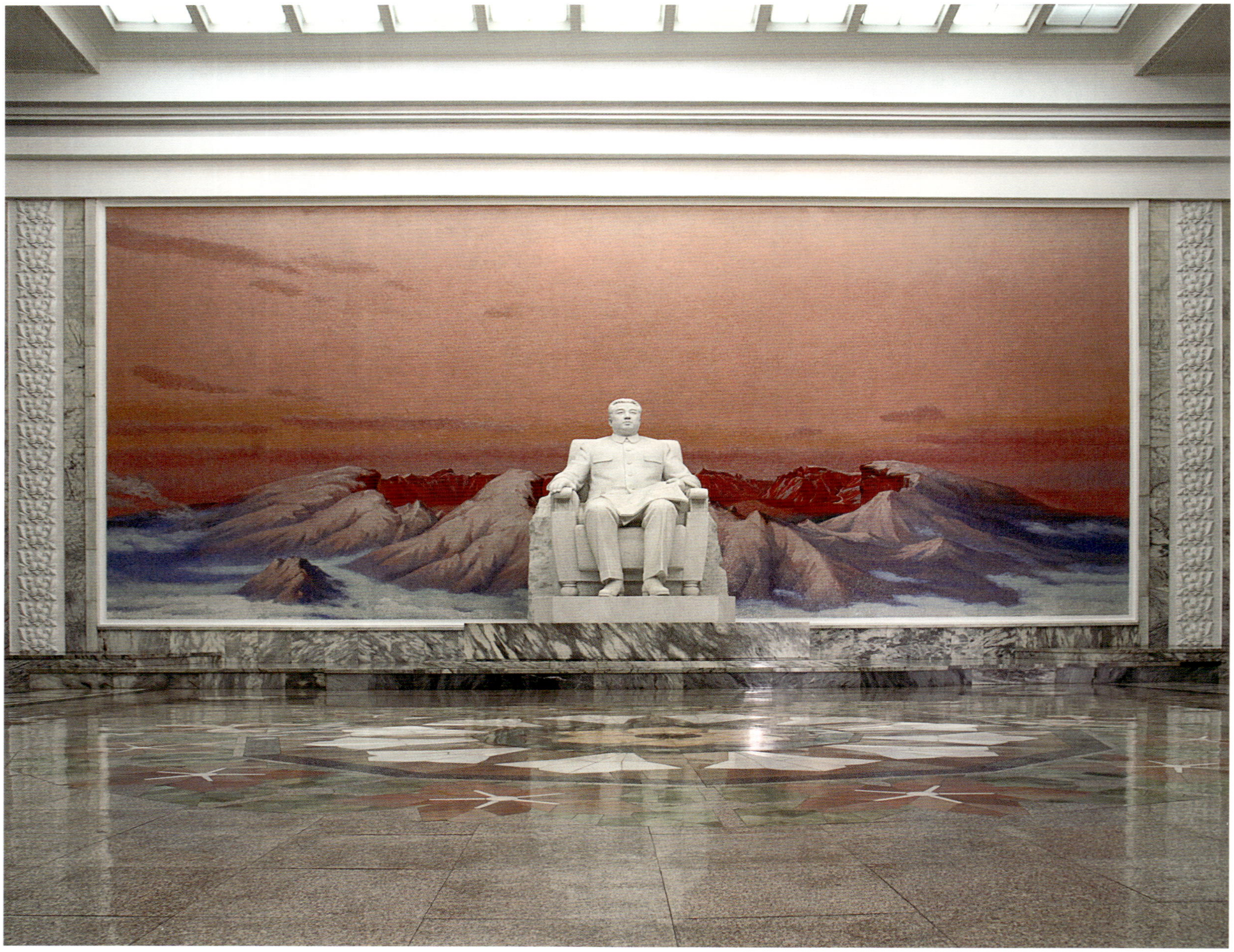

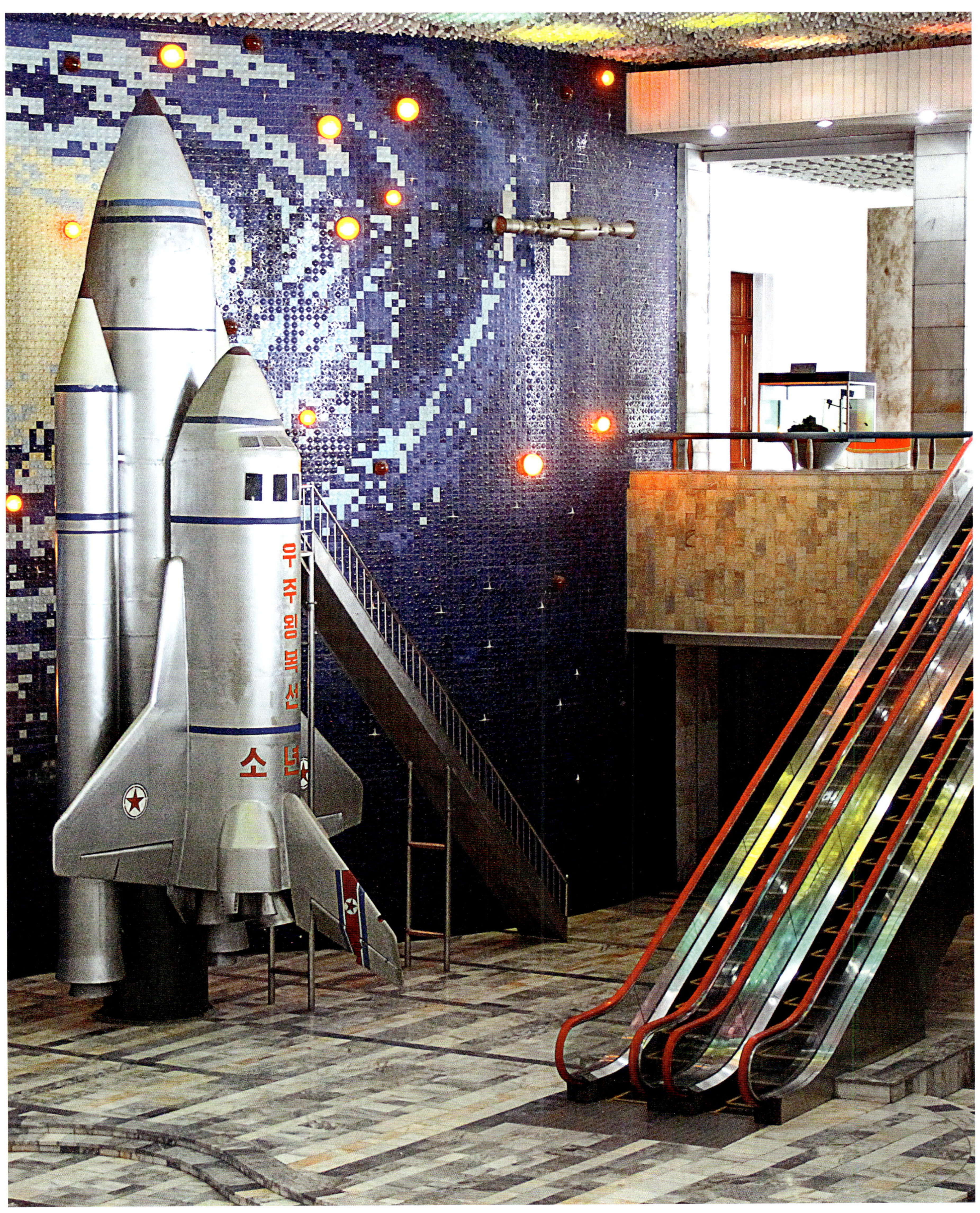
우주왕복선
소년

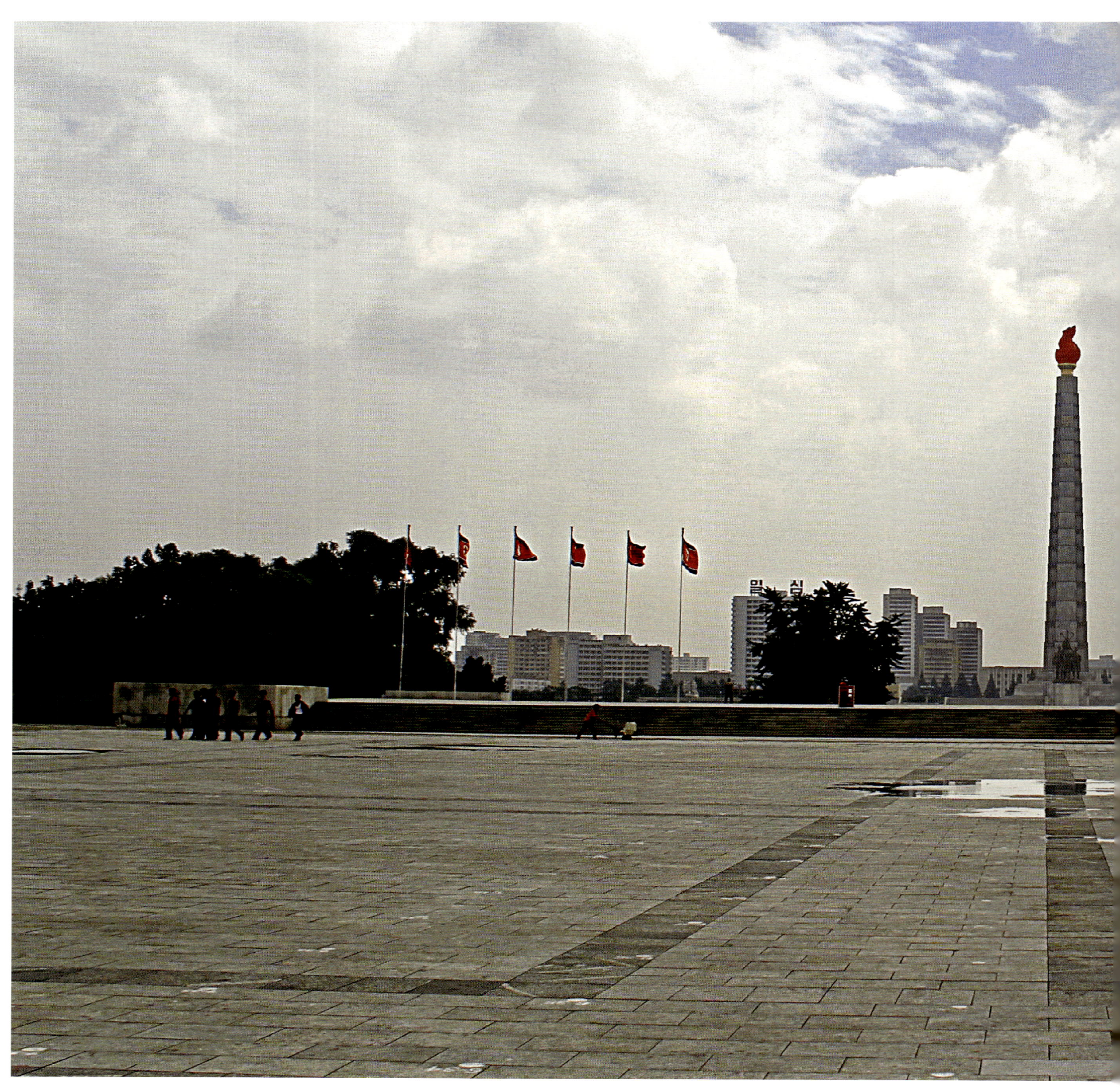

The Juche Tower symbolizes North Korea's state ideology. Juche (chuch'e) is a Korean word that loosely translates as "independence" or "self-reliance."
Der Juche-Turm symbolisiert die Staatsideologie Nordkoreas. Im Koreanischen bedeutet Juche (chuch'e) so viel wie Unabhängigkeit und Selbstständigkeit.
La tour du Juche symbolise la doctrine d'État de la Corée du Nord. Le mot coréen Juche (chuch'e) signifie indépendance et autonomie.

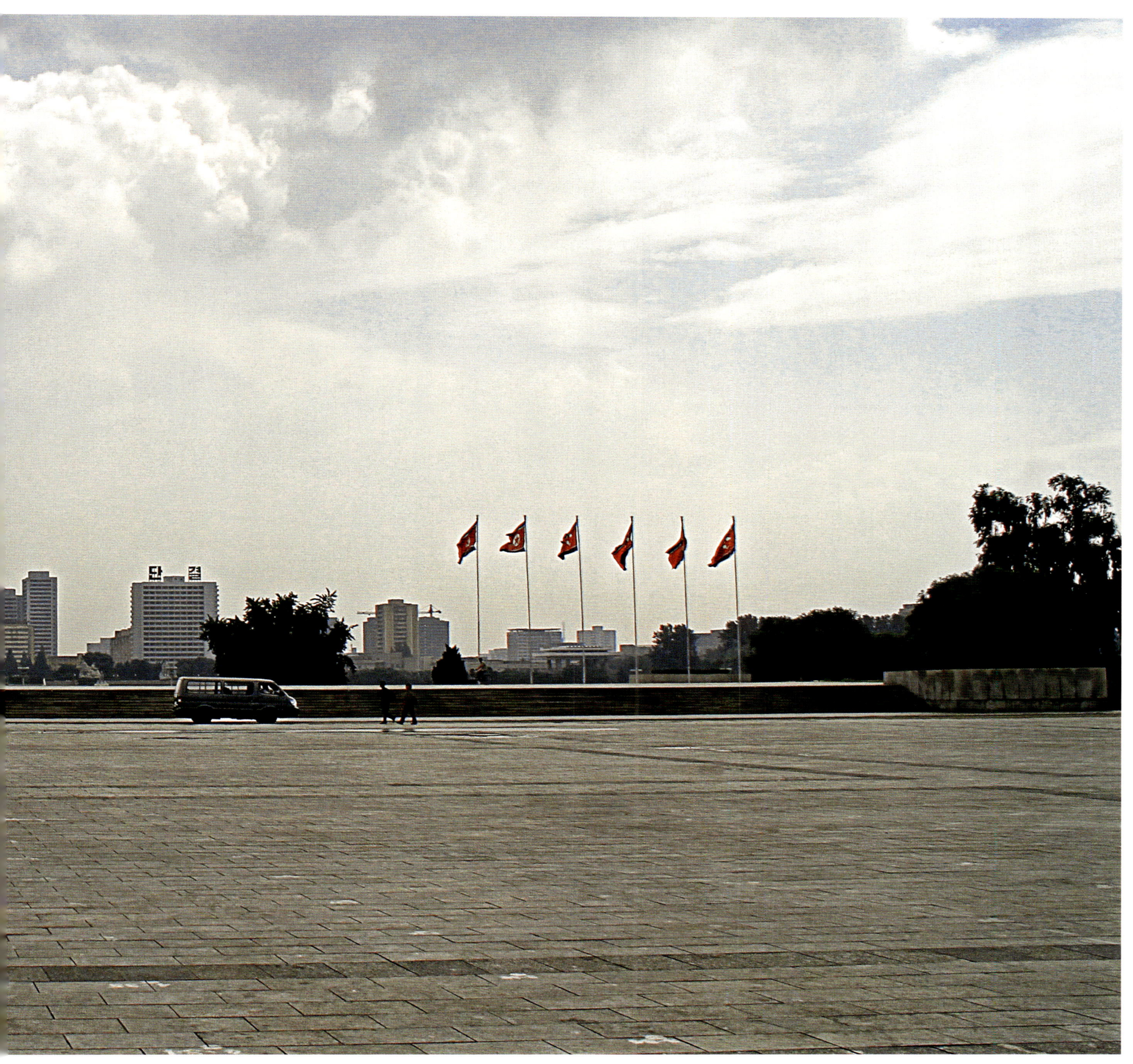
단결

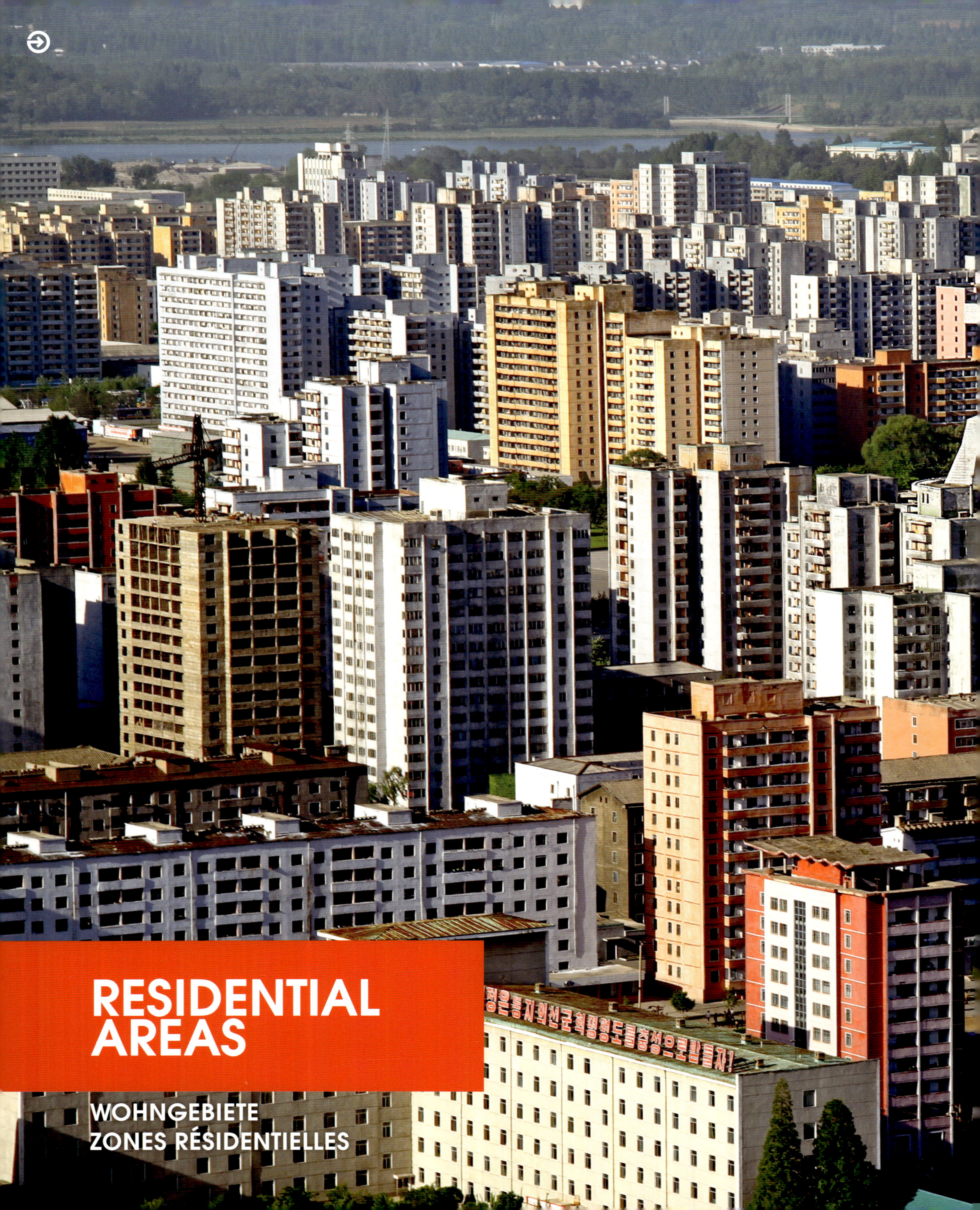

RESIDENTIAL AREAS

WOHNGEBIETE
ZONES RÉSIDENTIELLES

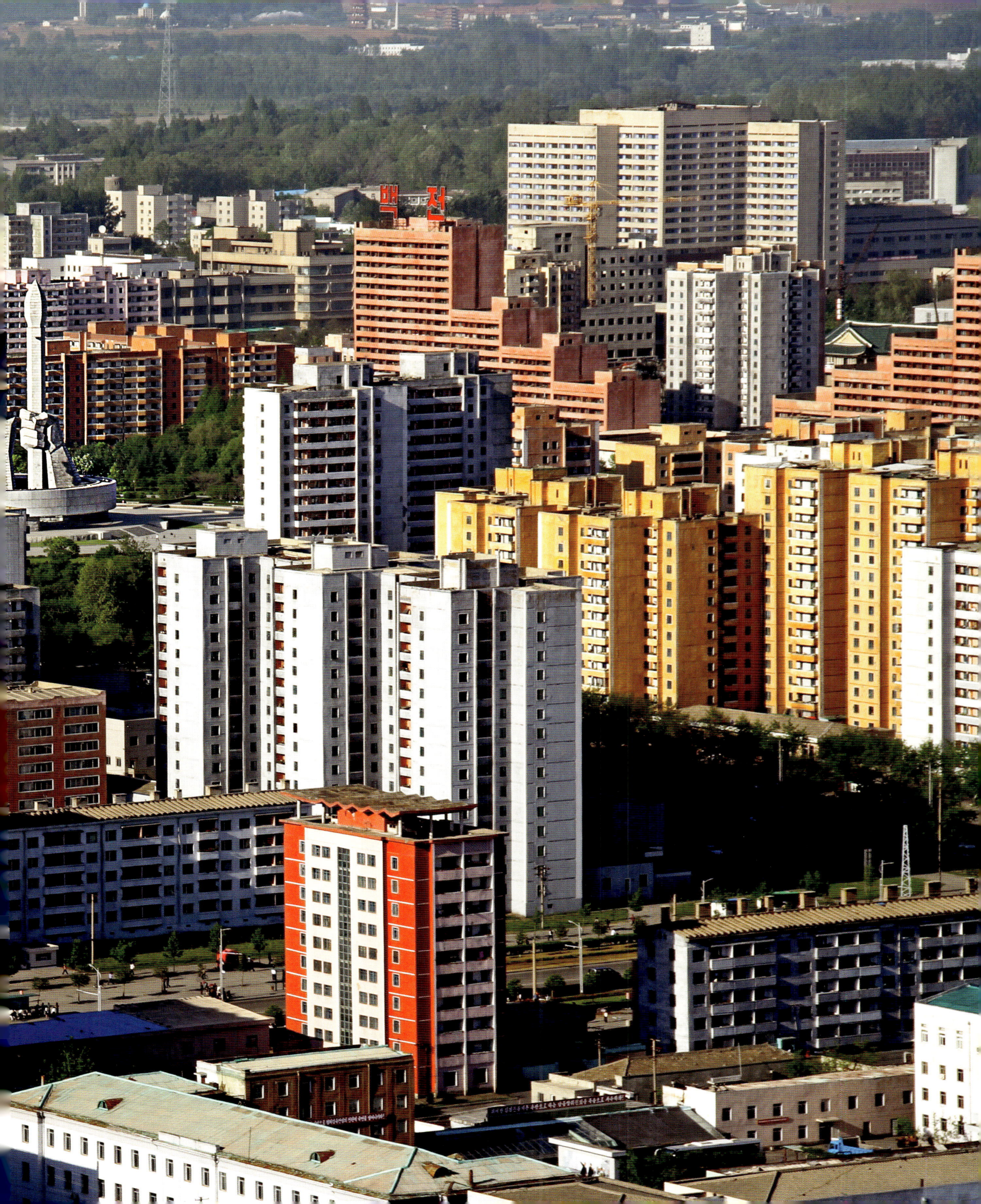
백 전

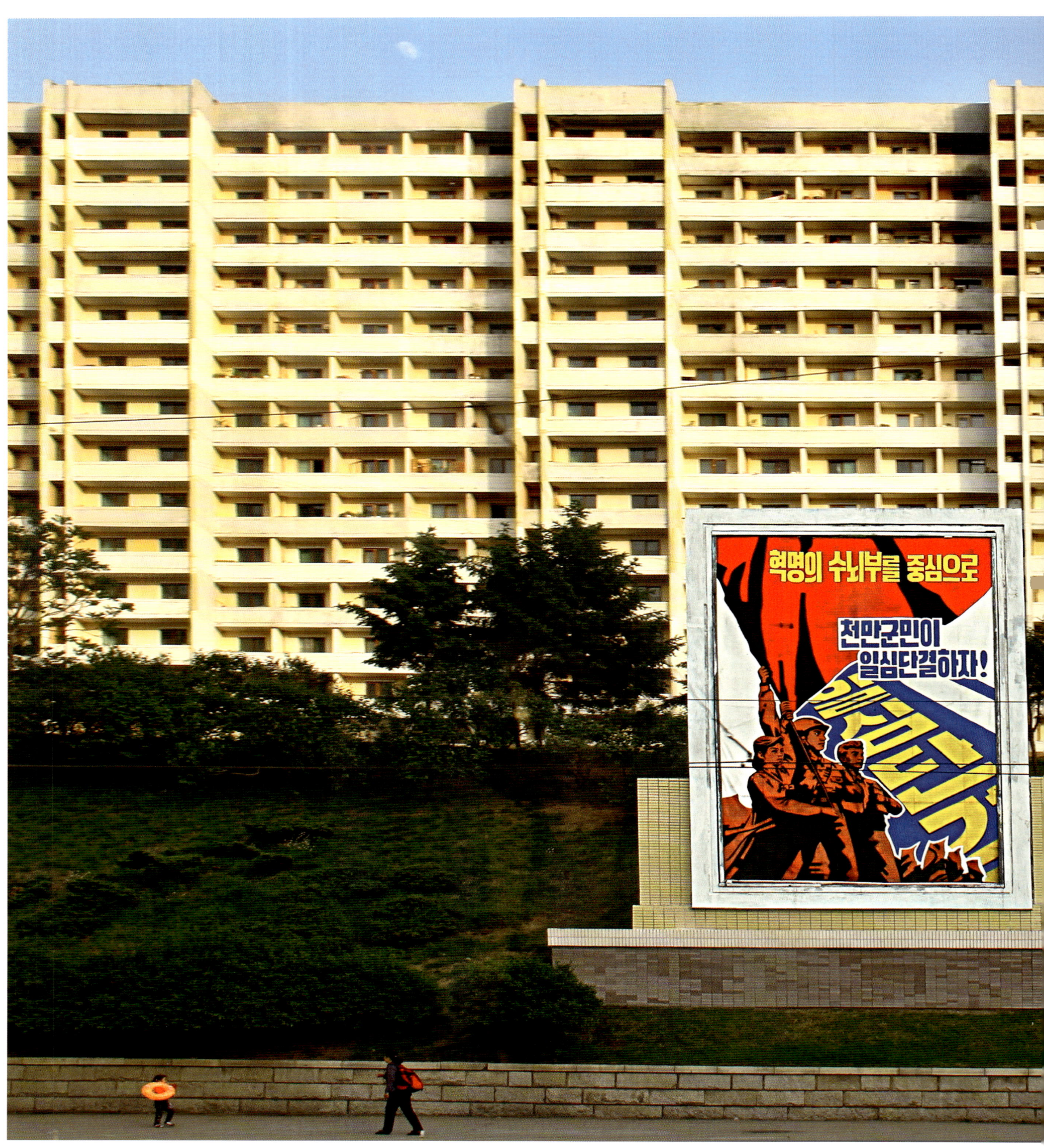

This is not a billboard ad but a call for people to remain on the alert.
Keine Werbeplakate: Hier wird zur Alarmbereitschaft aufgerufen.
Il ne s'agit pas de publicités mais d'une exhortation à se tenir en état d'alerte.

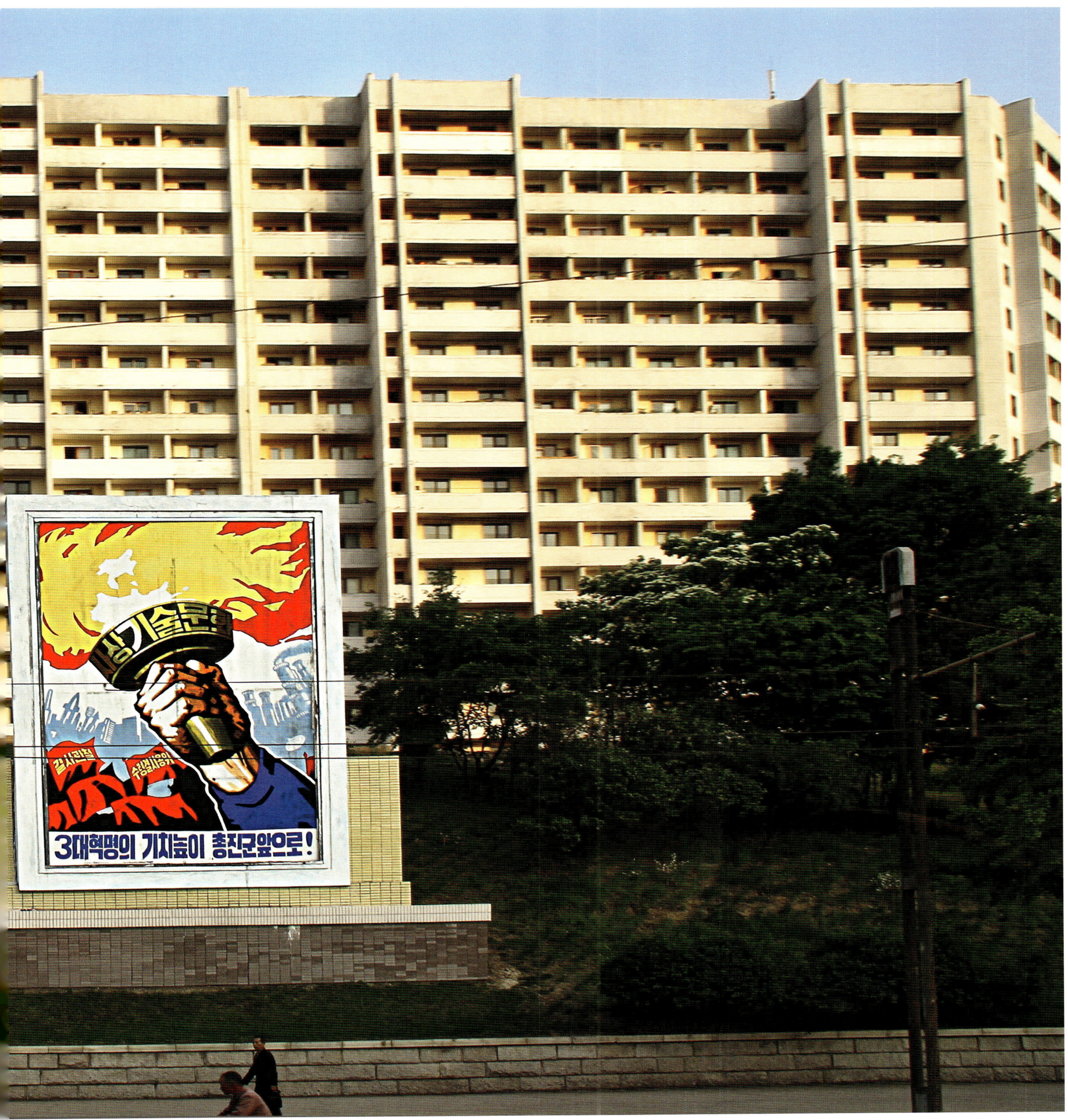
결사관철
수령결사옹위
3대혁명의 기치높이 총진군앞으로!

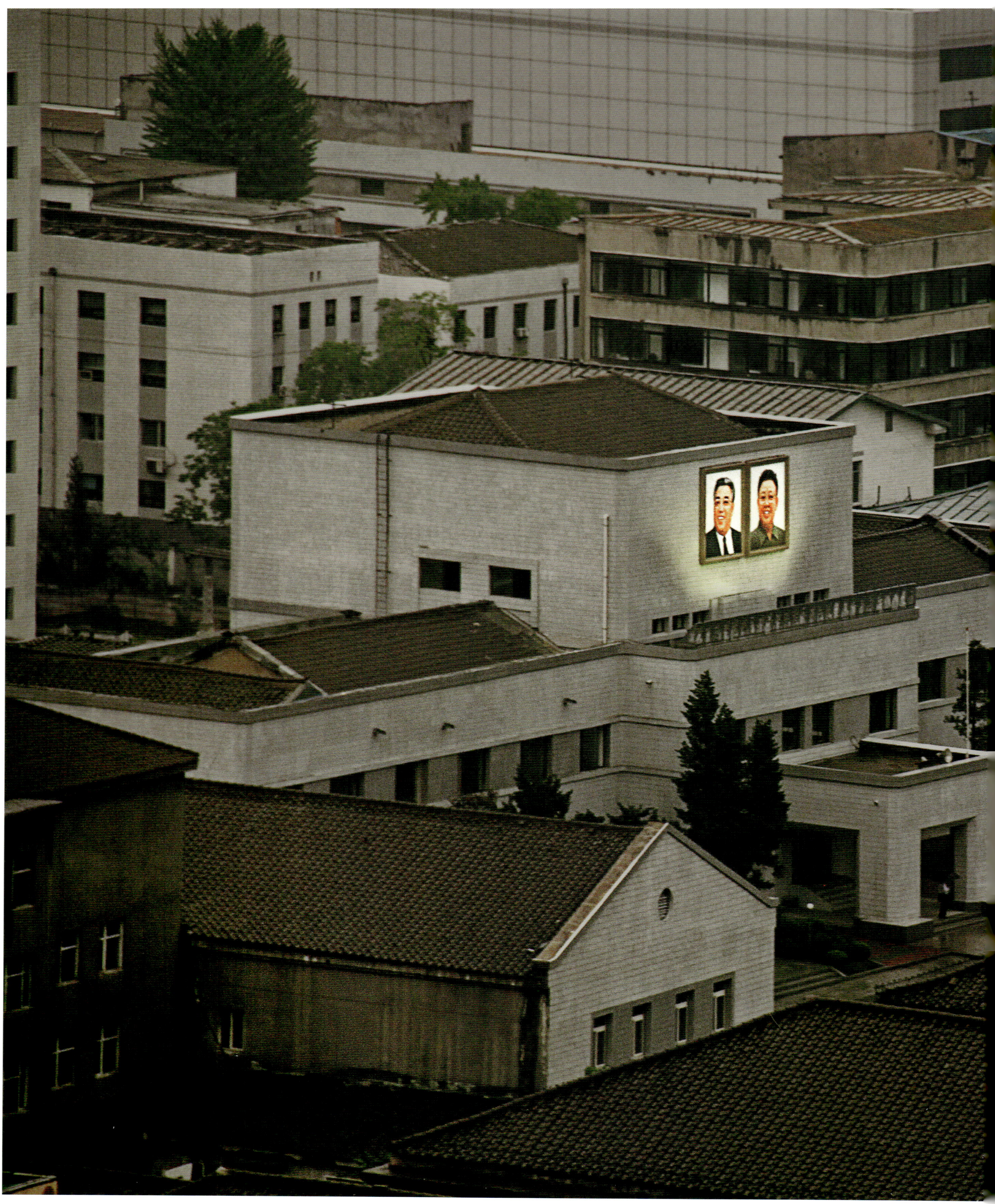

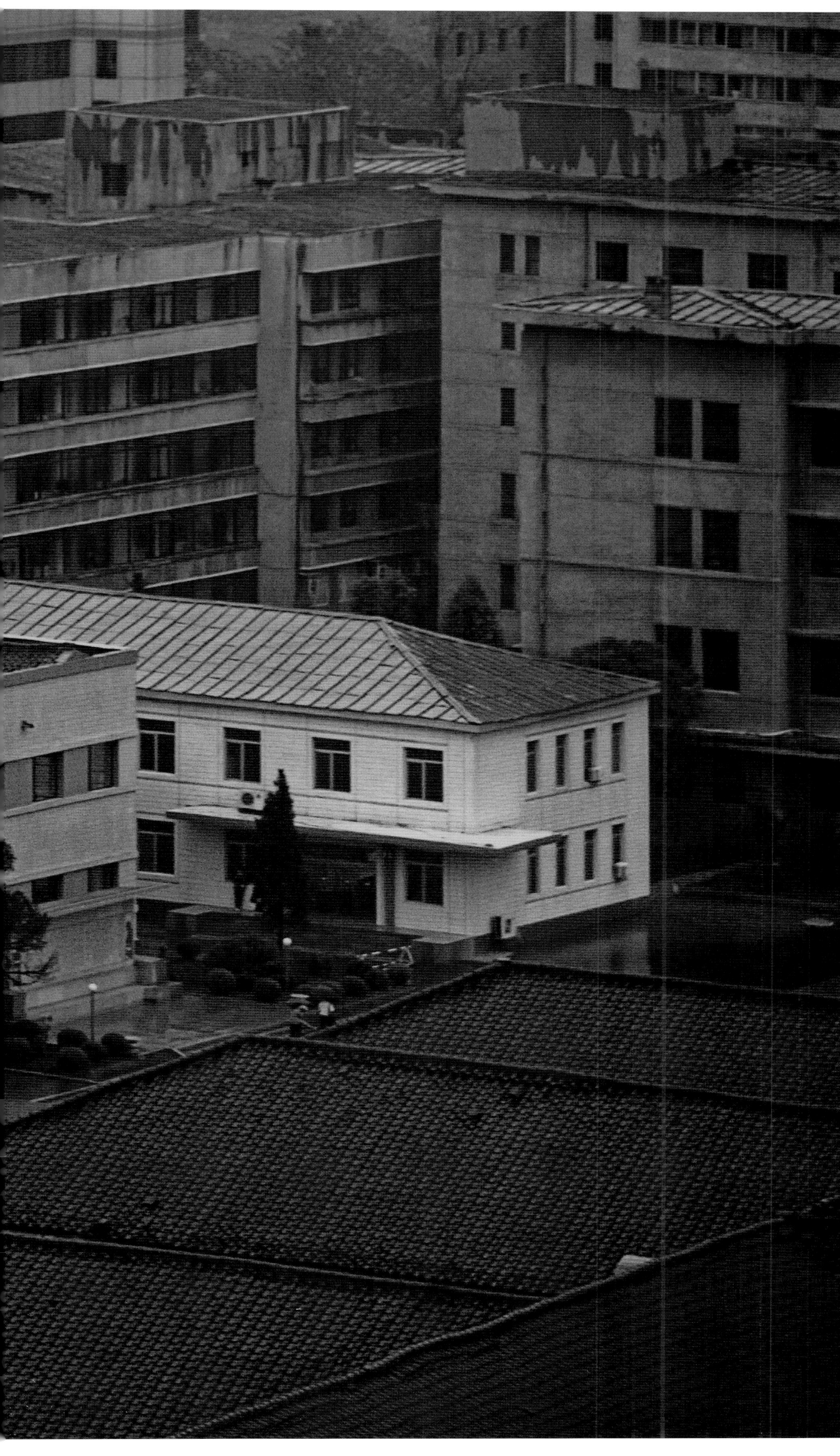

Lit up, the "Eternal Leaders" are often the only sources of light in the dark night.
Die illuminierten „Ewigen Führer" sind oft eine der wenigen Lichtquellen in der Dunkelheit.
Les effigies illuminées des « dirigeants éternels » sont souvent les seules sources de lumière une fois la nuit venue.

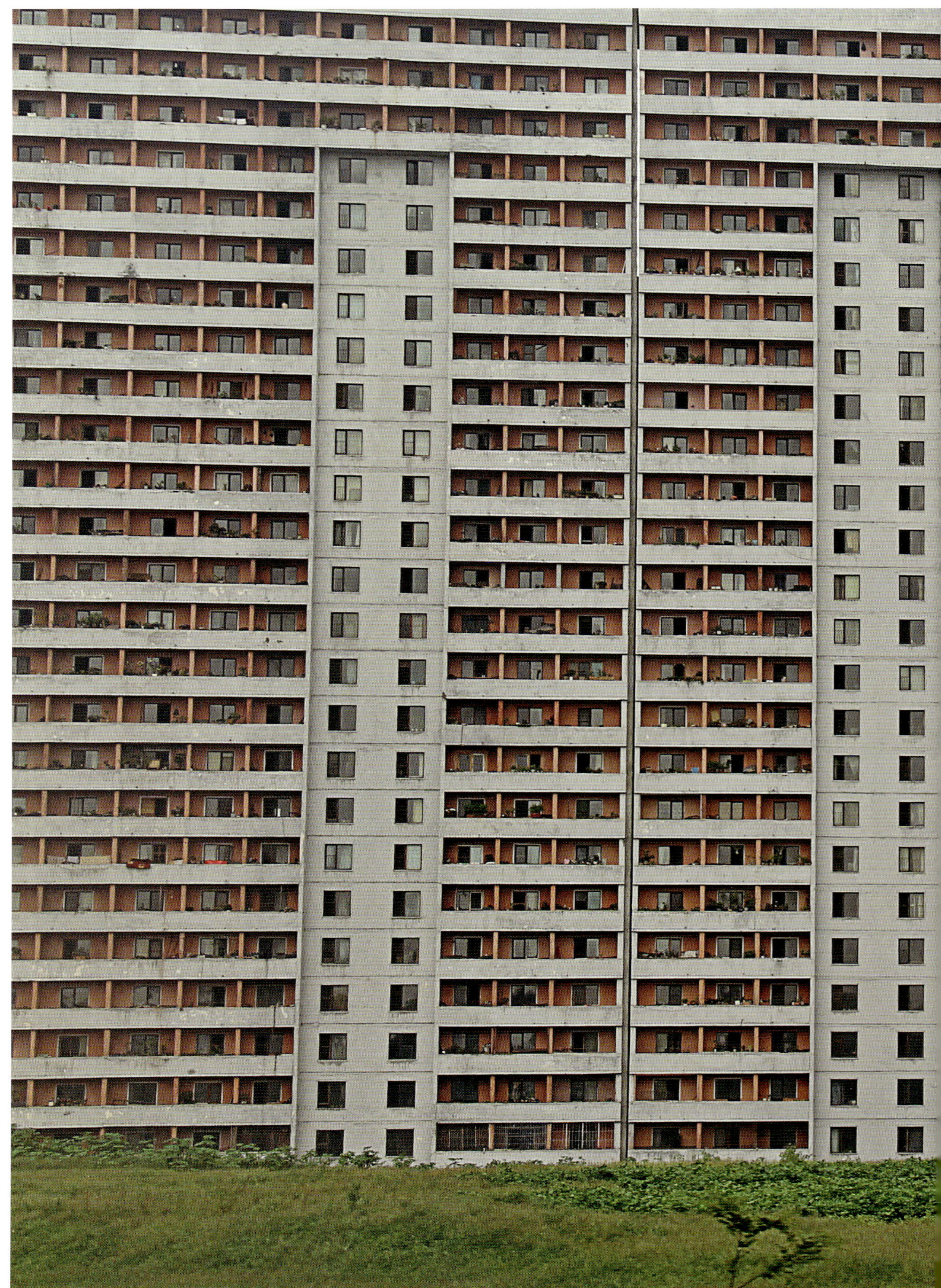

Three women arriving home. Residential buildings that house thousands of people reach for the sky like enormous honeycombs.
Drei Frauen kommen nach Hause. Wie riesige Waben recken sich Wohnblocks für Tausende gen Himmel.
Trois femmes rentrant chez elles. Semblables à des ruches gigantesques, des tours d'habitation s'élancent à la conquête des nuages.

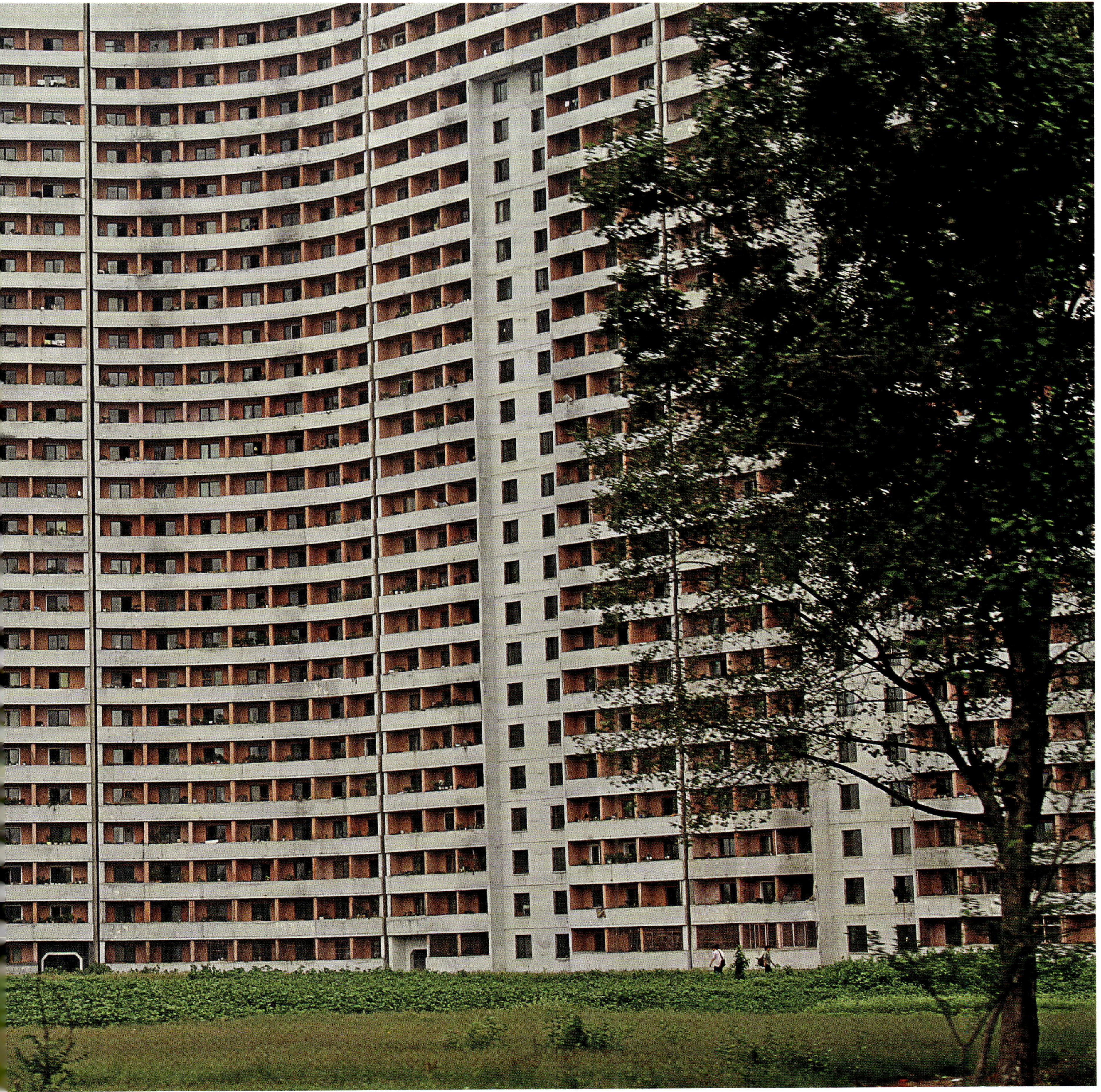

Kaesŏng is the fifth largest city in North Korea. Its broad streets, most of which are empty, end abruptly.
Kaesŏng ist die fünftgrößte Stadt des Landes. Die Straßen enden abrupt. Sie sind breit – und vor allem leer.
Kaesŏng est la cinquième ville du pays par sa population. Larges, mais surtout désertes, les rues s'arrêtent sans transition.

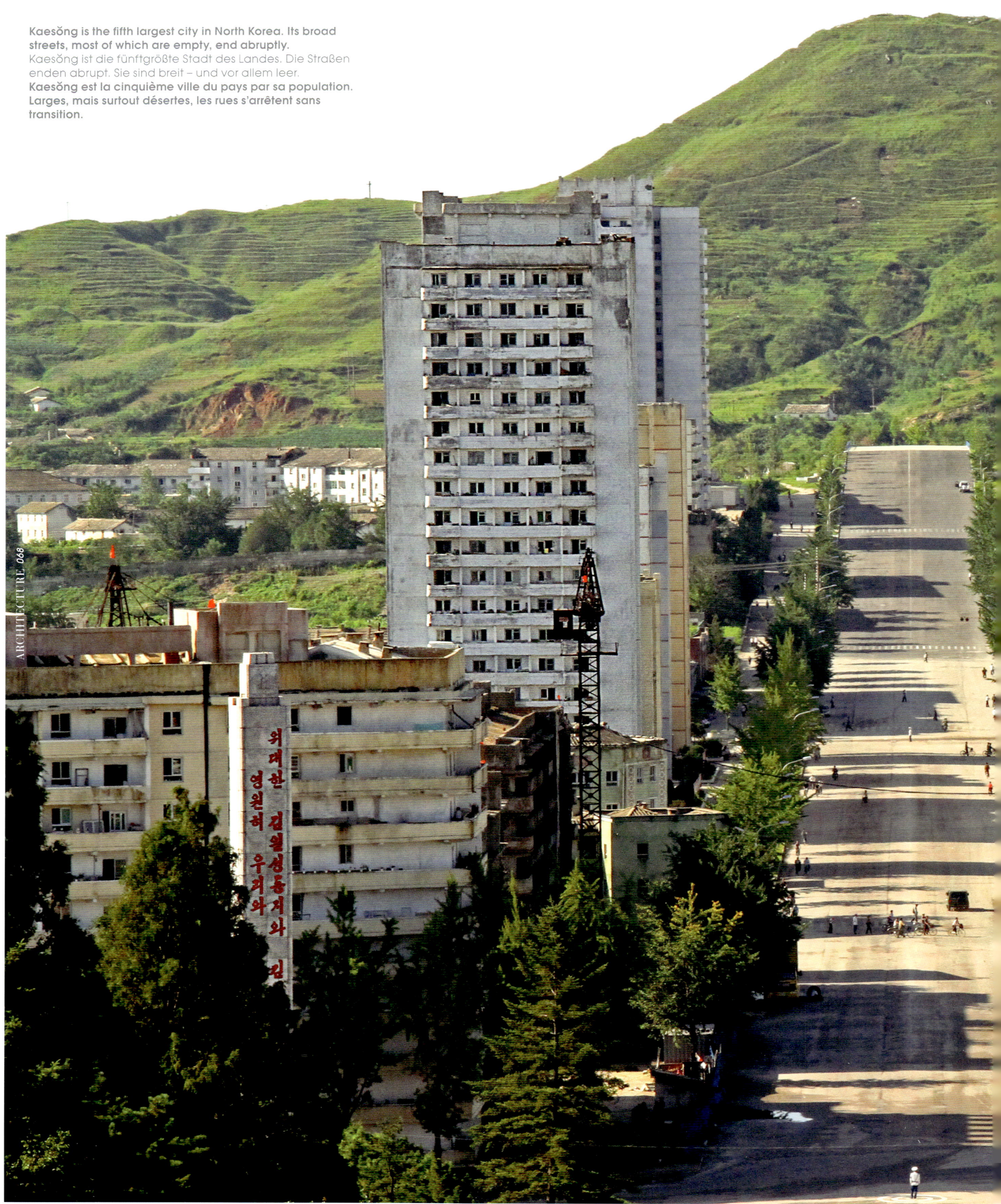

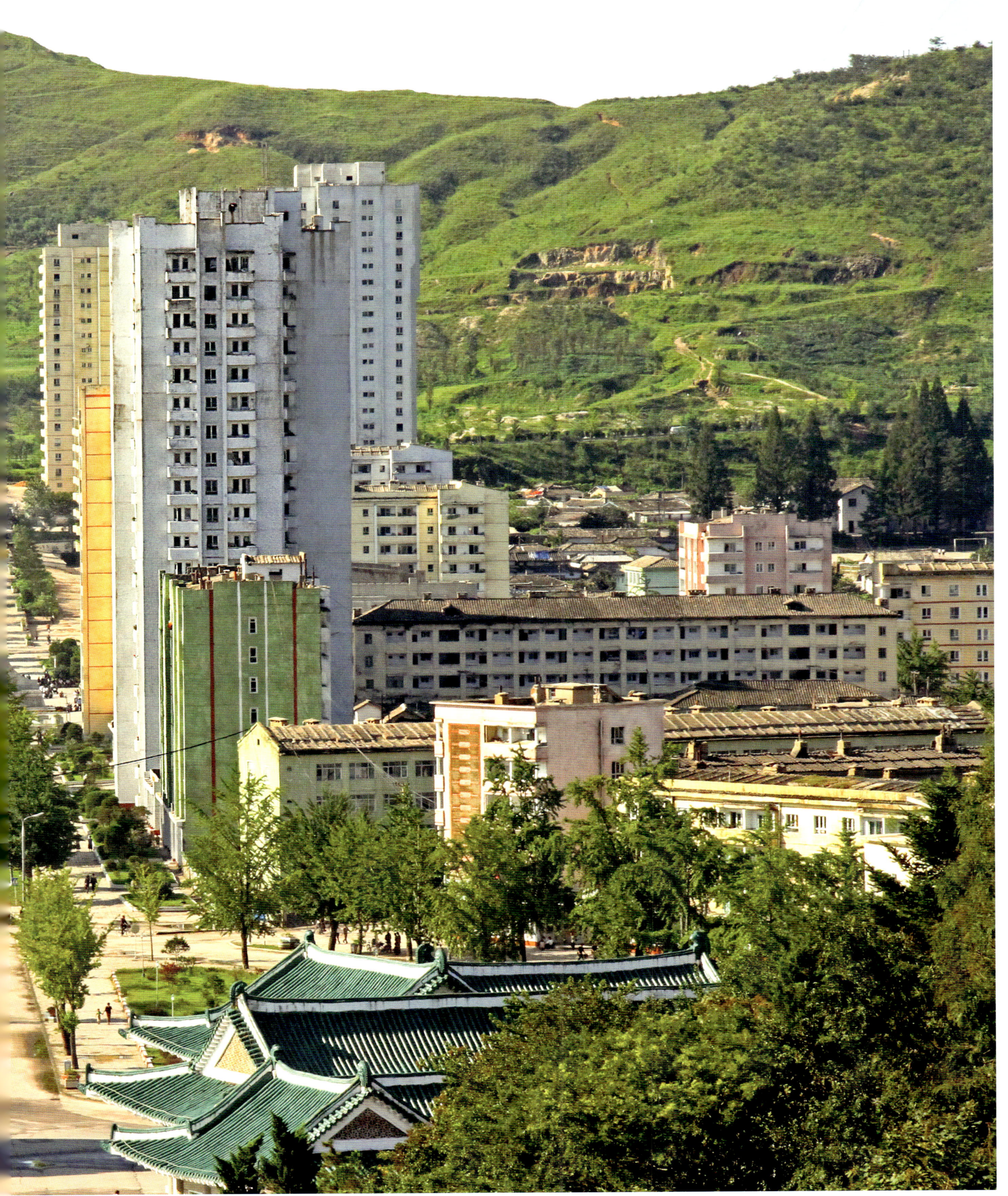

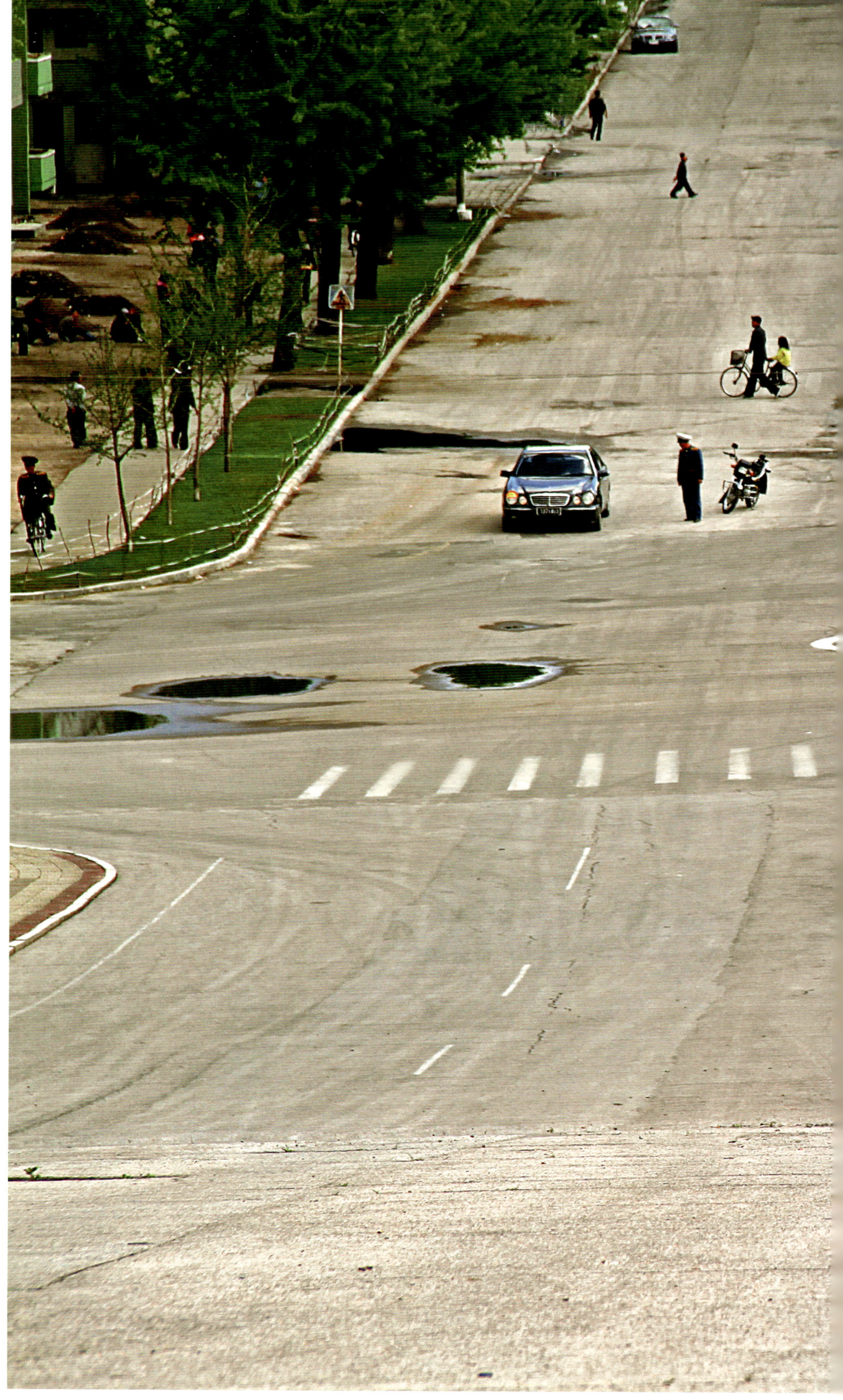

The Mercedes emblem and pink rubber boots are details of a familiar everyday scene: a family crosses the street safely by properly using the crosswalk.
Mercedesstern und rosa Gummistiefel sind Details einer vertrauten Alltagsszene: Um sicher über die Straße zu kommen, benutzt eine Familie ordnungsgemäß den Zebrastreifen.
Étoile de Mercedes et bottes en caoutchouc roses, détails tirés d'une scène de la vie quotidienne : pour traverser en toute sécurité, une famille emprunte, comme il se doit, le passage protégé.

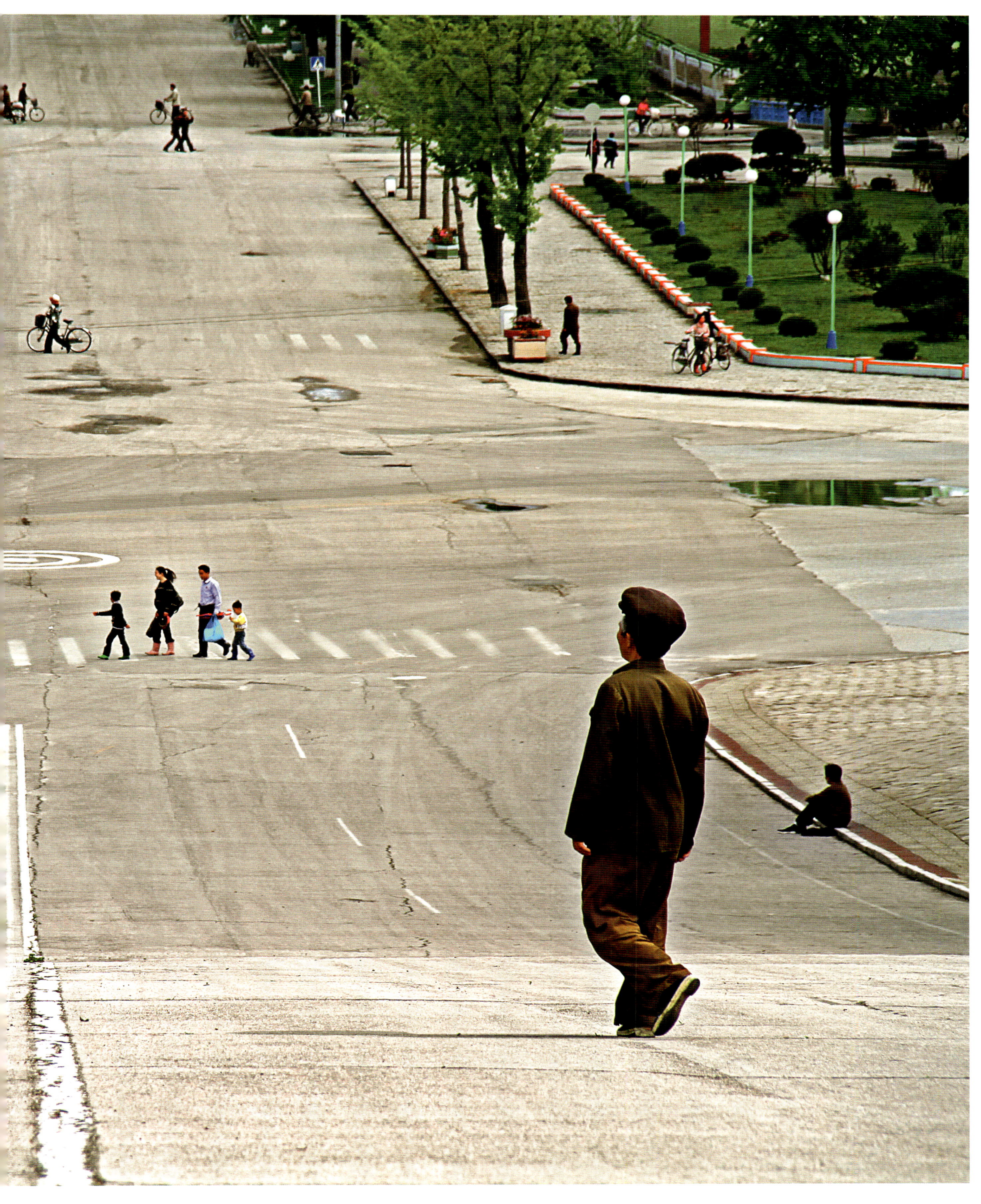

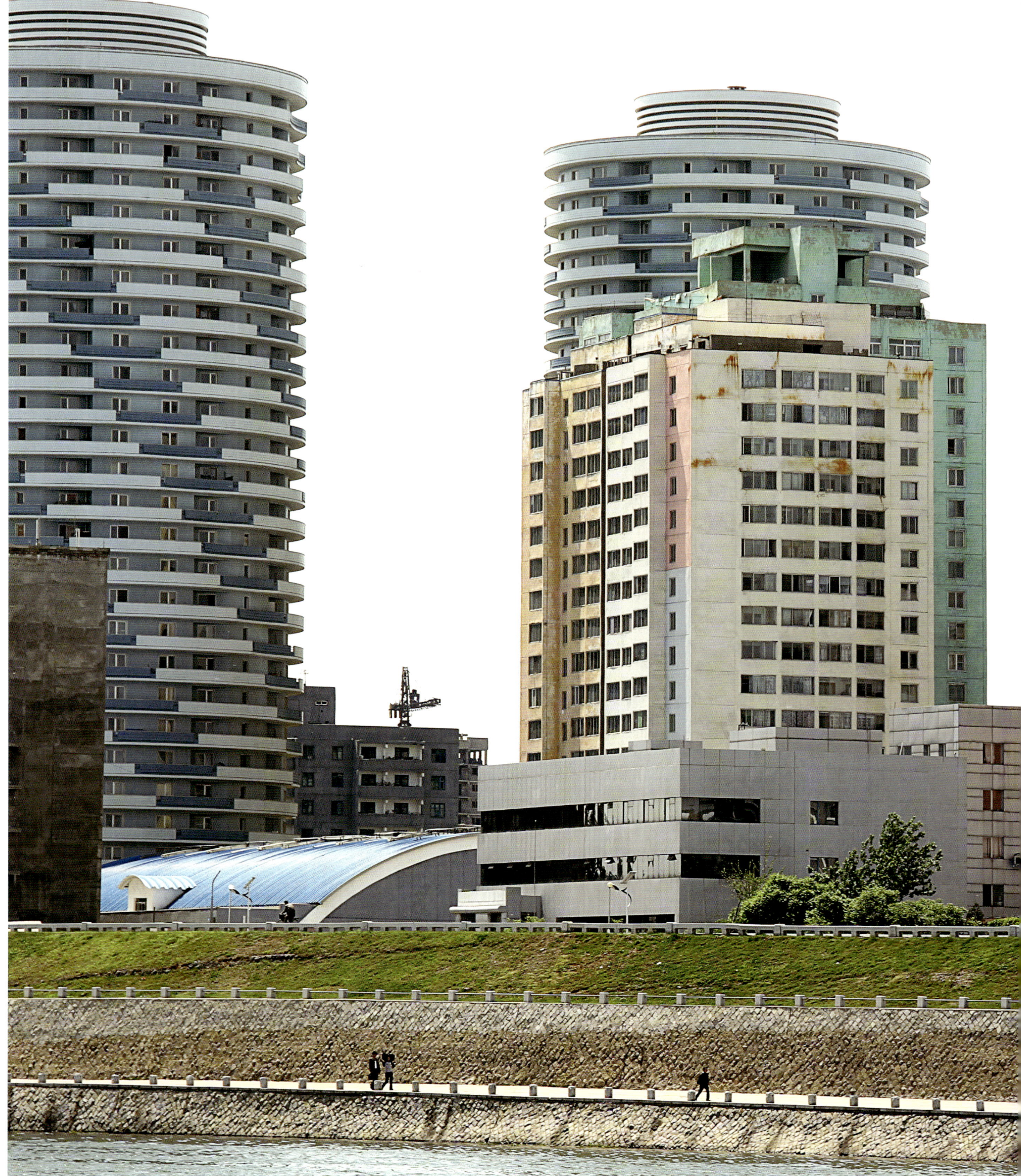

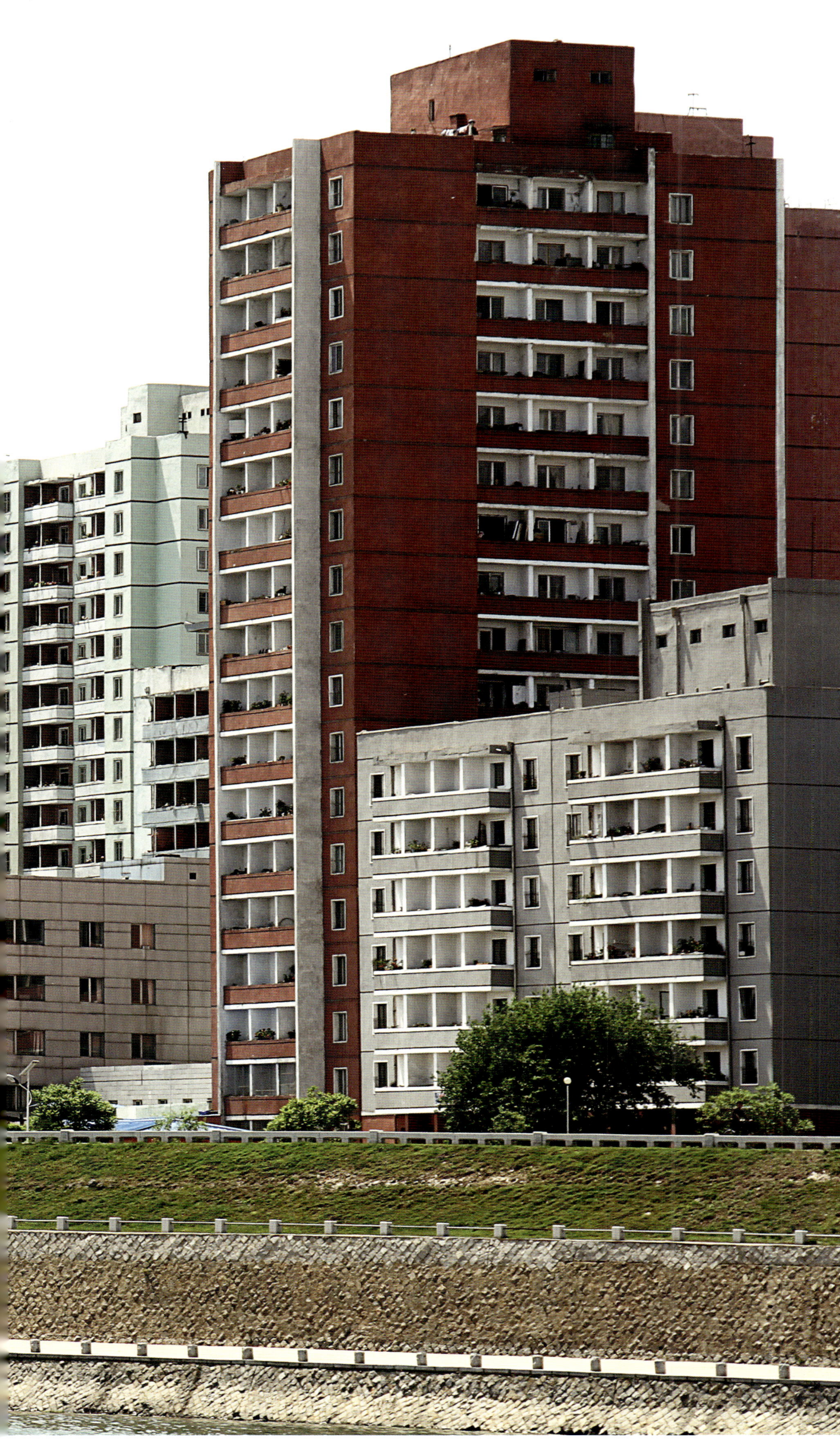

Strolling along the river walk
Spaziergang an der Uferpromenade
Promenade sur les berges

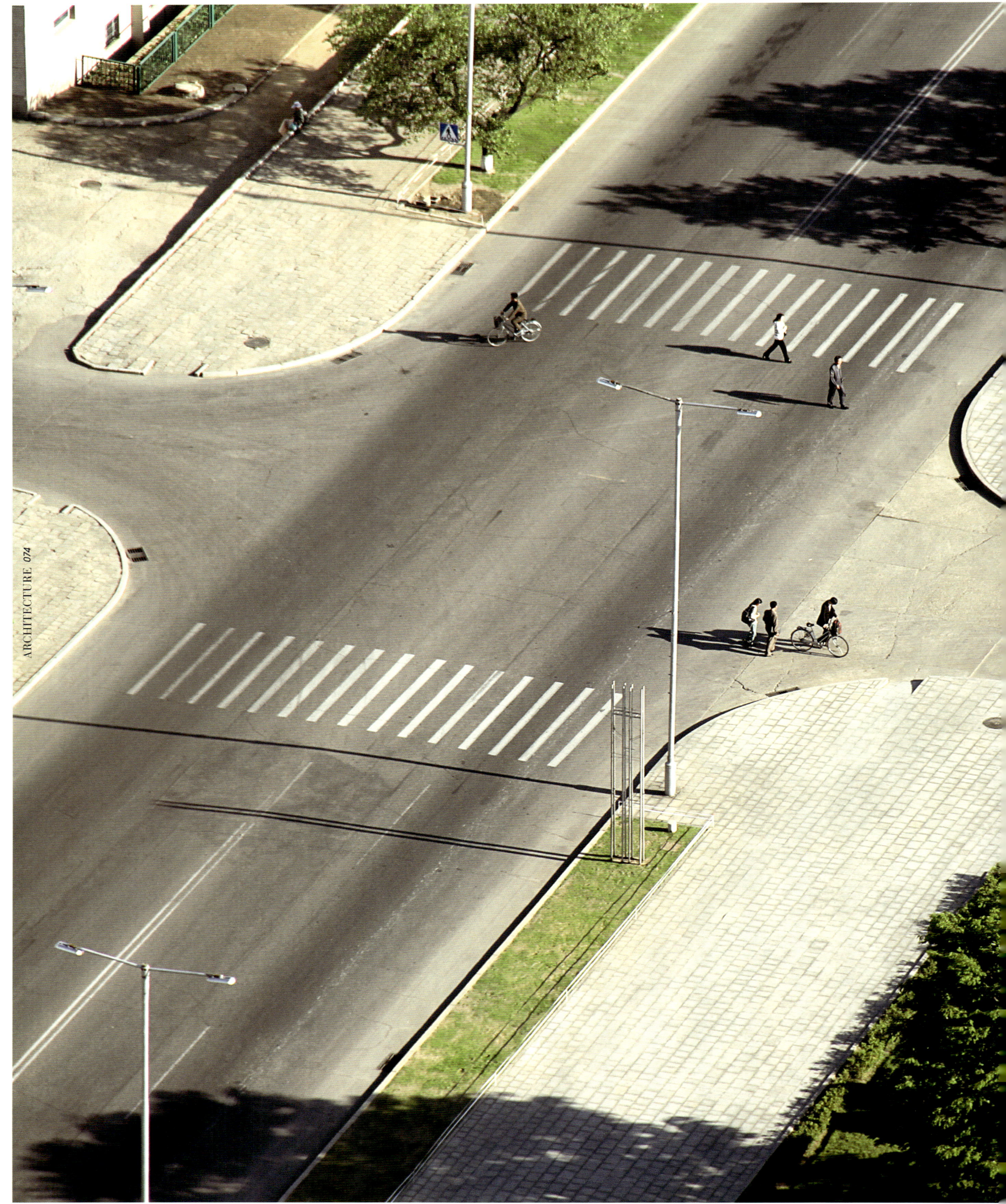

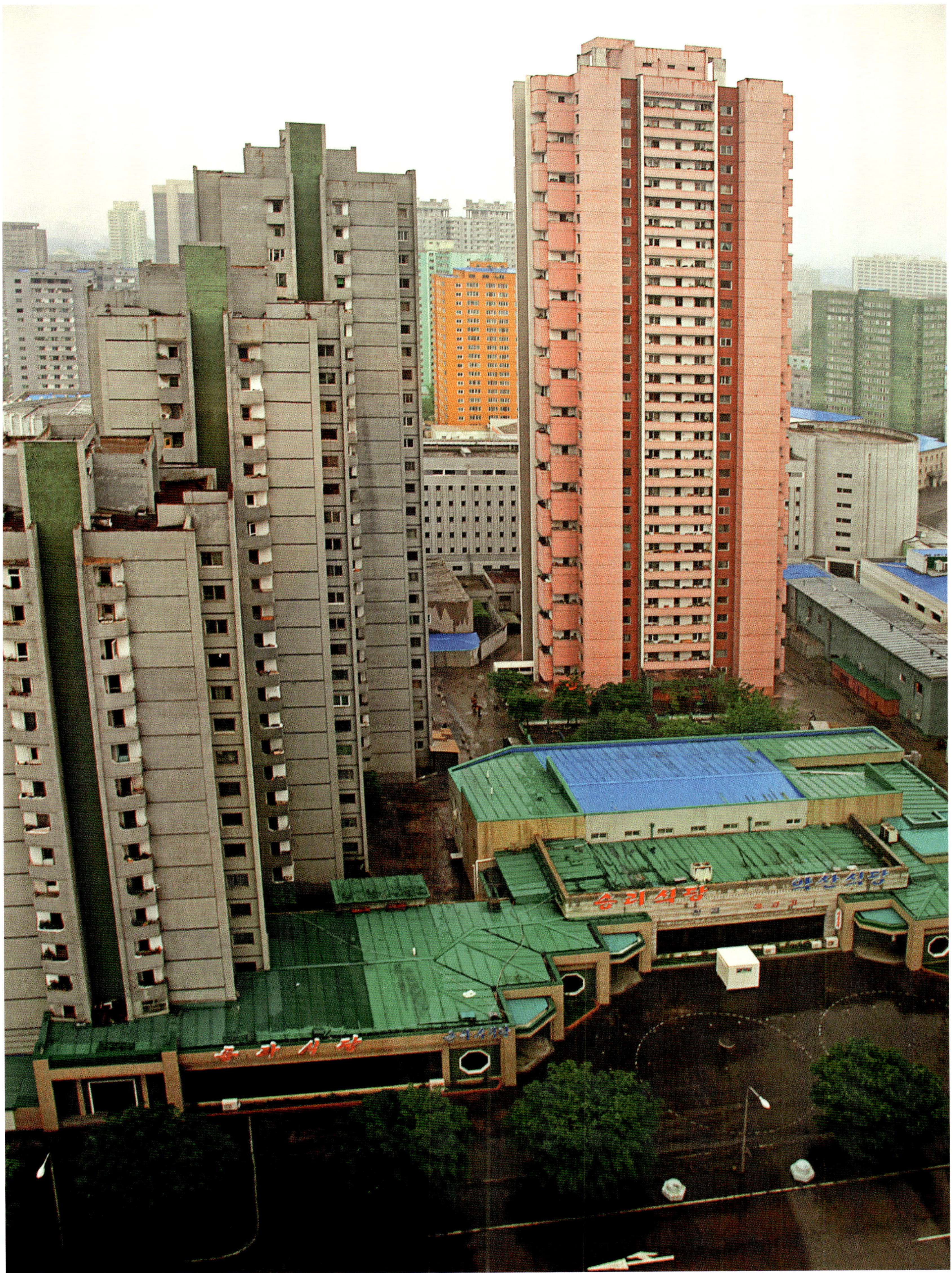
승리식당

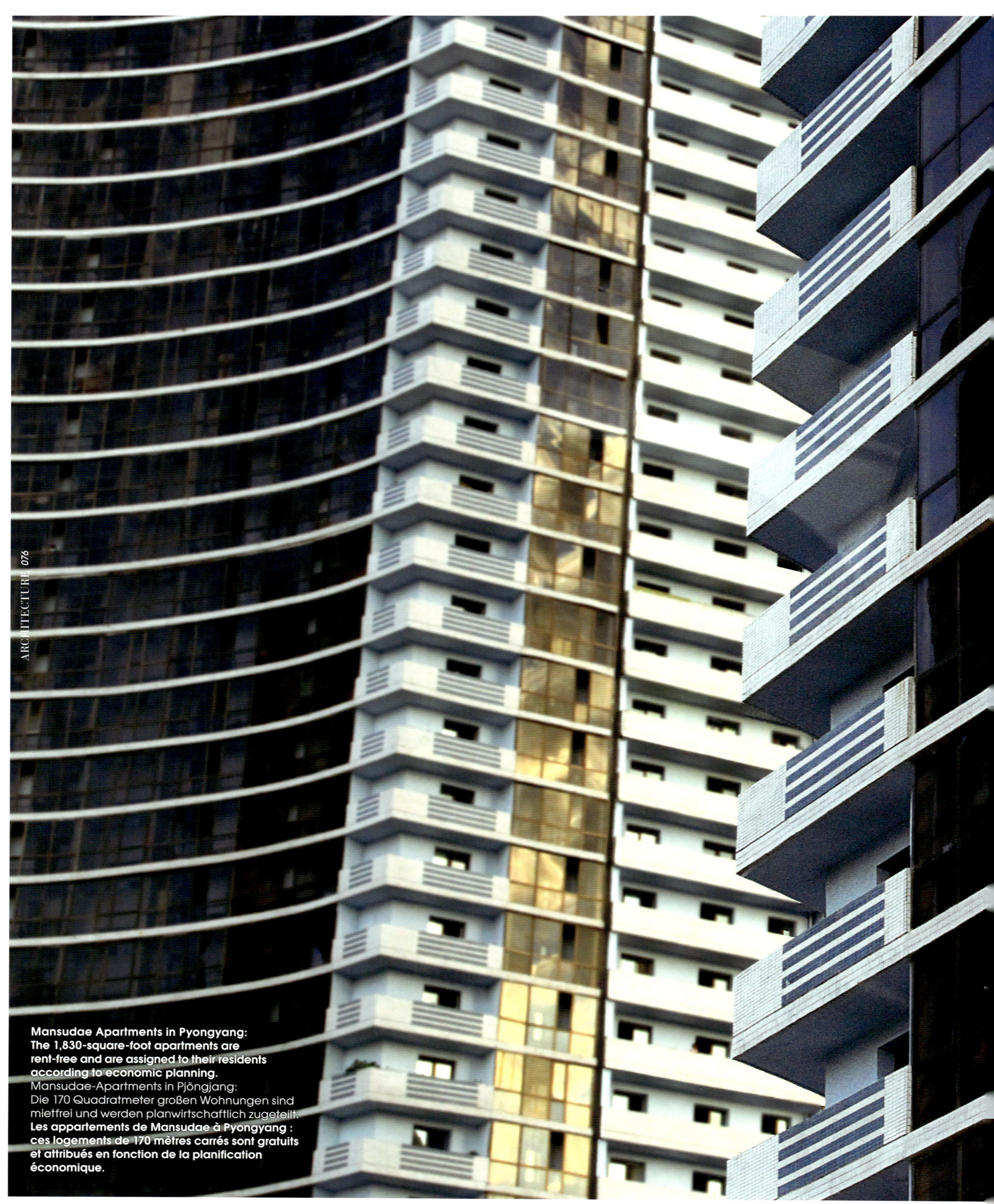

Mansudae Apartments in Pyongyang: The 1,830-square-foot apartments are rent-free and are assigned to their residents according to economic planning.
Mansudae-Apartments in Pjöngjang: Die 170 Quadratmeter großen Wohnungen sind mietfrei und werden planwirtschaftlich zugeteilt.
Les appartements de Mansudae à Pyongyang : ces logements de 170 mètres carrés sont gratuits et attribués en fonction de la planification économique.

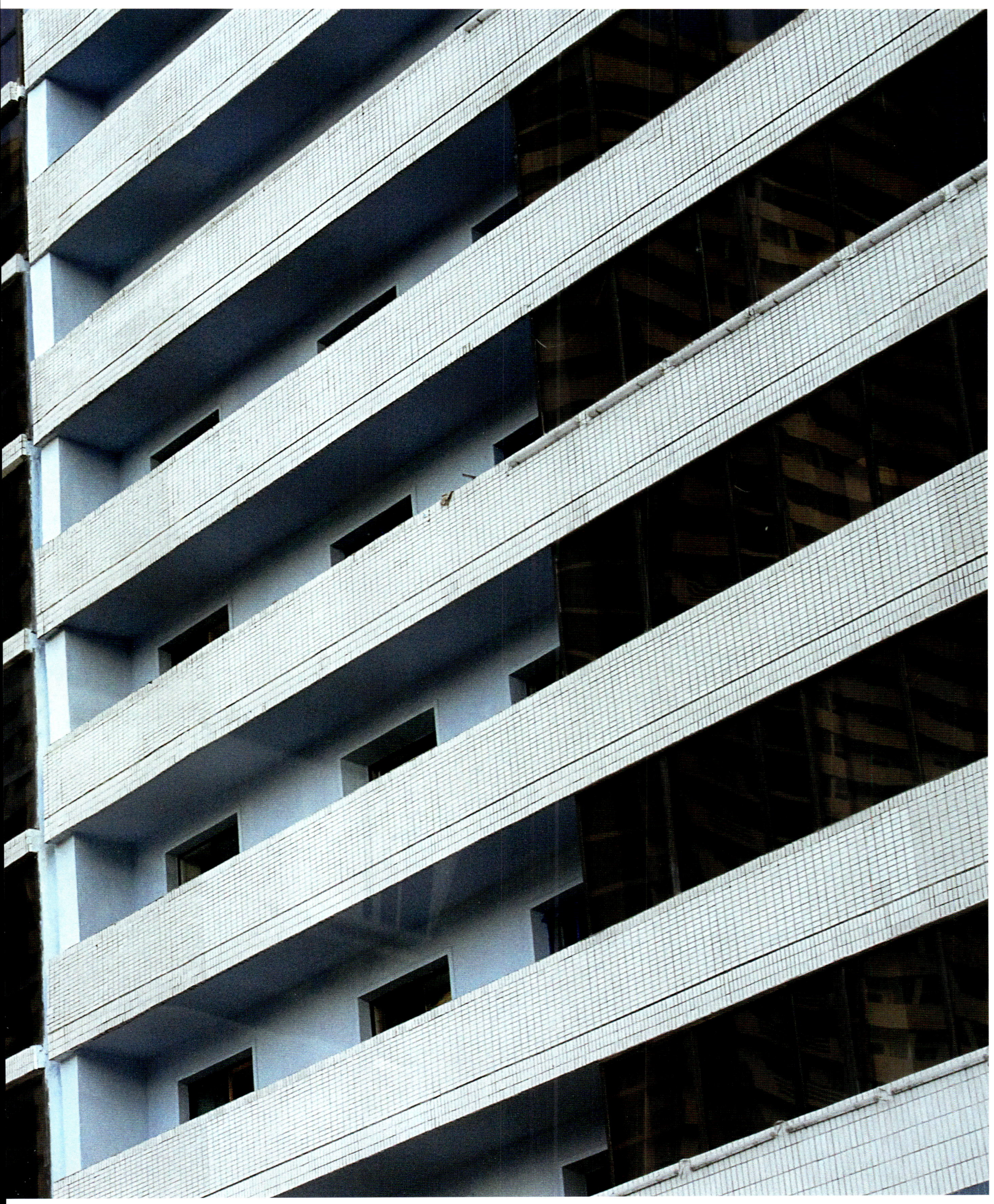

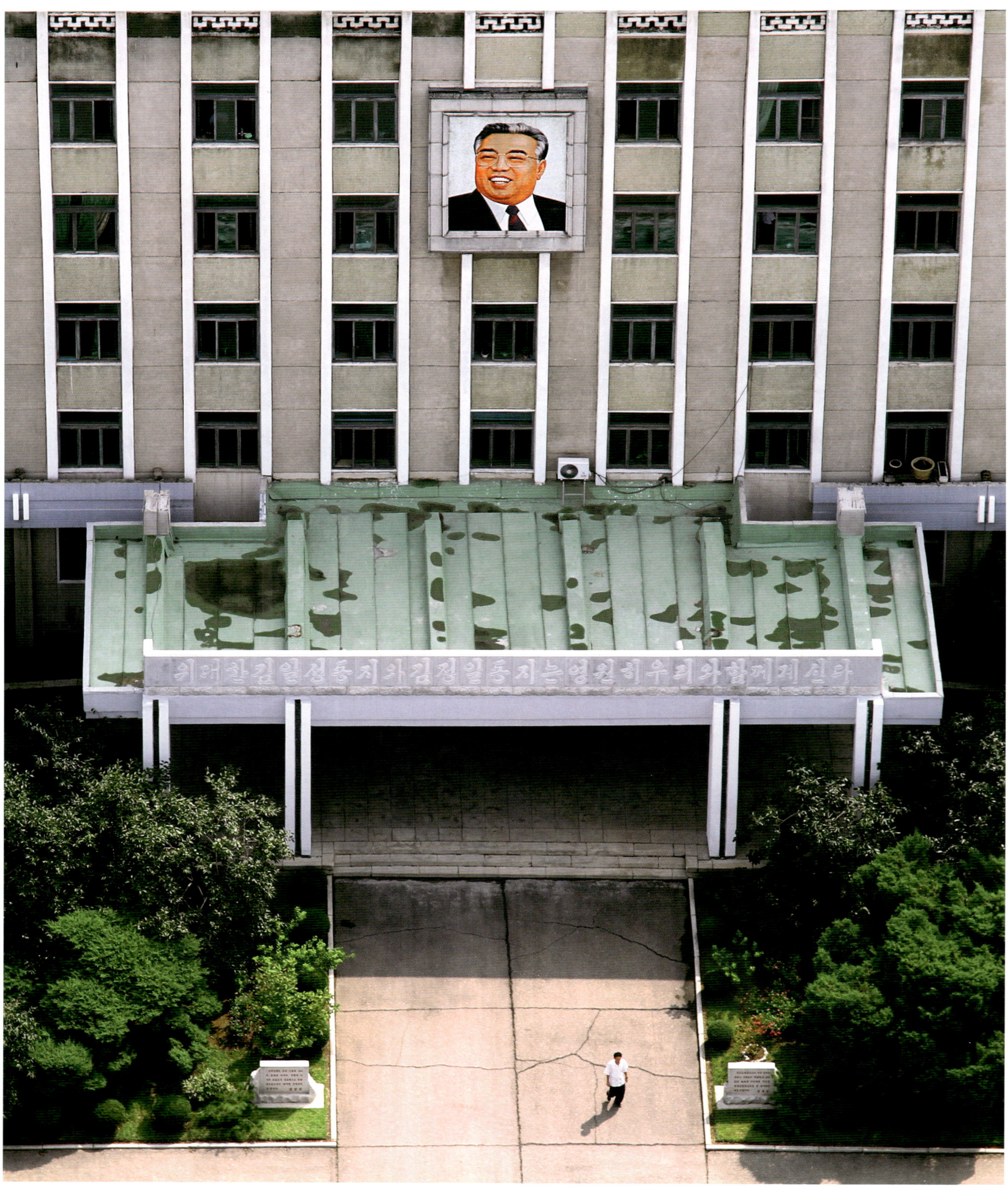

Left: The “Eternal Leaders” look down on the residents from on high.
Right: Capturing a smile
Links: Von hoch oben blicken die „Ewigen Führer“ überall auf die Einwohner herab.
Rechts: Momentaufnahme eines Lächelns
À gauche : En tout lieu, les « présidents éternels » veillent de leur piédestal sur les habitants.
À droite : Sourire pris sur le vif

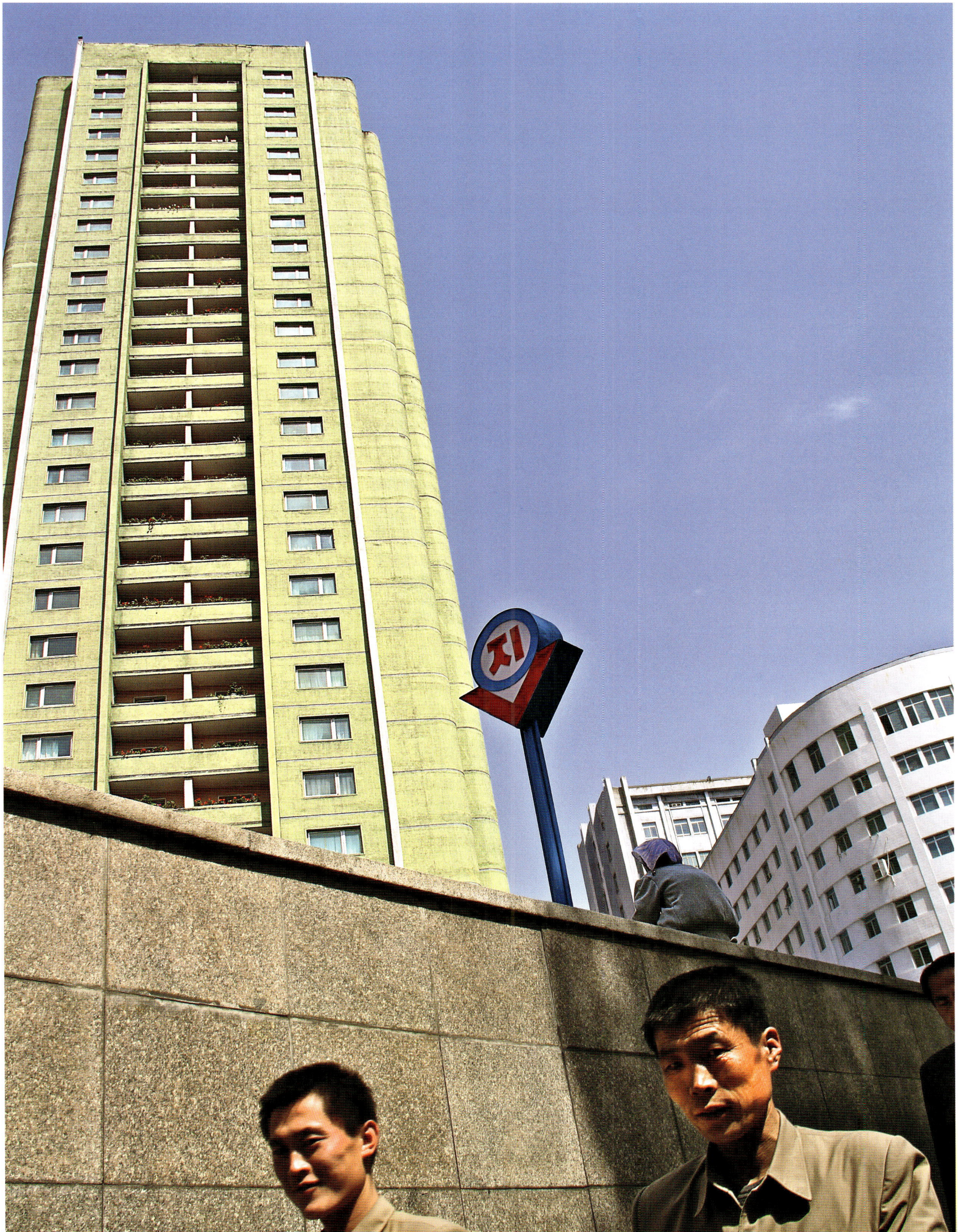

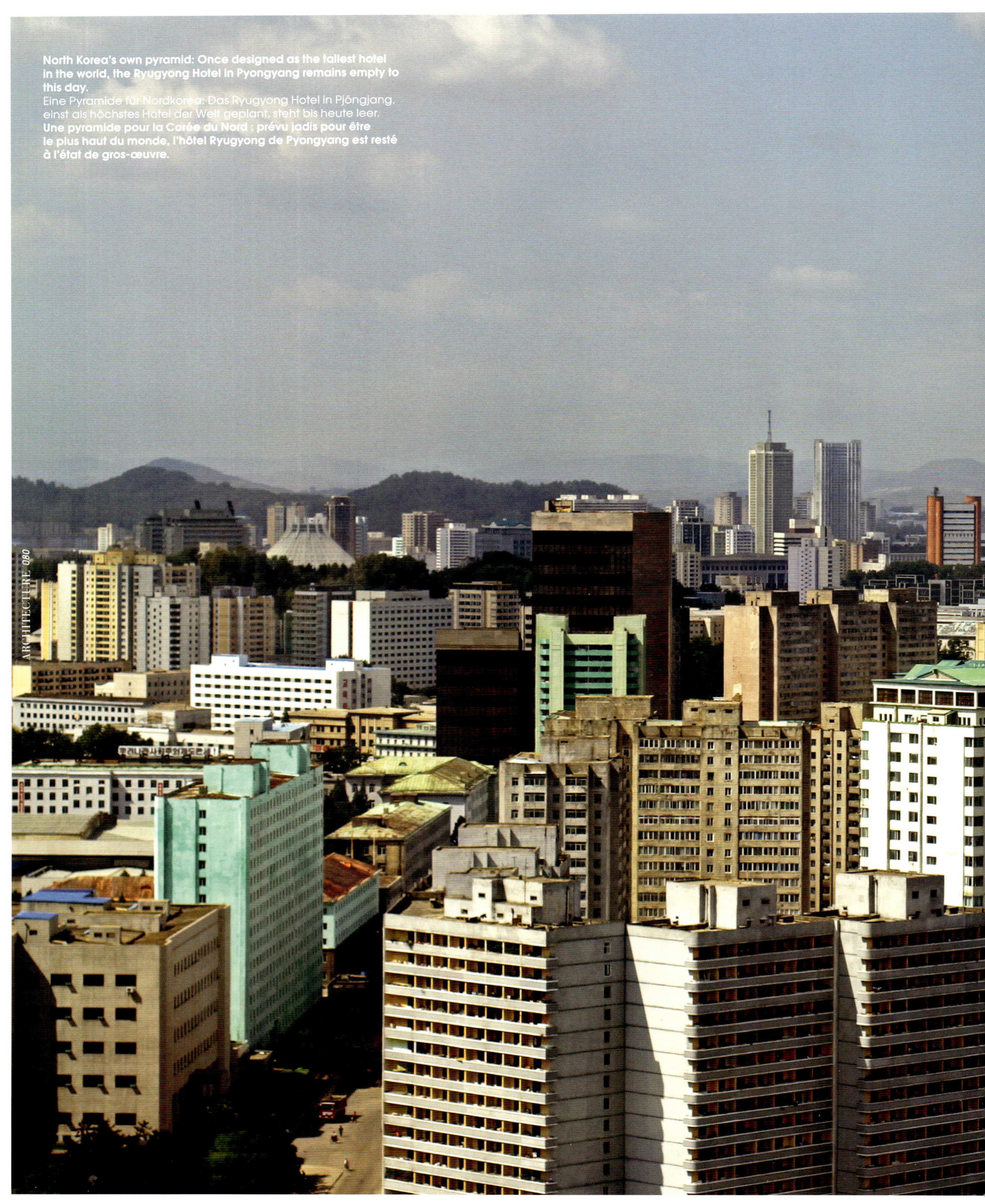

North Korea's own pyramid: Once designed as the tallest hotel in the world, the Ryugyong Hotel in Pyongyang remains empty to this day.
Eine Pyramide für Nordkorea: Das Ryugyong Hotel in Pjöngjang, einst als höchstes Hotel der Welt geplant, steht bis heute leer.
Une pyramide pour la Corée du Nord : prévu jadis pour être le plus haut du monde, l'hôtel Ryugyong de Pyongyang est resté à l'état de gros-œuvre.

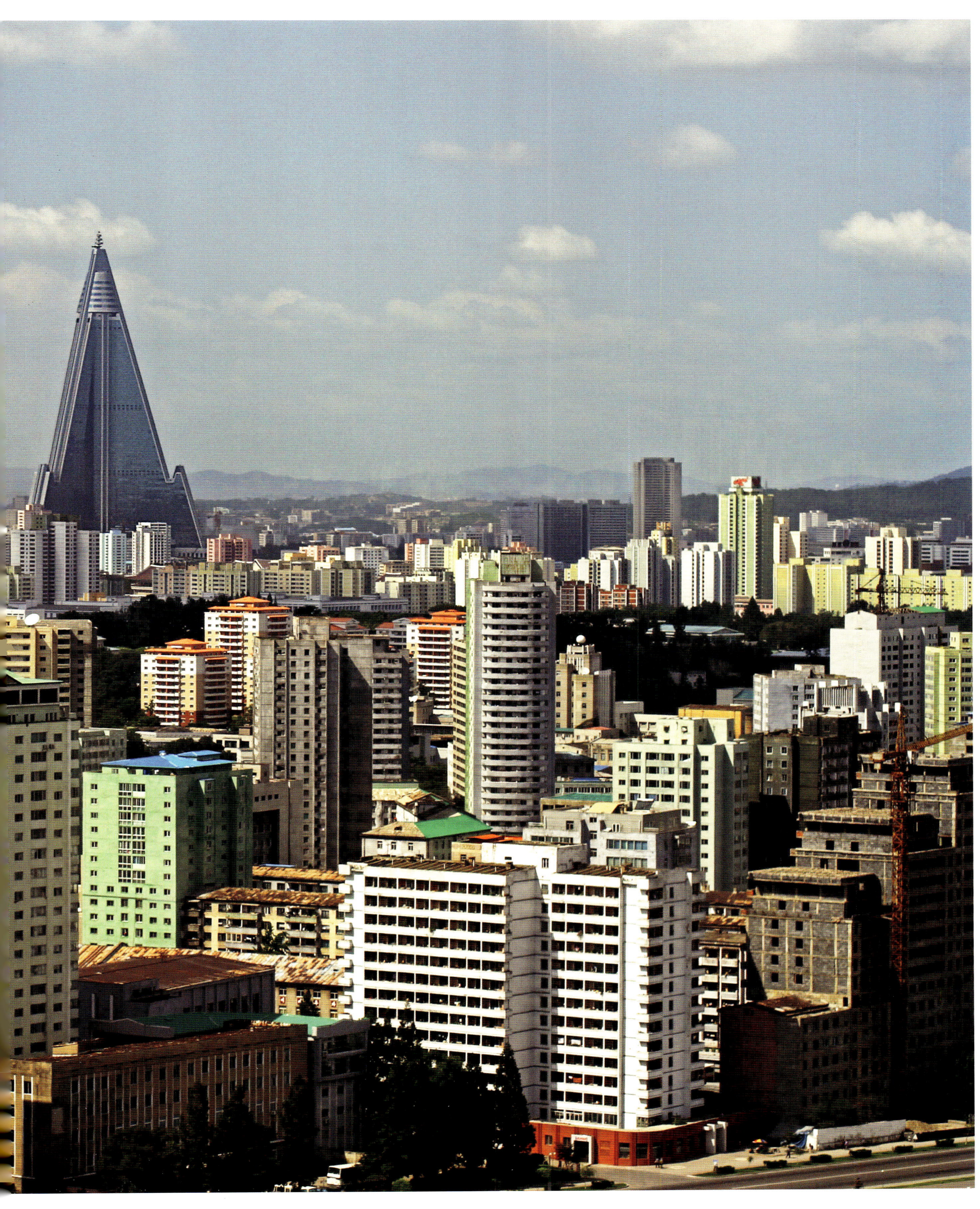

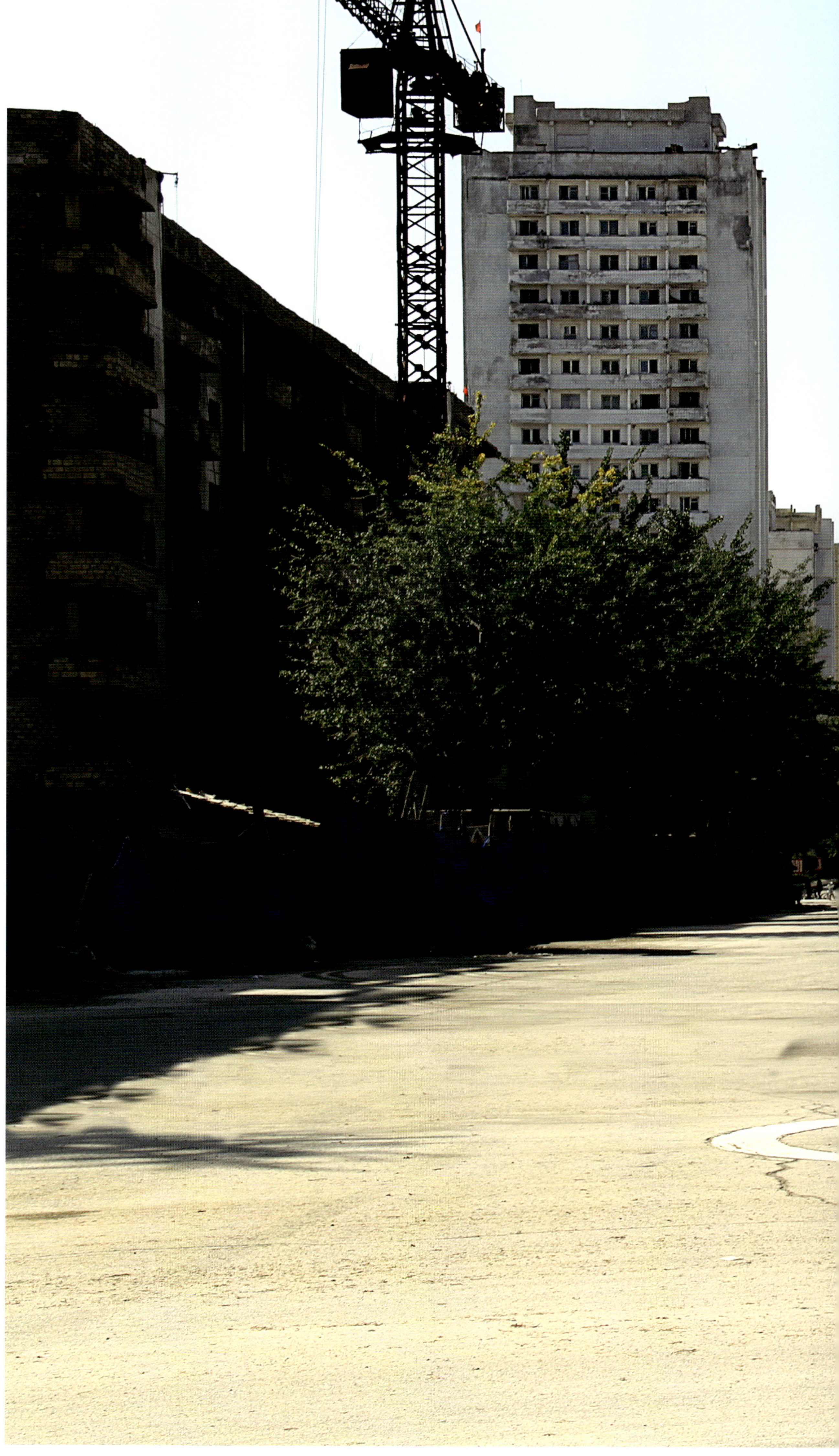

Picture of dignity: A traffic cop stands on a deserted street in Kaesŏng. Once the royal capital, this city is now a special economic zone.

Würdevoll: Verkehrspolizist auf autofreier Straße in Kaesŏng. Die ehemalige Hauptstadt des Königreichs ist heute Sonderwirtschaftszone.

Cet agent de la circulation sur une chaussée déserte de Kaesŏng incarne la dignité même. Ancienne capitale du royaume, cette ville est à l'heure actuelle une zone économique spéciale.

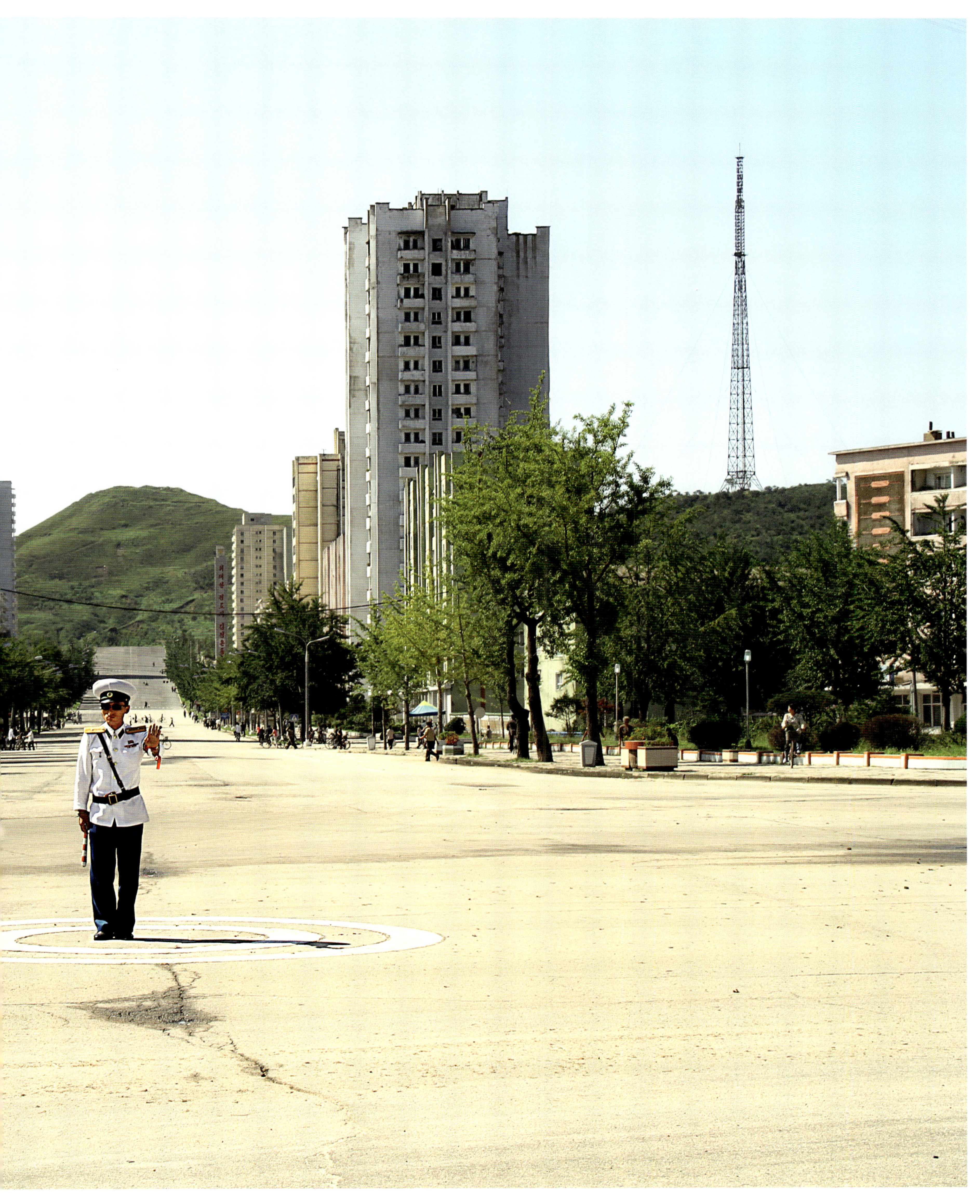

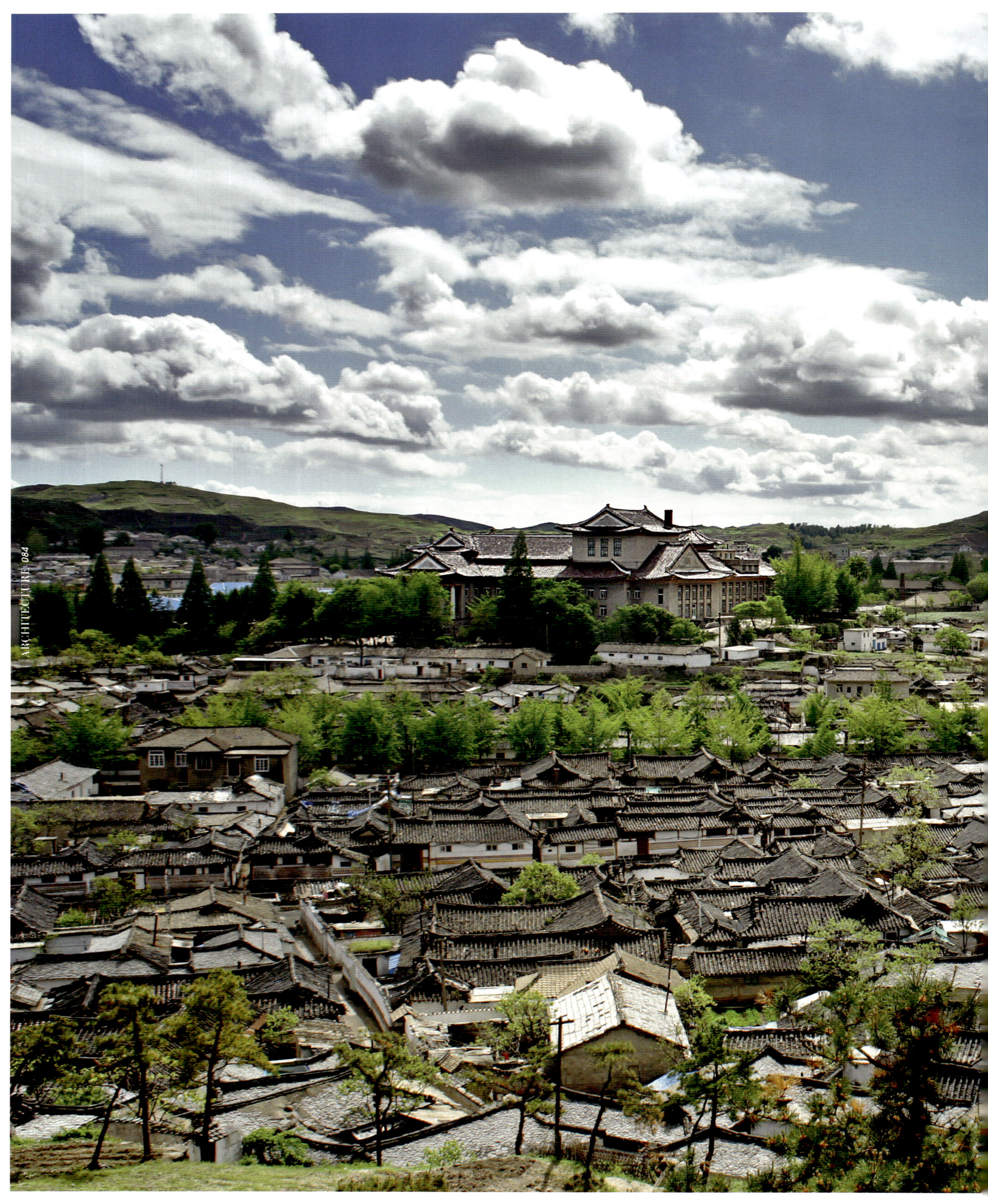

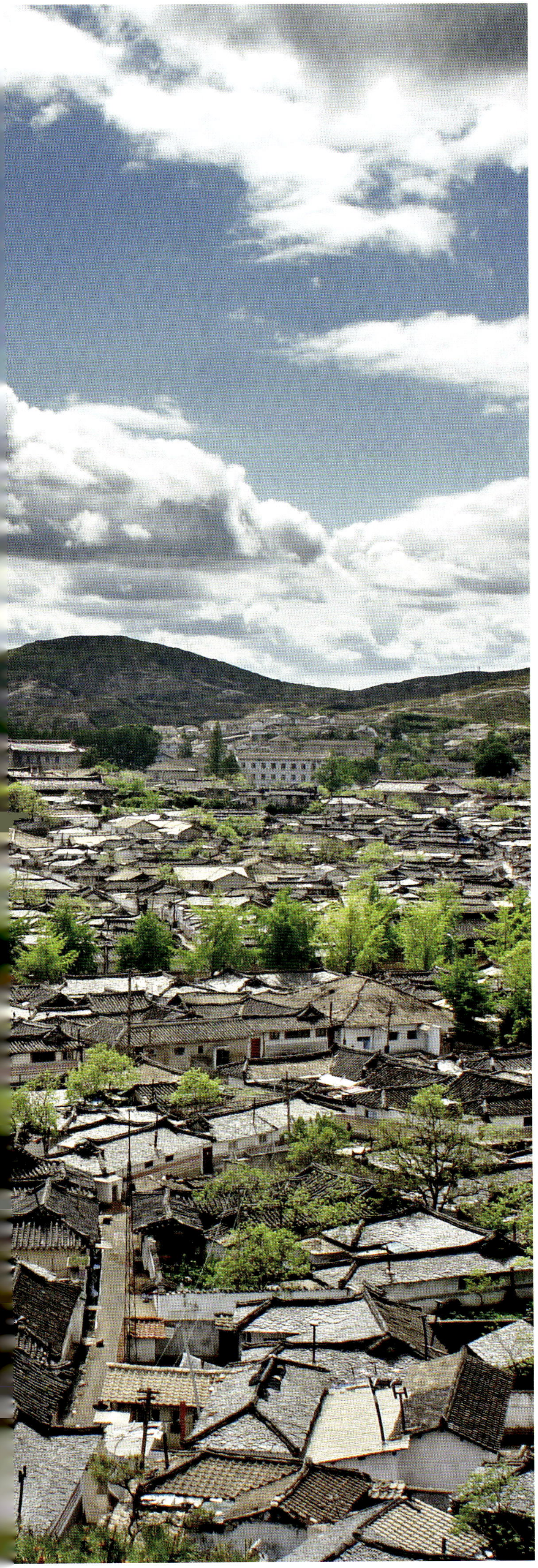

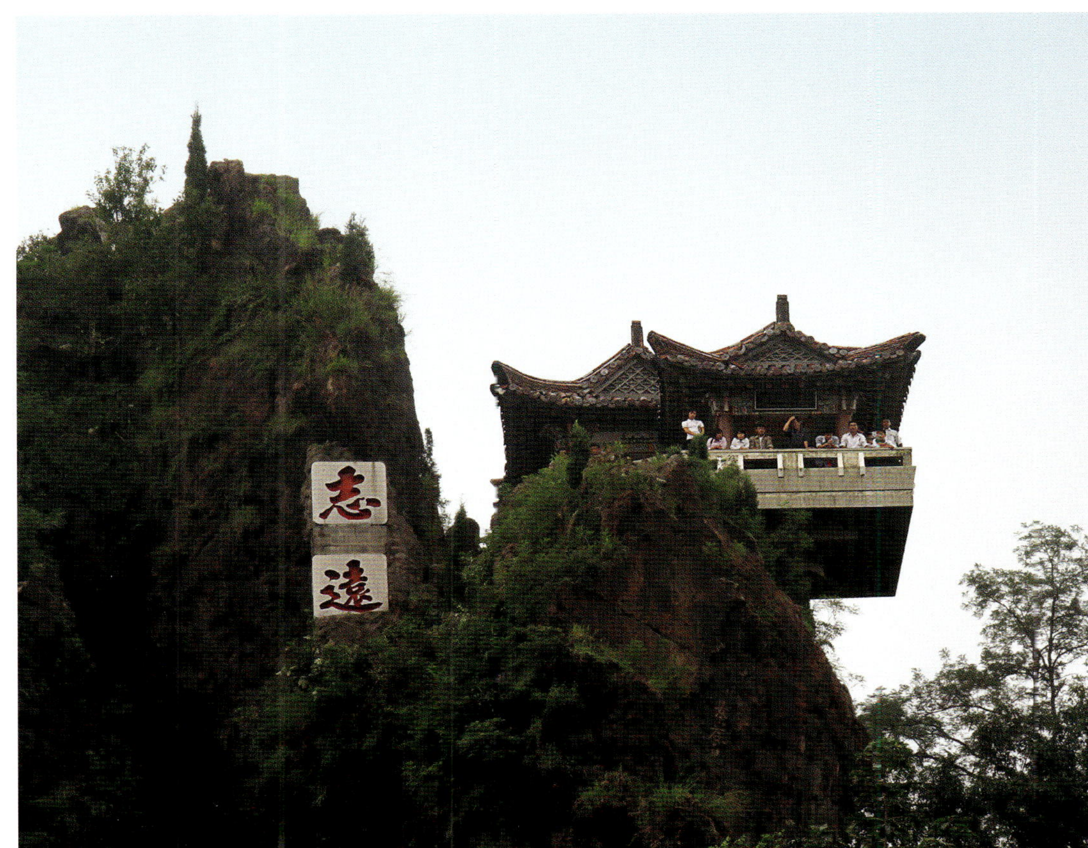

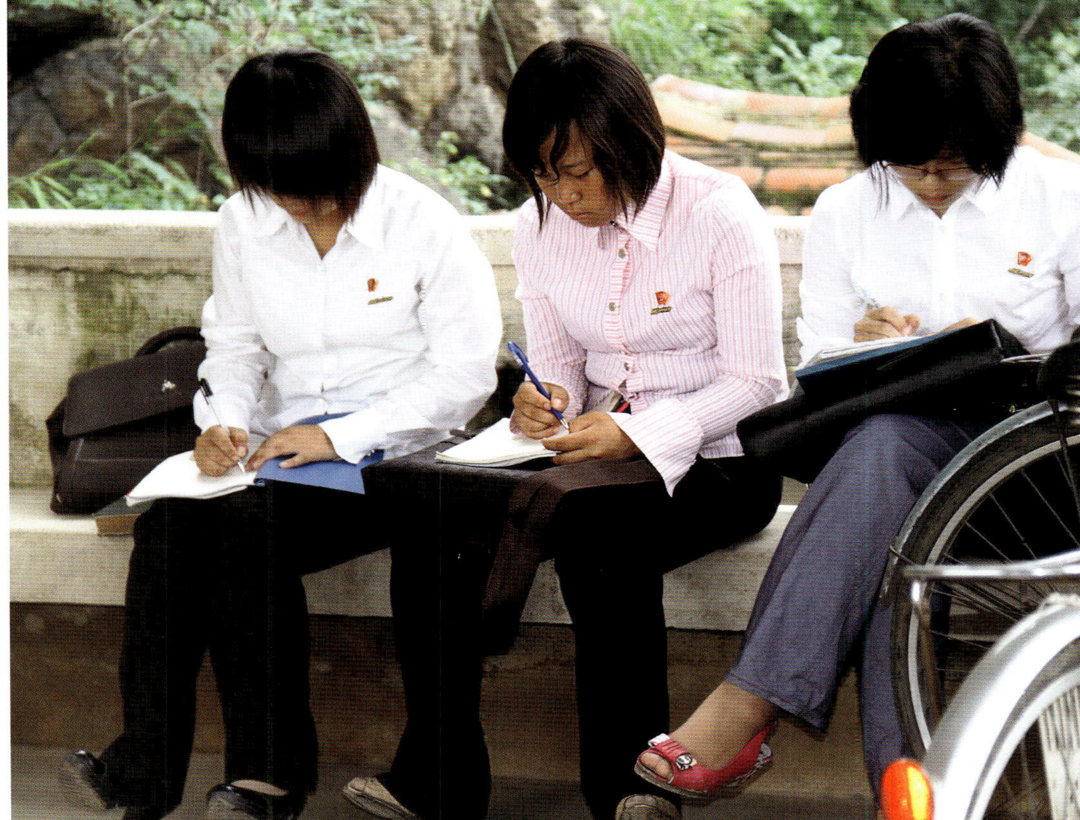

Left: Kaesŏng is the only city in North Korea that was not destroyed in the war, because it lay in the American occupation zone.
Right: Children go to school in Sariwŏn's "flying classrooms."
Links: Kaesŏng wurde als einzige nordkoreanische Stadt nicht im Krieg zerstört, da sie im amerikanisch besetzten Teil lag.
Rechts: Schüler lernen im „fliegenden Klassenzimmer" in Sariwŏn.
À gauche : Kaesŏng est la seule ville de Corée du Nord qui n'ait pas été détruite pendant la guerre car elle se trouvait dans la zone d'occupation américaine.
À droite : Des élèves apprennent leurs leçons dans « la classe volante » à Sariwŏn.

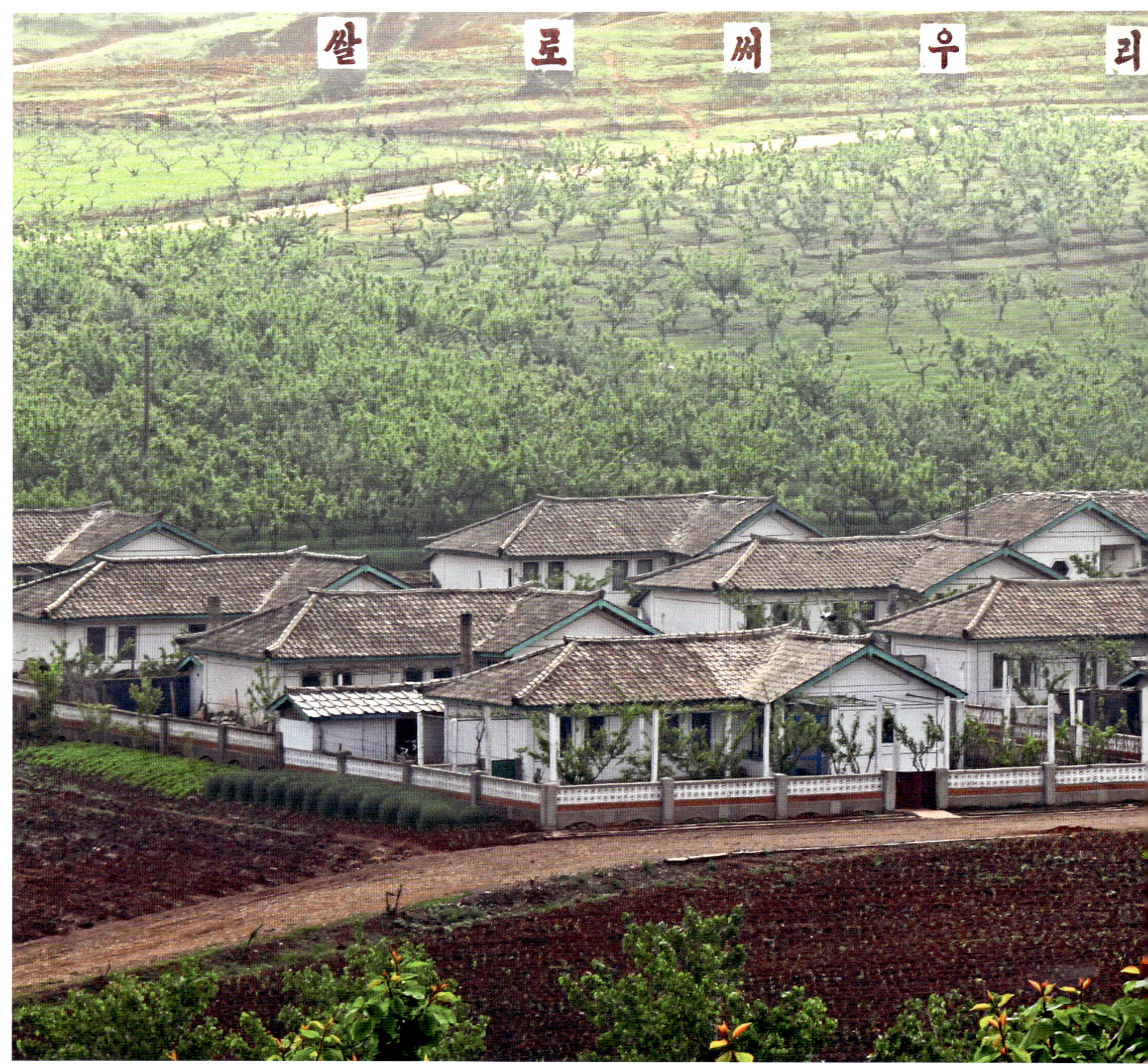

Migok Cooperative in North Hwanghae Province. The characters celebrate the Juche ideology and say: "Our rice glorifies our party."

Migok-Kooperative in der Hwanghae-pukto-Provinz: Die Schriftzeichen feiern die Juche-Ideologie – „Mit Reis halten wir unsere Partei hoch."

La coopérative de Migok, dans la province du Hwanghae du Nord : les idéogrammes célèbrent la doctrine du Juche – « Avec du riz, nous soutenons notre parti. »

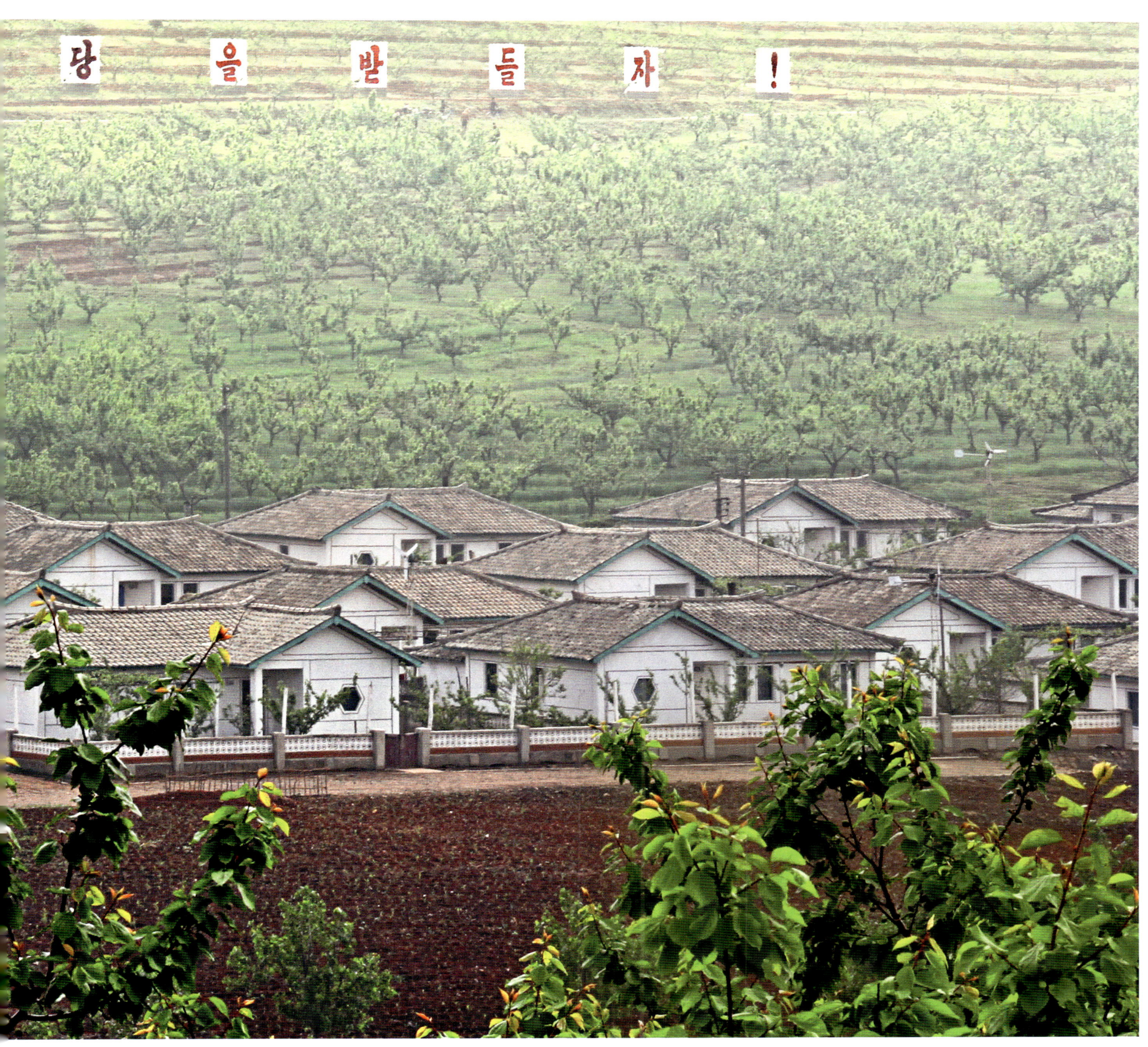
당 을 받 들 자 !

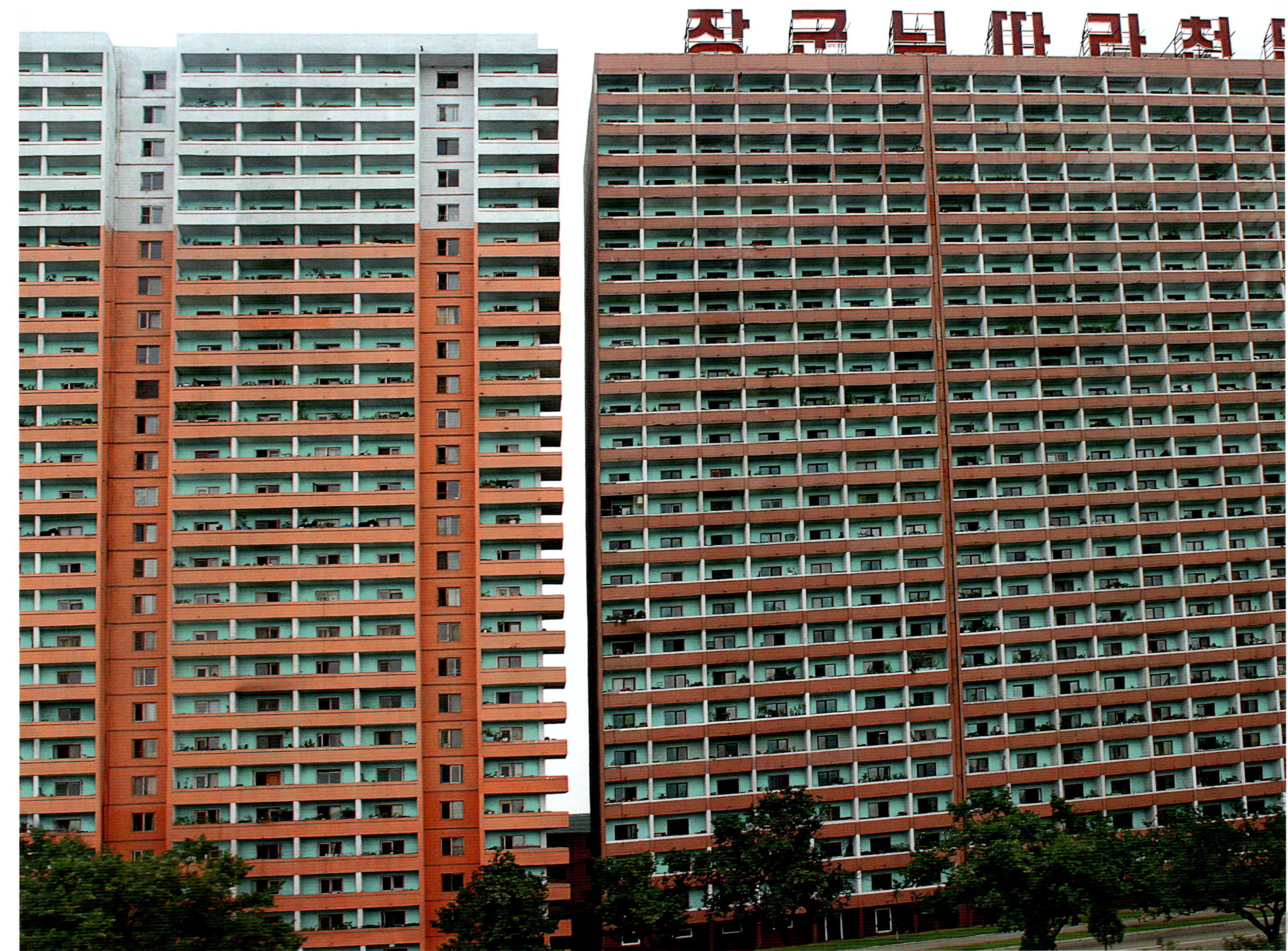

"We will follow our general forever."
„Für immer folgen wir unserem General."
« Nous suivons notre général à tout jamais. »

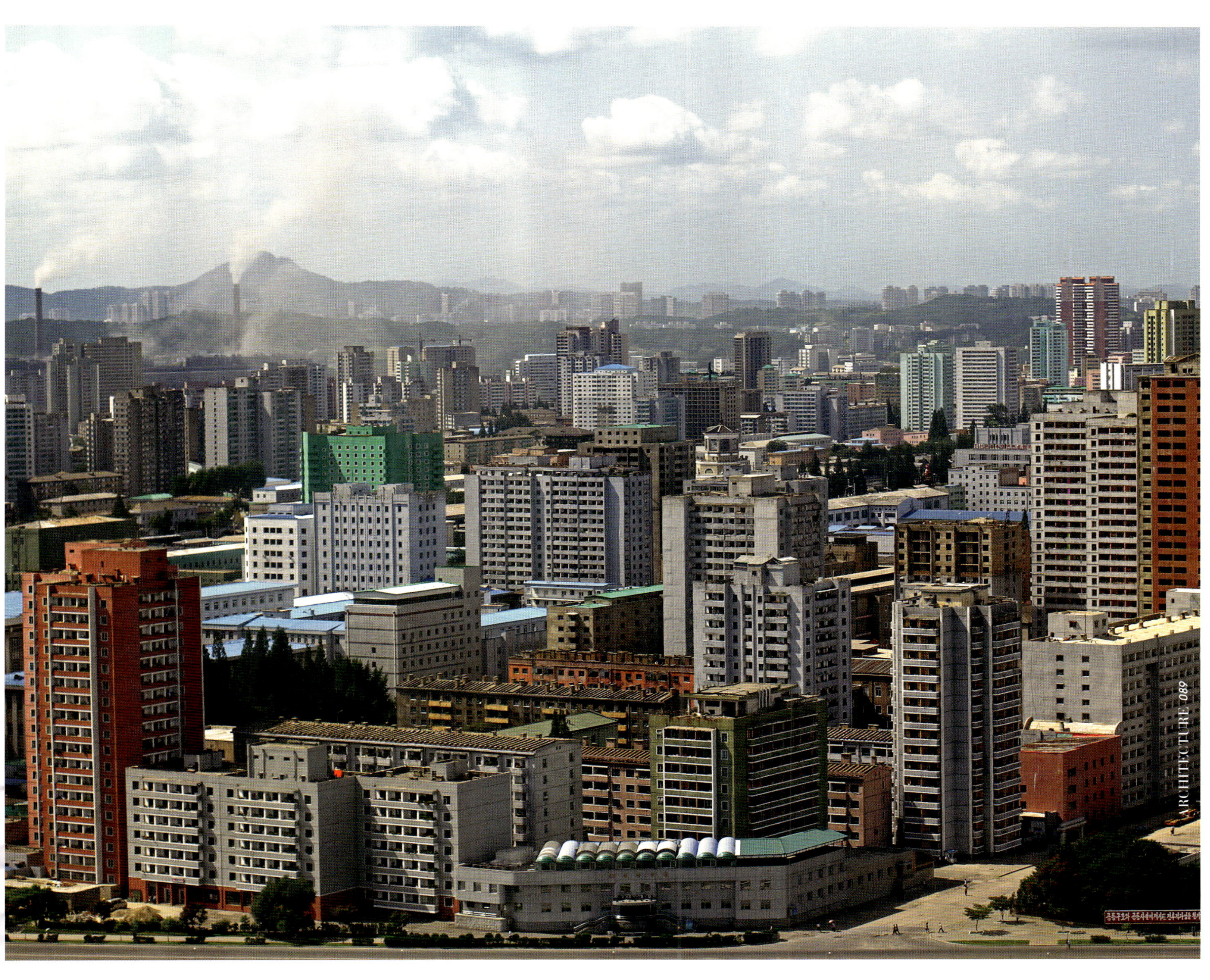

The Juche state ideology is a form of Marxist nationalism. The country's own independence takes precedence over global communist interests. Even urban planning is based on Juche teachings, subordinating the individual to the collective.

Die Staatsideologie Juche ist eine Art marxistischer Nationalismus. Über den weltkommunistischen Interessen steht die eigene Unabhängigkeit. Auch die Städteplanung folgt der Juche-Lehre: Der Einzelne ordnet sich der Gemeinschaft unter.

Le Juche est une sorte de nationalisme marxiste, selon lequel l'indépendance nationale prime sur les intérêts du communisme dans le monde entier. Cette doctrine d'État se reflète jusque dans l'urbanisme, qui subordonne l'individu à la communauté.

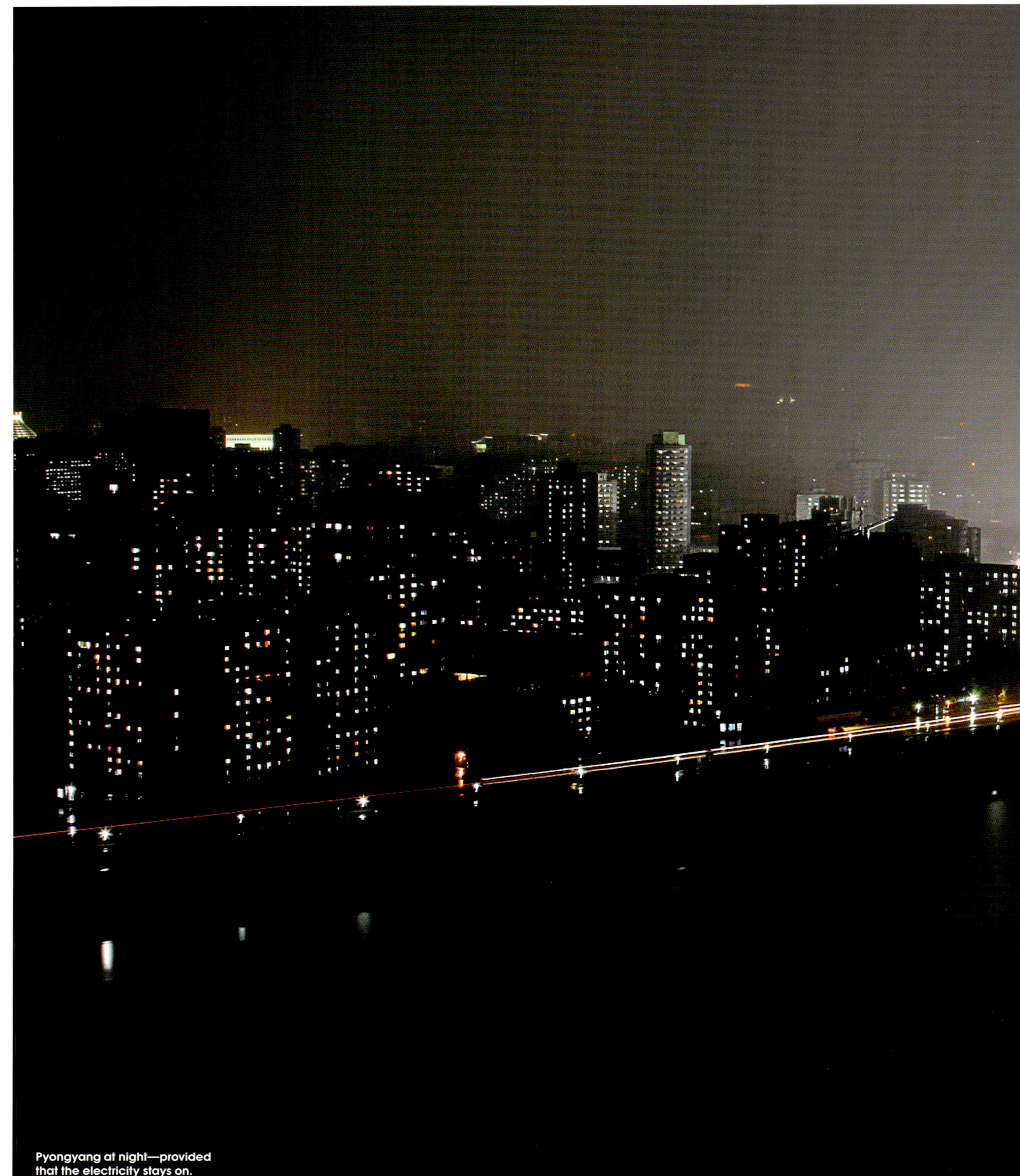

Pyongyang at night—provided that the electricity stays on.
Pjöngjang bei Nacht – sofern der Strom fließt.
Pyongyang la nuit, tant qu'il y a du courant.

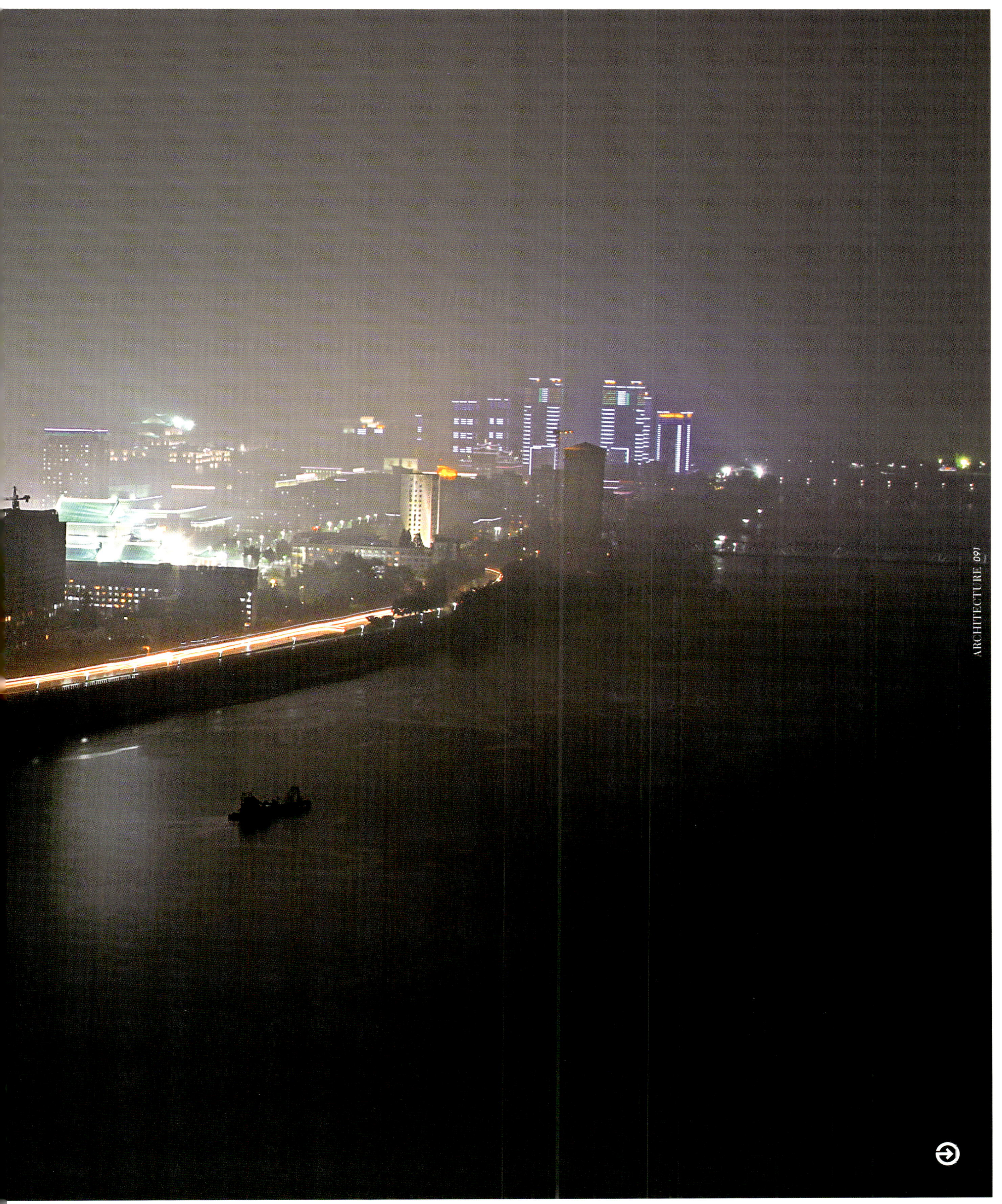

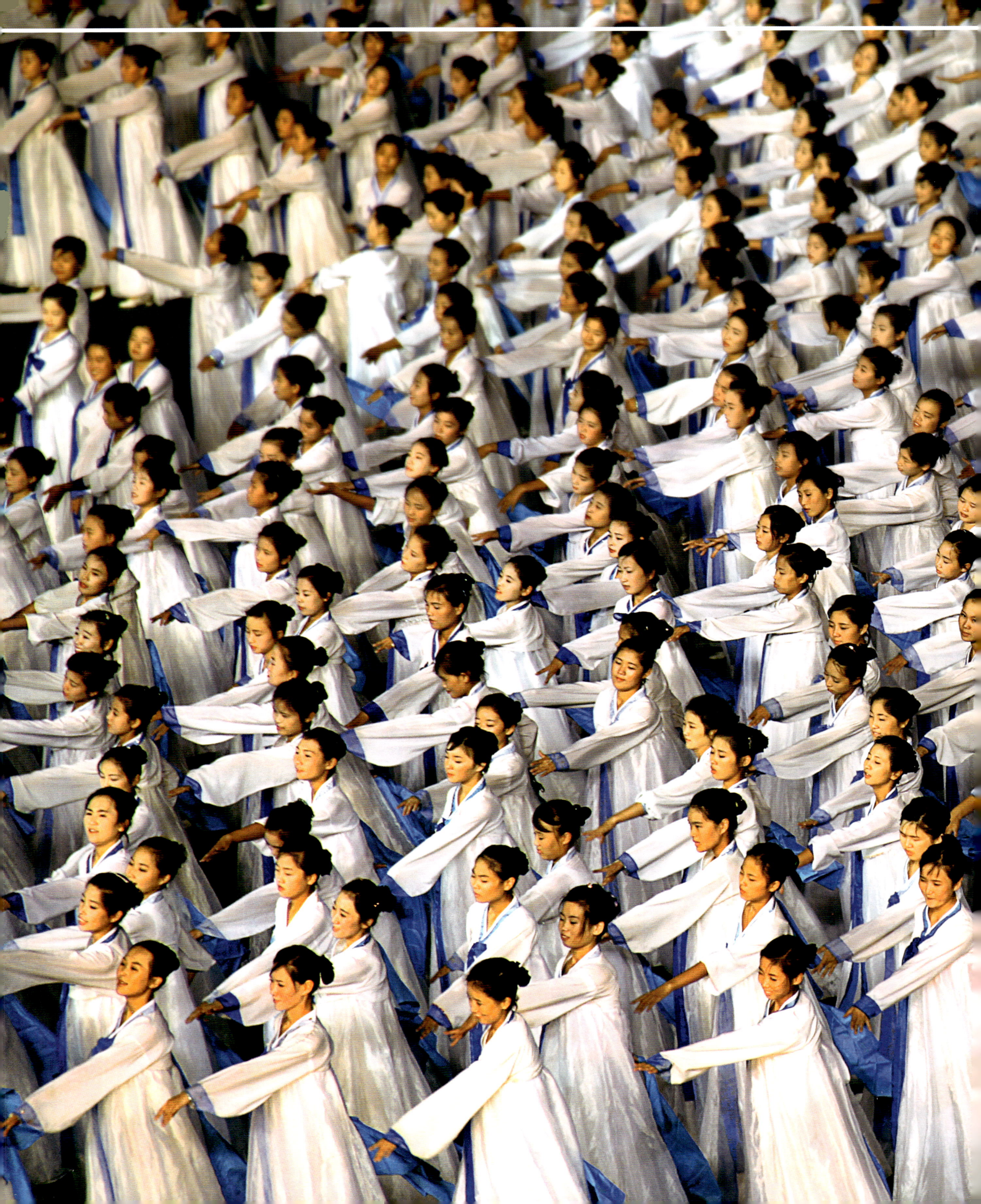

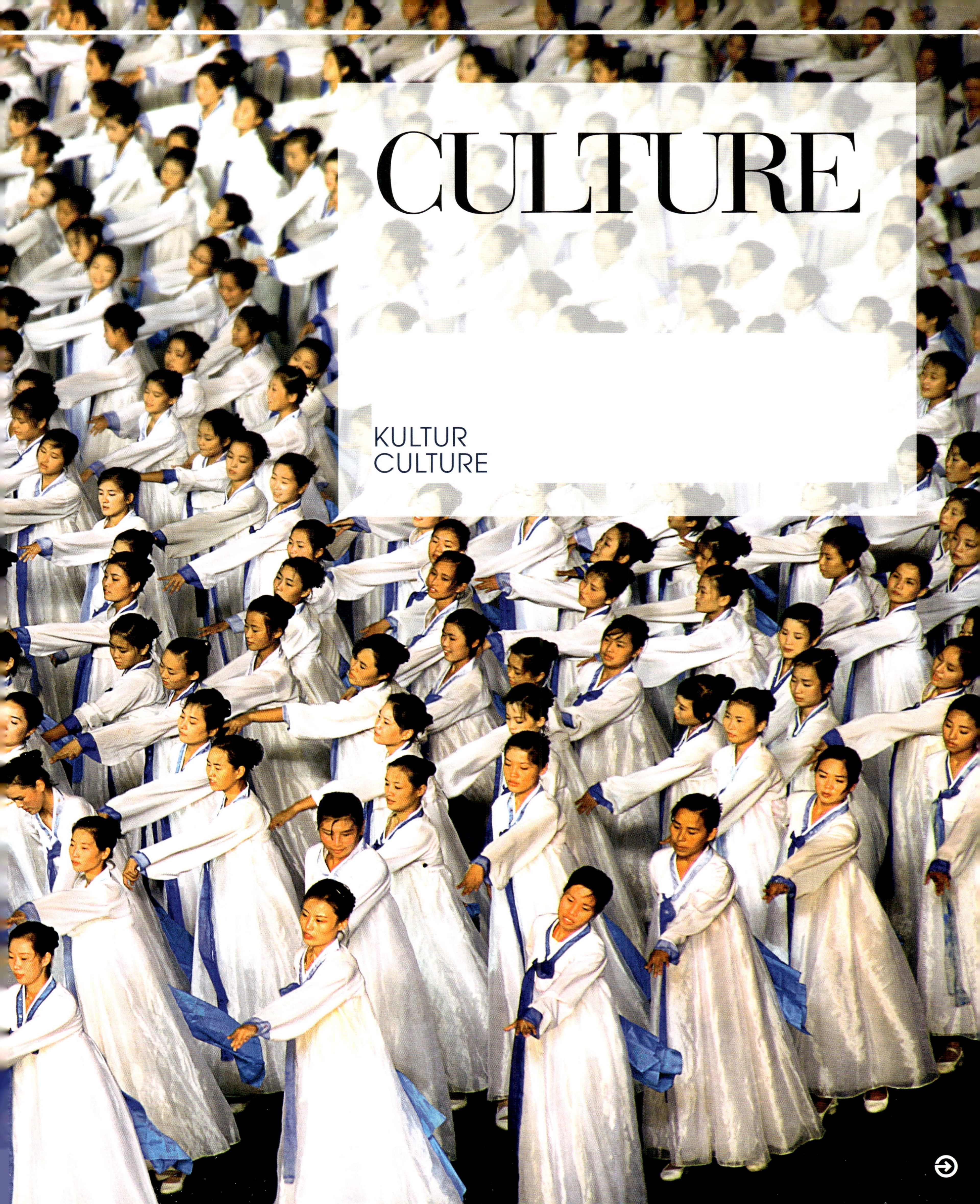

CULTURE

KULTUR
CULTURE

In North Korea, the individual exists only in relation to the collective. This concept is certainly an alien one to Westerners. Huge crowds form visually stunning slogans during vast spectacles such as the well known Arirang Festival. The precise mass choreography depicts symbols of the state's Juche ideology, which stands for political sovereignty, economic self sufficiency, and military independence. The precisely synchronized dancing, the oversized human mosaics, and the meticulously coordinated waves formed by thousands of participants have even made it into the Guinness Book of World Records. Propaganda and an anachronistic personality cult frame everyday life in North Korea.

In Nordkorea ist die Existenz des Individuums nur im Zusammenhang mit dem Kollektiv denkbar. Aus westlicher Sicht erscheint das sicher befremdlich. Bei Gigaveranstaltungen, wie dem bekannten Arirang-Festival, formen riesige Menschenmengen bildgewaltige Parolen. Die präzisen Massenchoreografien zeigen Symbole der Staatsideologie Juche, die für politische Souveränität, wirtschaftliche Selbstversorgung und militärische Eigenständigkeit steht. Sogar ins Guinnessbuch der Rekorde haben es die exakten Synchrontänze, das überdimensionale Menschenmosaik und die minutiös kalkulierten Wellenbewegungen Tausender Mitwirkender geschafft. Auch der nordkoreanische Alltag wird von anachronistischem Personenkult und Propaganda flankiert.

En Corée du Nord, l'individu ne se conçoit pas en dehors de la collectivité, ce qui est assurément déroutant pour les Occidentaux. Lors de manifestations de masse, comme le célèbre festival Arirang, d'immenses foules forment des messages en images. Les chorégraphies mettent en avant des symboles du Juche, la doctrine d'État, qui repose sur la souveraineté nationale, l'autosuffisance de l'économie et l'autonomie militaire. Les danses parfaitement rodées, les gigantesques mosaïques humaines et les mouvements ondoyants soigneusement étudiés de milliers de gymnastes figurent même dans le Livre Guinness des records. En Corée du Nord, le quotidien rime avec culte de la personnalité anachronique et propagande.

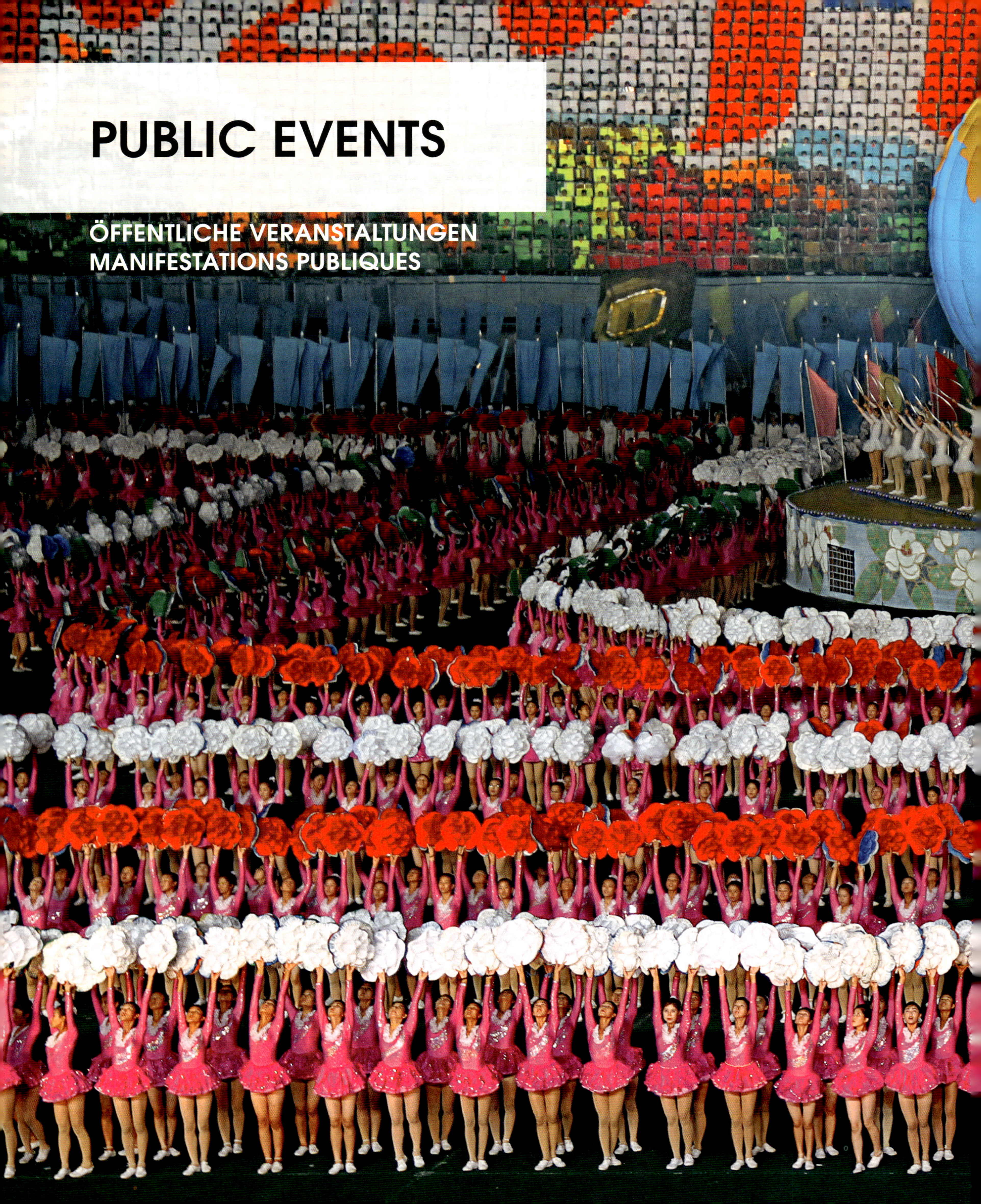

PUBLIC EVENTS

ÖFFENTLICHE VERANSTALTUNGEN
MANIFESTATIONS PUBLIQUES

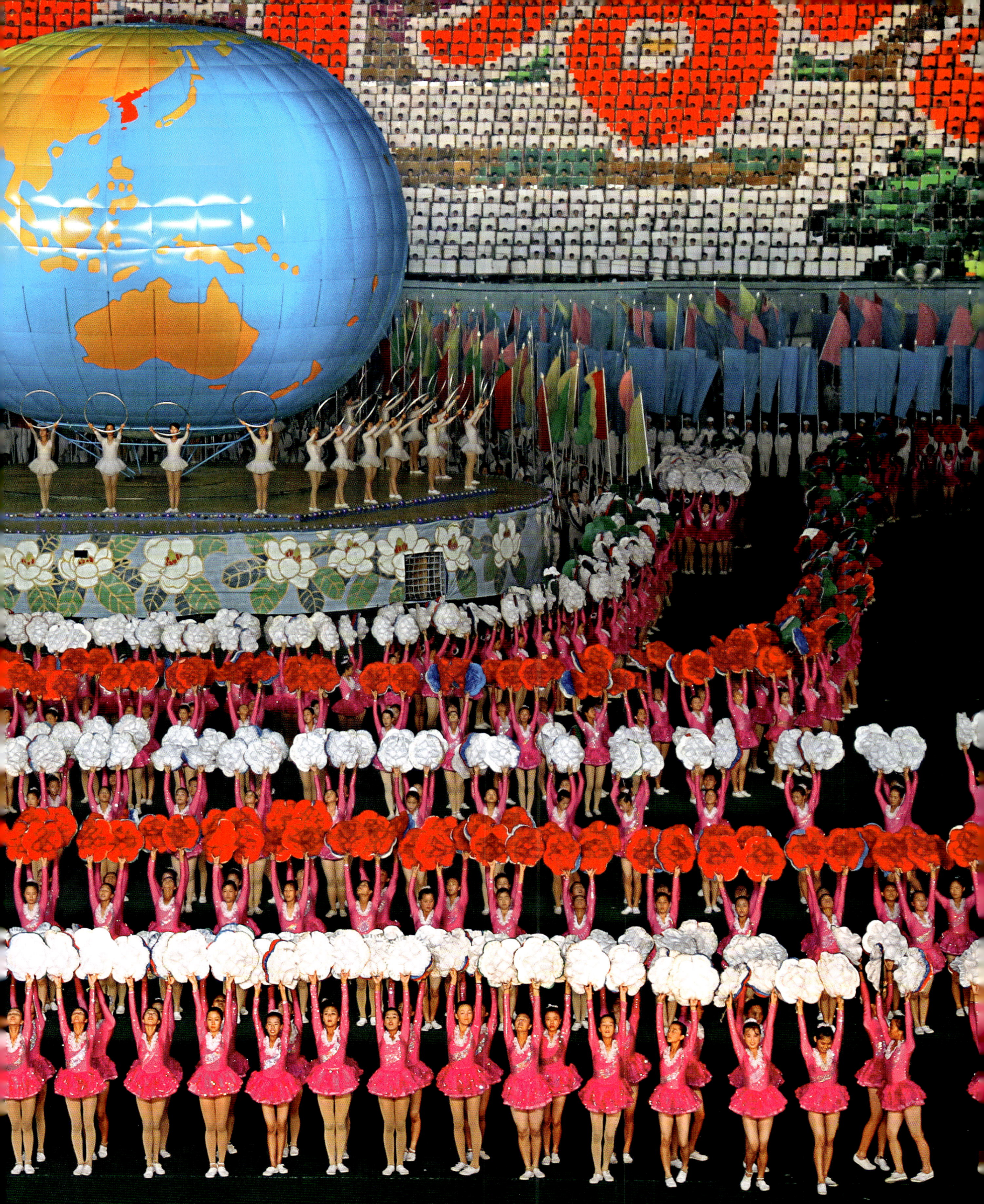

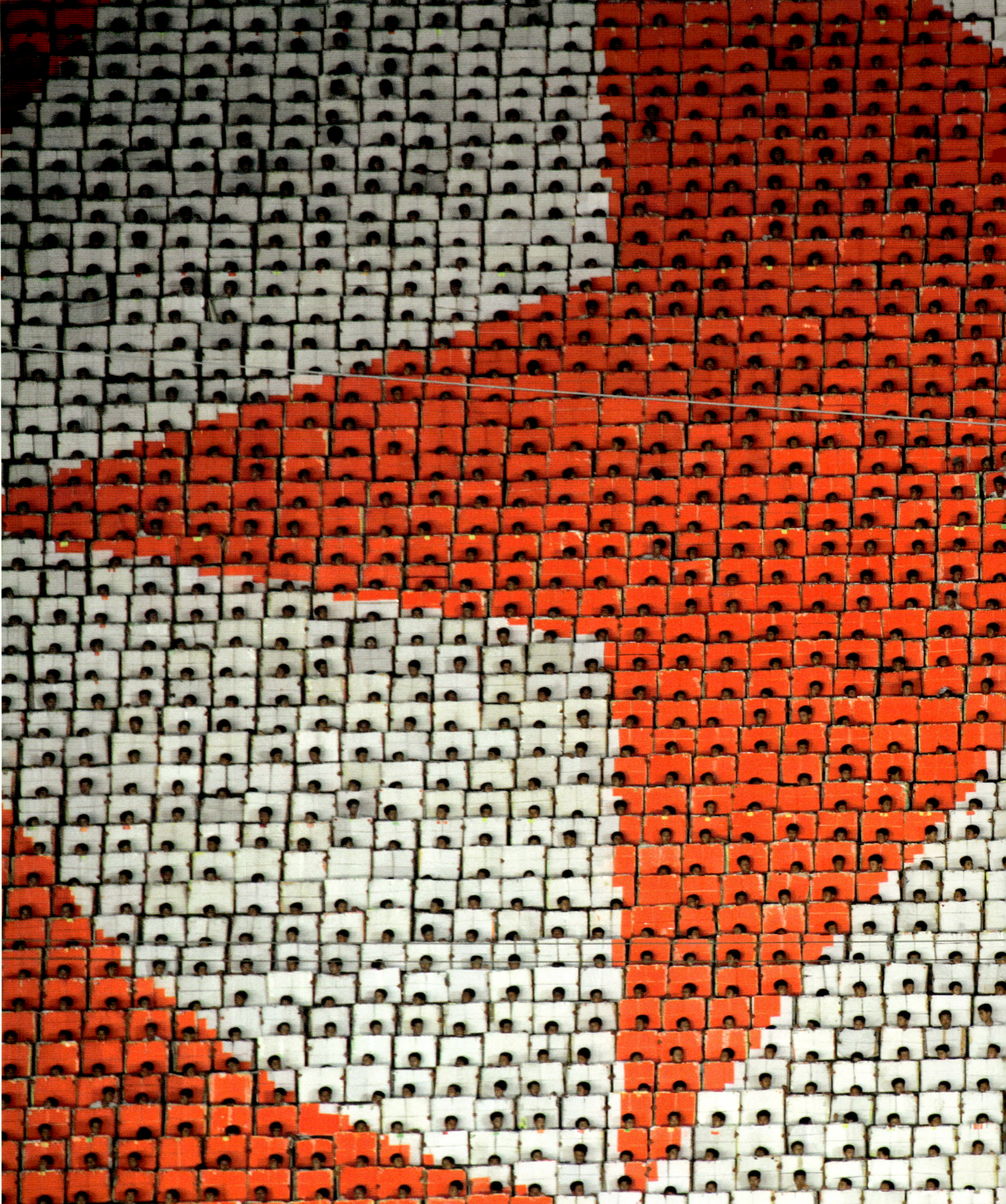

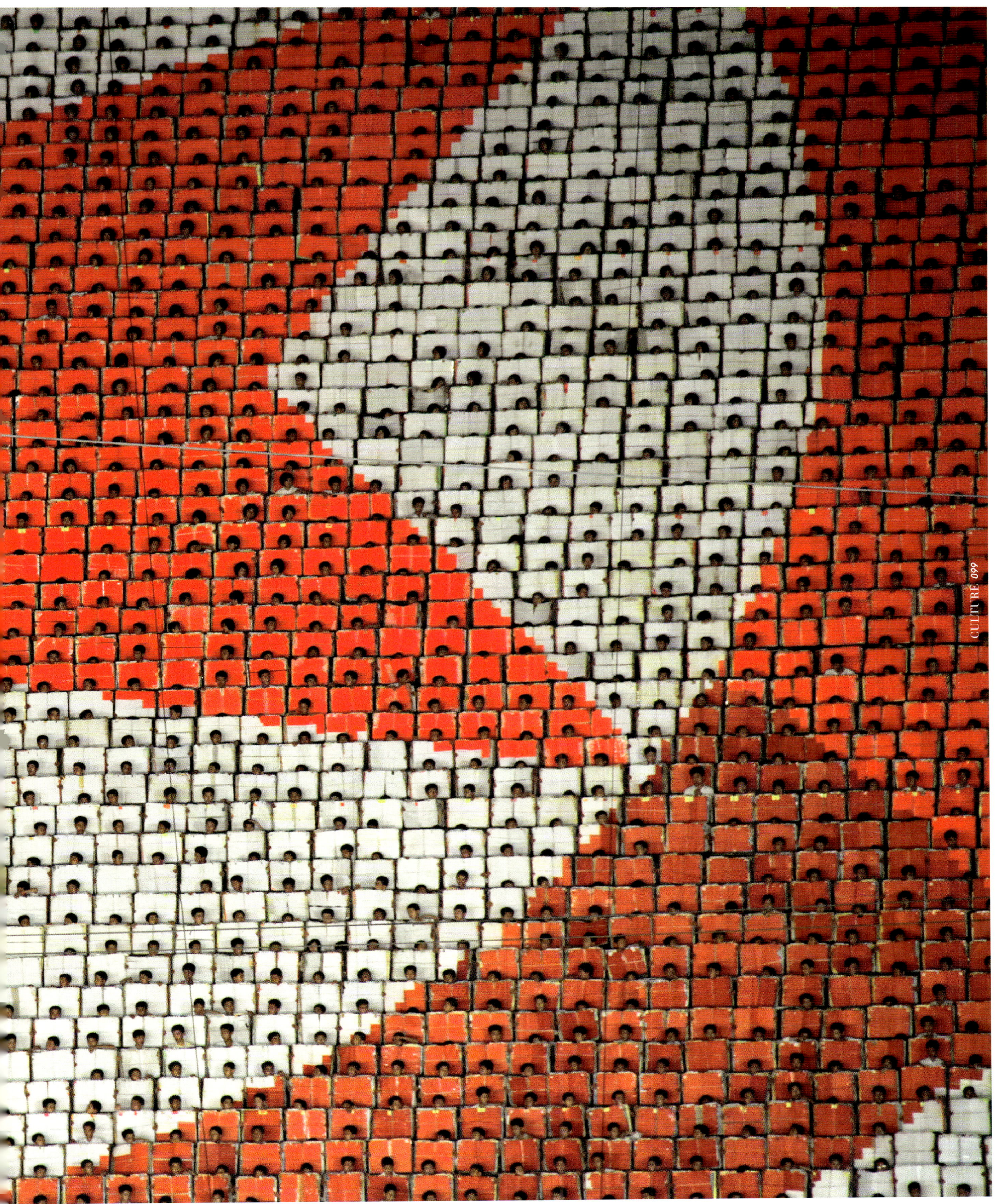

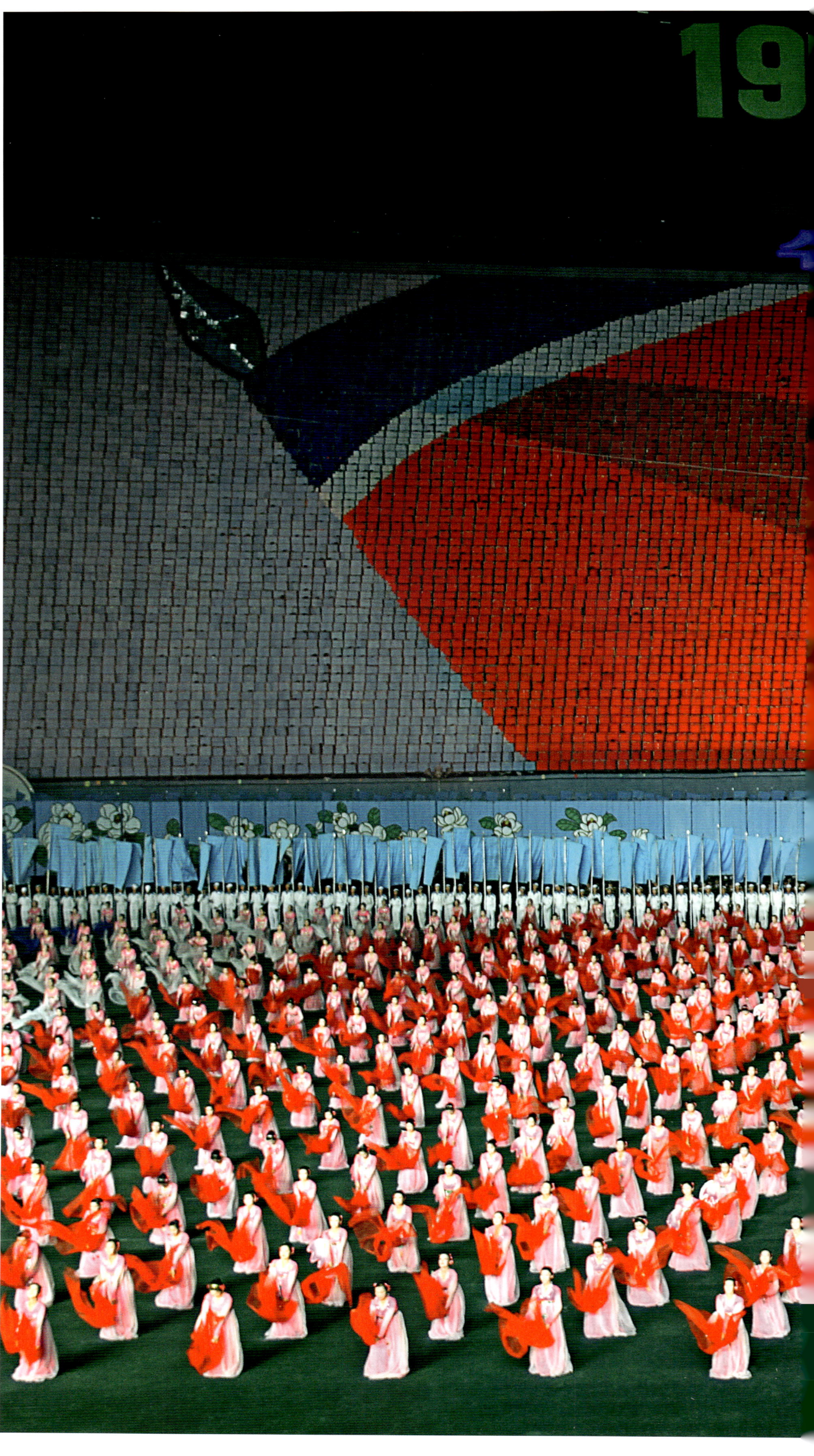

The Arirang mass festival, which takes its name from a traditional Korean folksong, reenacts the history of North Korea. More than 100,000 people are said to participate in this extravaganza, held in the May Day Stadium. The Arirang Festival has been in the Guinness Book of World Records since 2007, where it is described as the biggest event of its kind.

Während der Massenveranstaltung Arirang, benannt nach einem alten koreanischen Volkslied, wird die Geschichte Nordkoreas dargestellt. Angeblich wirken über 100 000 Menschen im Stadion „Erster Mai" an der pompösen Selbstinszenierung mit. Das Arirang-Festival ist seit 2007 im Guinnessbuch der Rekorde als größte Veranstaltung seiner Art verzeichnet.

Pendant le festival Arirang, manifestation de masse qui doit son nom à une vieille chanson populaire coréenne, on retrace l'histoire de la Corée du Nord. Plus de 100 000 personnes participeraient à cette pompeuse auto-mise en scène dans le stade du Premier-Mai. Le festival Arirang figure depuis 2007 dans le Livre Guinness des records au titre de plus grande manifestation dans sa catégorie.

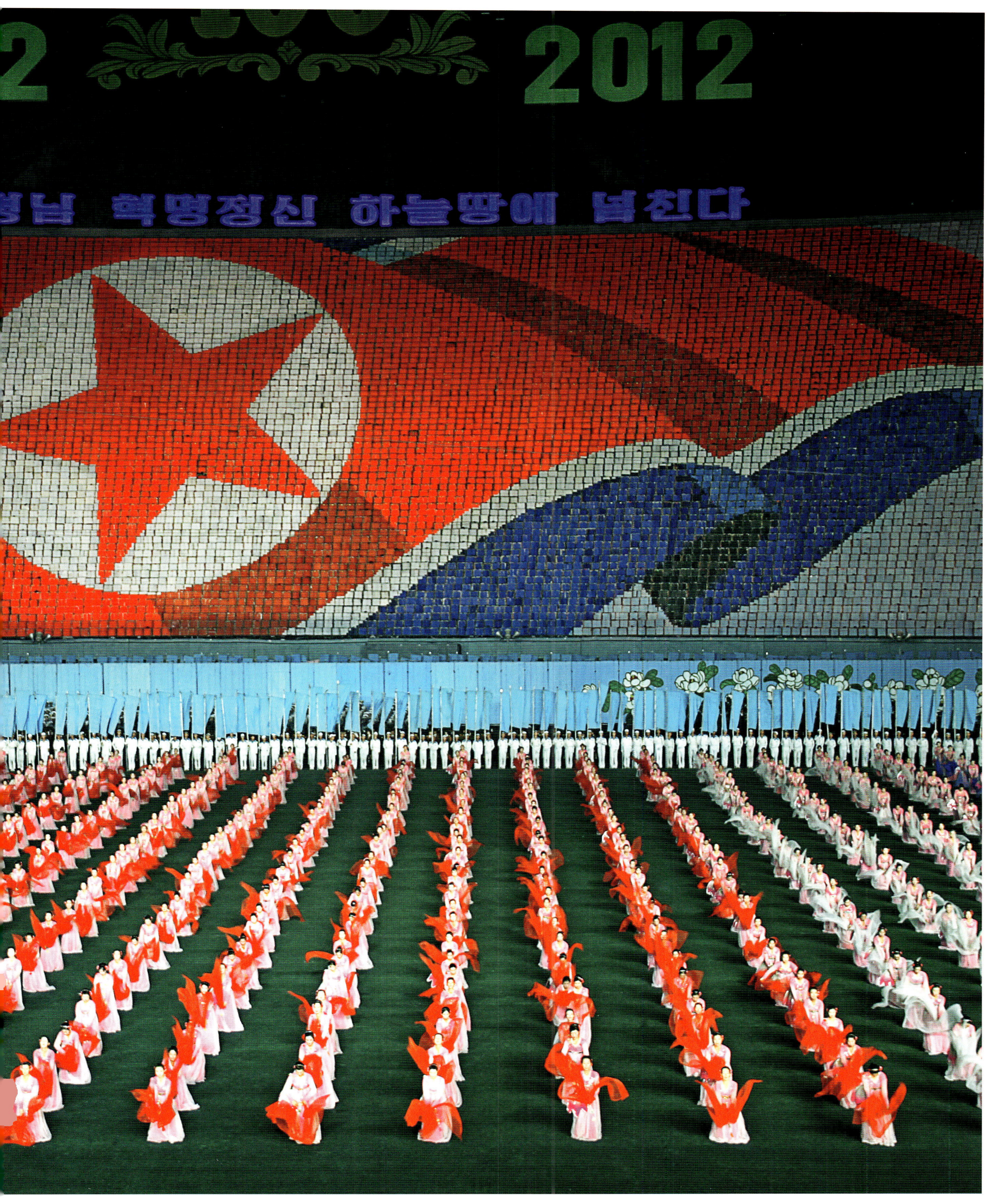
2012
혁명정신 하늘땅에 넘친다

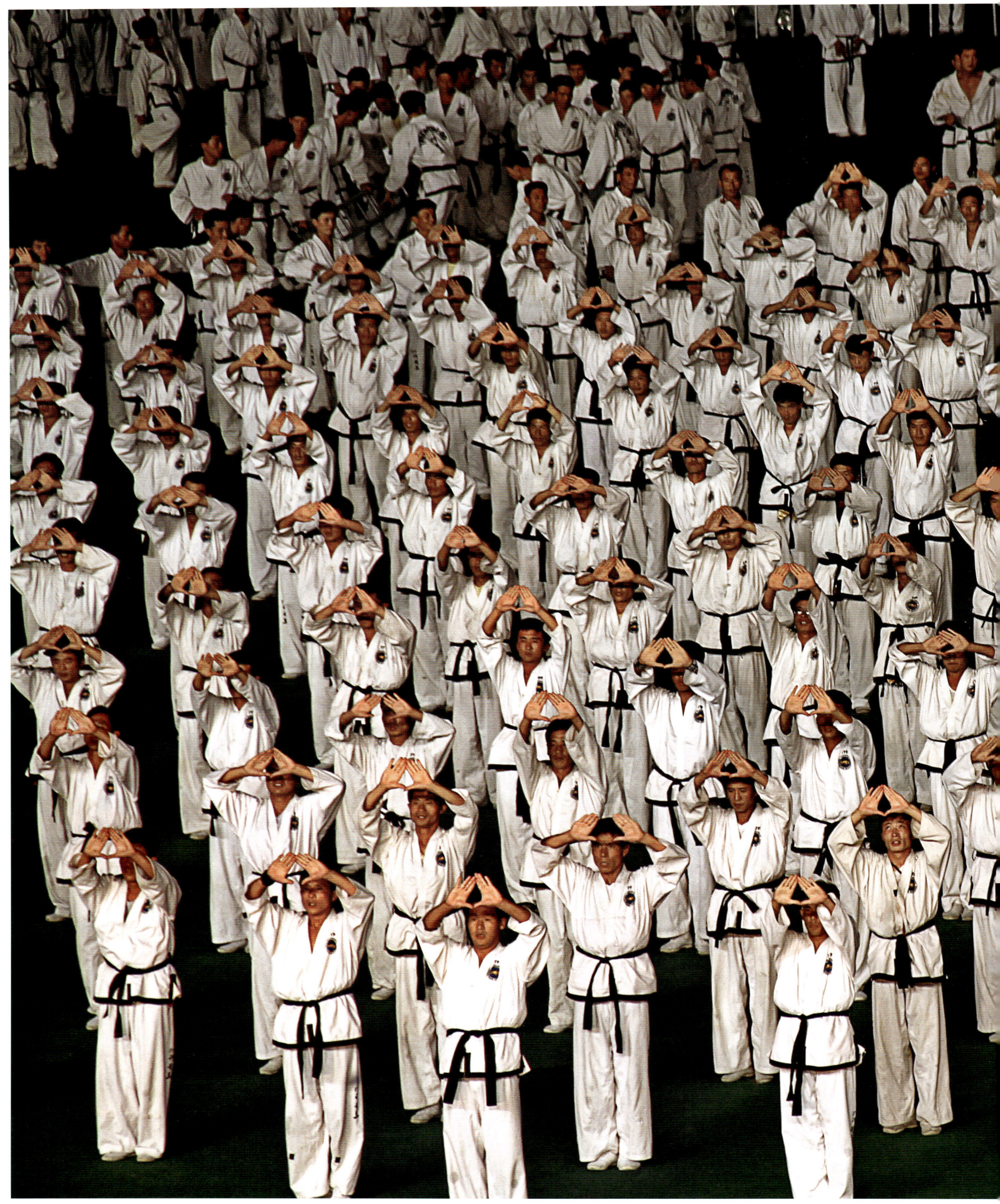

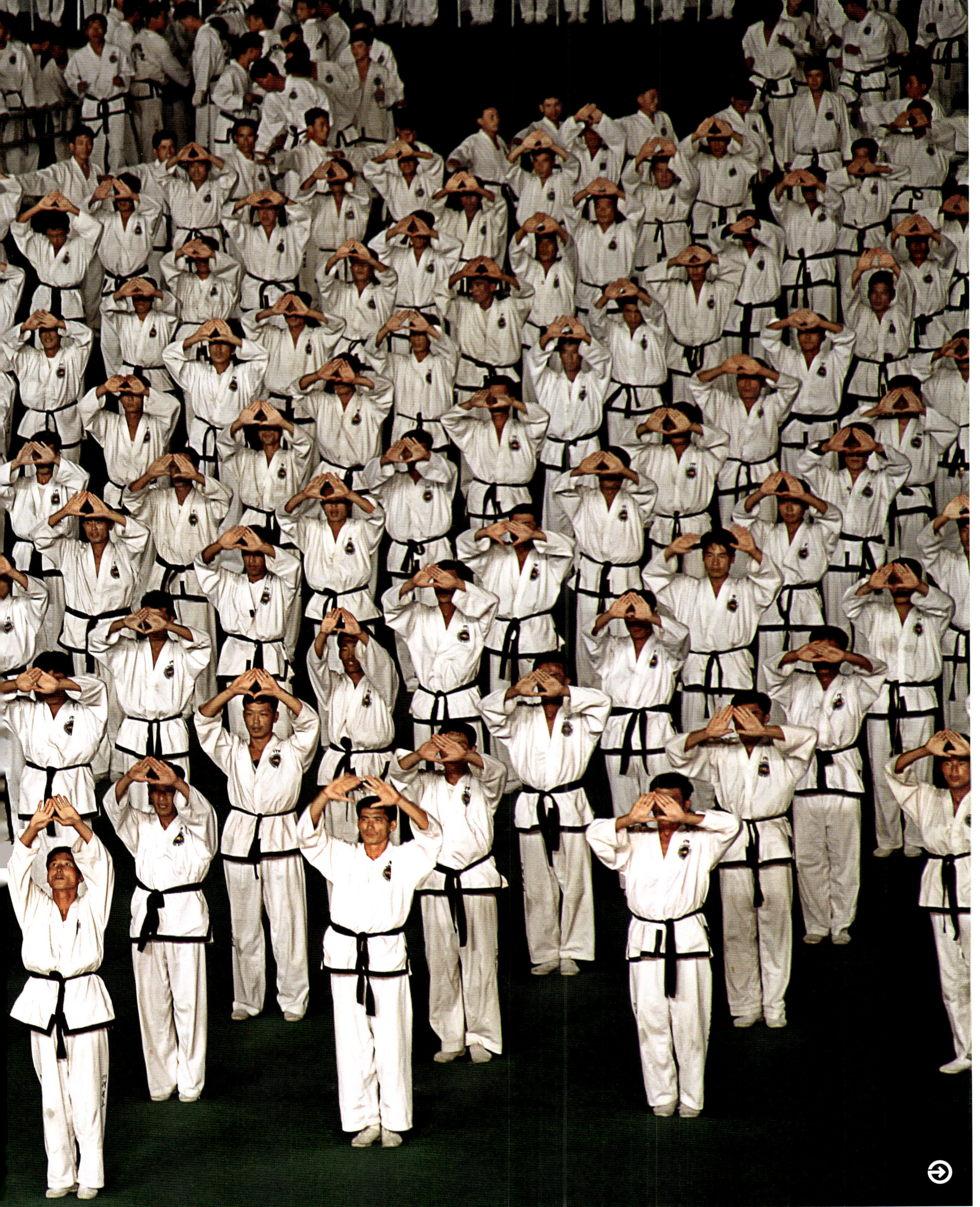

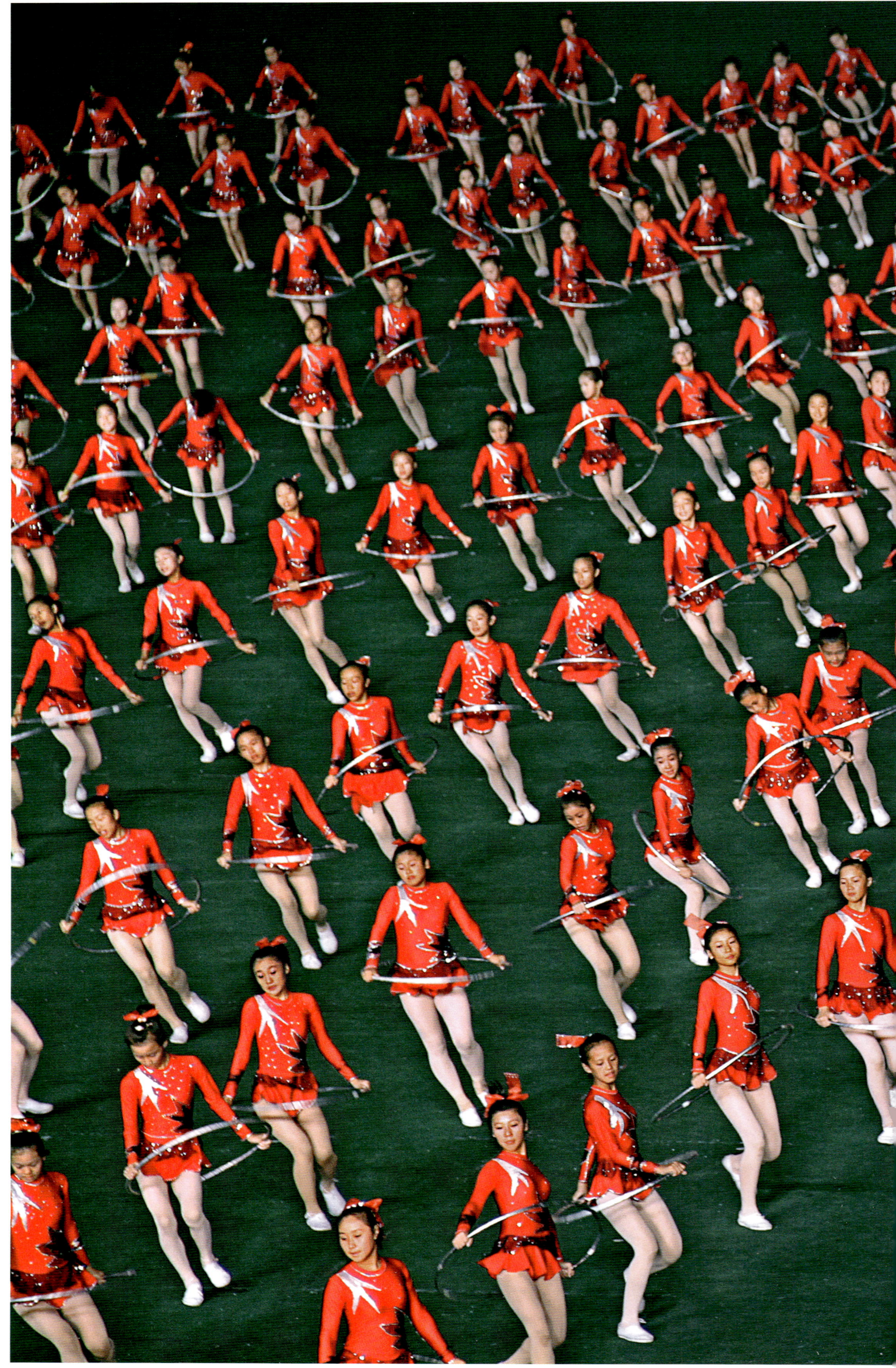

A group of girls at the Arirang Festival
Mädchengruppe beim Arirang-Festival
Groupe de jeunes filles dans le cadre du festival Arirang

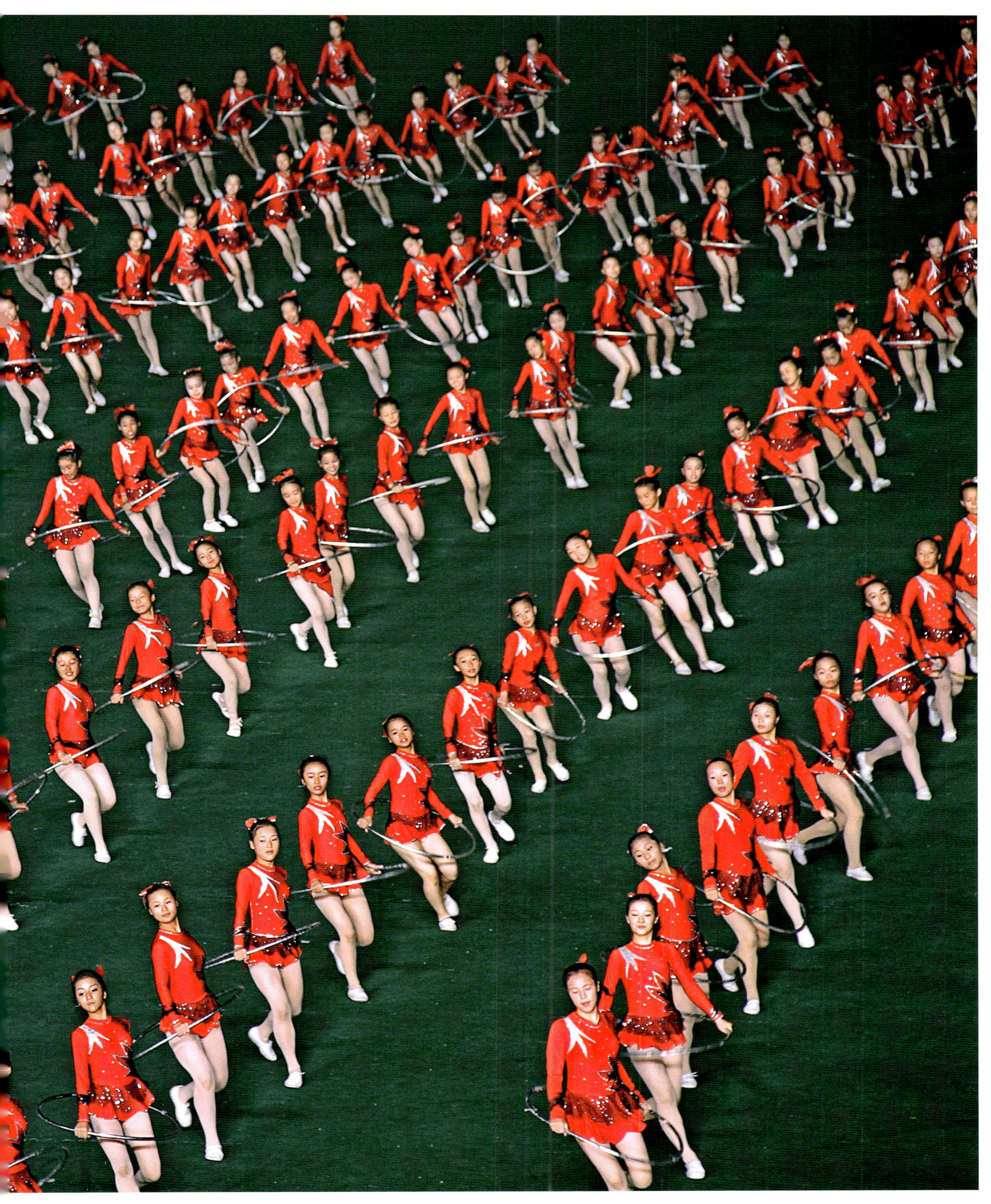

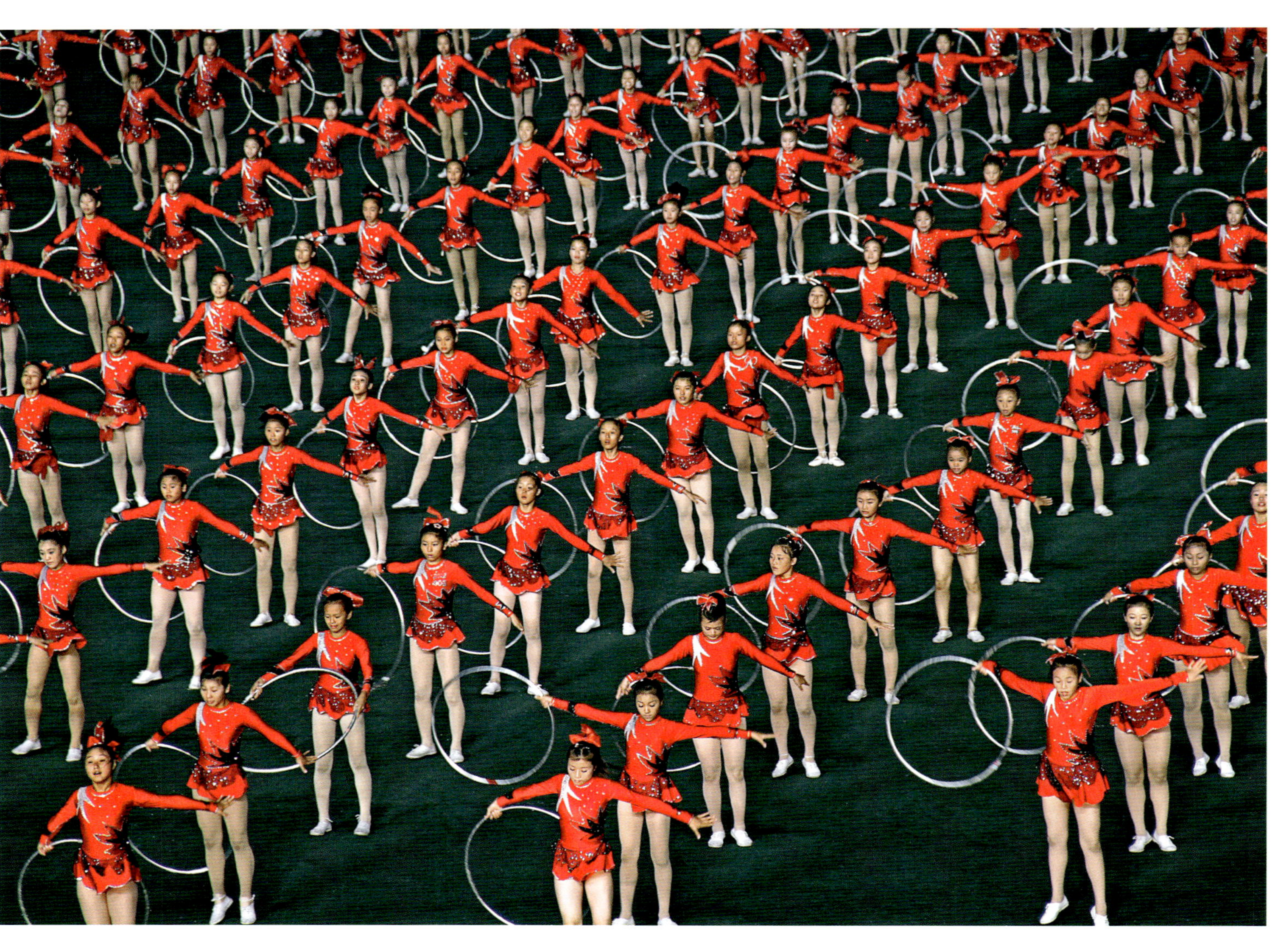

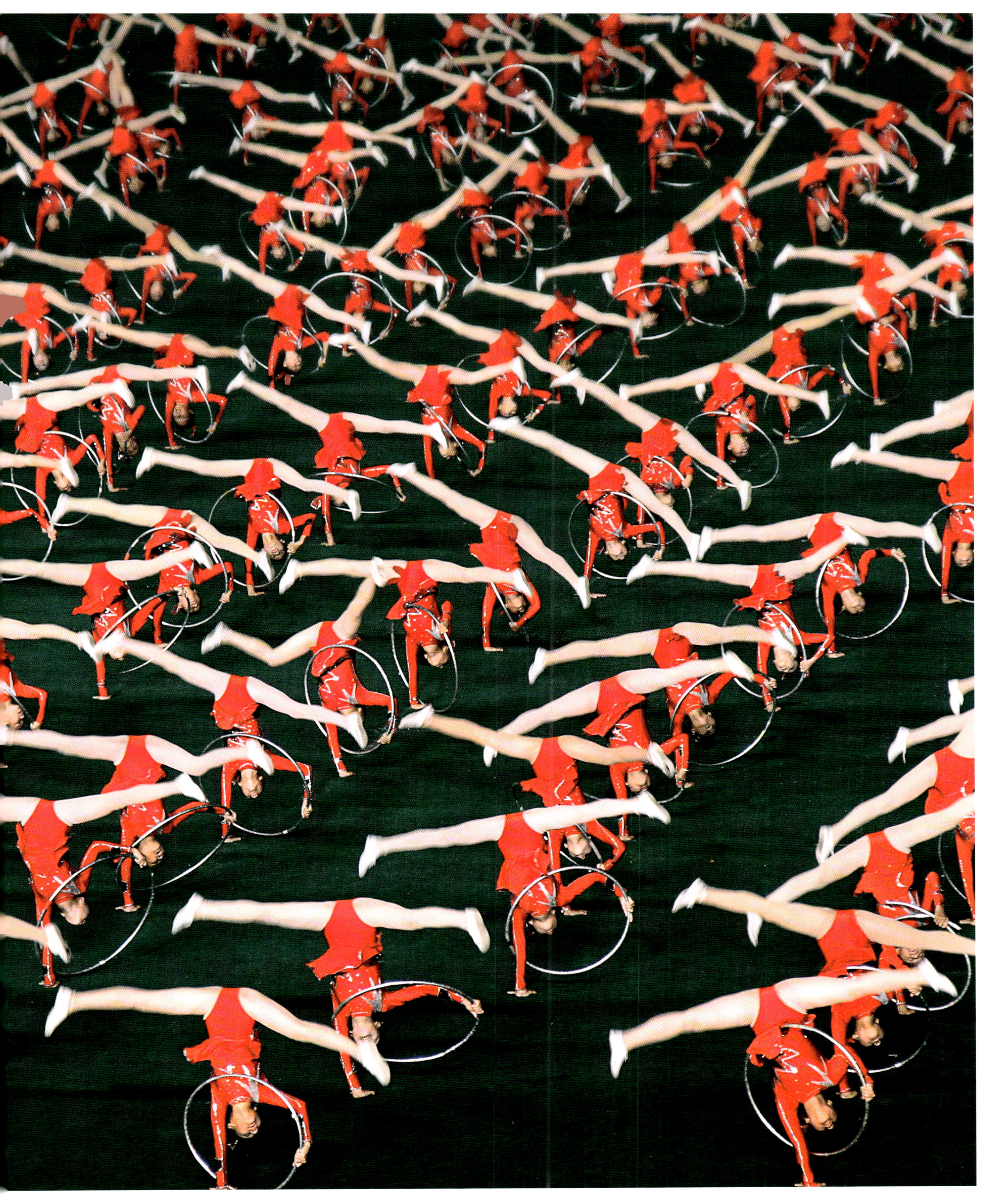

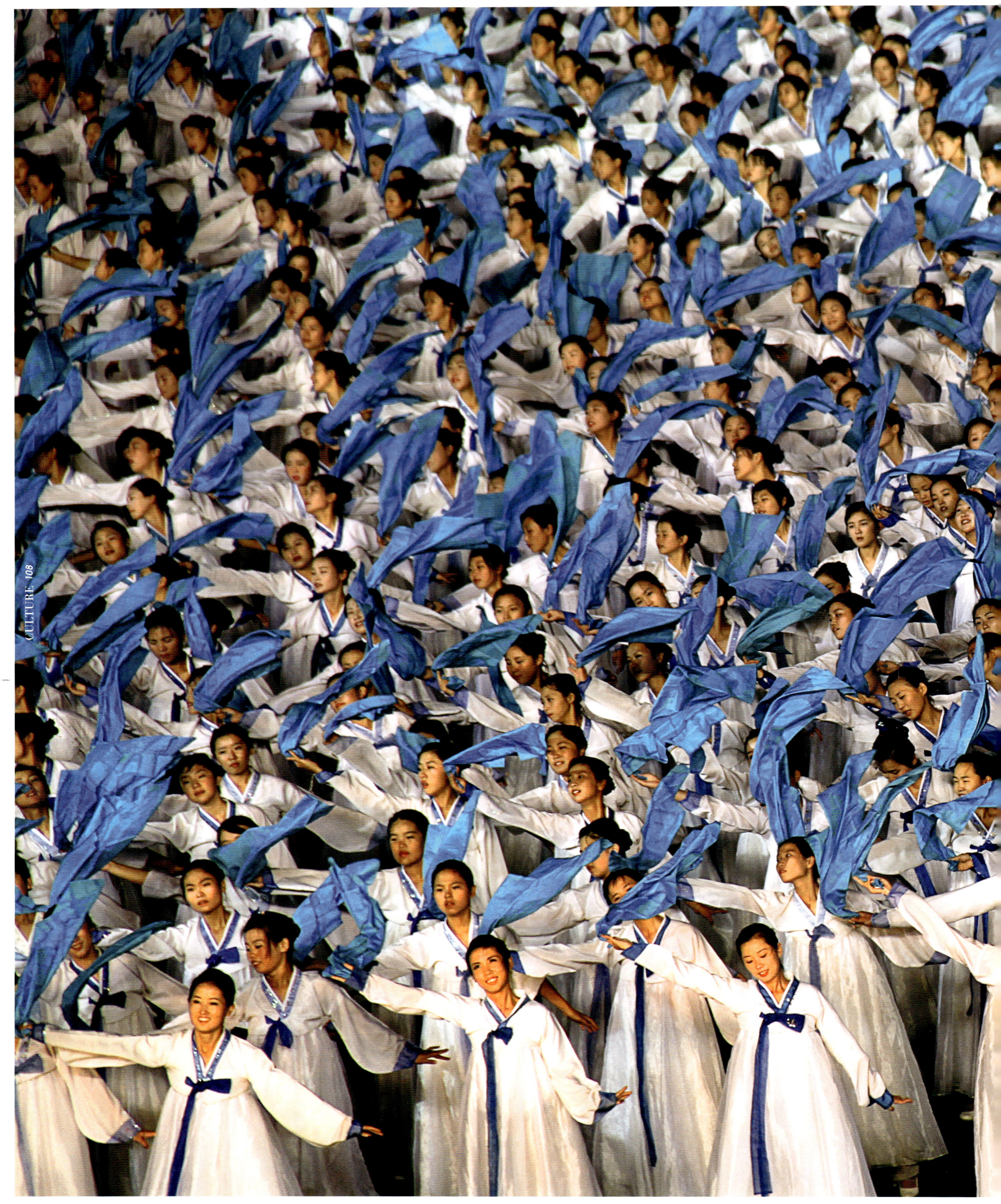

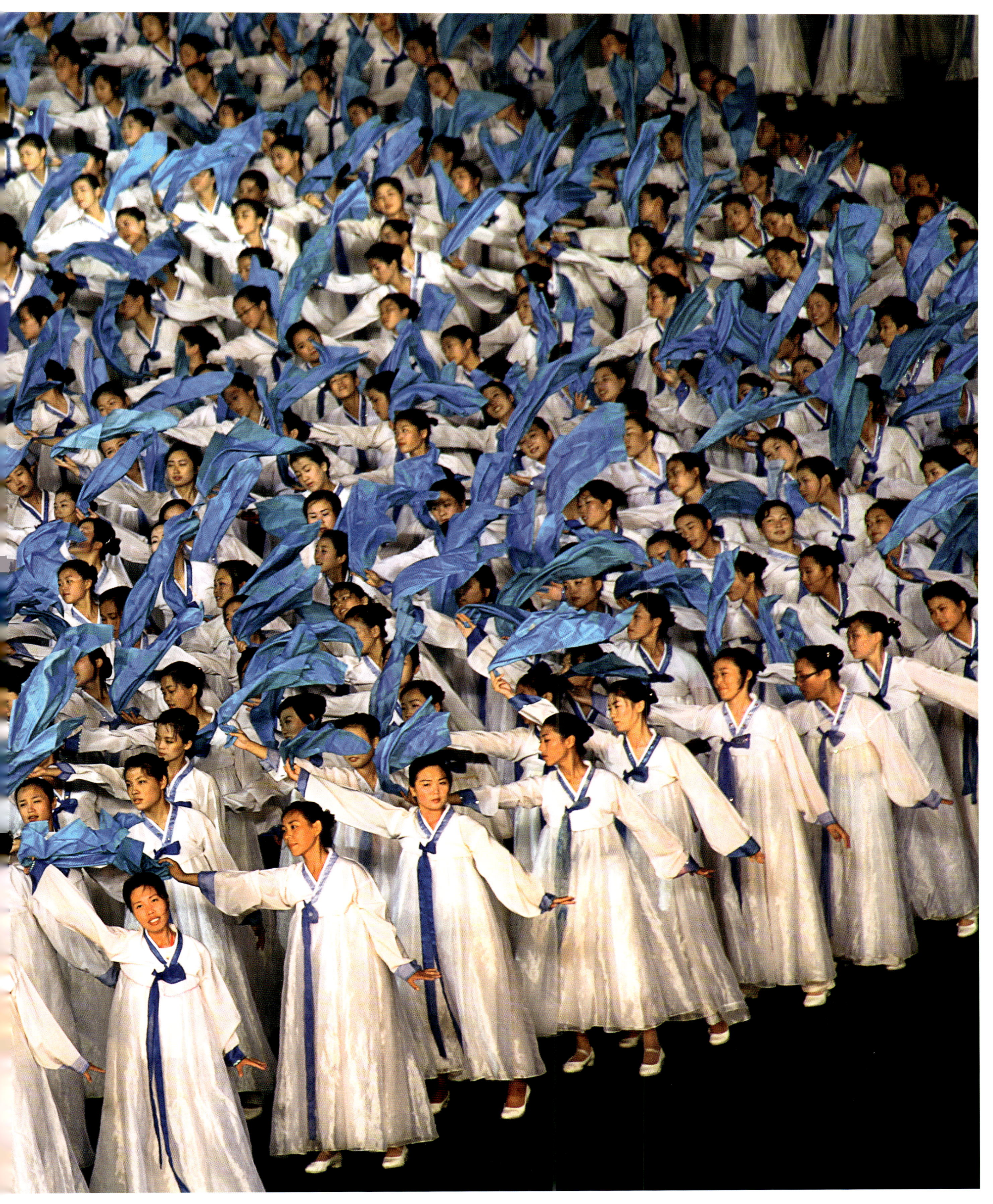

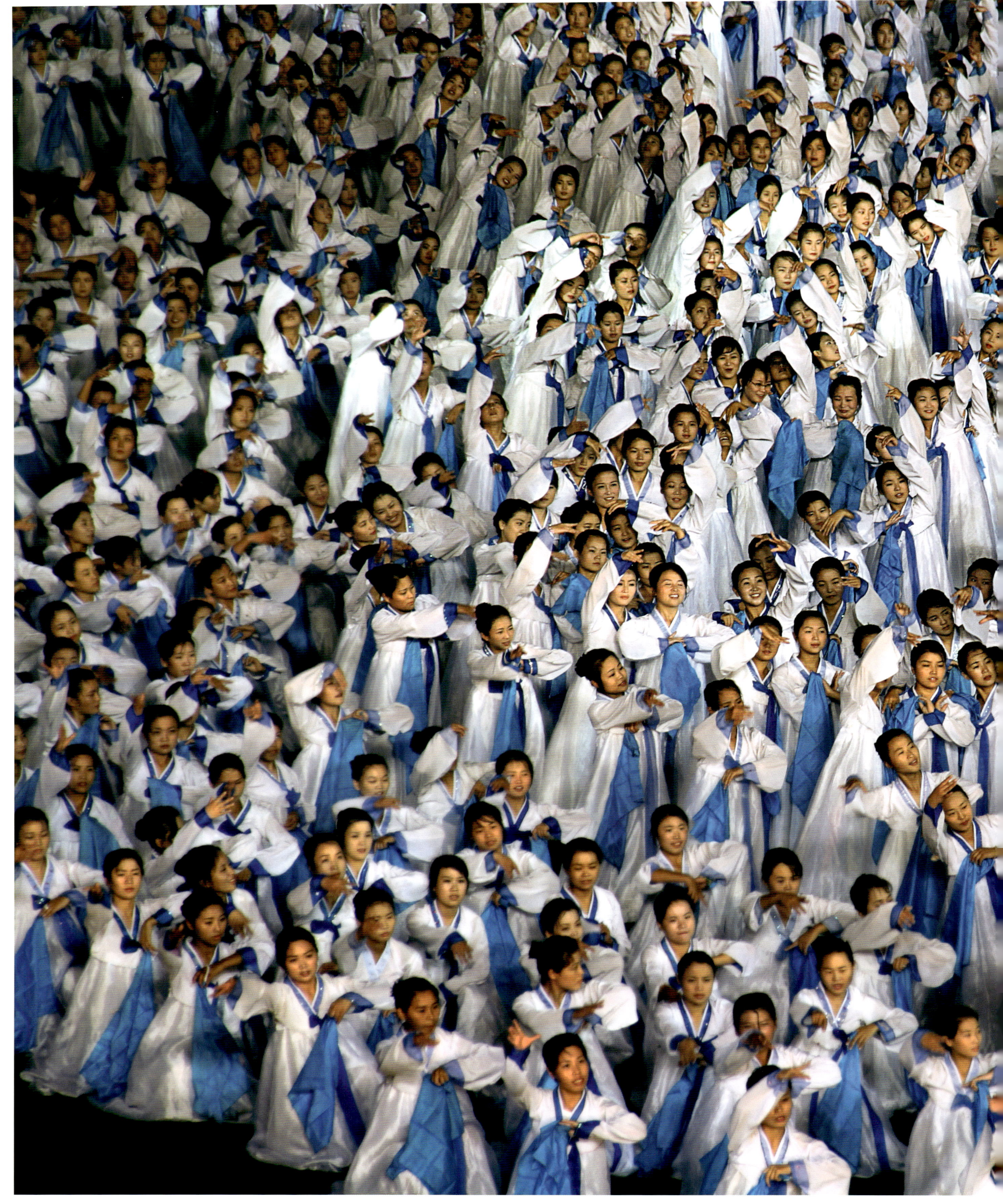

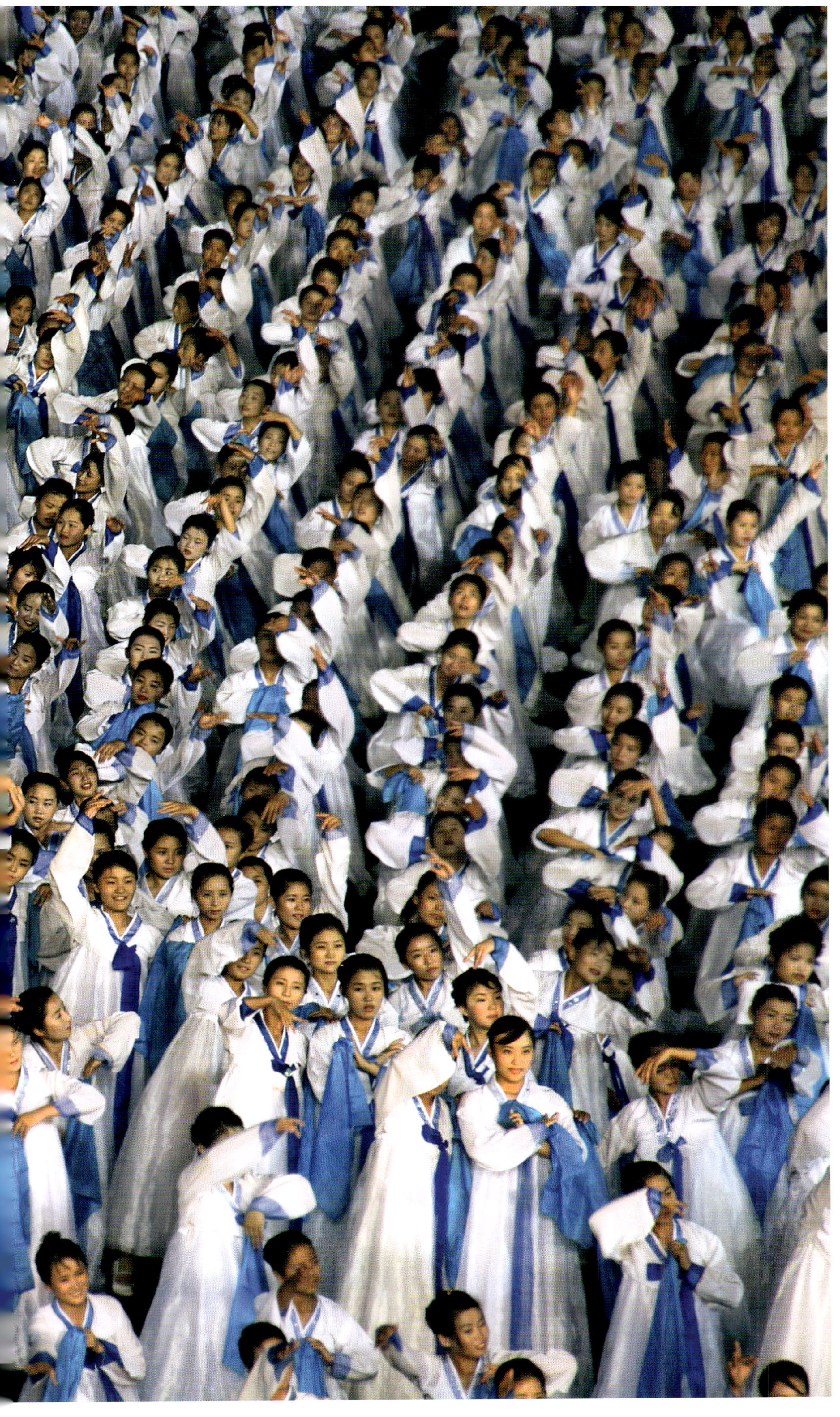

Arirang is the unofficial national anthem of both North Korea and its southern neighbor. The song expresses joy and sorrow throughout history and in the lives of all Koreans. A kind of cultural DNA, it is deeply rooted in the Korean soul.
Arirang ist die inoffizielle Nationalhymne sowohl Nord- als auch Südkoreas. Das Lied verkörpert Freude und Leid in der Geschichte und im Leben aller Koreaner. Als kulturelle DNA ist es tief in der koreanischen Seele verwurzelt.
Arirang est l'hymne officieux des deux Corées. Ce chant incarne la joie et la souffrance dans l'histoire et dans la vie de tous les Coréens. Sorte d'ADN culturel, il est profondément ancré dans l'âme coréenne.

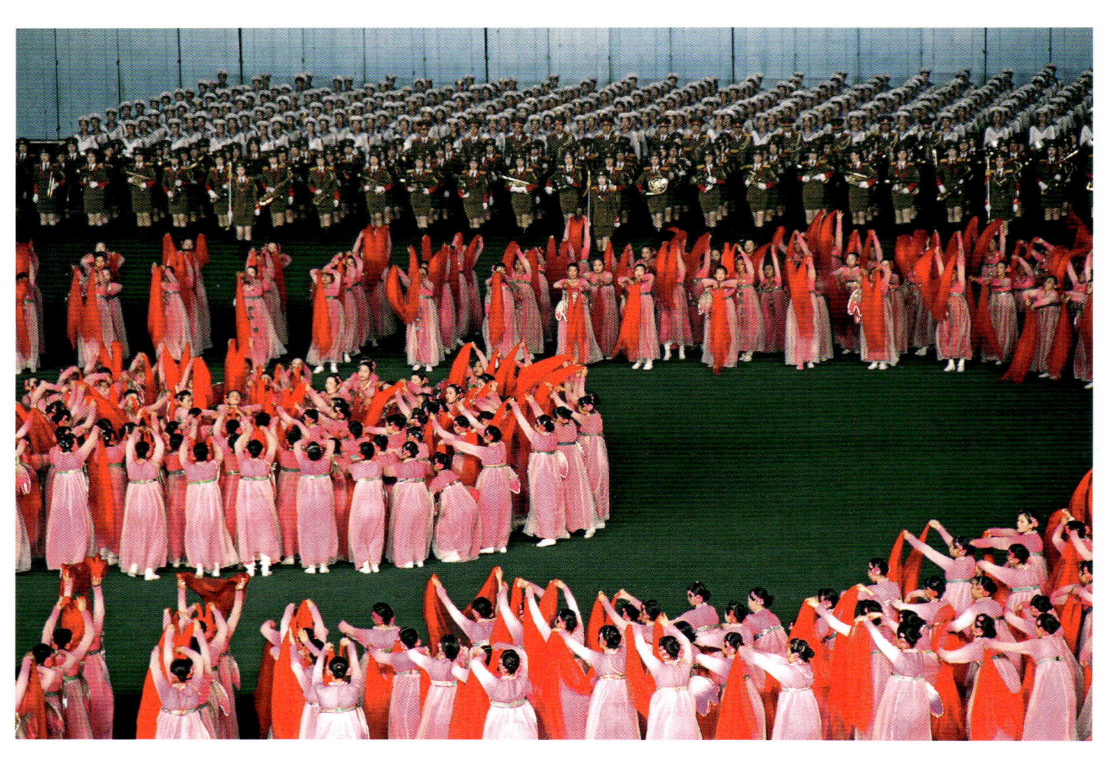

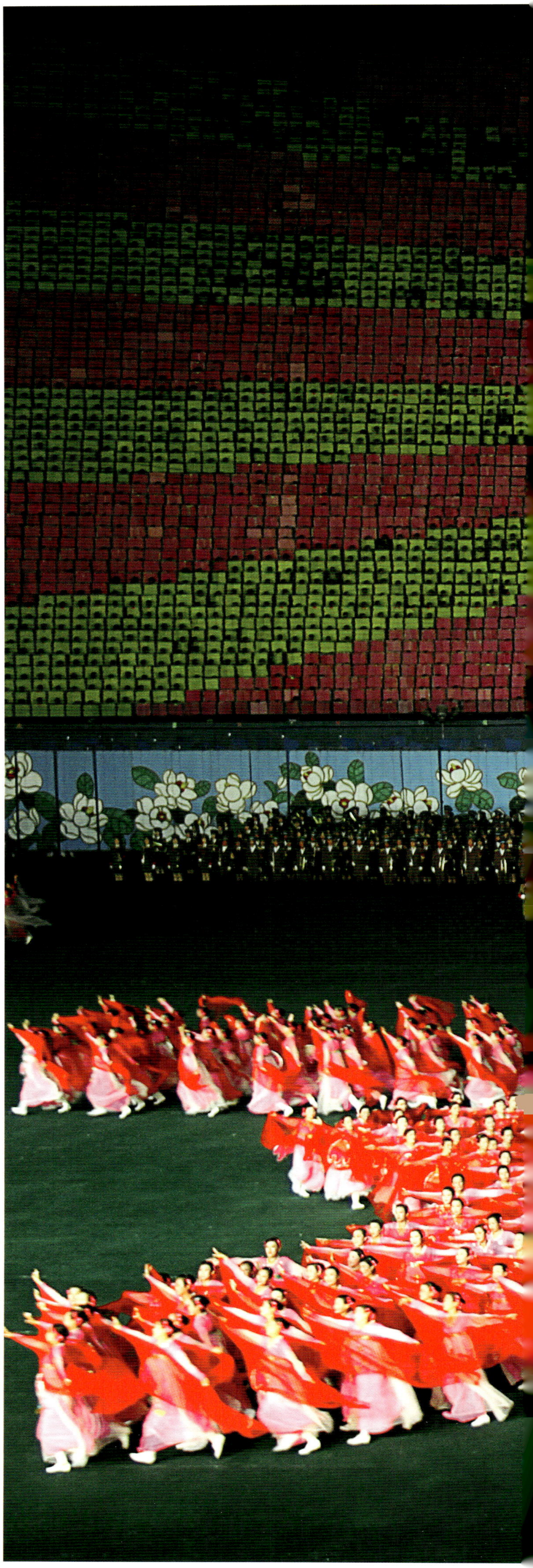

Every single human being contributes to the grand total: The star represents the revolution, and its rays call upon the people to pass on their traditions. The hydroelectric power plant reflects the country's independent industry. Ears of rice symbolize agriculture, and the red ribbon stands for the unbreakable bonds of Korean unity. The characters spell out the name of the nation.
Der Mensch als kleinstes Bildelement: Im Staatswappen steht der Stern für die Revolution. Die Strahlen fordern die Weitergabe der Tradition und im Wasserwerk spiegelt sich die unabhängige Industrie. Reisähren symbolisieren die Landwirtschaft und die entschlossene Einheit aller Koreaner zeigt sich im roten Band. Die Schriftzeichen stehen für den Staatsnamen.
L'être humain comme unité de base de l'image : sur le drapeau nord-coréen, l'étoile représente la révolution, dont le rayonnement favorise la transmission de la tradition. Le barrage hydroélectrique évoque l'autosuffisance de l'industrie, tandis que les épis de riz figurent l'agriculture, et la bande rouge l'unité inébranlable des Coréens. L'inscription correspond à la dénomination officielle du pays.

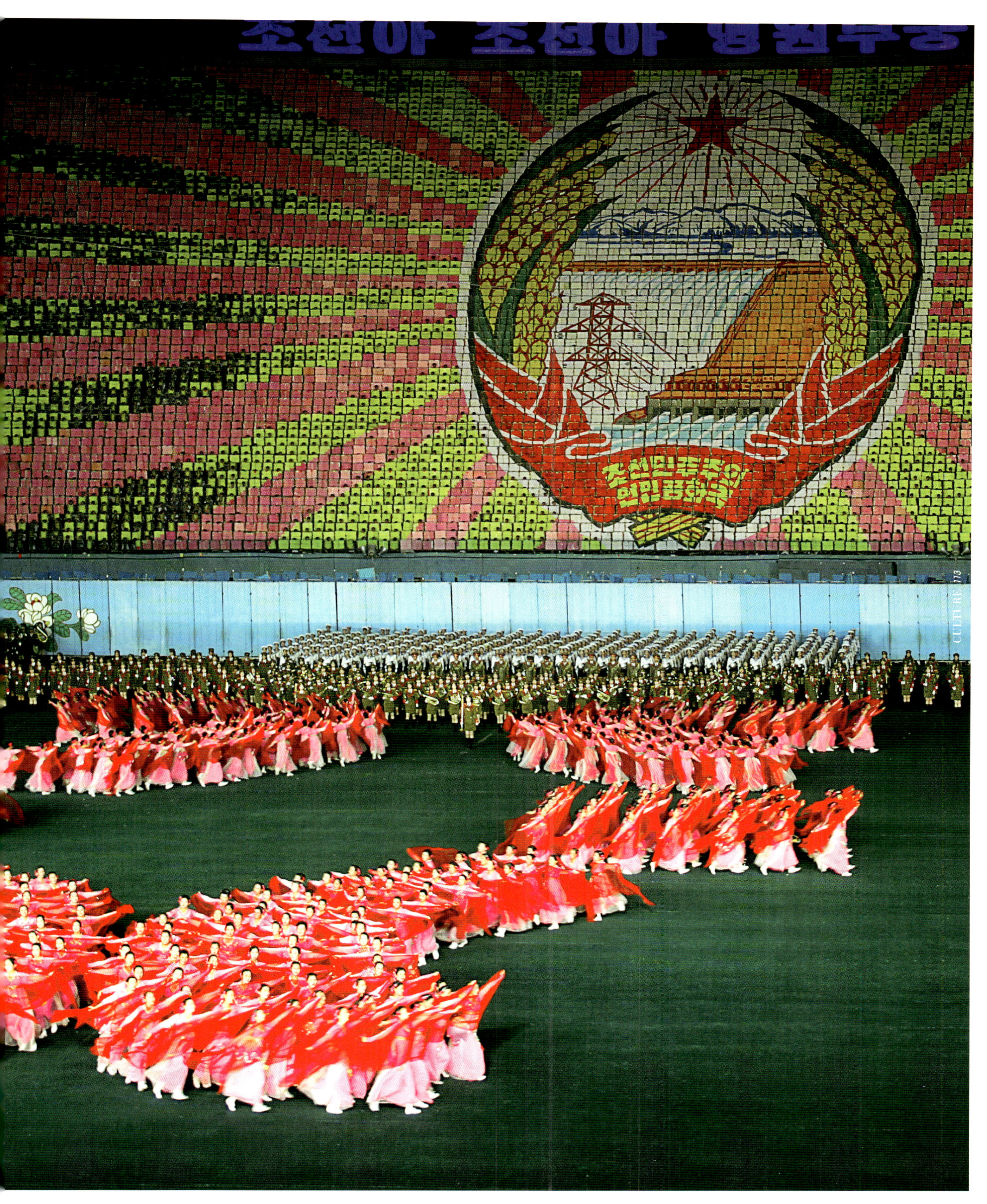
조선아 조선아 영원무궁
조선민주주의
인민공화국

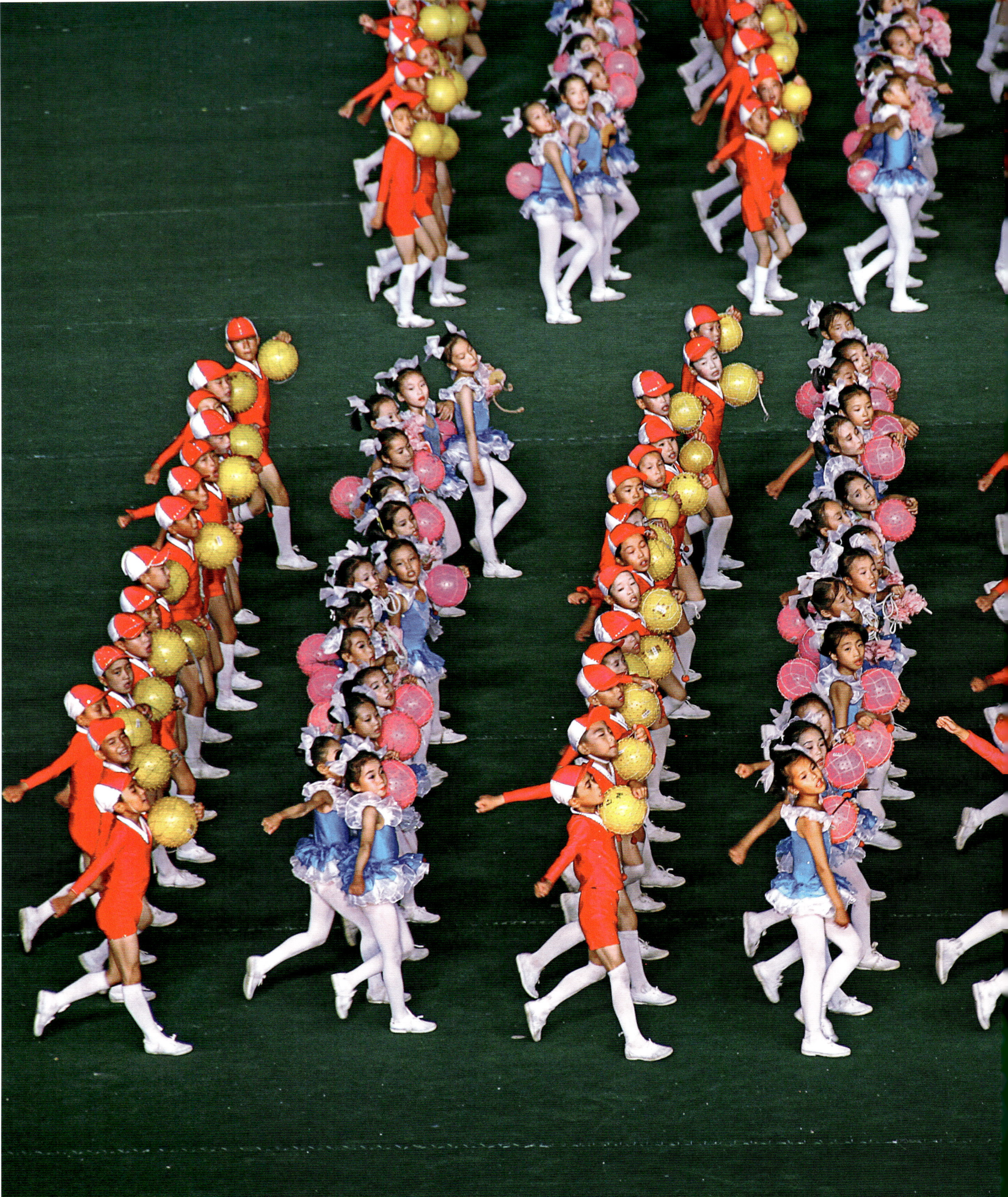

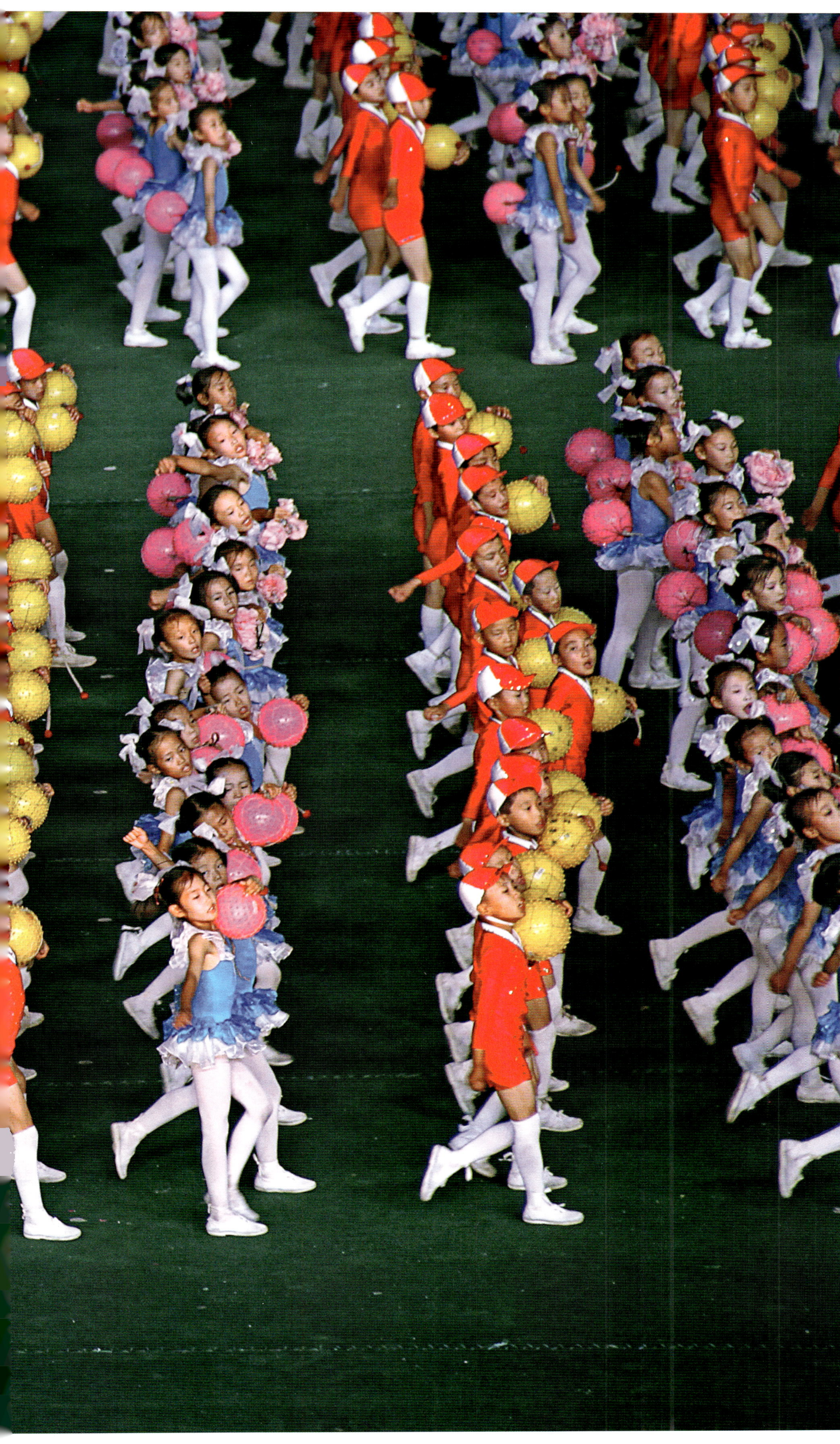

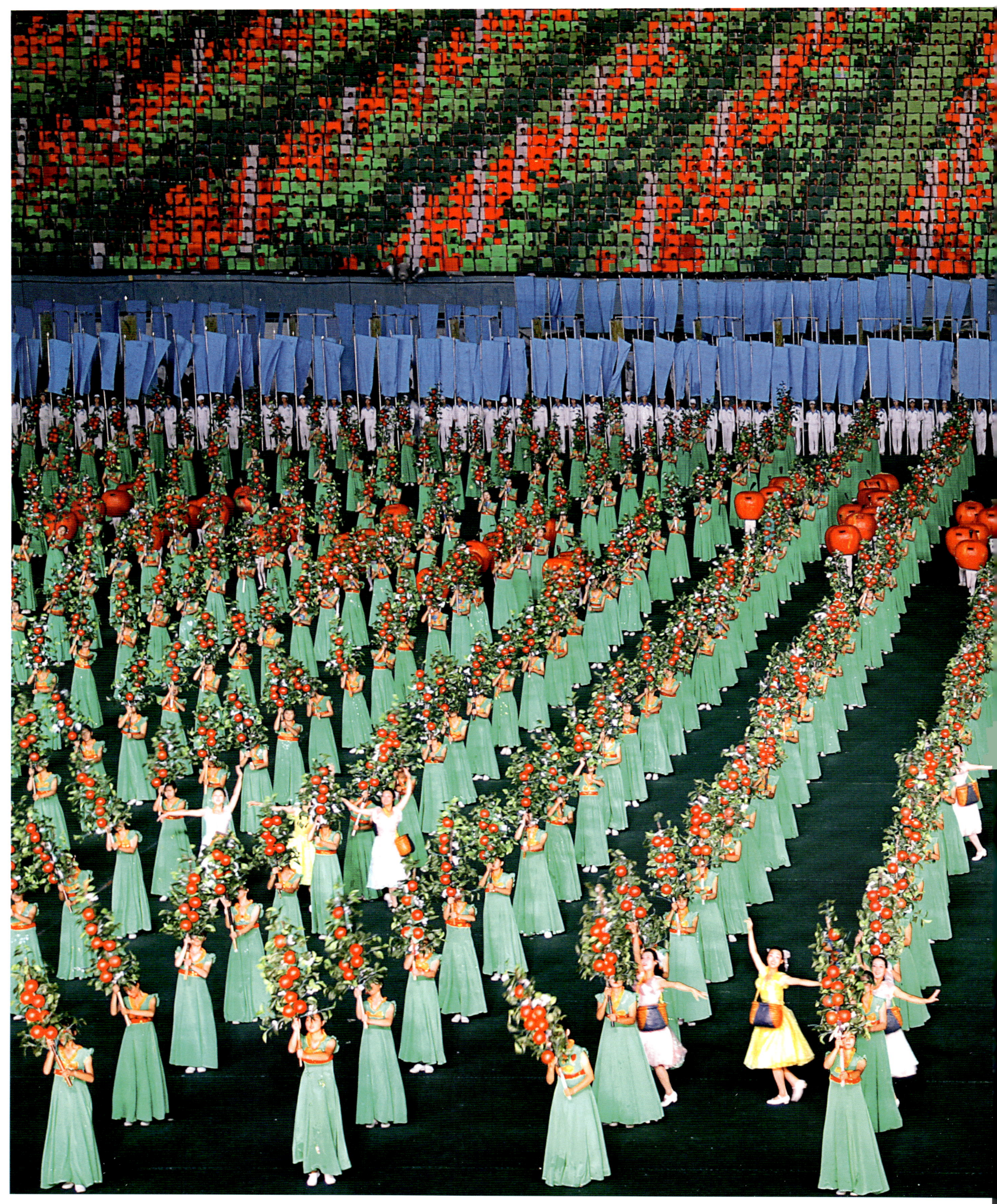

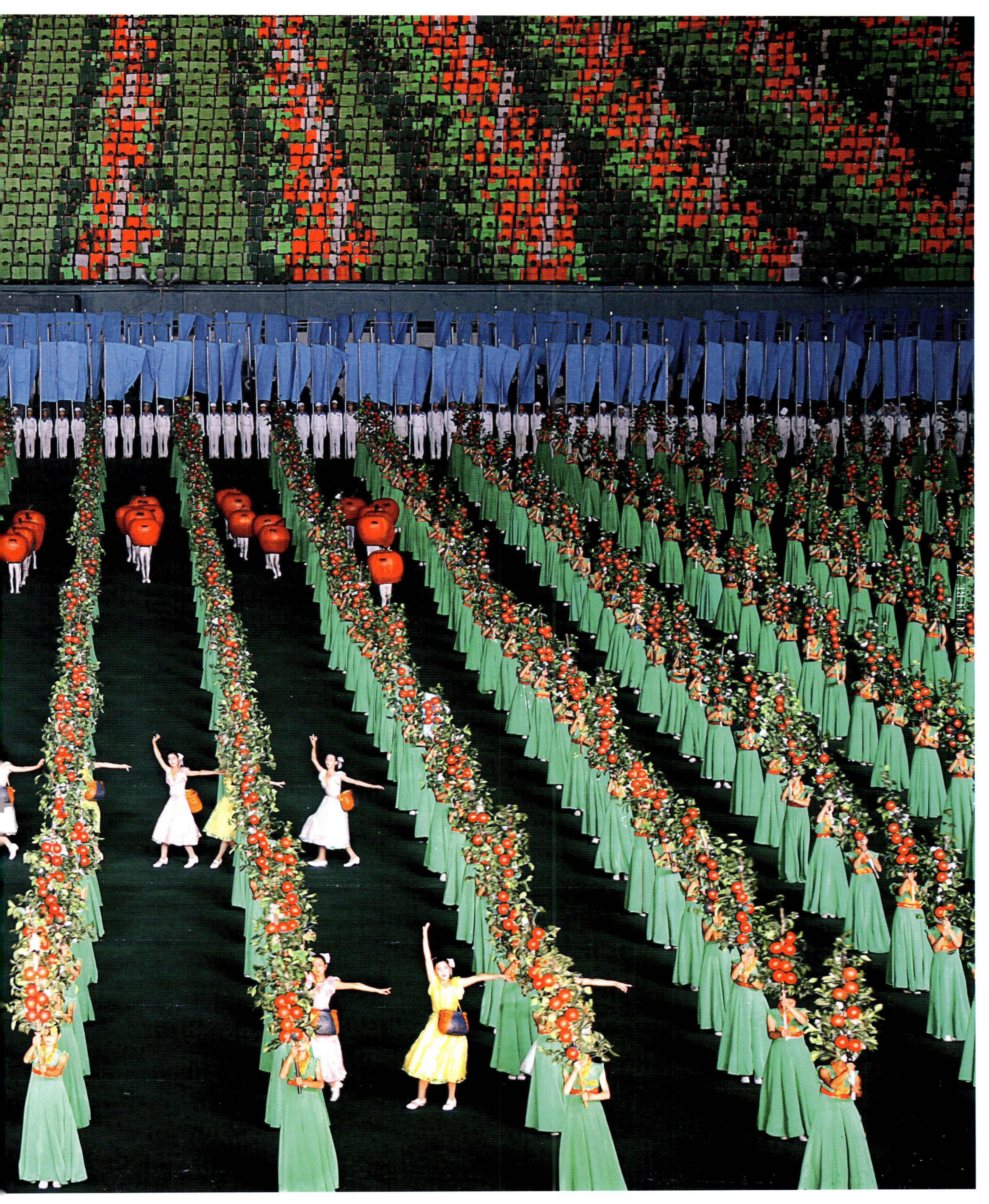

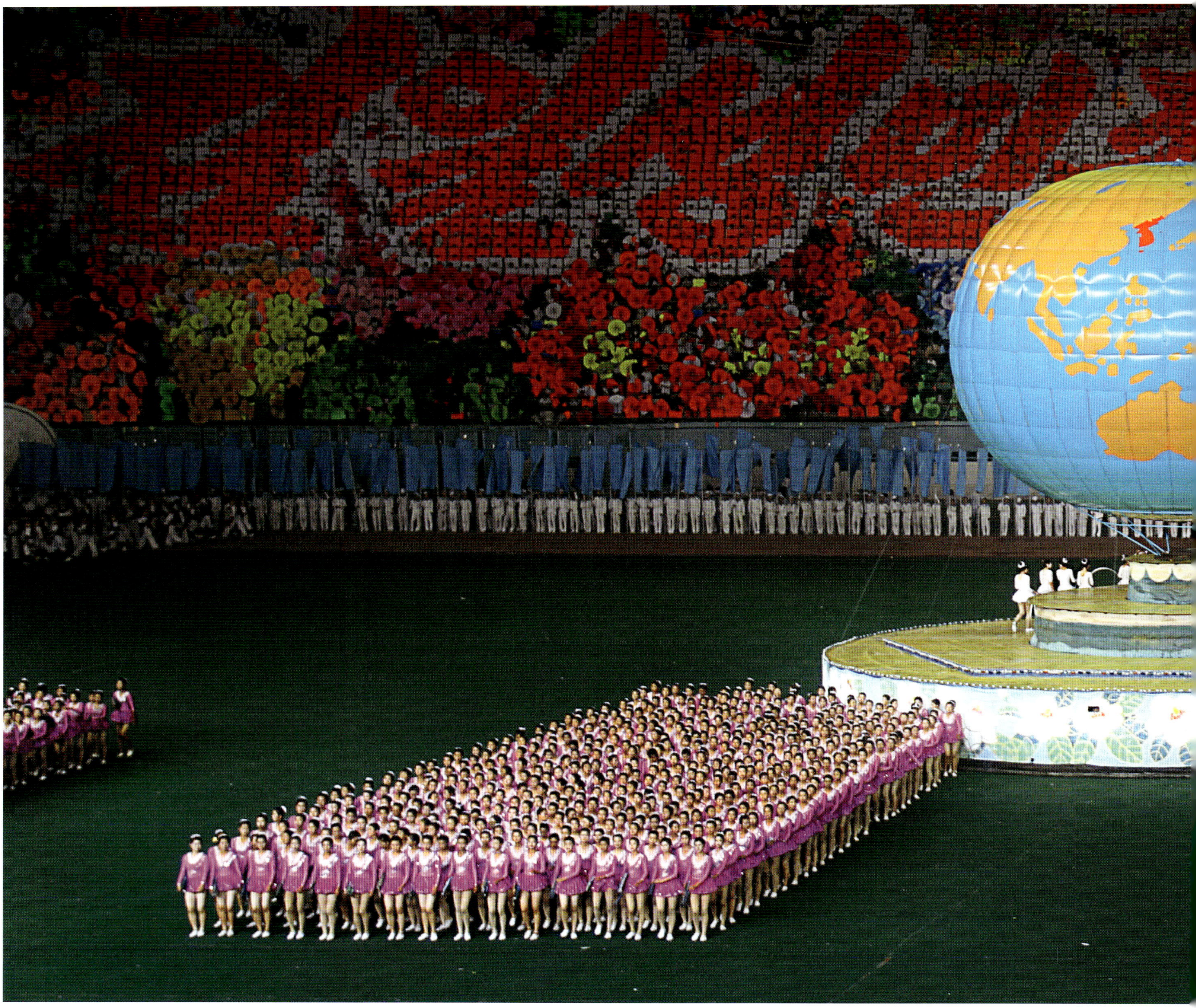

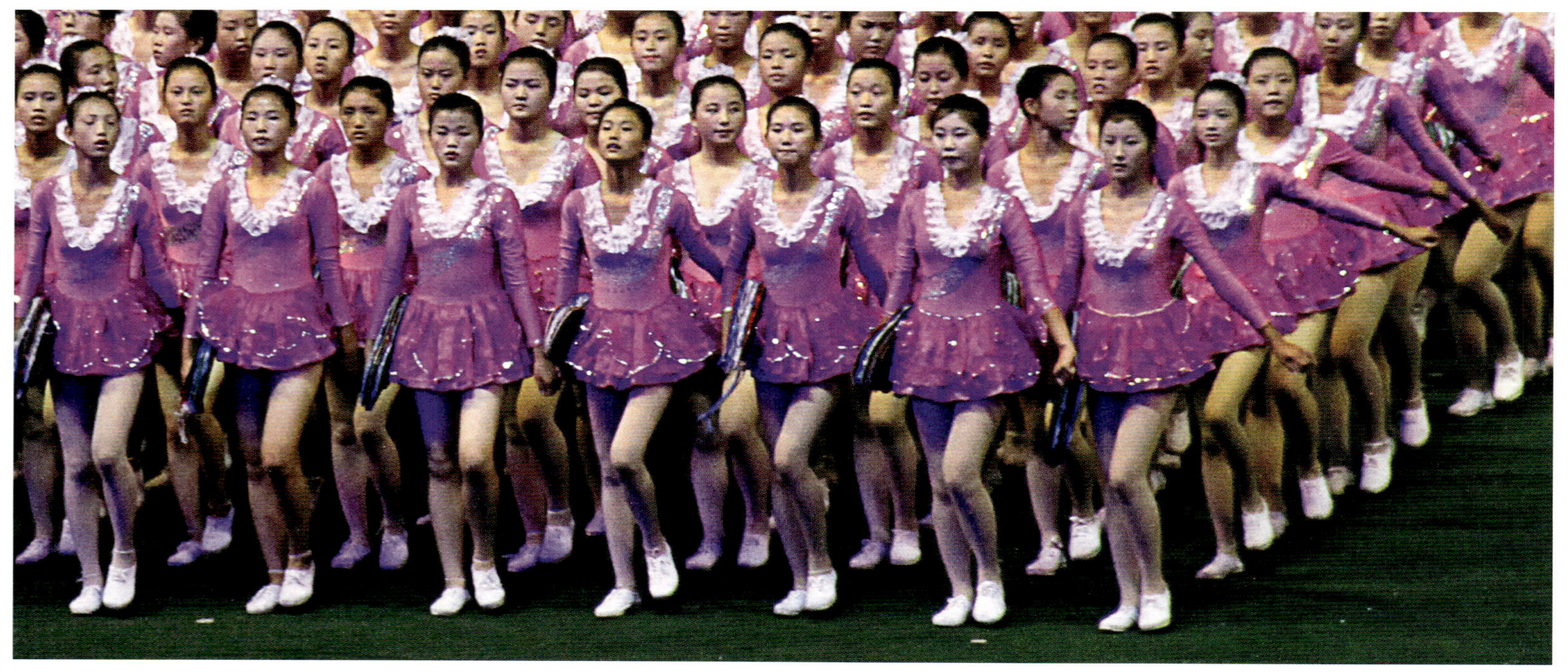

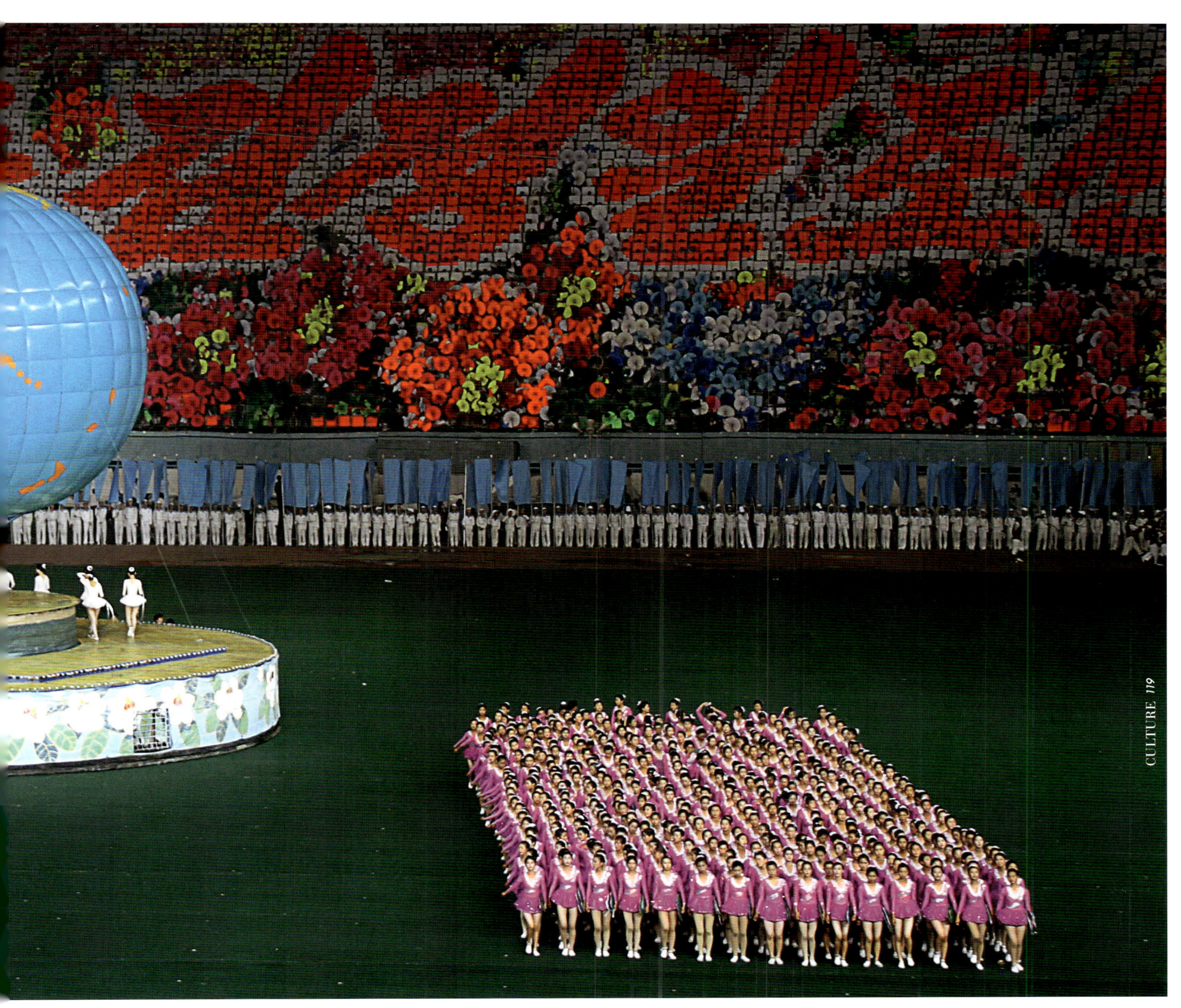

Arirang is a tragic folksong about separation and lost love.
It is a national symbol of Korea's past and its worrisome present.
Das tragische Volkslied Arirang über Trennung und verlorene Liebe ist ein nationales Symbol für Koreas Vergangenheit und für seine besorgniserregende Gegenwart.
Chant populaire tragique sur les thèmes de la séparation et de l'amour perdu, Arirang est un symbole du passé de la Corée et de son présent préoccupant.

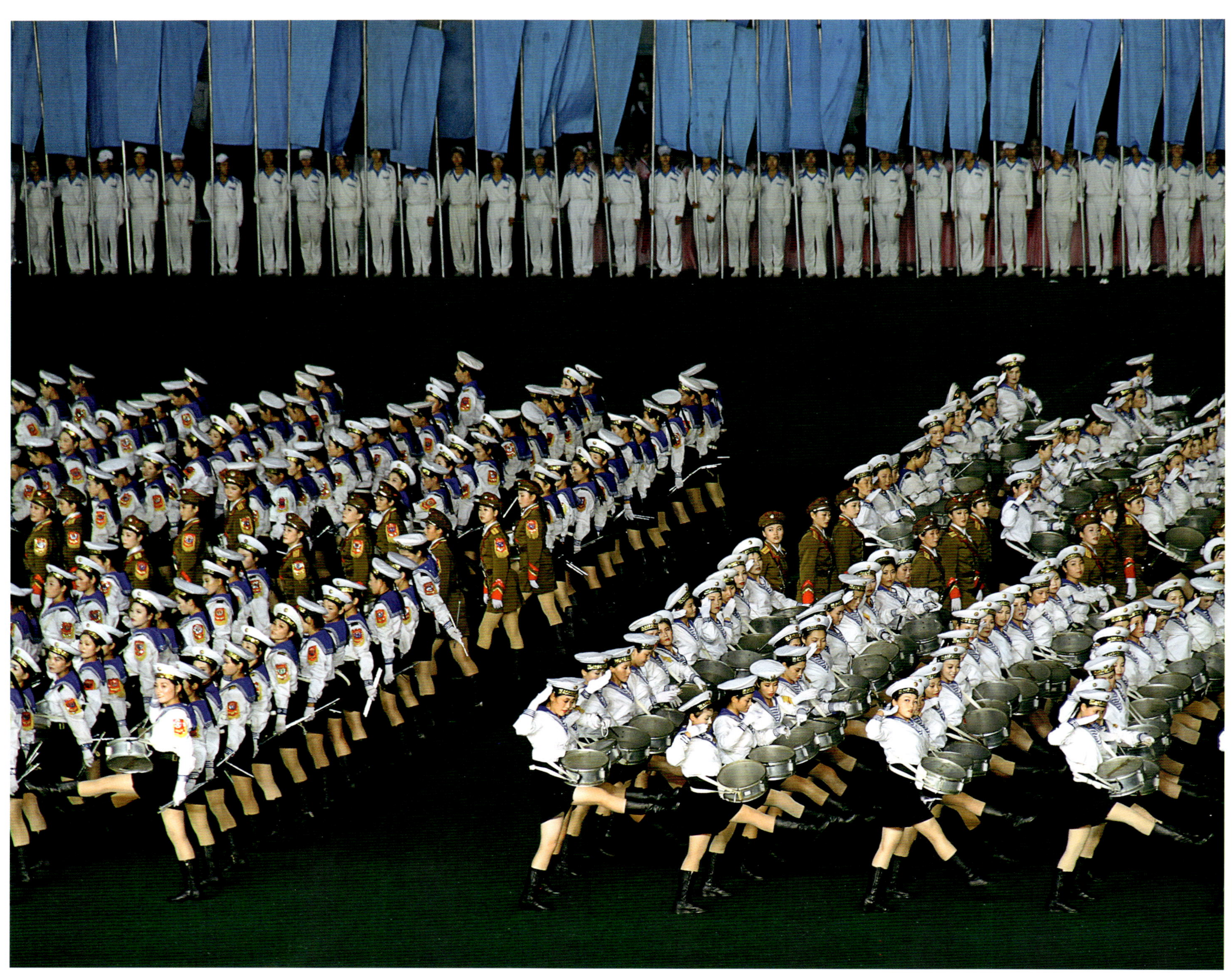

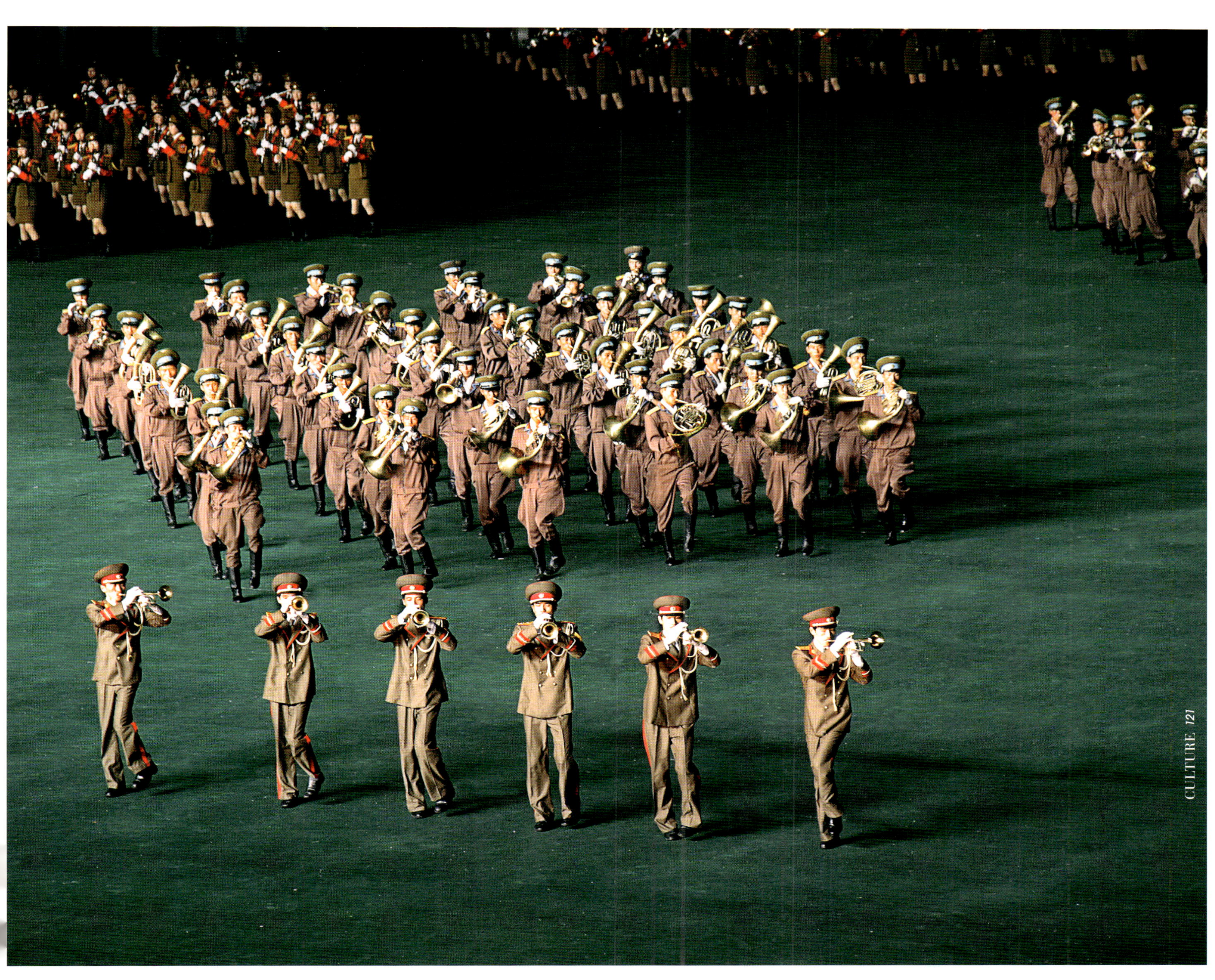

Arirang also represents Korea's struggle for independence from Japan.
Arirang steht auch für Koreas Unabhängigkeitskampf gegen Japan.
Arirang symbolise également la lutte de la Corée pour s'affranchir de la tutelle du Japon.

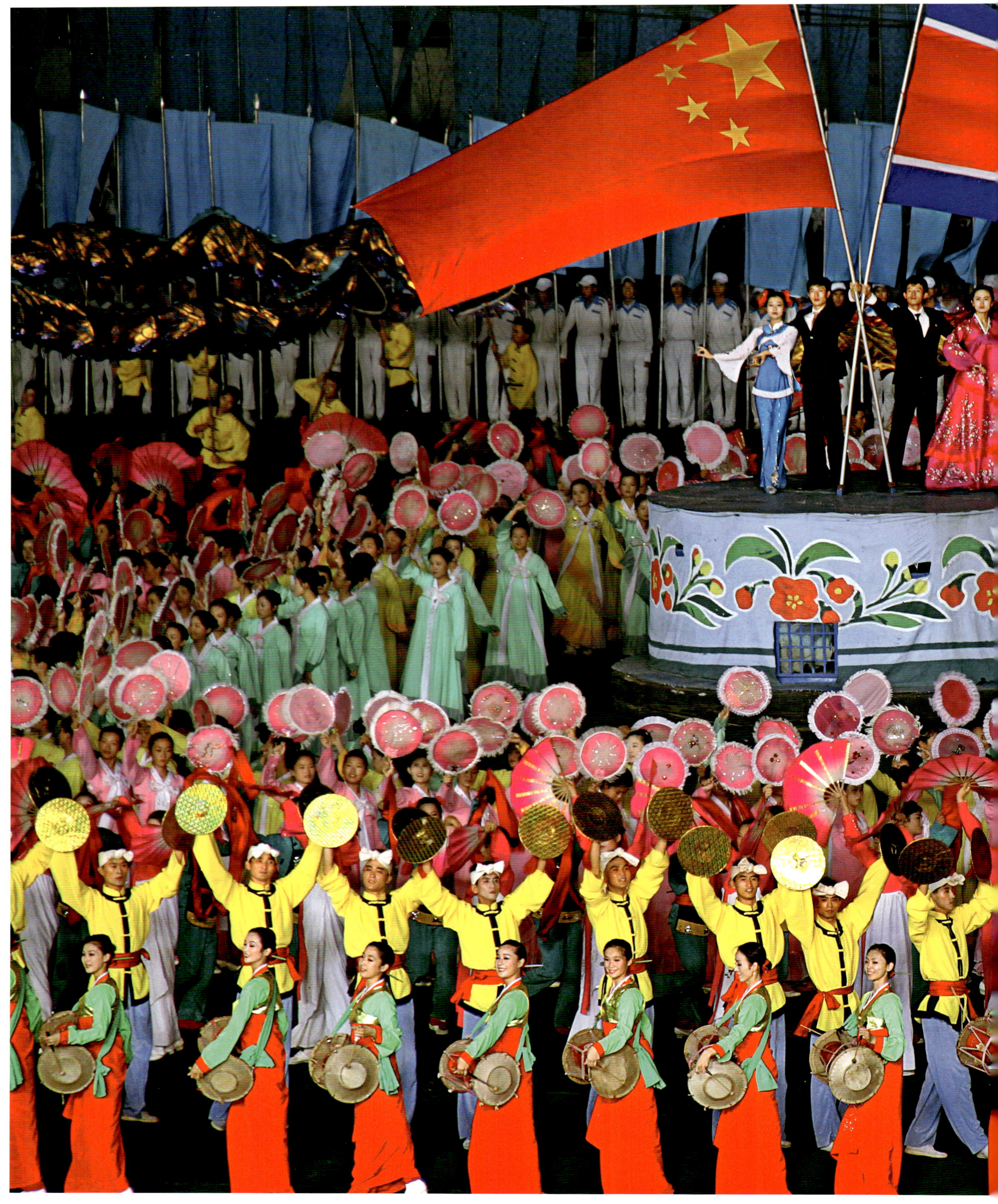

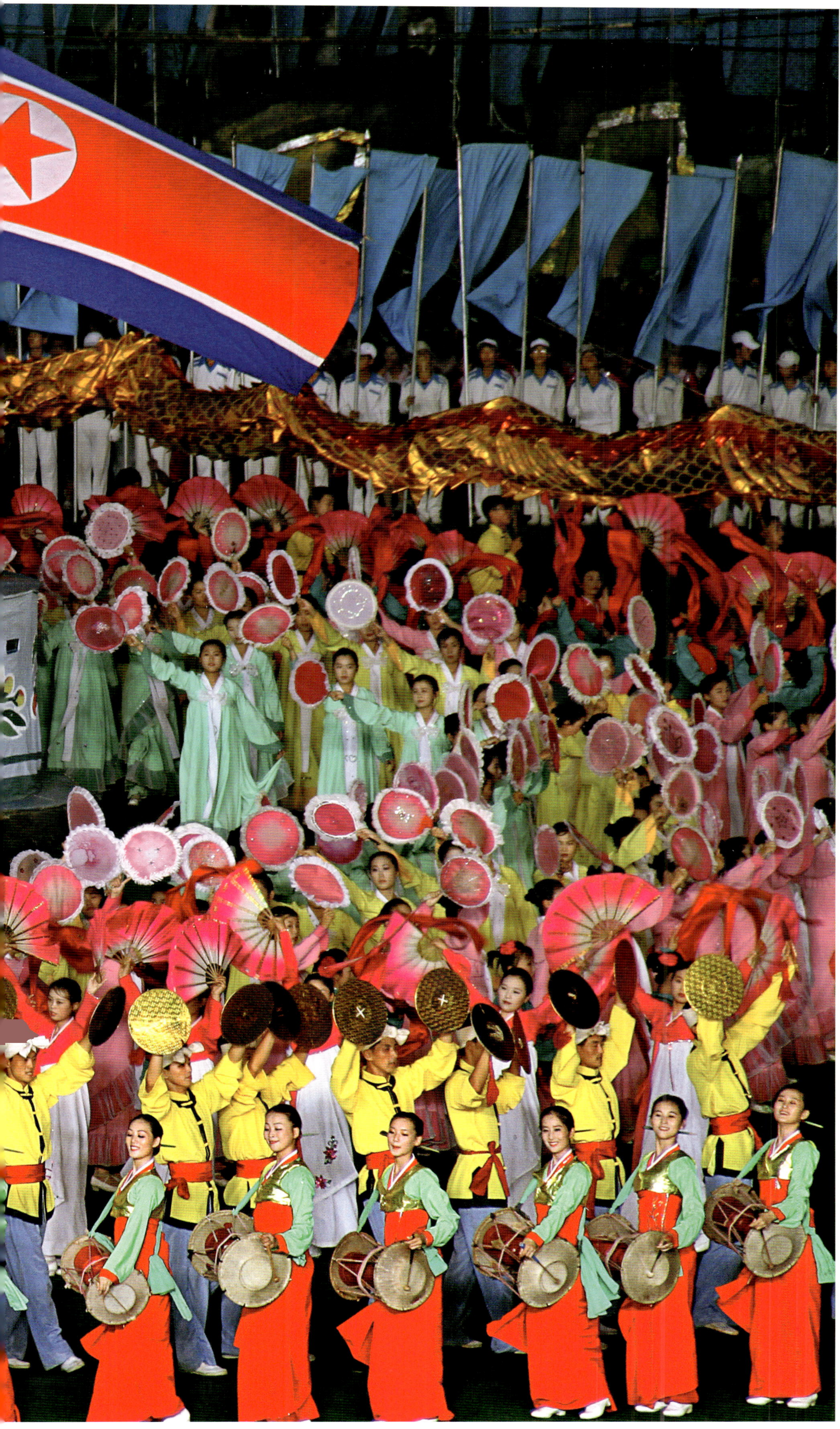

North Korea and its protector: China
Nordkorea und die Schutzmacht China
La Corée du Nord et sa puissance protectrice, la Chine

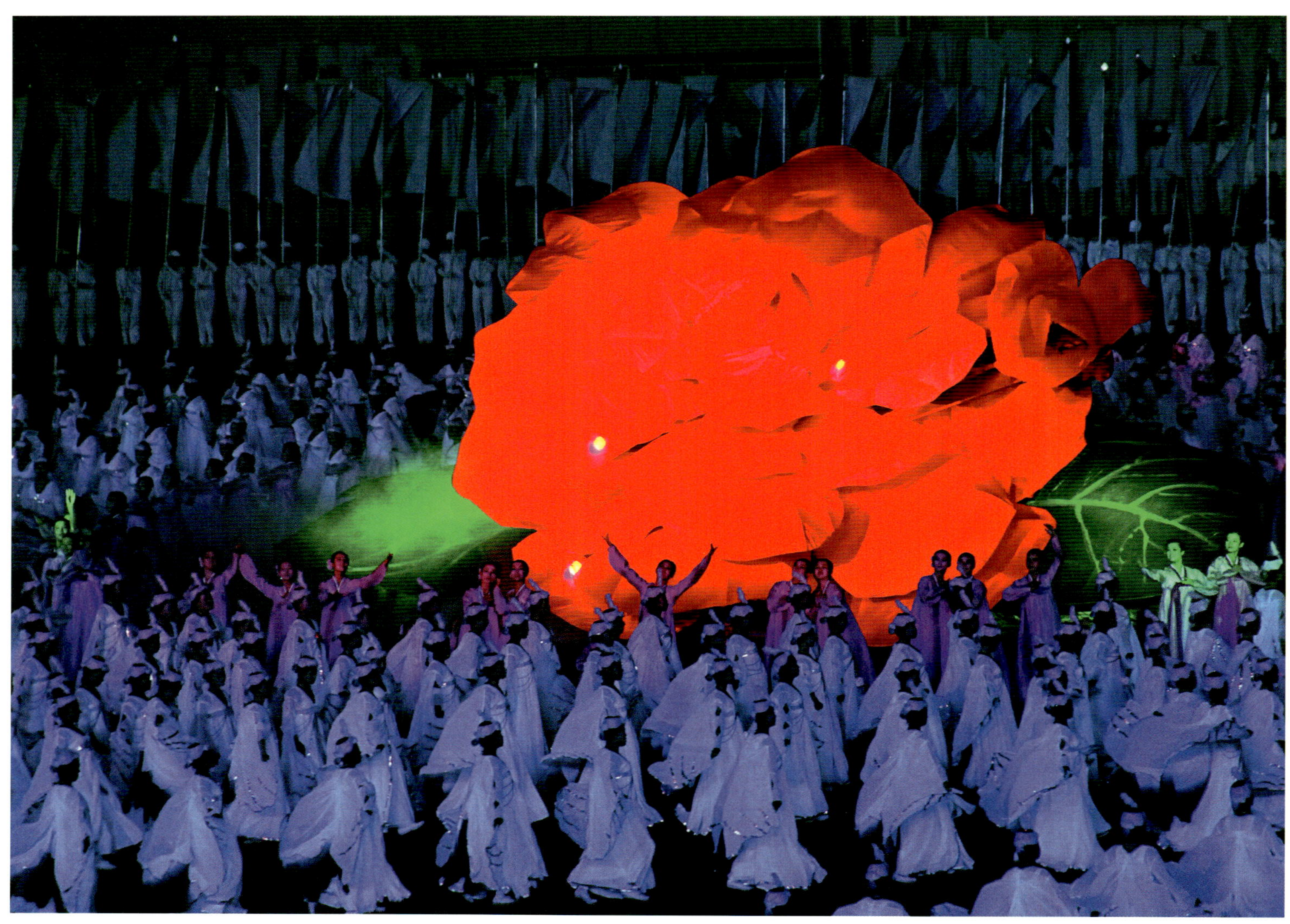

In Arirang festival's performance, the tragedy of North and South Korea being divided reminds of "Romeo and Juliet."
Die historische Tragik der Trennung in Nord- und Südkorea verleihen Arirang einen „Romeo und Julia"-Charakter.
La tragédie historique de la partition en Corée du Nord et Corée du Sud donne au festival d'Arirang un petit air de Roméo et Juliette.

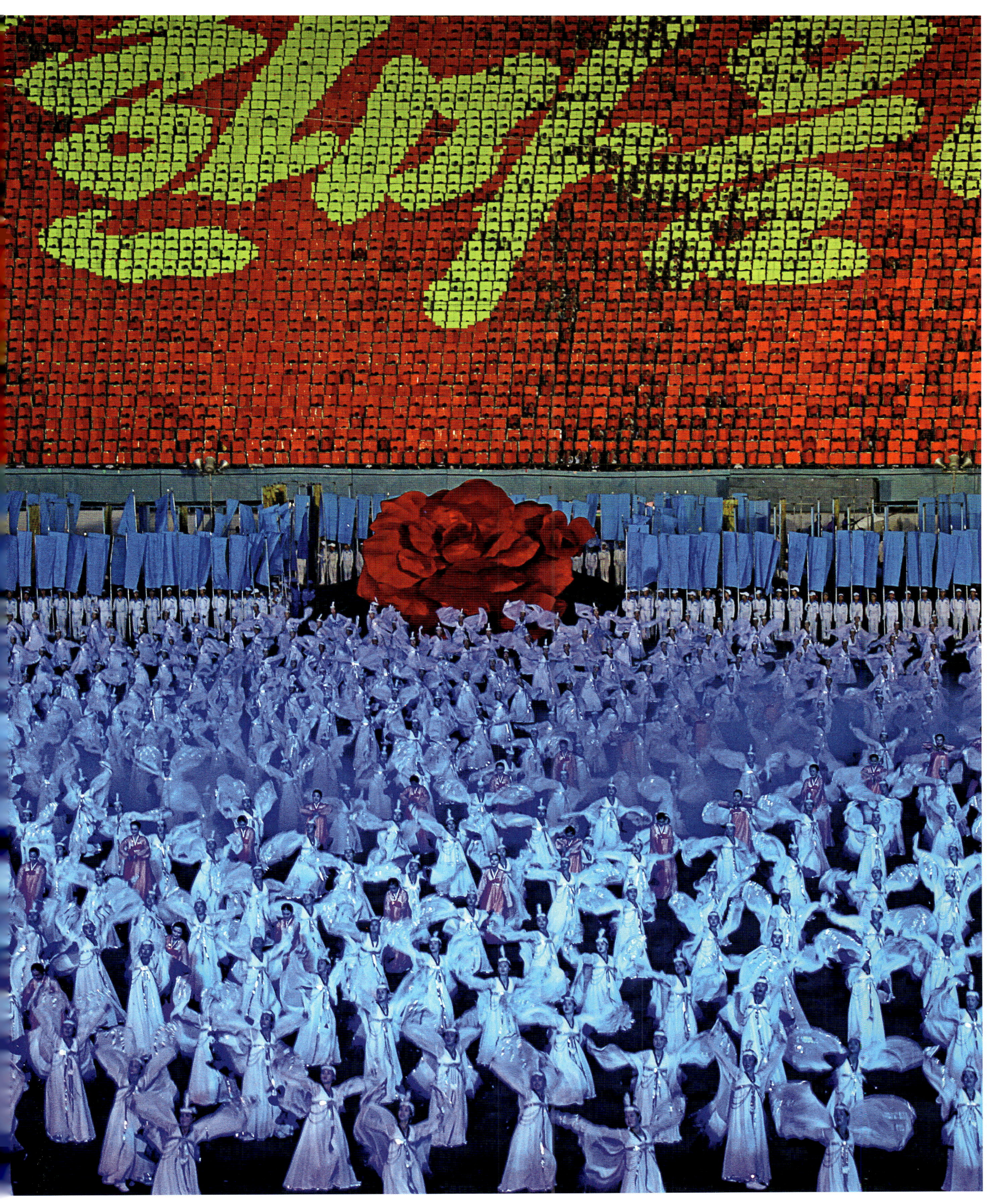

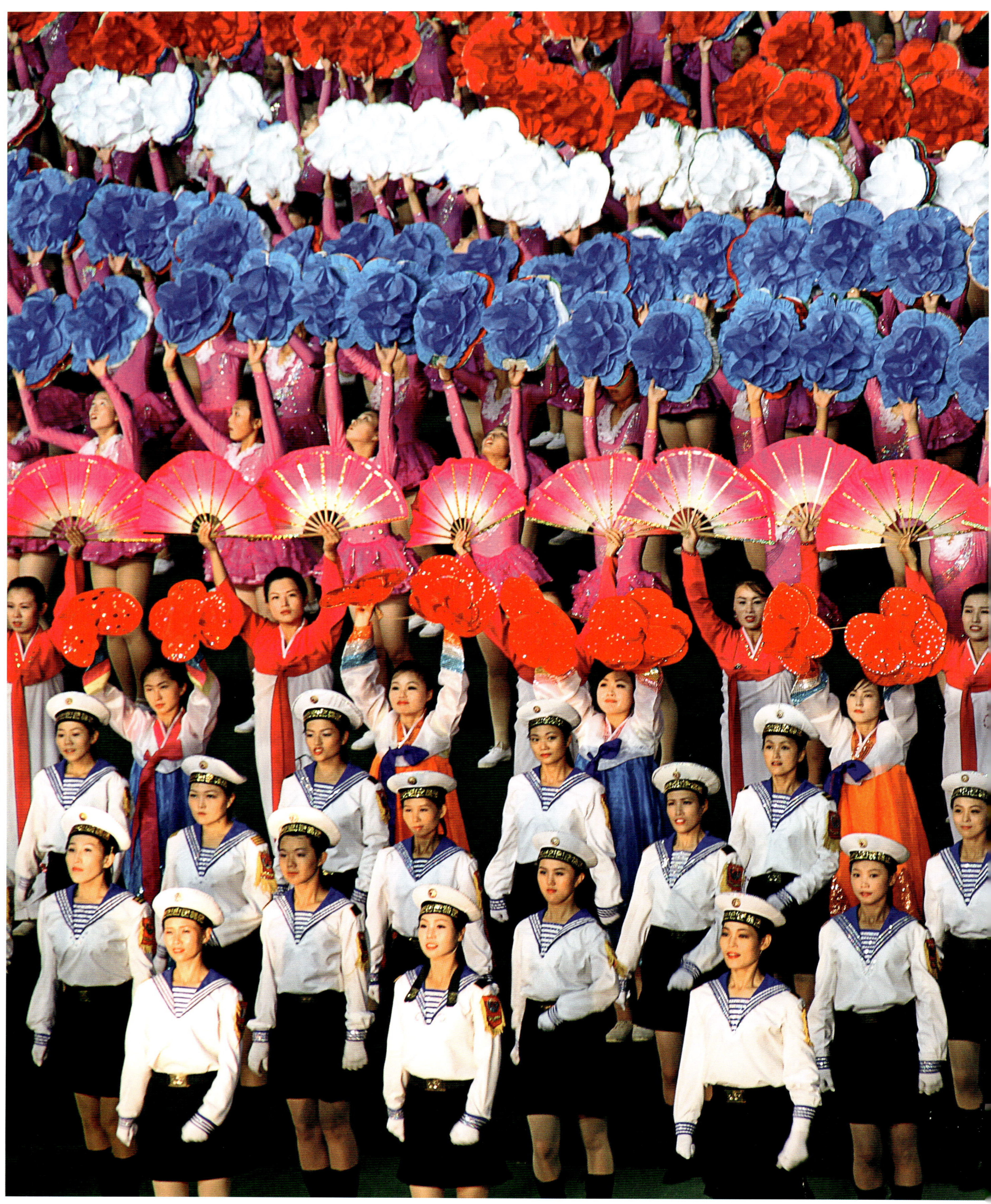

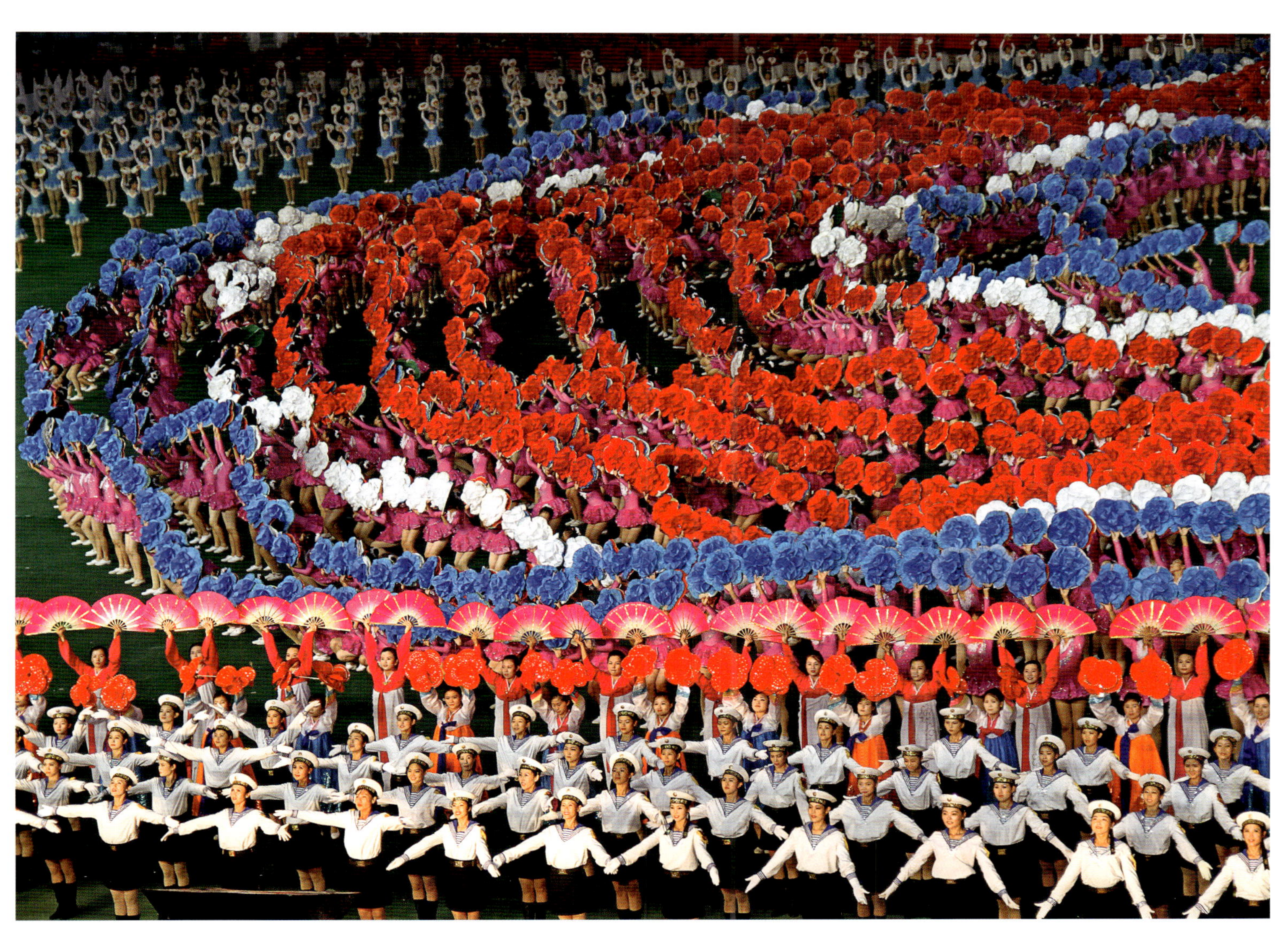

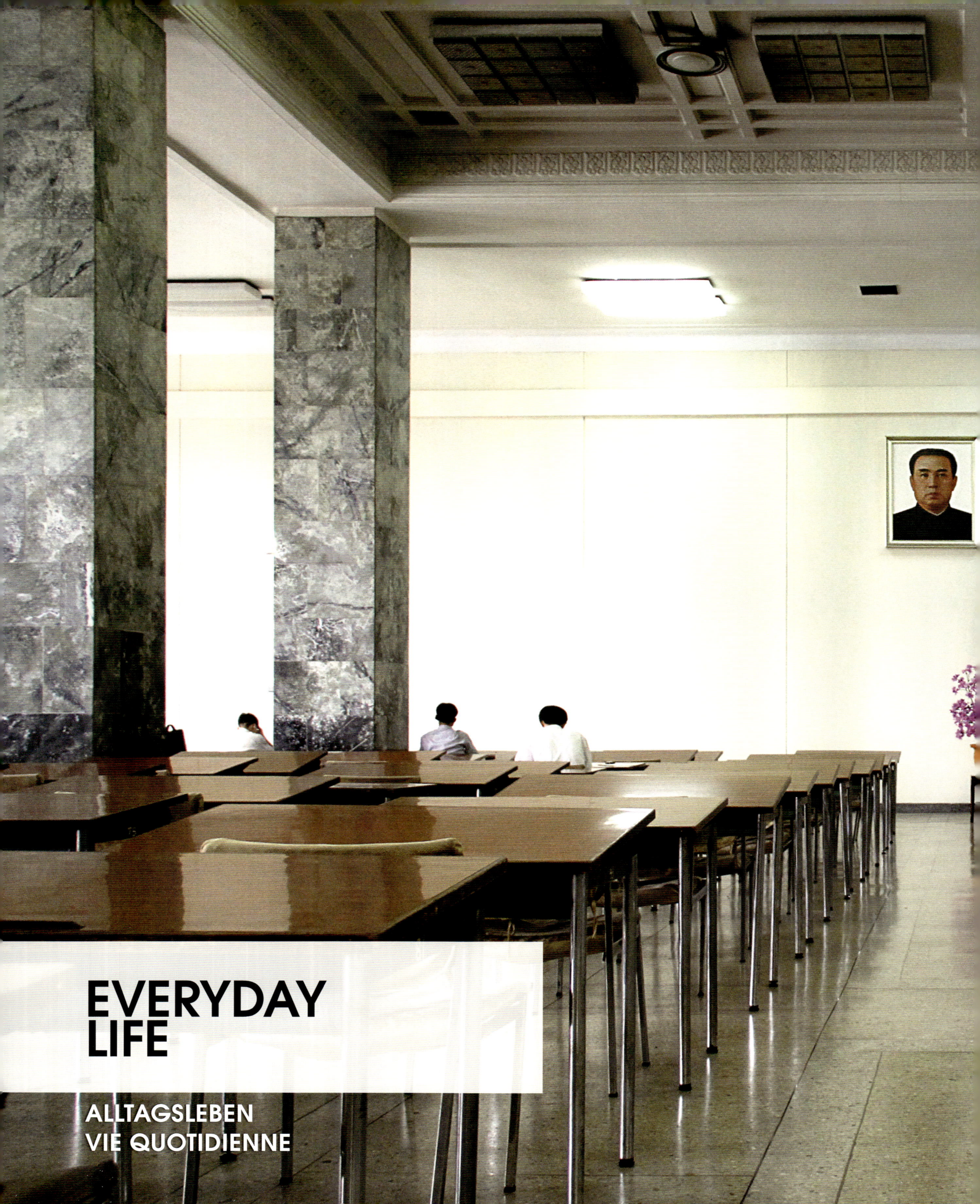

EVERYDAY LIFE

ALLTAGSLEBEN
VIE QUOTIDIENNE

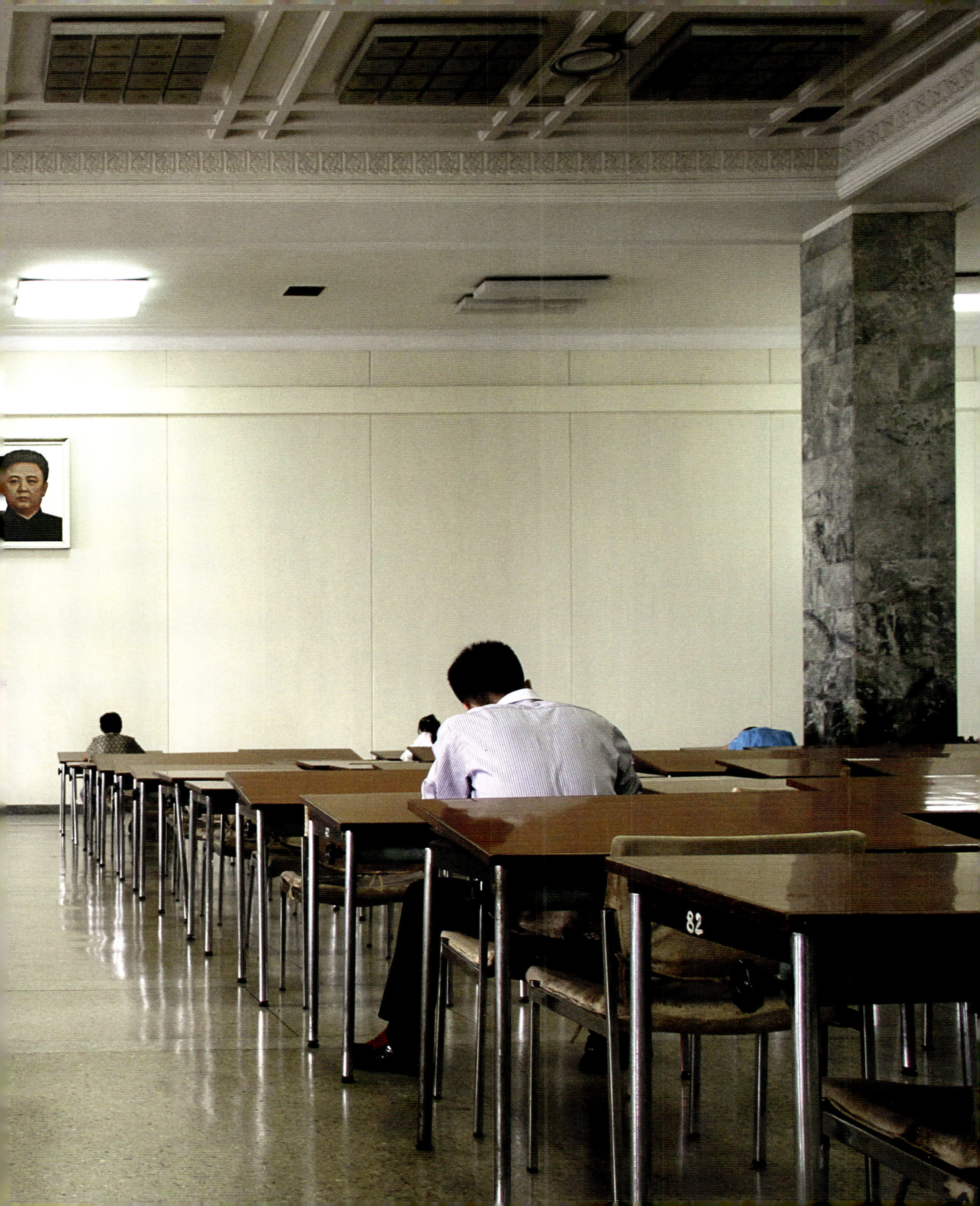
82

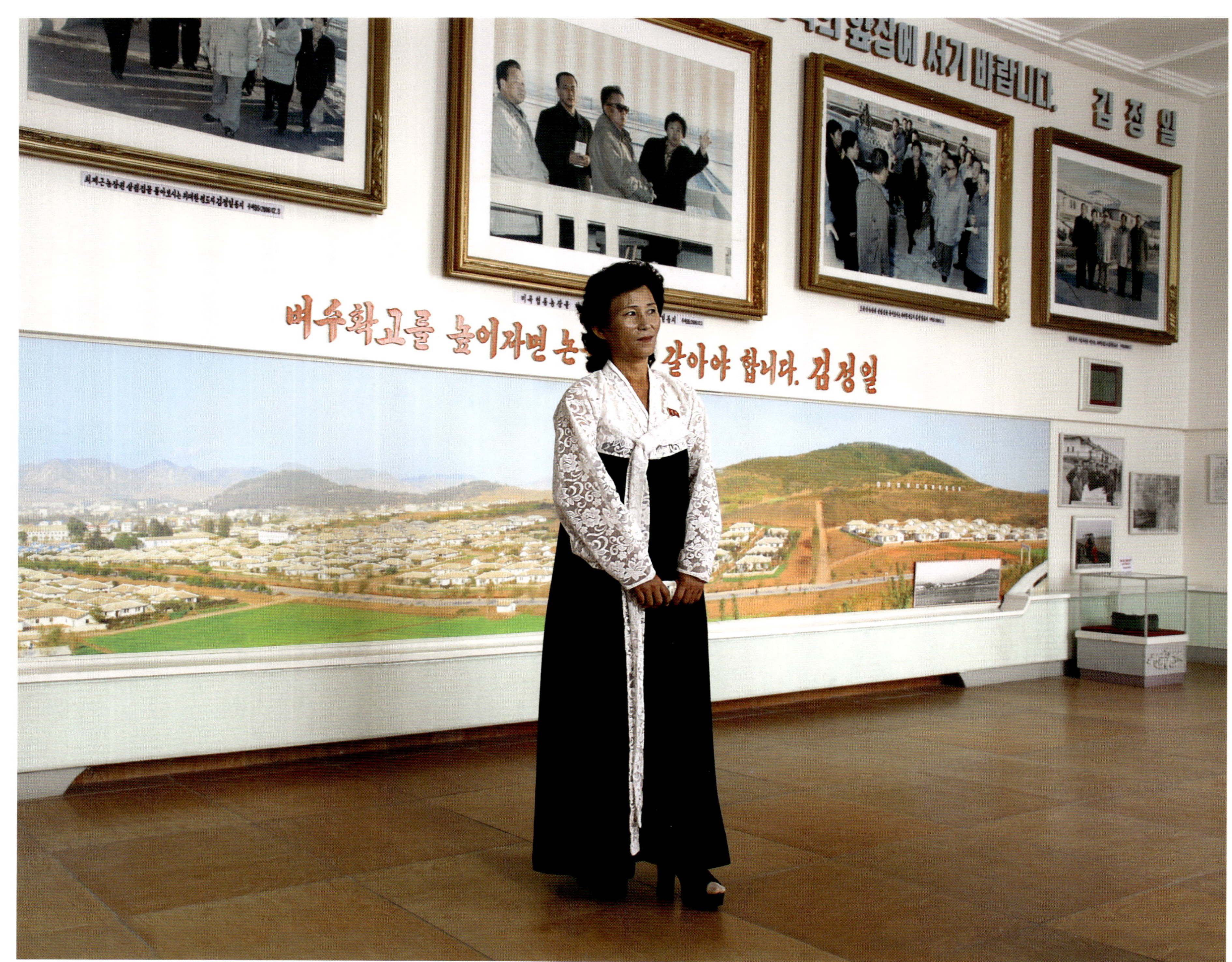

Museum of the Migok farming collective: Director Kim Yong-ae describes a day in the life of the 2,000 farmers who work in the agricultural production cooperative.

Museum der Migok-Kooperative: Leiterin Kim Yong-ae erklärt den Tagesablauf der 2 000 Bauern in der landwirtschaftlichen Produktionsgenossenschaft.

Musée de la coopérative de Migok : Kim Yong-ae présente l'emploi du temps quotidien des 2 000 paysans de la coopérative de production agricole.

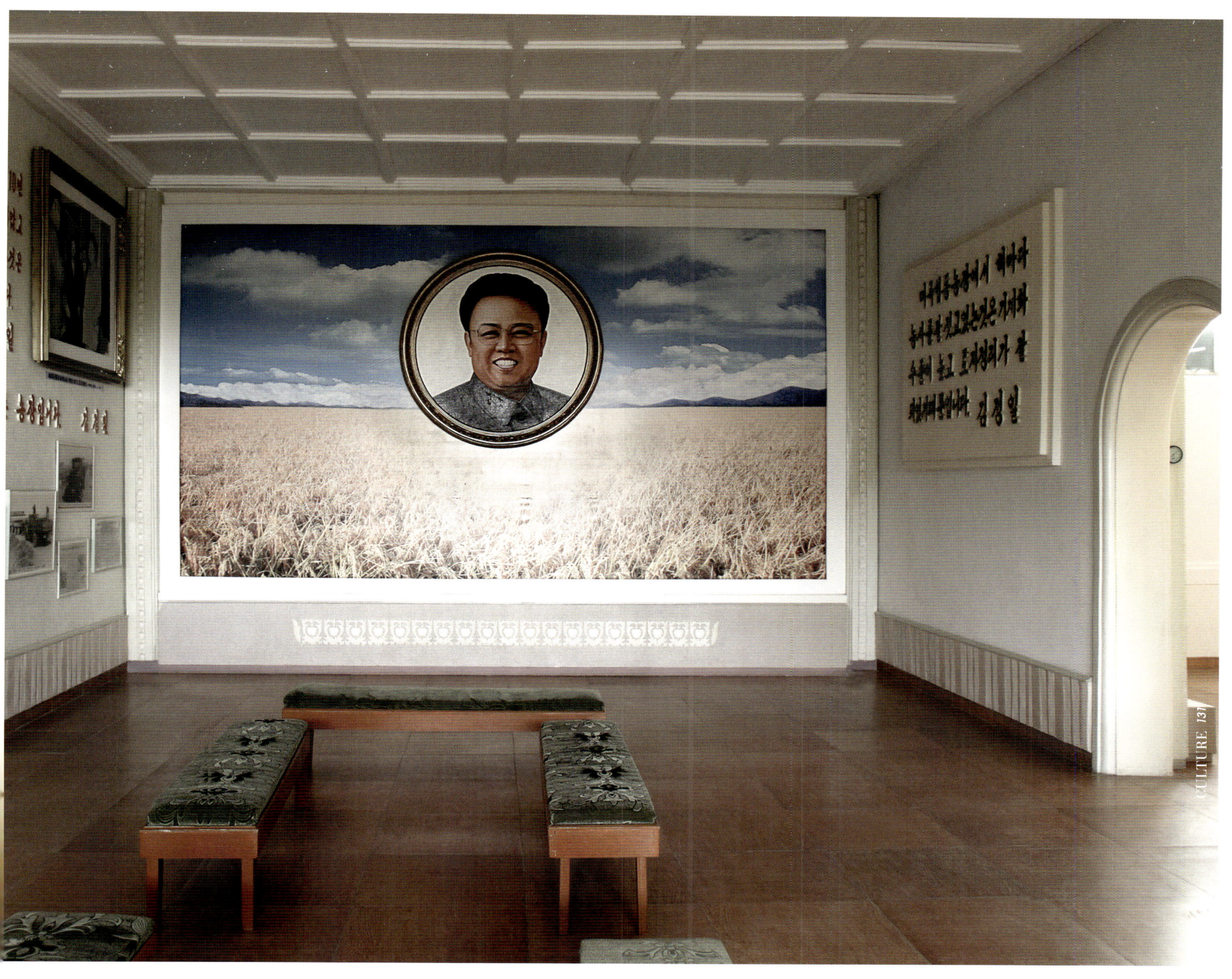

Migok farmworkers take great pride in Kim Il-sung's 89 visits to the production cooperative.
Der ganze Stolz der Migok-Kooperative: 89 Mal besuchte Kim Il-sung die Produktionsgenossenschaft.
Toute la fierté de la coopérative de production de Migok : les 89 visites que lui a rendues Kim Il-sung.

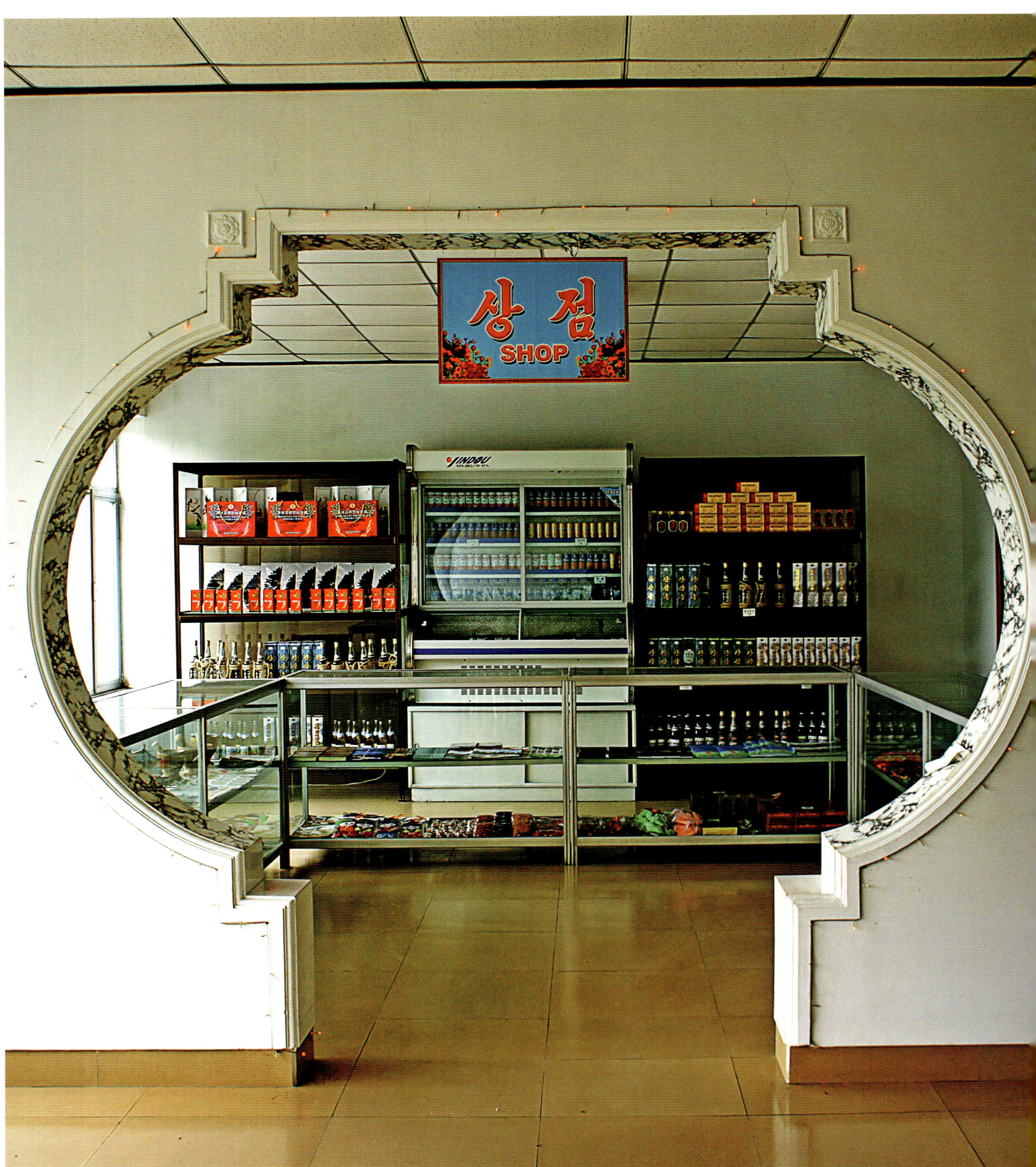
상점
SHOP
YINDOU

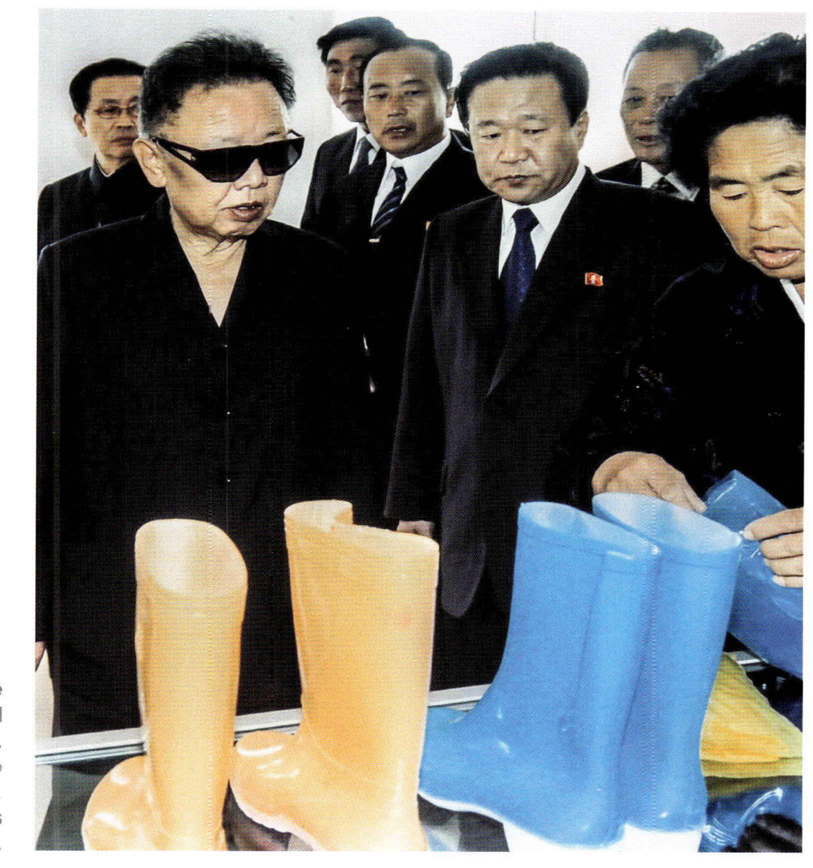

These rubber boots were elevated to the status of relic simply because the "Beloved Leader" cast his eye on them.
Allein der Blick des „Geliebten Führers" erhob diese Gummistiefel zu einer Reliquie.
Un regard du « cher dirigeant » a élevé ces bottes en caoutchouc au rang de reliques.

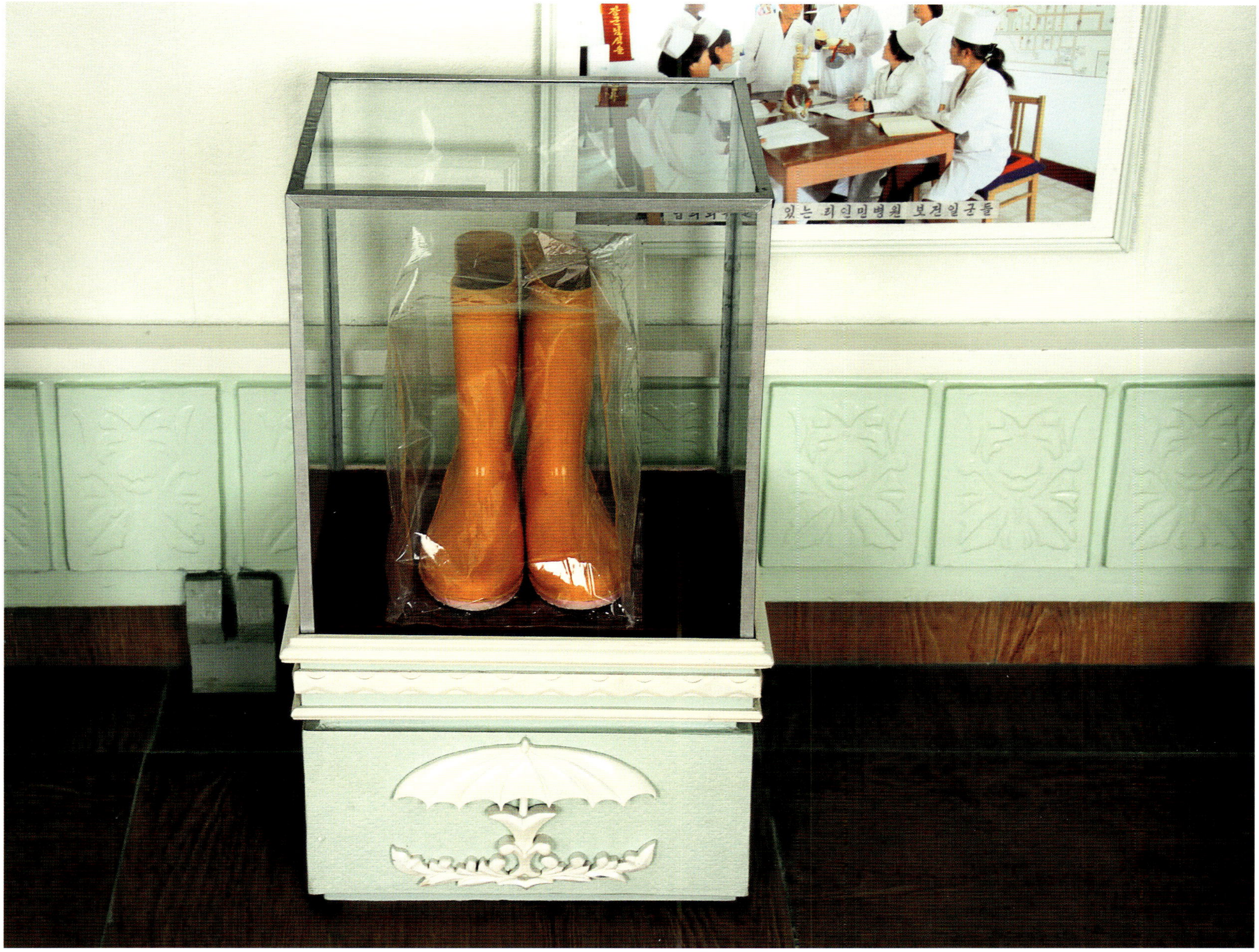

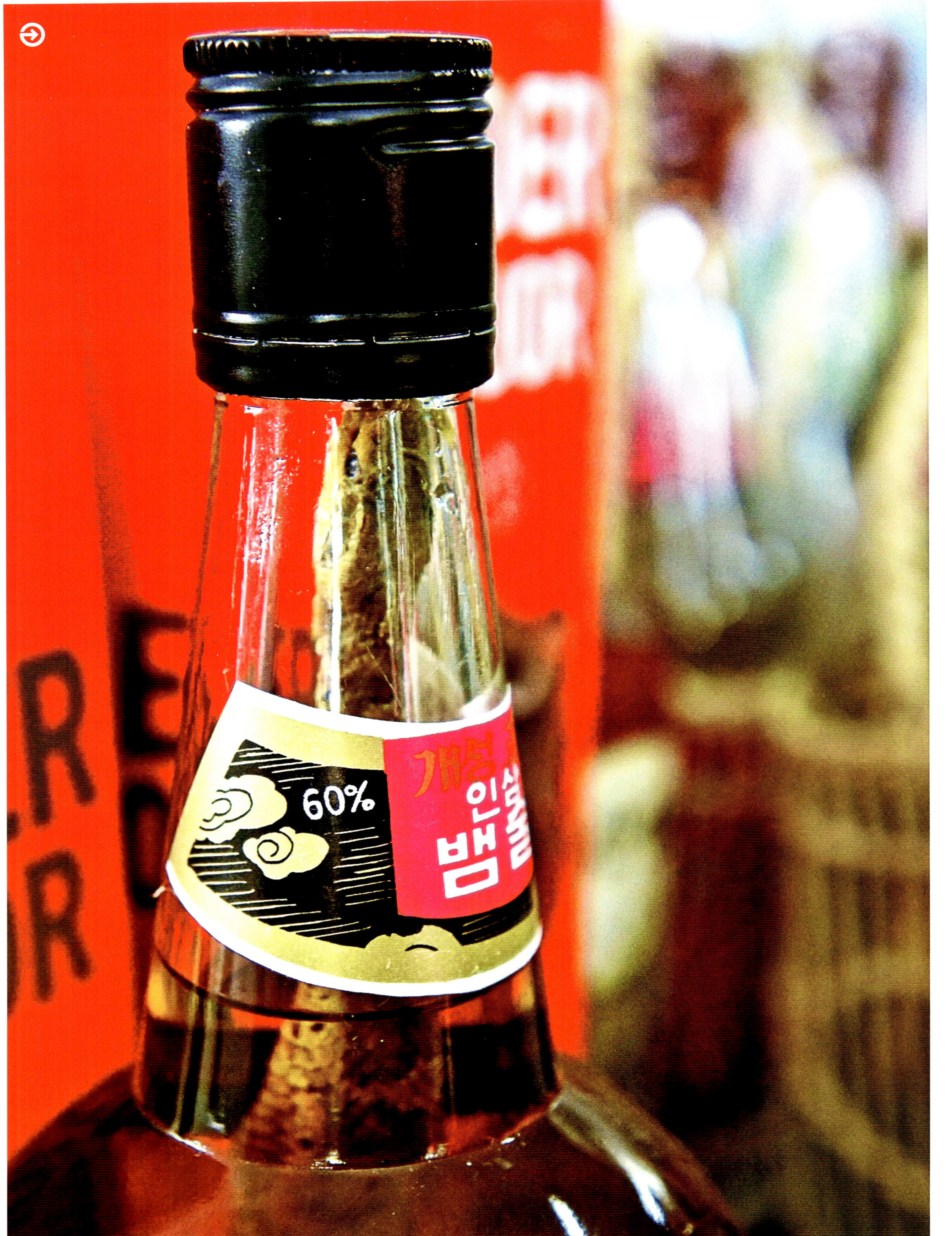
60%

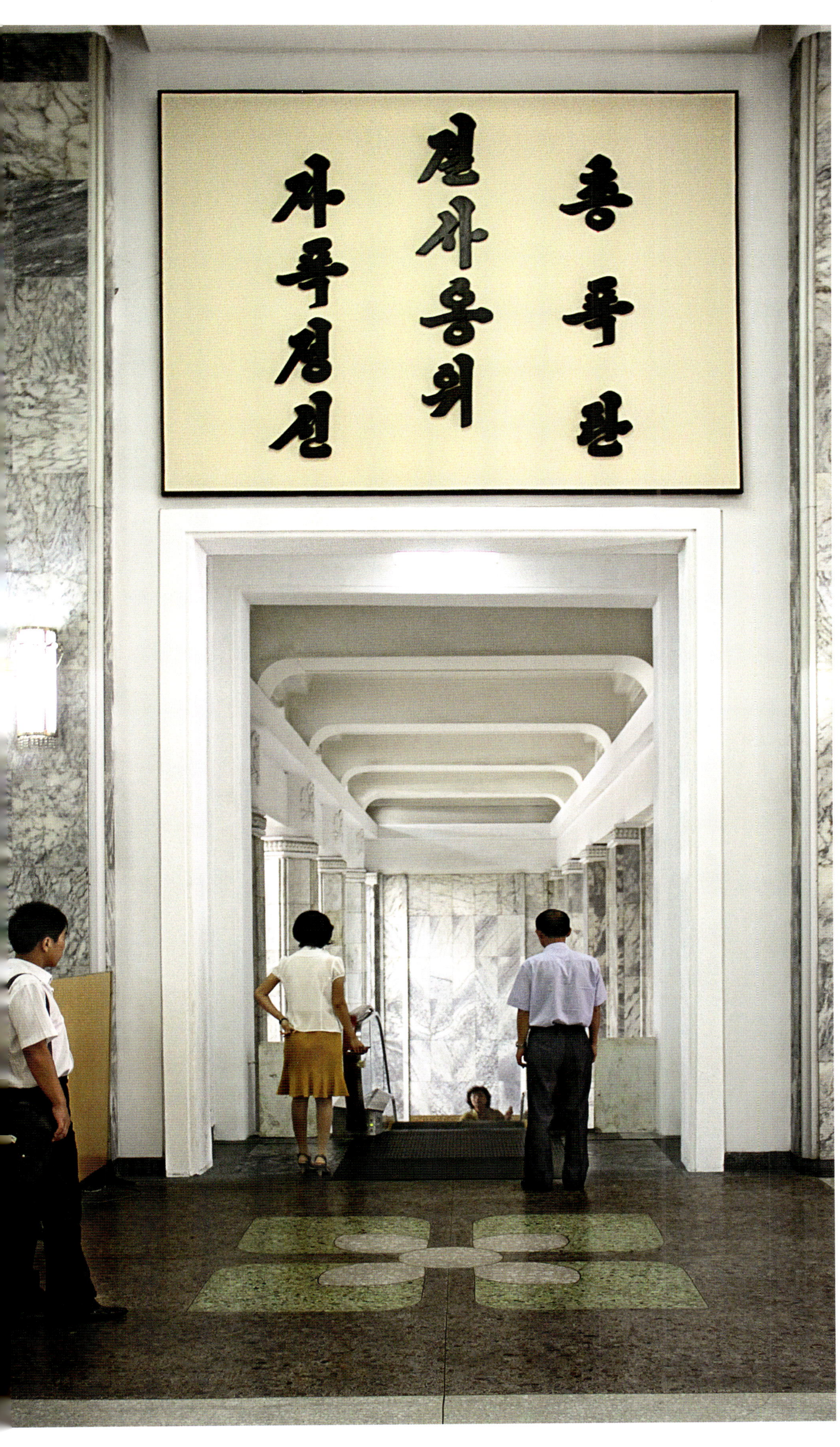

Left: Snake wine, a national tradition
Right: In the Grand People's Study Hall, Pyongyang. The magnolia blossoms on the floor are an oft-repeated floral motive and represent love, wisdom, and peace.

Links: Landestypischer Schlangenschnaps
Rechts: In der großen Studienhalle des Volkes, Pjöngjang. Die Magnolien am Boden – das immer wieder auftauchende Blumenornament – symbolisieren Liebe, Weisheit und Frieden.

À gauche : L'alcool de serpent, une spécialité nationale
À droite : Intérieur de la Grande Maison des études du peuple, à Pyongyang. Ornement floral récurrent, les fleurs de magnolias représentées sur le sol symbolisent l'amour, la sagesse et la paix.

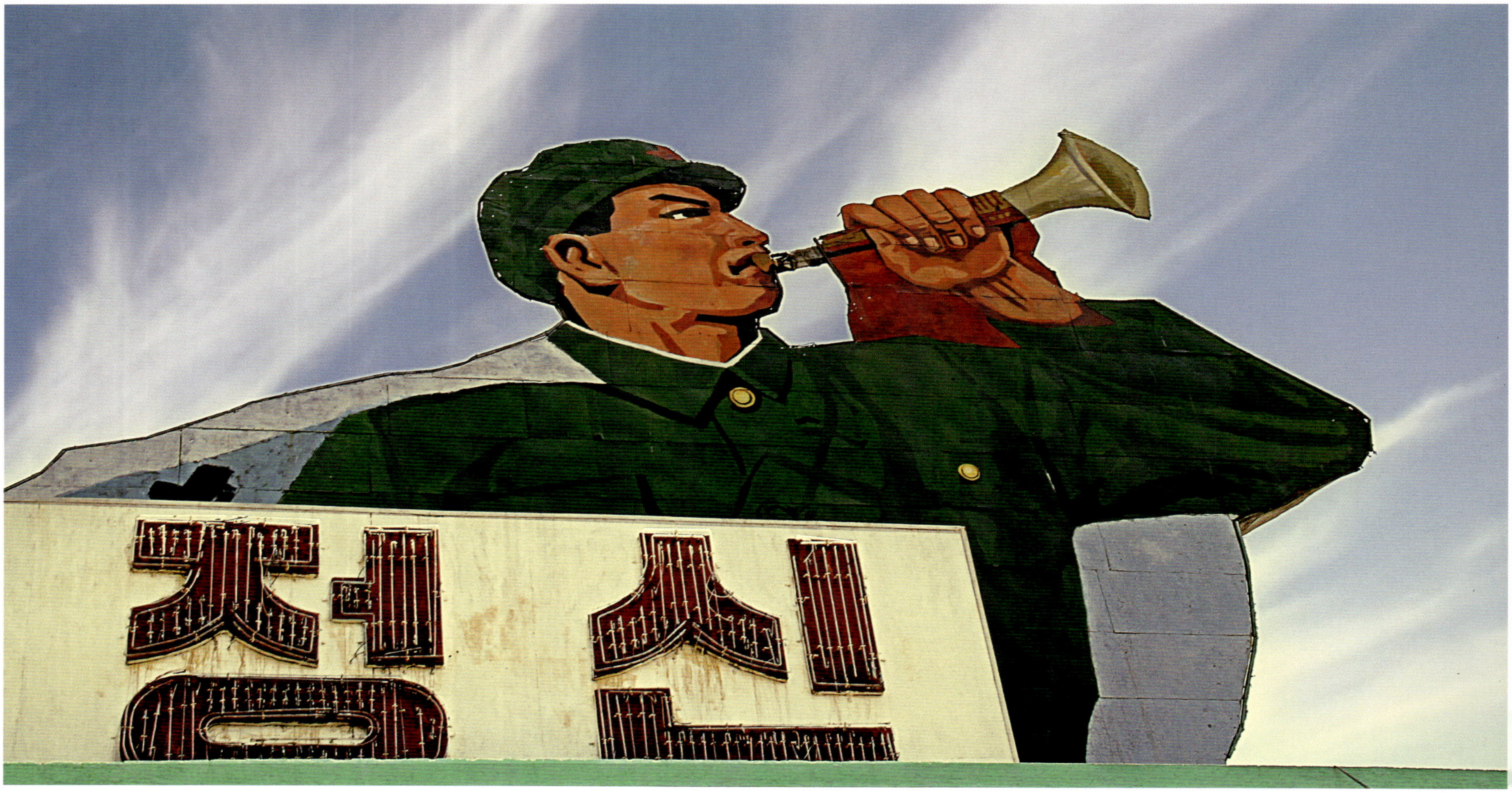

정신
CNC선반 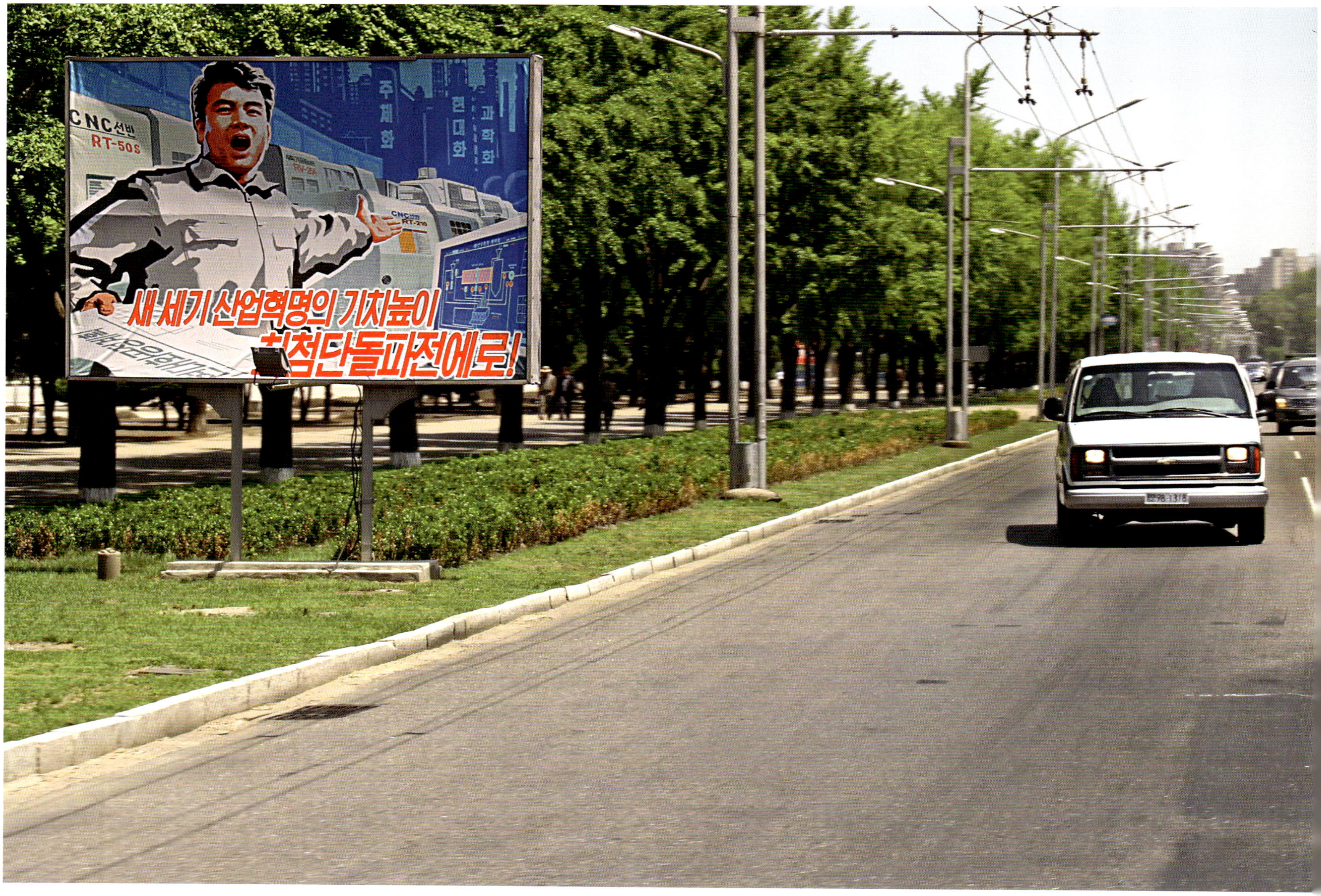
RT-50S
주체화
현대화
과학화
새 세기 산업혁명의 기치높이
첨단돌파전에로!

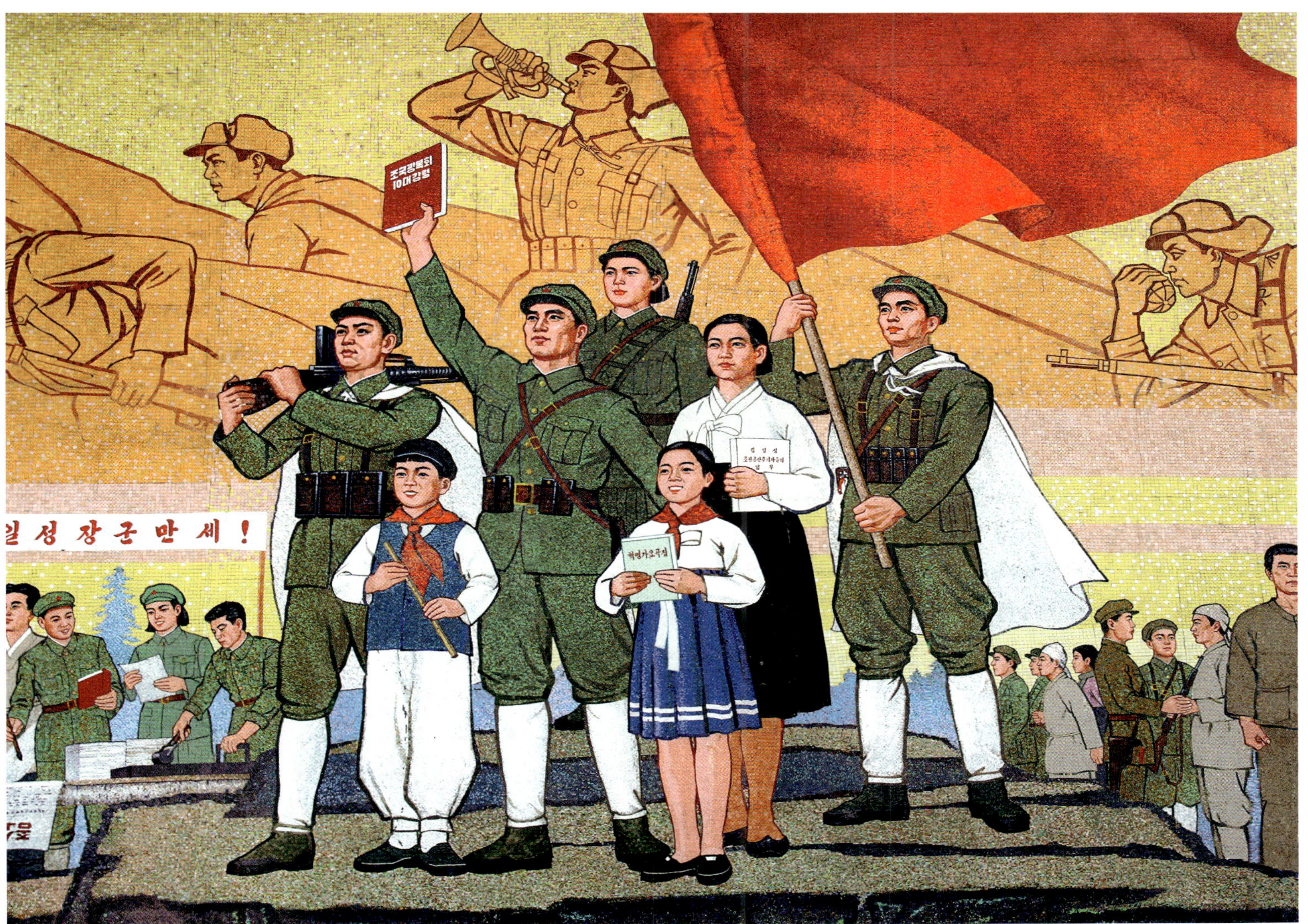

Roof framework, poster, mosaic: propaganda made of metal, paper, and stone
Dachgestell, Plakat, Mosaik: Stimmungsmache in Blech, Papier und Stein
Enseigne de toit, affiche et mosaïque : la propagande faite métal, papier et pierre

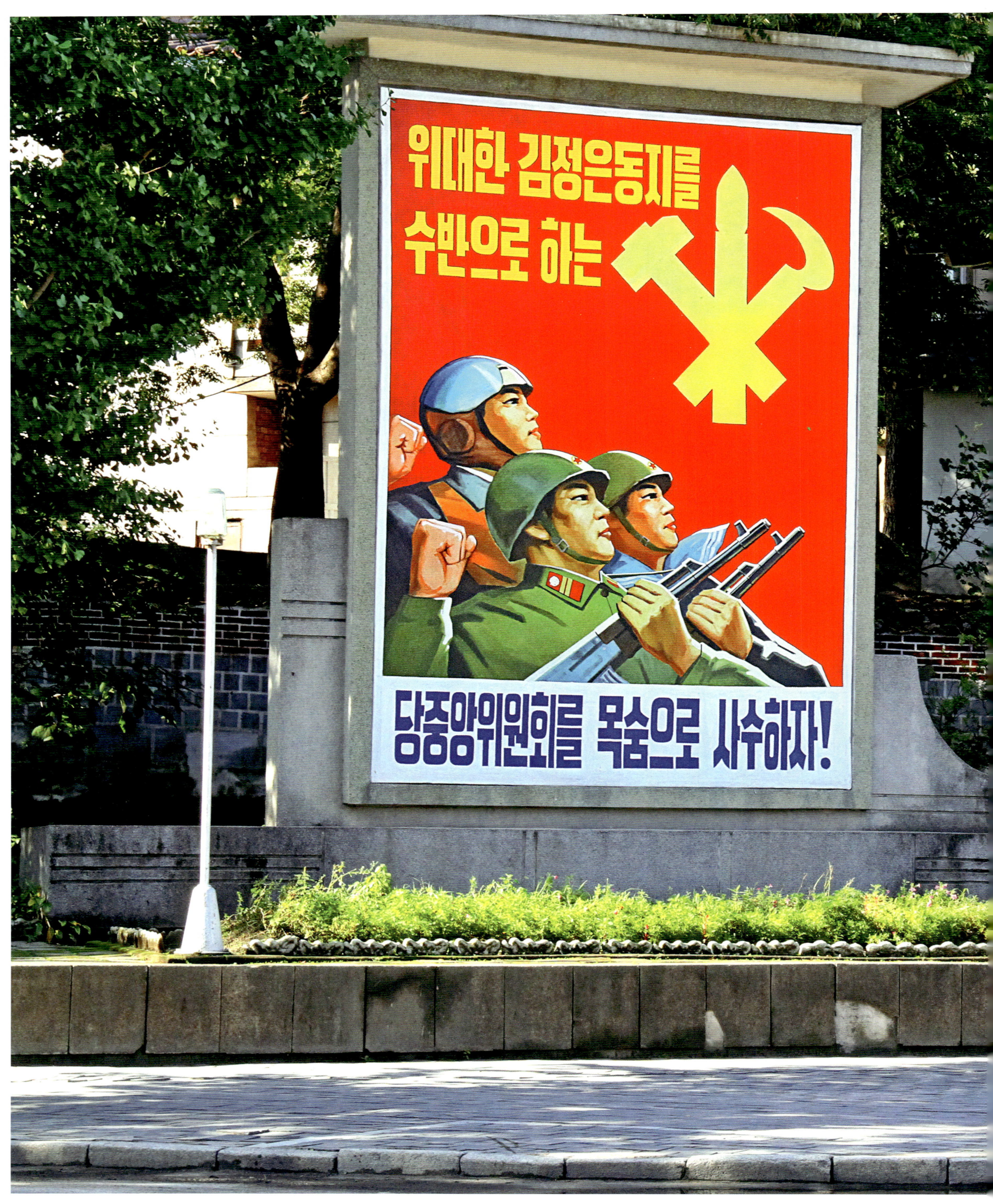
위대한 김정은동지를
수반으로 하는
당중앙위원회를 목숨으로 사수하자!

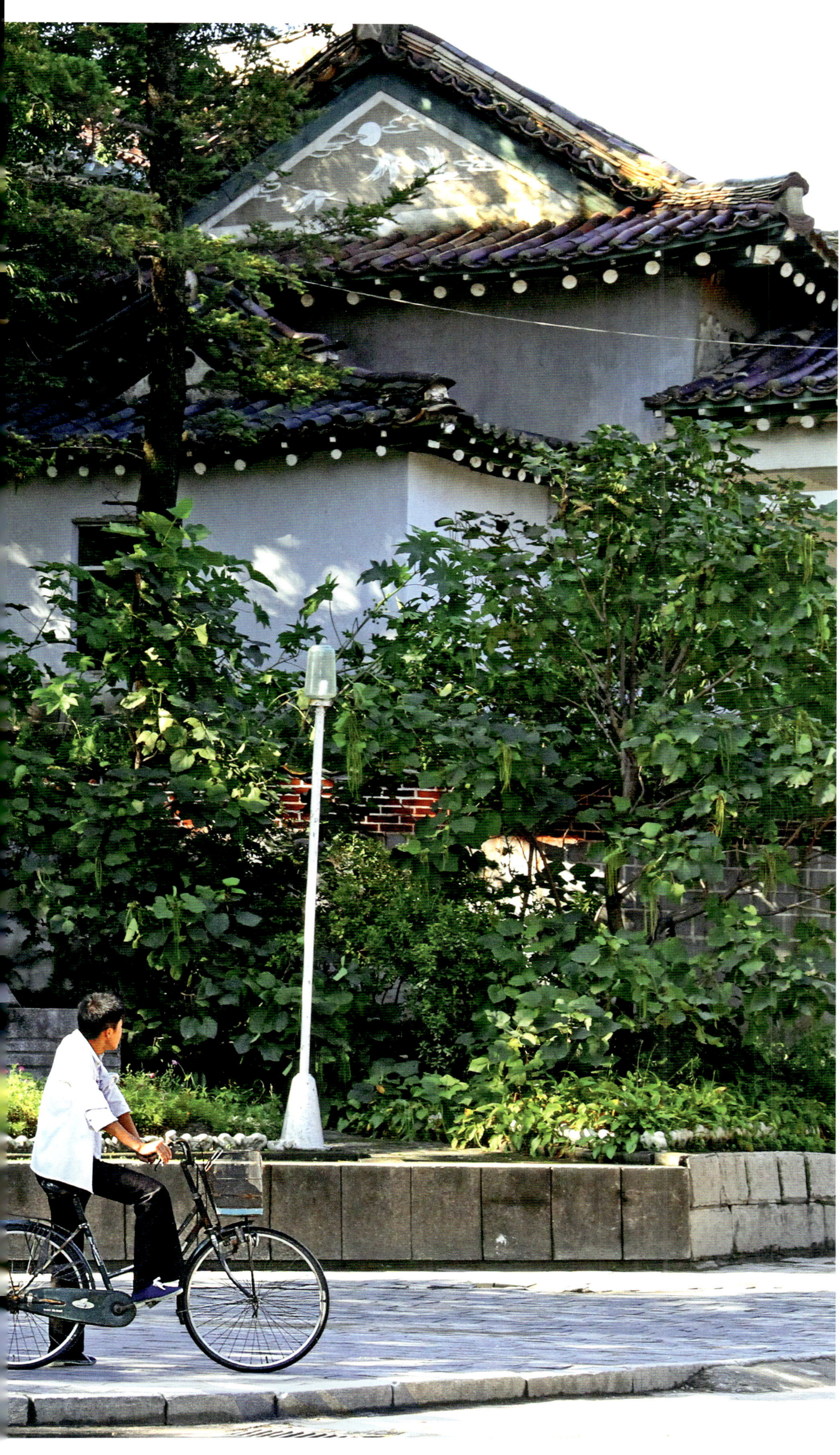

North and South Korea signed an armistice agreement in 1953 but never followed it up with a peace treaty. This poster is located in Kaesŏng, a mere six miles from the border between the two countries.
1953 wurde ein Waffenstillstandsabkommen unterzeichnet, dem nie ein Friedensvertrag folgte. Das Plakat befindet sich nur zehn Kilometer von der Grenze zwischen Nord und Süd entfernt in Kaesŏng.
La signature d'un armistice en 1953 n'a jamais été suivie d'un traité de paix. Cette affiche est placardée à seulement dix kilomètres de la frontière intercoréenne, à Kaesŏng.

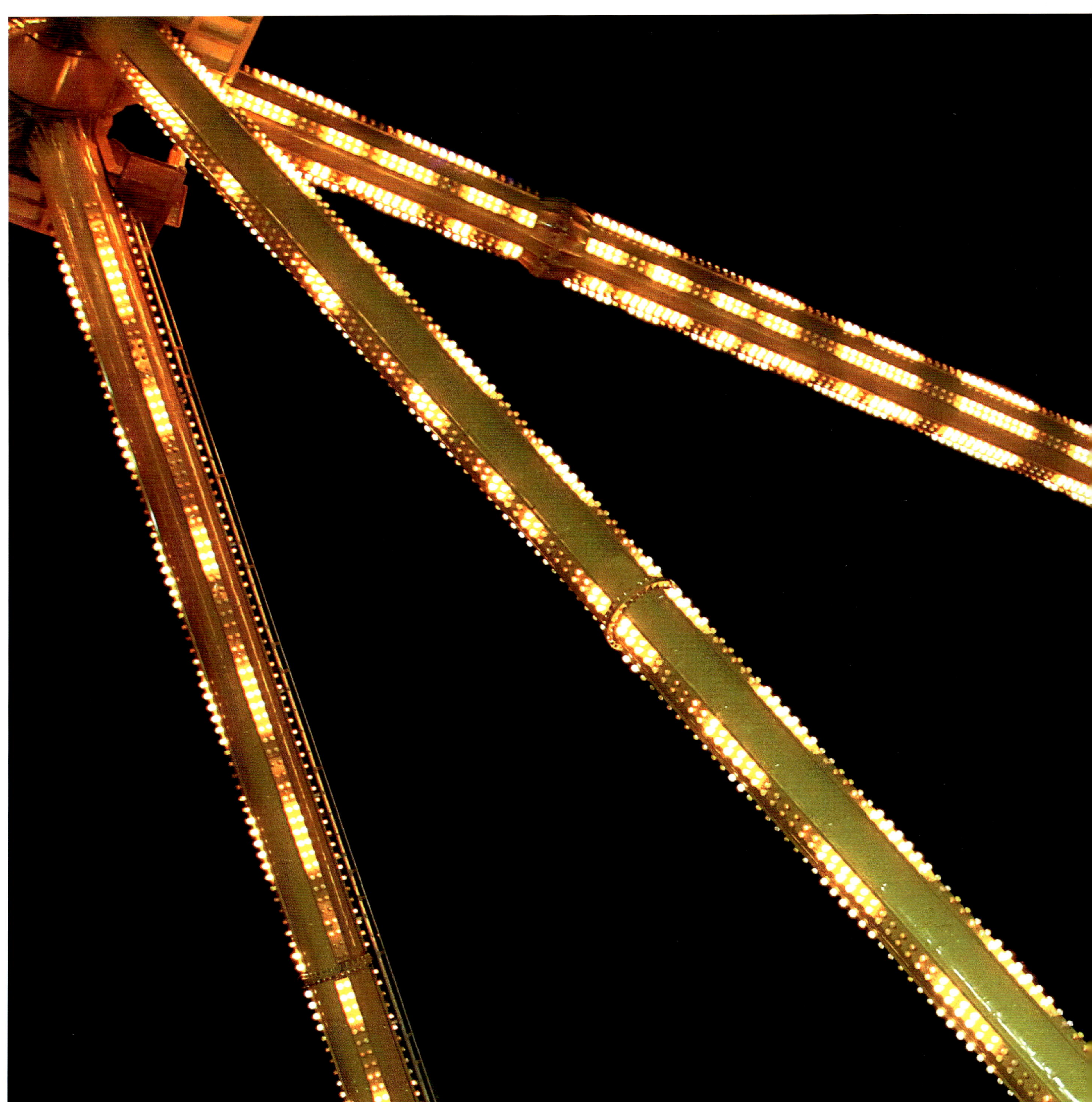

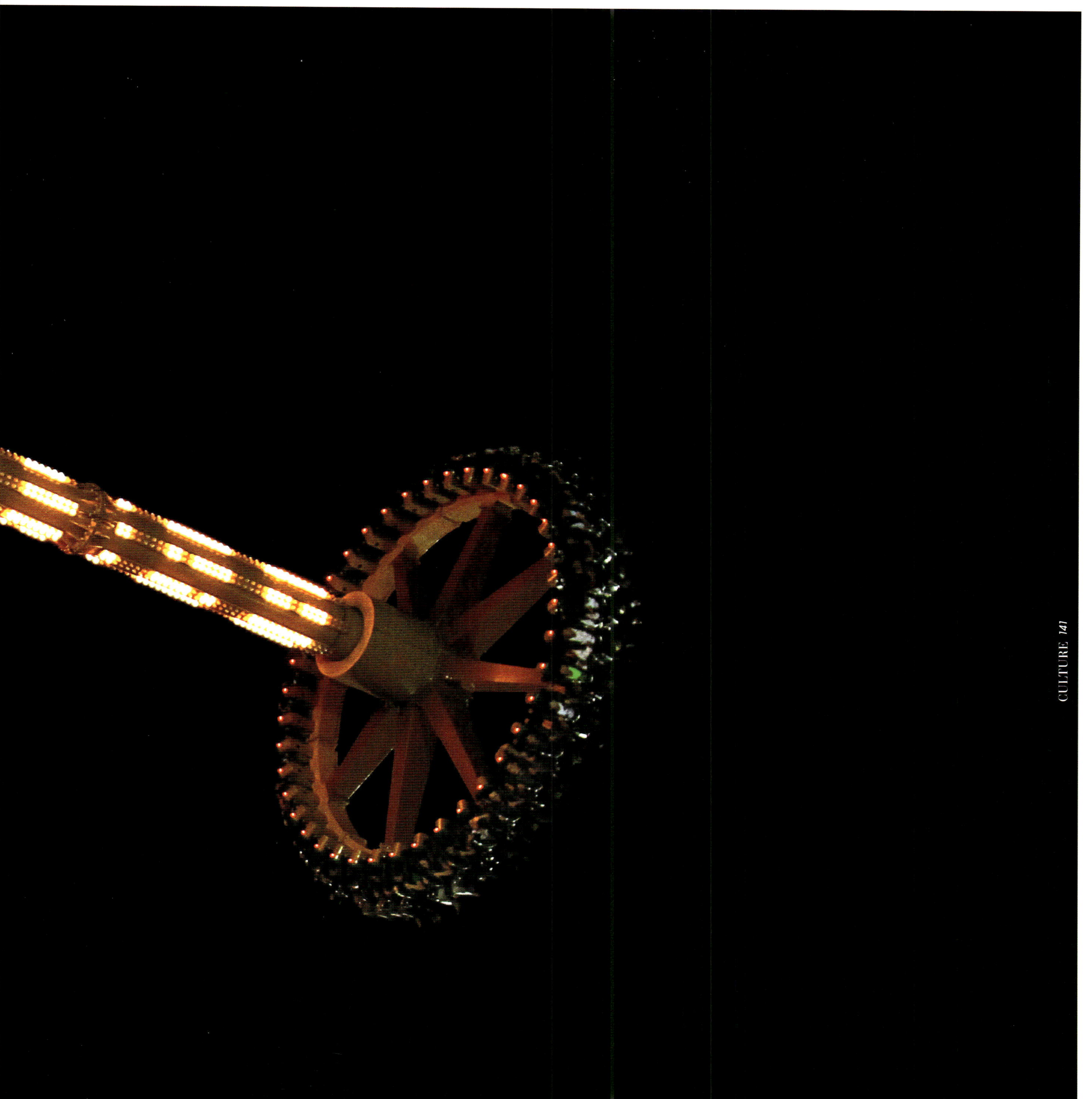

Kaeson amusement park in Pyongyang
Kaeson-Vergnügungspark in Pjöngjang
Le parc d'attractions de Kaeson, à Pyongyang

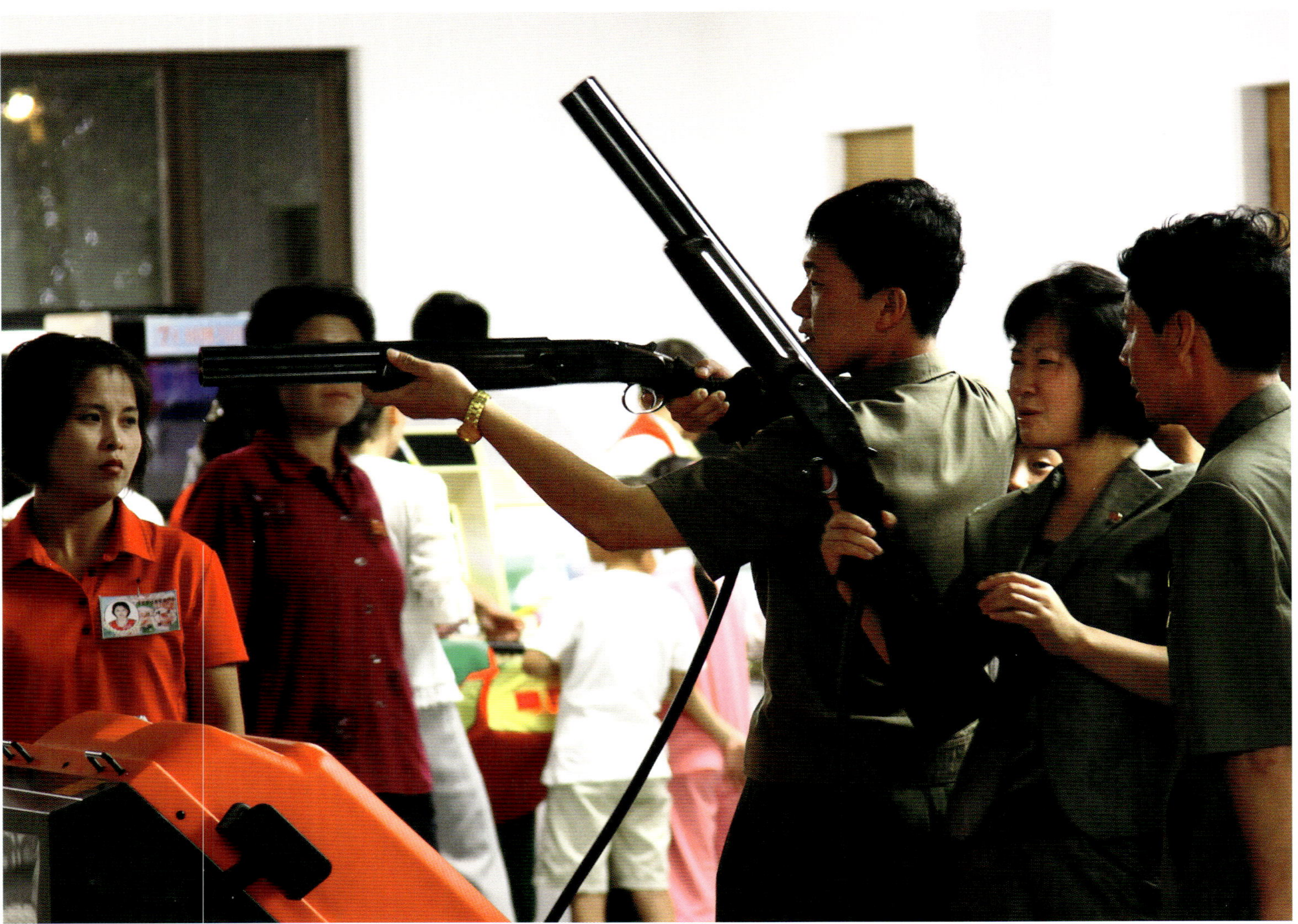

Arcade and other attractions
Spielhalle und andere Attraktionen
Maison de jeux et manèges

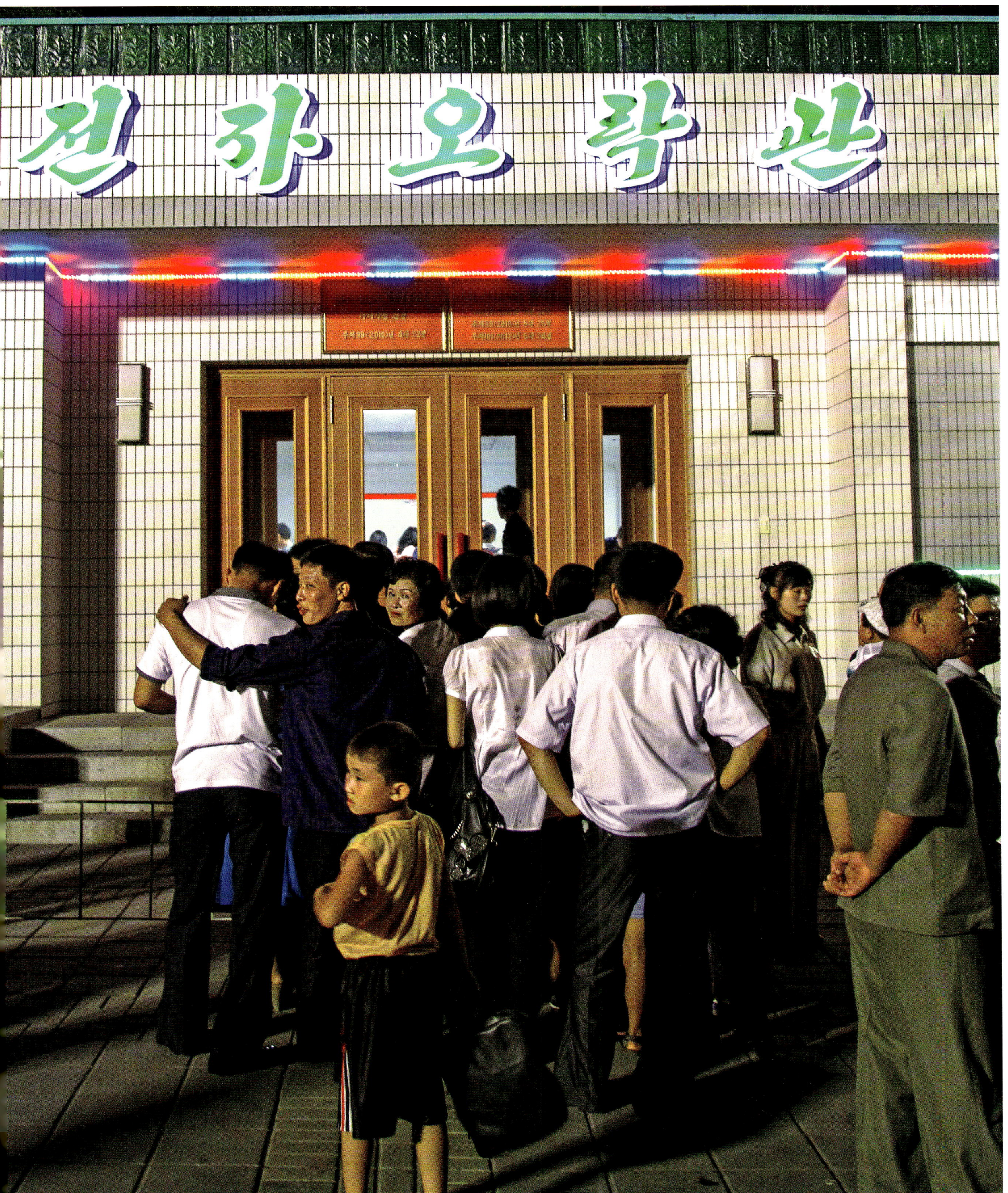
전자오락관
주체99(2010)년 4월 22일

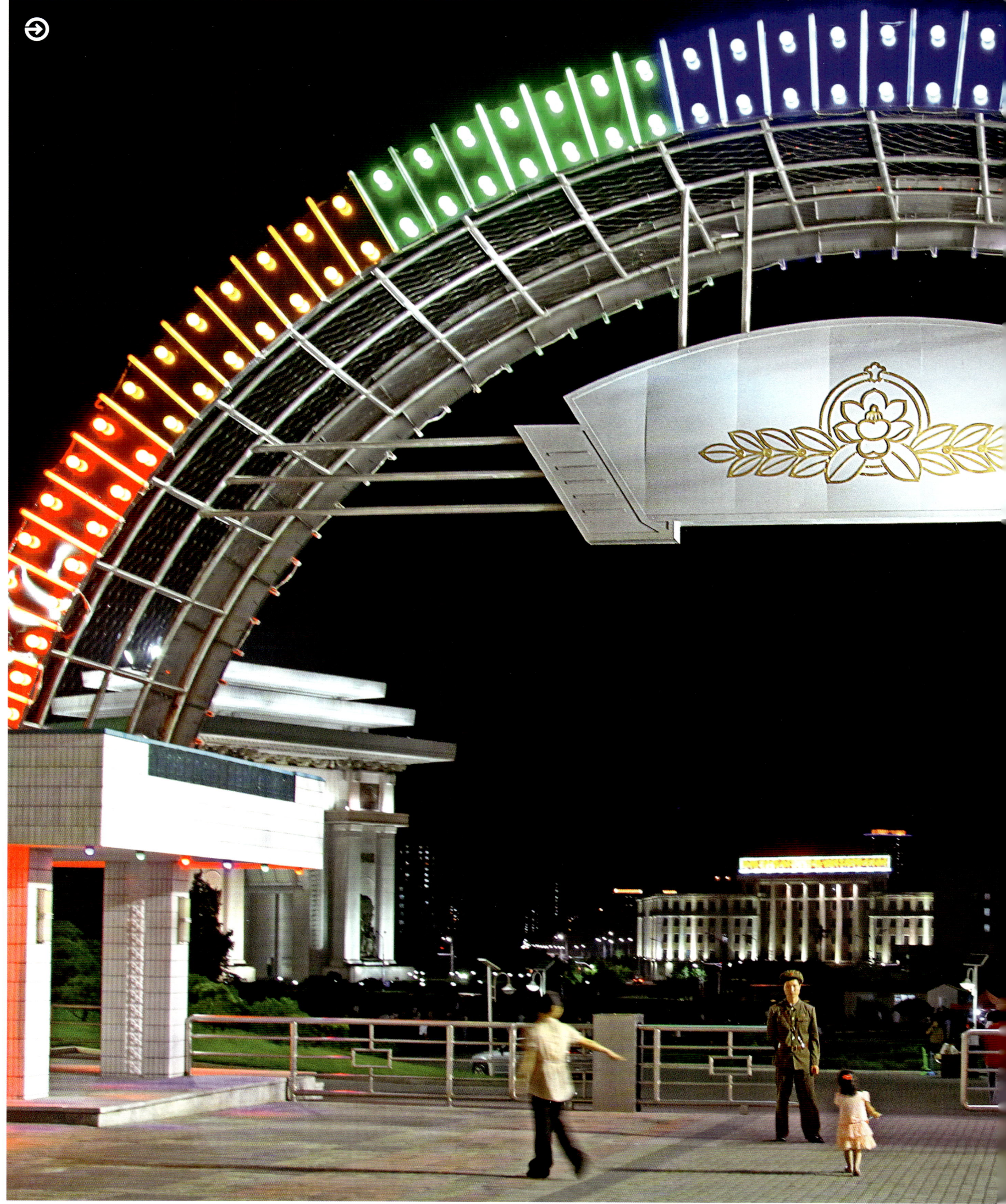

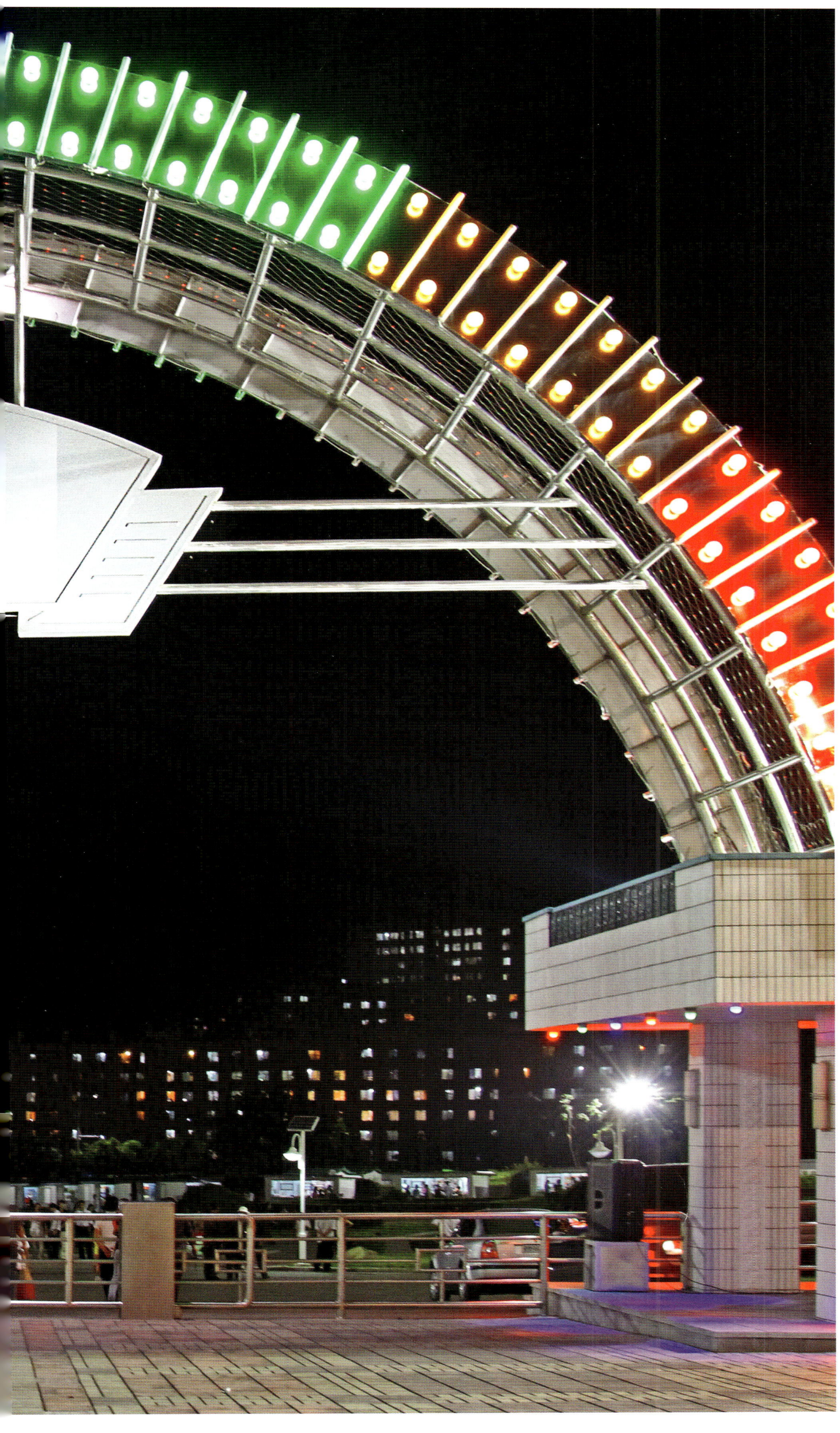

Lone security guard in front of the "Gateway to Fun"
Einsamer Wächter vor dem „Tor ins Vergnügen"
Gardien esseulé devant la « Porte de l'amusement »

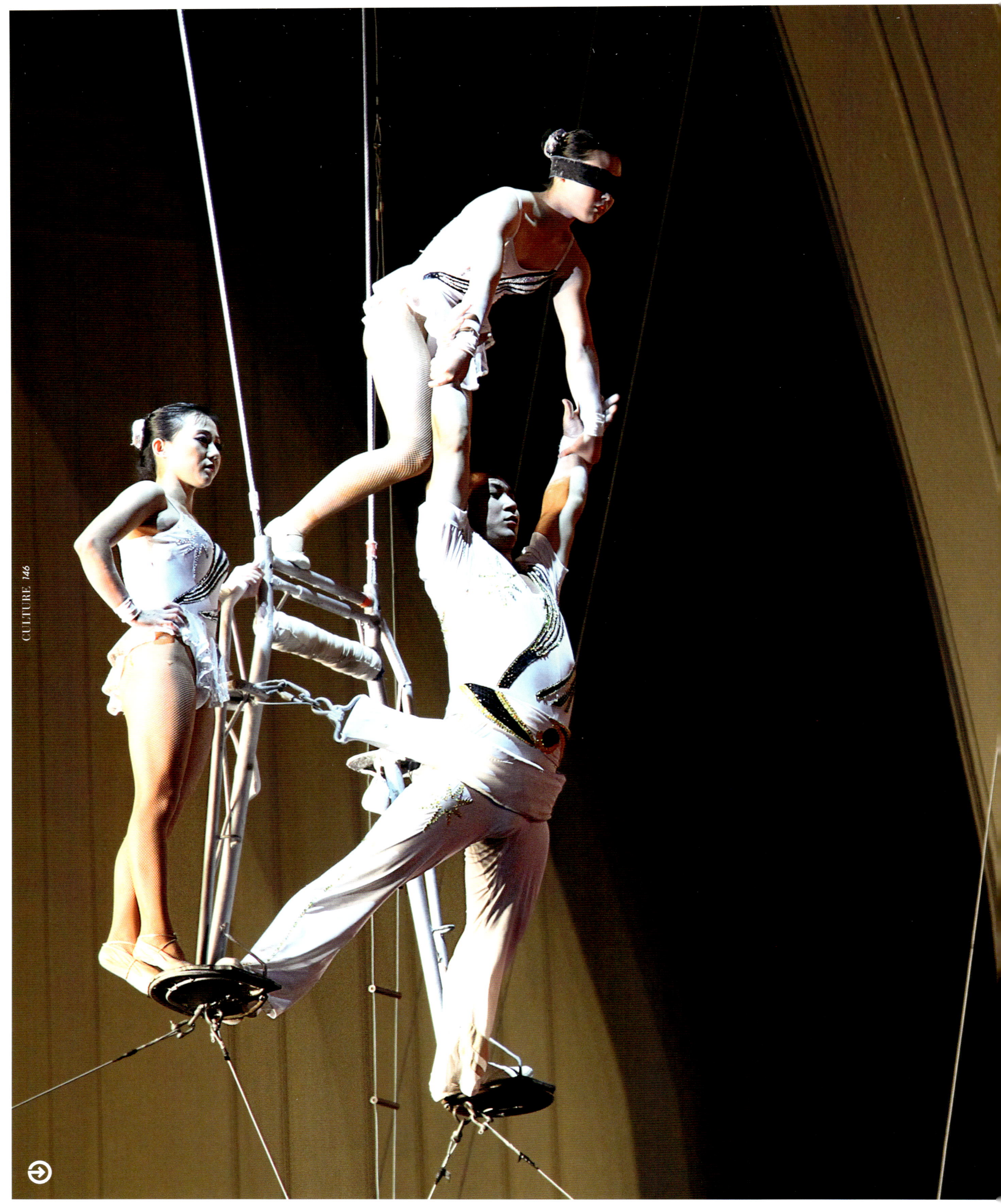

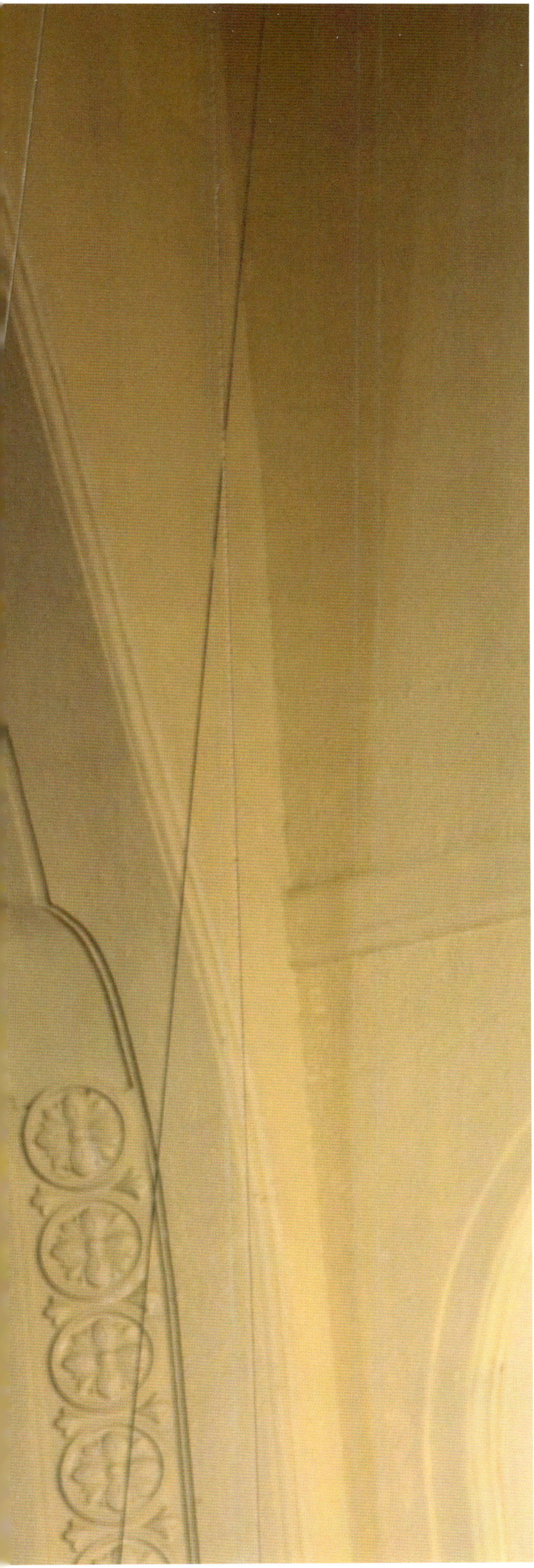

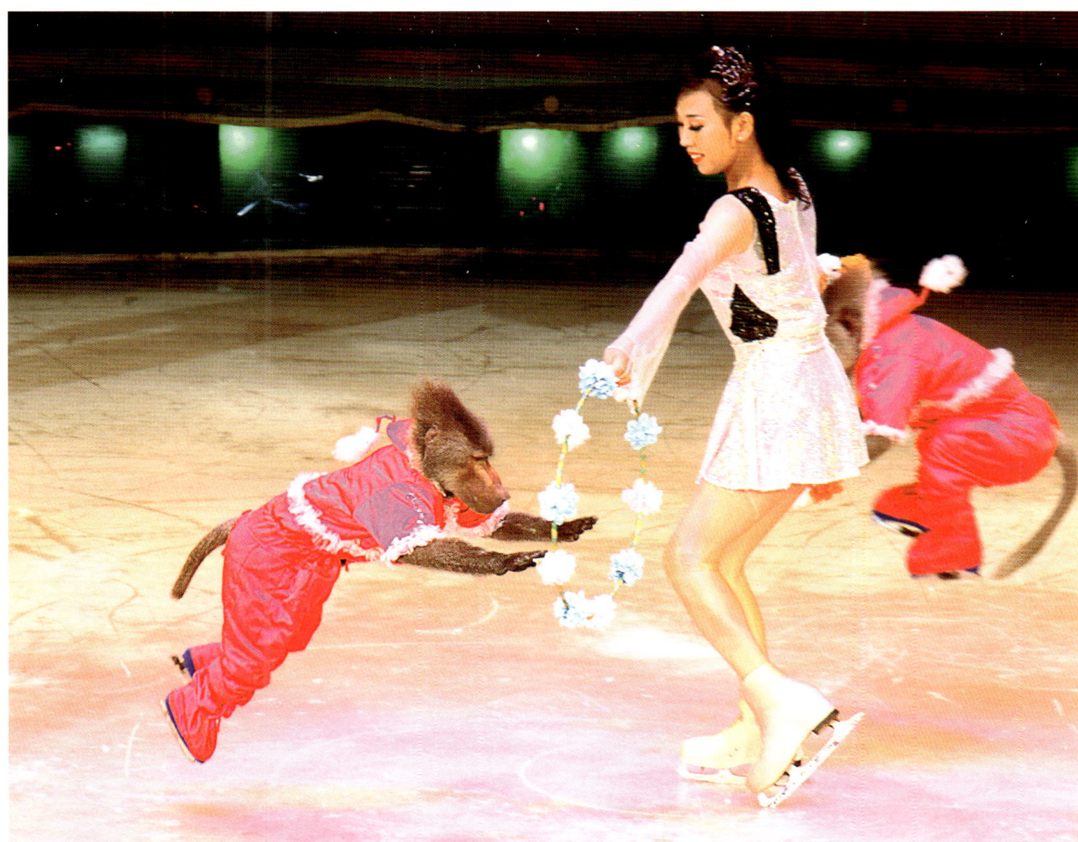

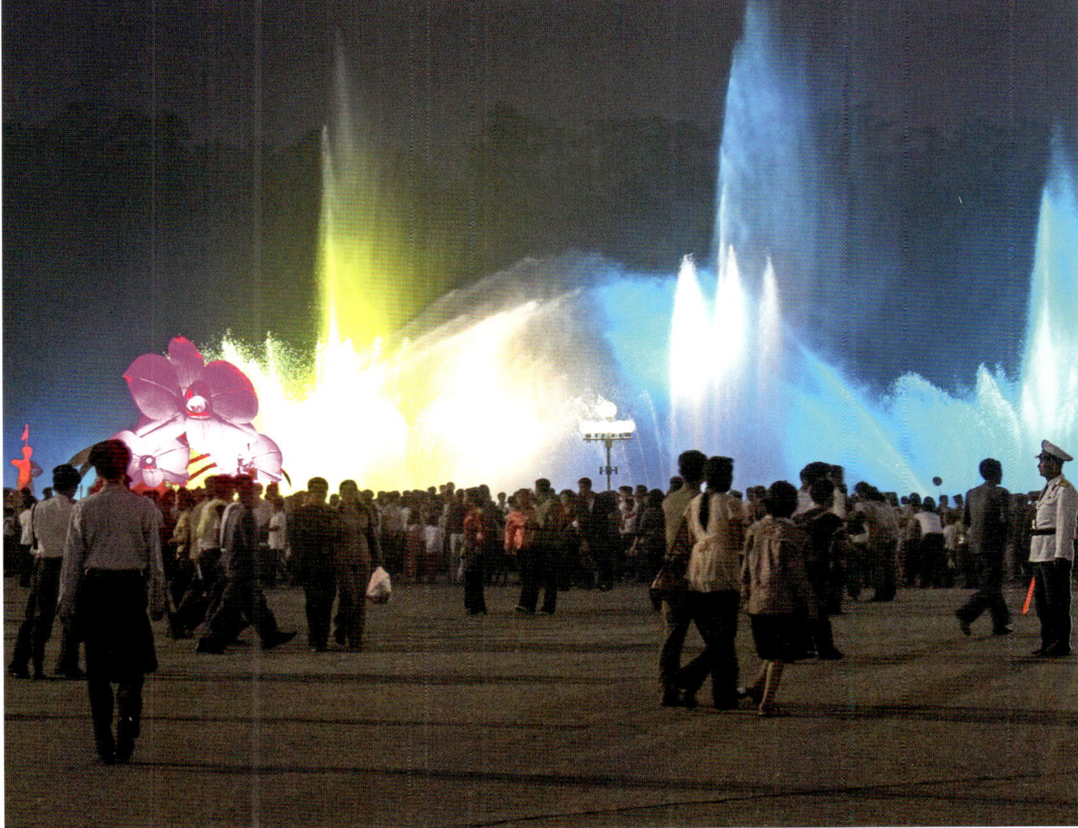

The "Flying Girls" performing at the circus
Zirkusvorstellung mit den „fliegenden Mädchen"
Spectacle de cirque avec les « jeunes filles volantes »

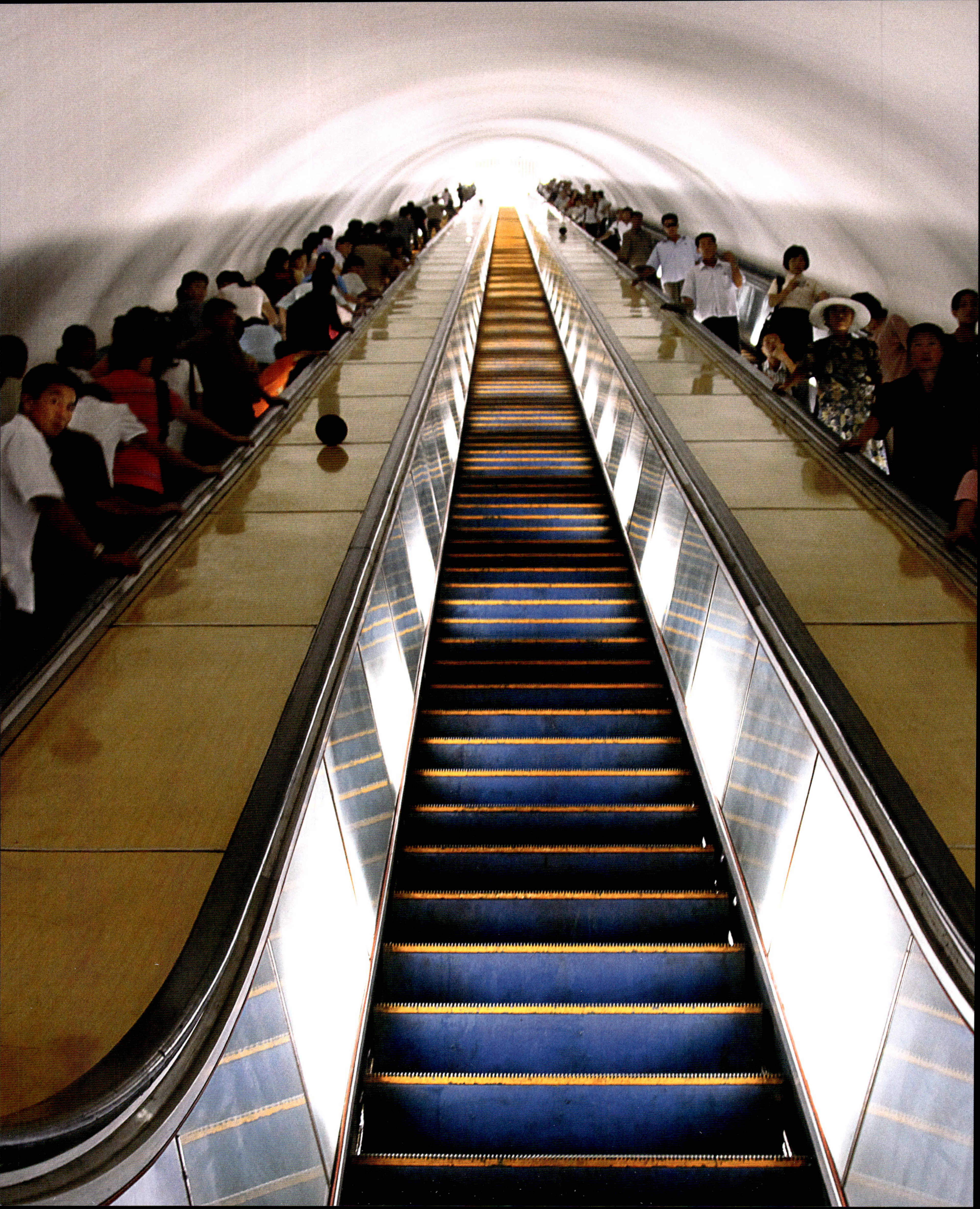

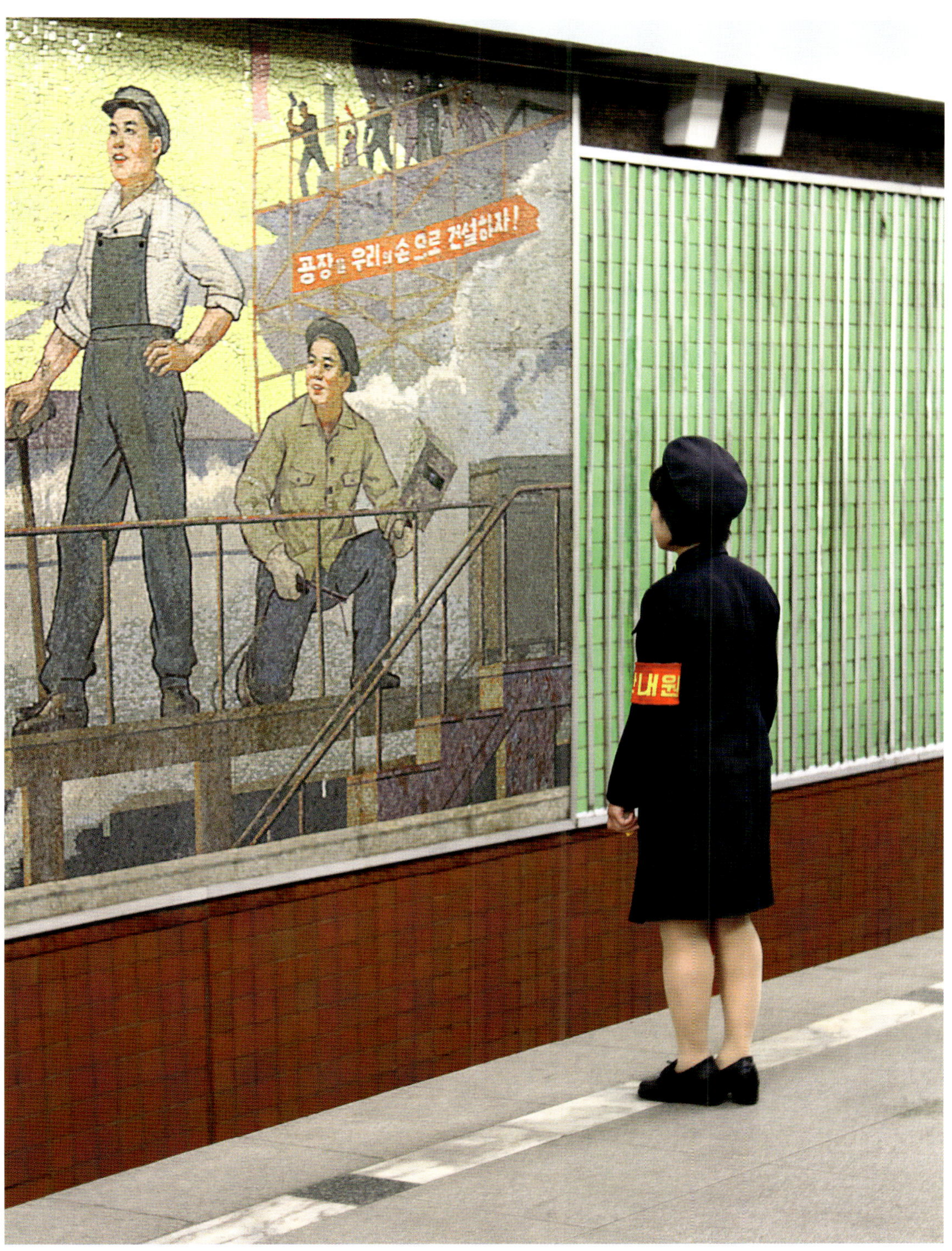

Left: No one uses the middle
escalator in the metro station.
Who is it reserved for?
Right: Office worker at the
"Resurrection" station in Pyongyang
Links: In der Metrostation bleibt die
mittlere Rolltreppe frei.
Für wen ist sie reserviert?
Rechts: Angestellte an der Haltestelle
„Wiederauferstehung", Pjöngjang
À gauche : Dans les stations de métro,
l'escalier mécanique central est désert.
À qui est-il réservé ?
À droite : Employée à la station
« Renouveau », à Pyongyang

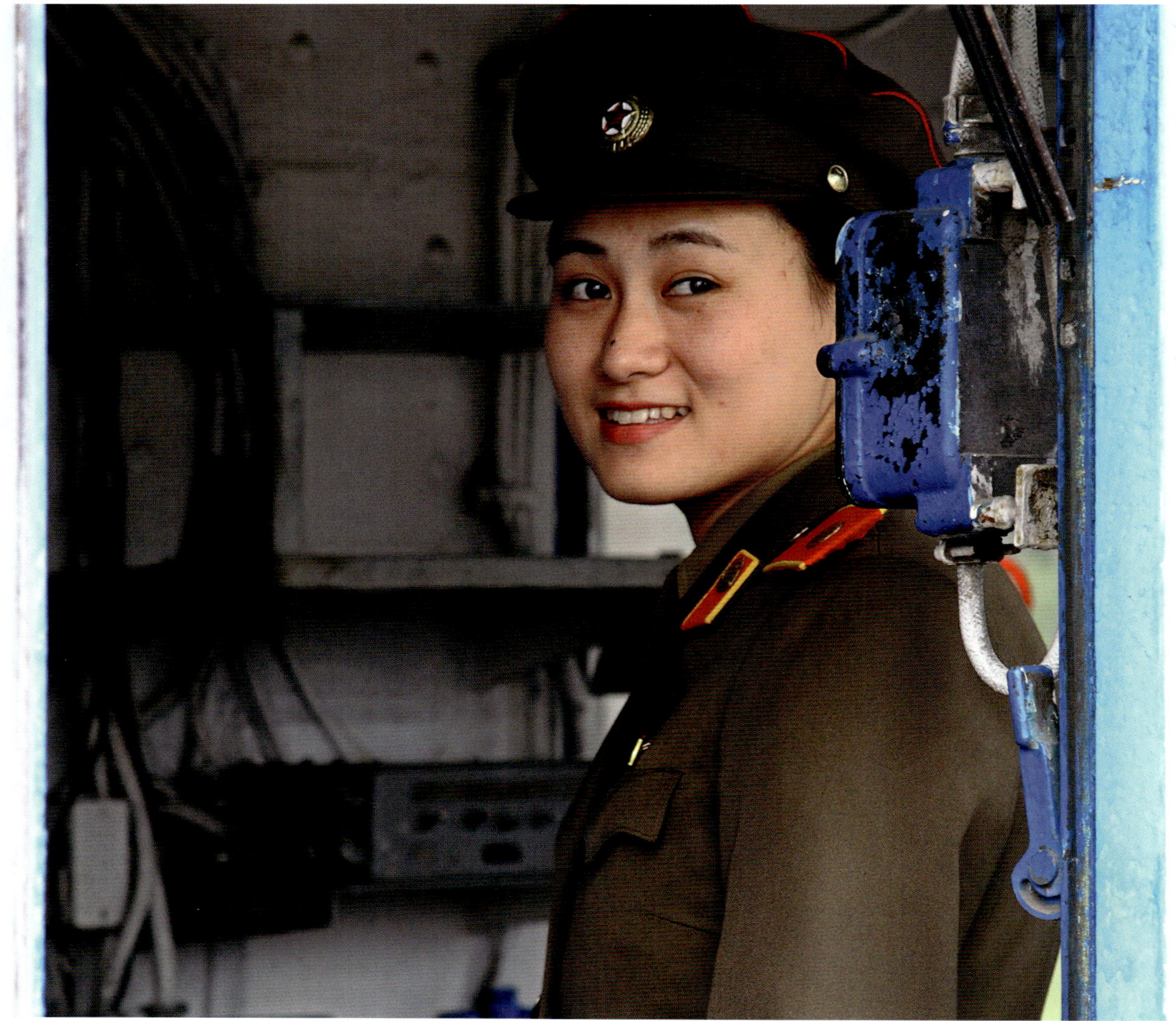

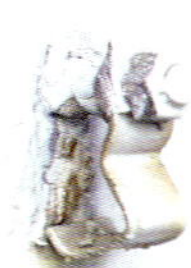

Former Berlin subway trains were recycled for service in the Pyongyang metro.
In Pjöngjangs Untergrund fahren ausrangierte Züge der Berliner U-Bahn.
Ce sont des wagons du métro de Berlin mis au rebut qui circulent dans les entrailles de Pyongyang.

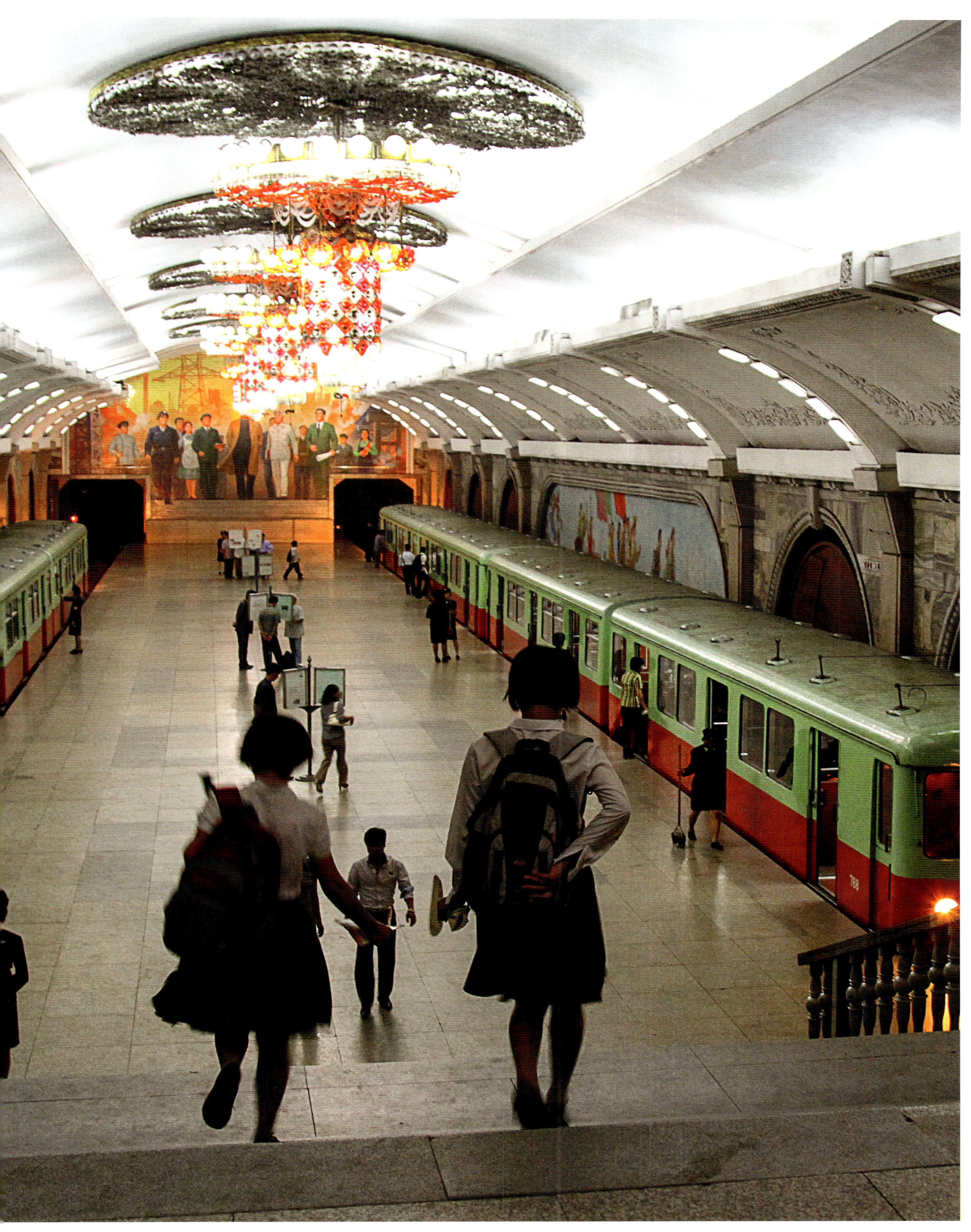

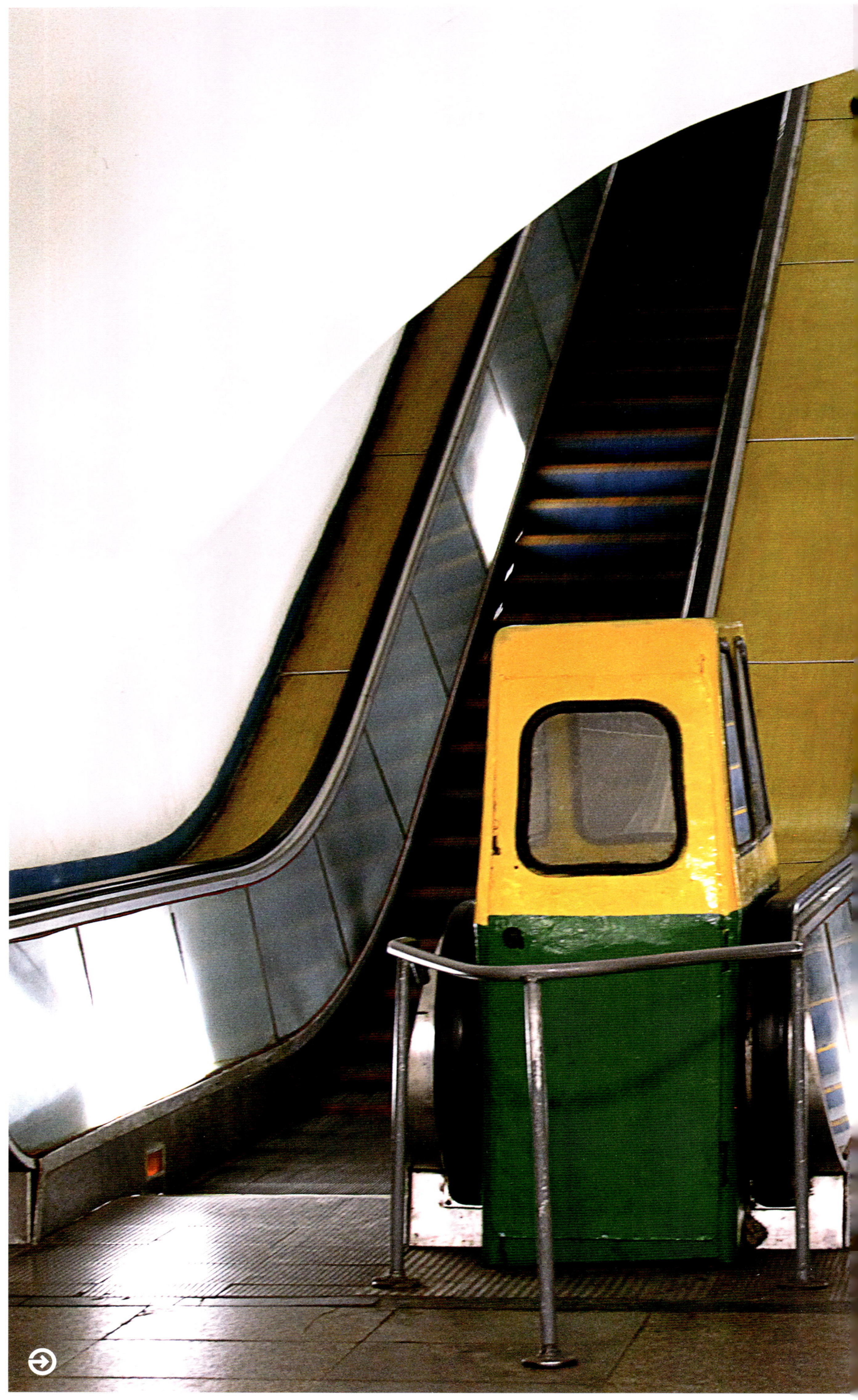

Metro stations have names like "Golden Field," "Triumphant Return," and "Paradise."
U-Bahn-Stationen tragen Namen wie „Goldenes Feld", „Triumphale Wiederkunft" und „Paradies".
Les stations de métro ont pour noms « Champ d'or », « Retour triomphal » ou encore « Paradis ».

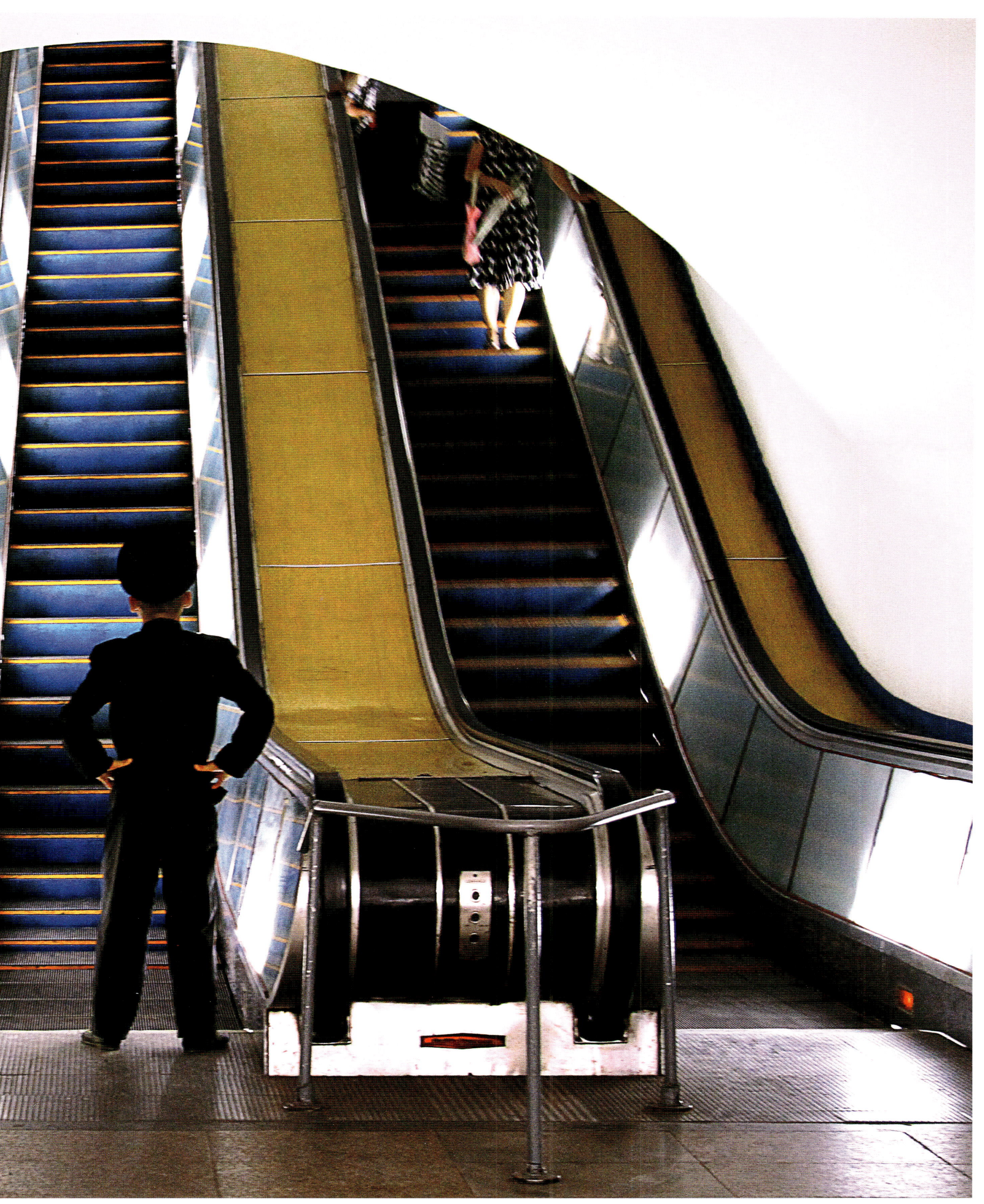

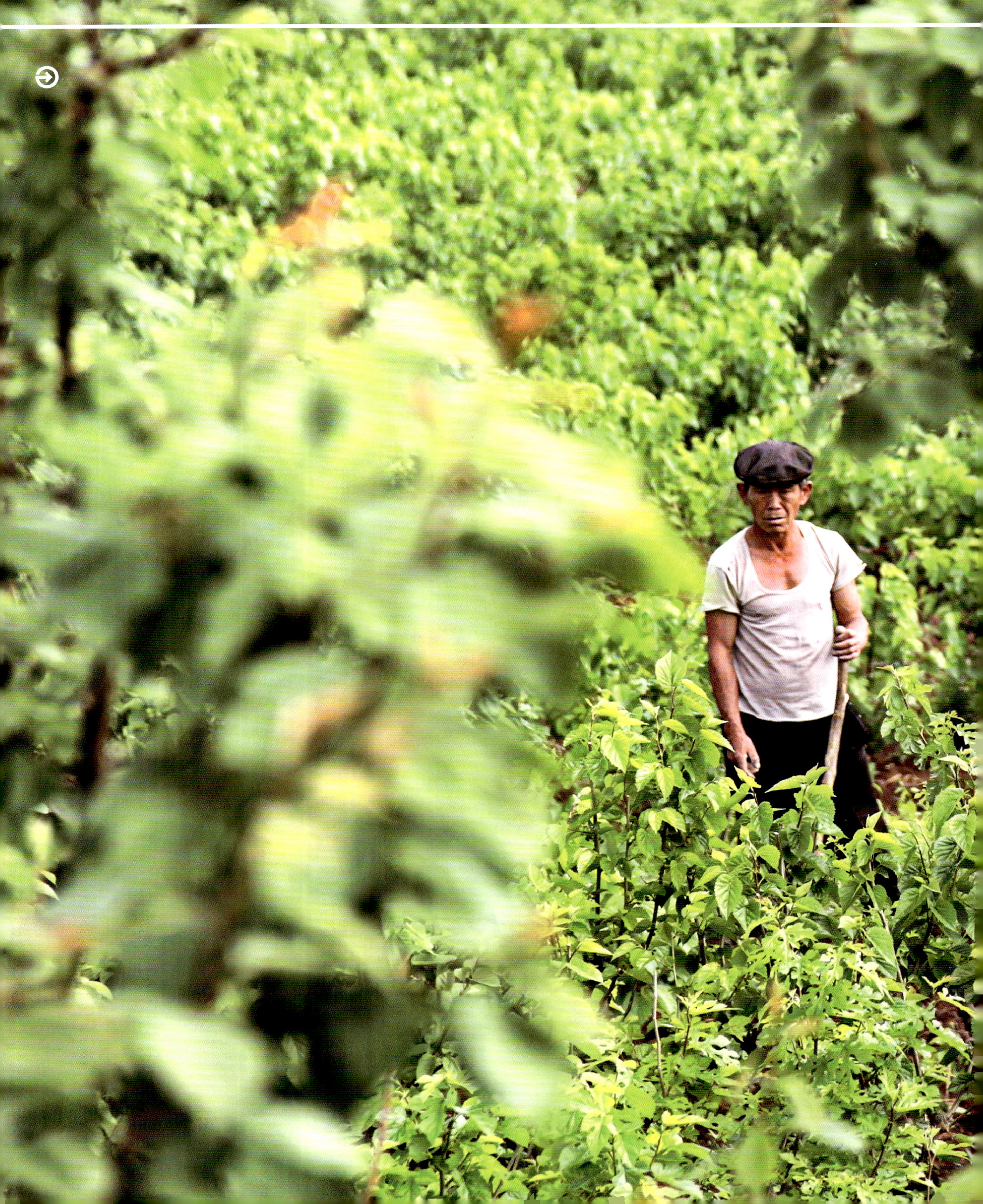

PEOPLE

MENSCHEN
GENS

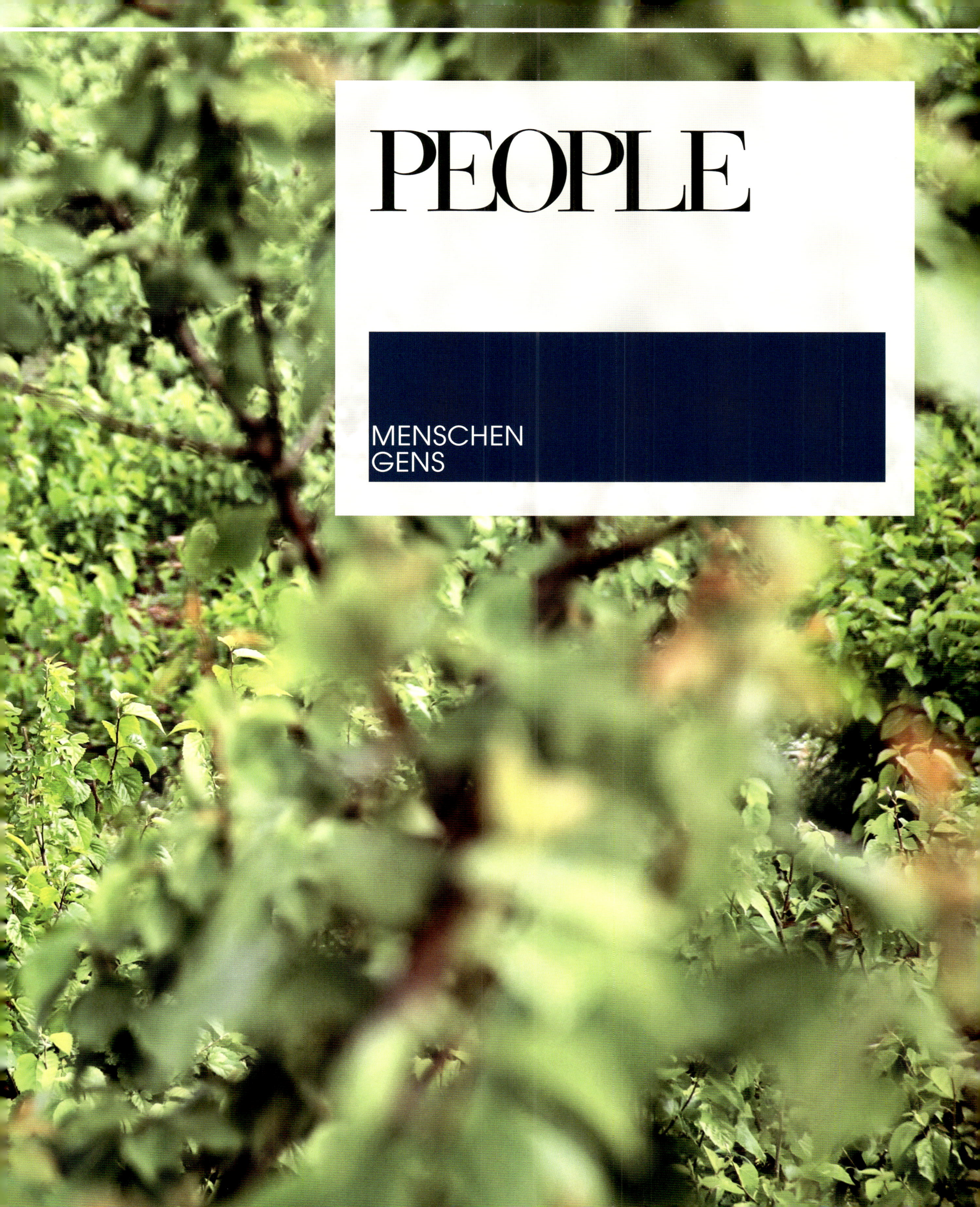

The Cold War is not yet over in this country. It can heat up again at any time, as has been regularly reported in the international media. However, apart from the political saber rattling, what do we know about the 24 million inhabitants of North Korea? Today, the citizens of this country live in a world apart, in their own time. The following photos show daily life in the last remaining nation of this size that has remained untouched by globalization. The pictures invite us to take a peek behind the final piece of the Iron Curtain. Beyond the personality cult and the military presence, these images portray the human face of North Korea as the gulf widens between urban life in the capital and country life in the provinces.

Hier ist der Kalte Krieg noch nicht vorbei. Er kann jederzeit wieder heiß werden. Das berichten internationale Medien in regelmäßigen Abständen. Doch was wissen wir, abgesehen von dem politischen Säbelrasseln, über das 24-Millionen-Volk der Nordkoreaner? Bis heute leben die Menschen im Land in ihrer ganz eigenen Welt und Zeitrechnung. Die folgenden Bilder zeigen die Lebensweise der letzten verbliebenen Nation dieser Größe, an der die Globalisierung vollkommen vorbeigezogen ist. Sie laden ein, einen Blick hinter den letzten Eisernen Vorhang zu werfen. Inmitten von Personenkult und Militär porträtieren diese Aufnahmen das menschliche Antlitz Nordkoreas in der wachsenden Kluft zwischen Pjöngjang und der Provinz.

Dans ce pays, la guerre froide n’est pas encore terminée : elle peut repartir de plus belle, comme les médias internationaux le signalent régulièrement. Mais, en dehors des bruits de bottes, que savons-nous sur les 24 millions de Coréens du Nord ? Ceux-ci continuent d’évoluer dans un monde et une ère qui leur sont propres. Les photographies qui suivent révèlent le mode de vie de la dernière nation de cette taille qui n’ait pas été touchée par la mondialisation. Elles invitent à jeter un coup d’œil derrière le dernier rideau de fer. Par-delà le culte de la personnalité et la militarisation, ces prises de vue montrent le visage humain de la Corée du Nord, où se creuse le fossé entre Pyongyang et la province.

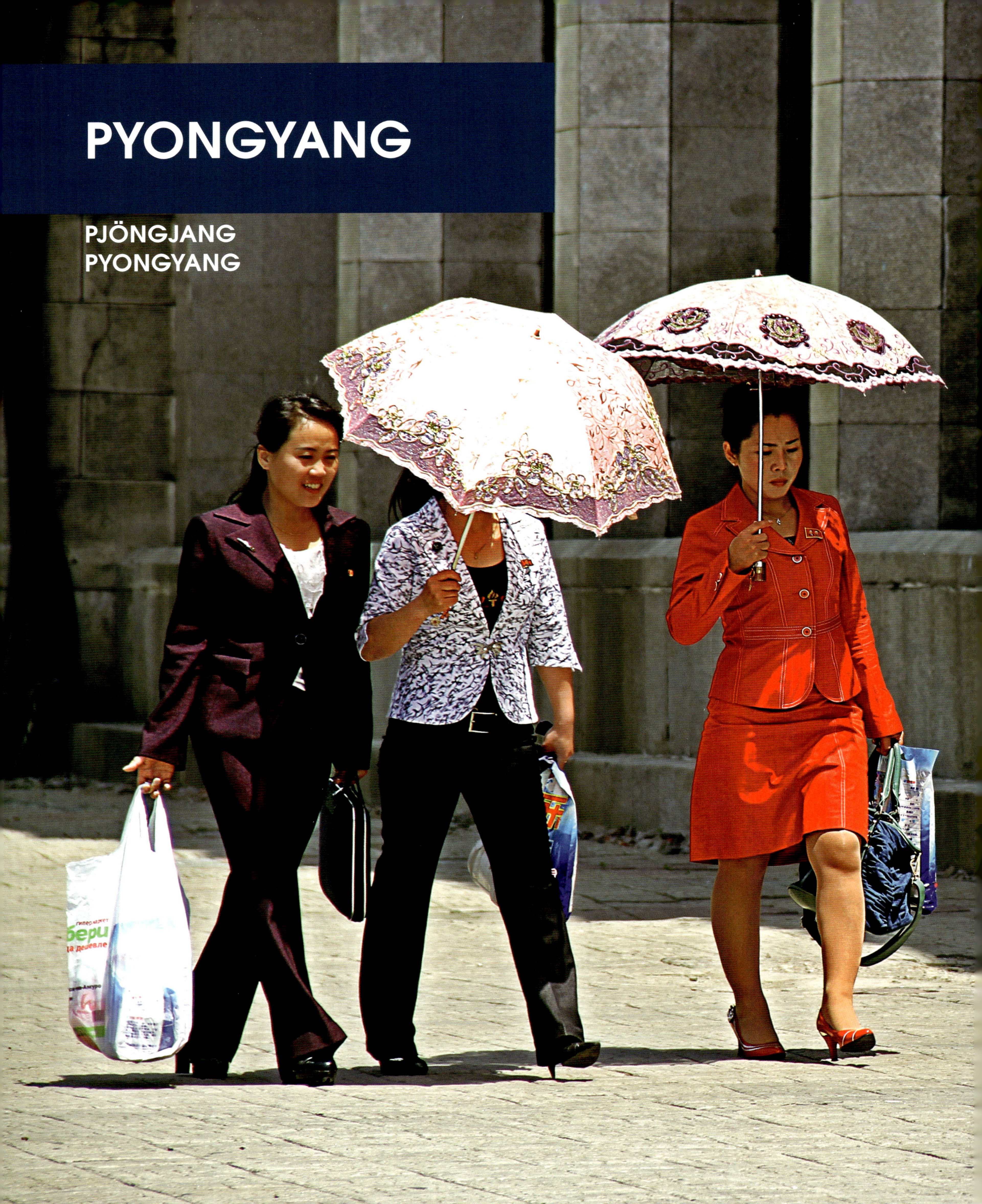

PYONGYANG

PJÖNGJANG
PYONGYANG

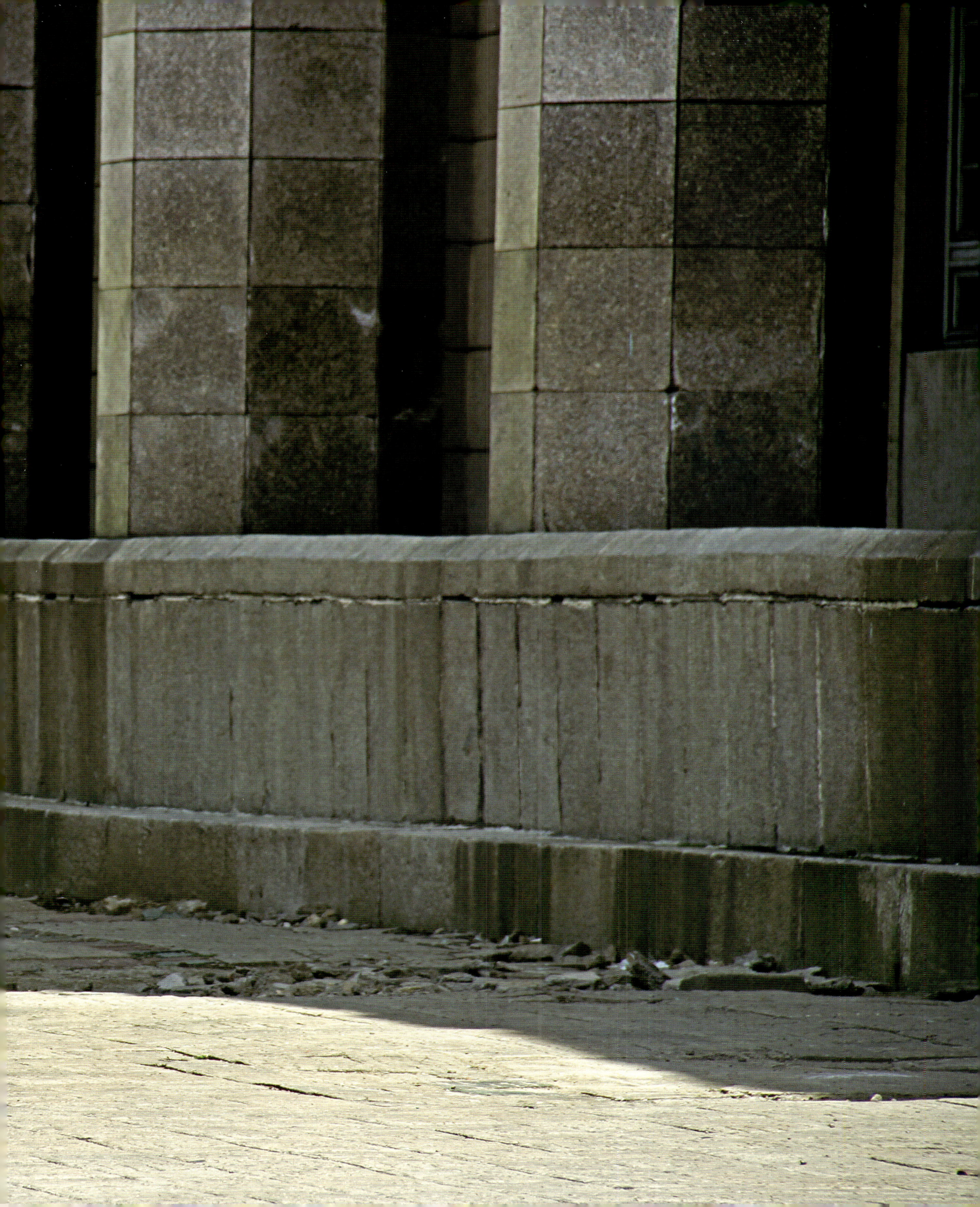

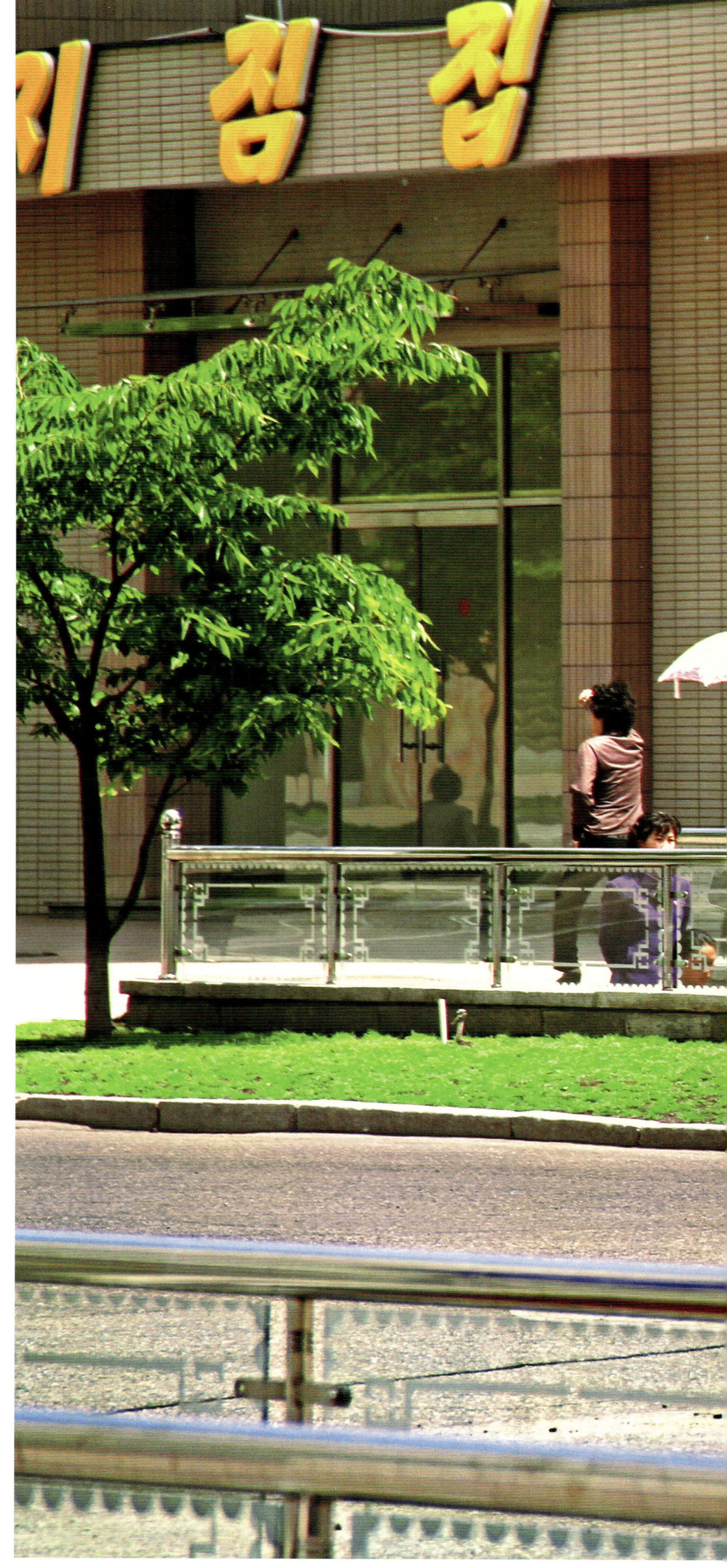

In the capital, meter maids are known as "Flowers of Pyongyang."
„Blumen Pjöngjangs": So werden in der Hauptstadt die Politessen genannt.
Une « fleur de Pyongyang », ainsi qu'on surnomme les contractuelles dans la capitale.

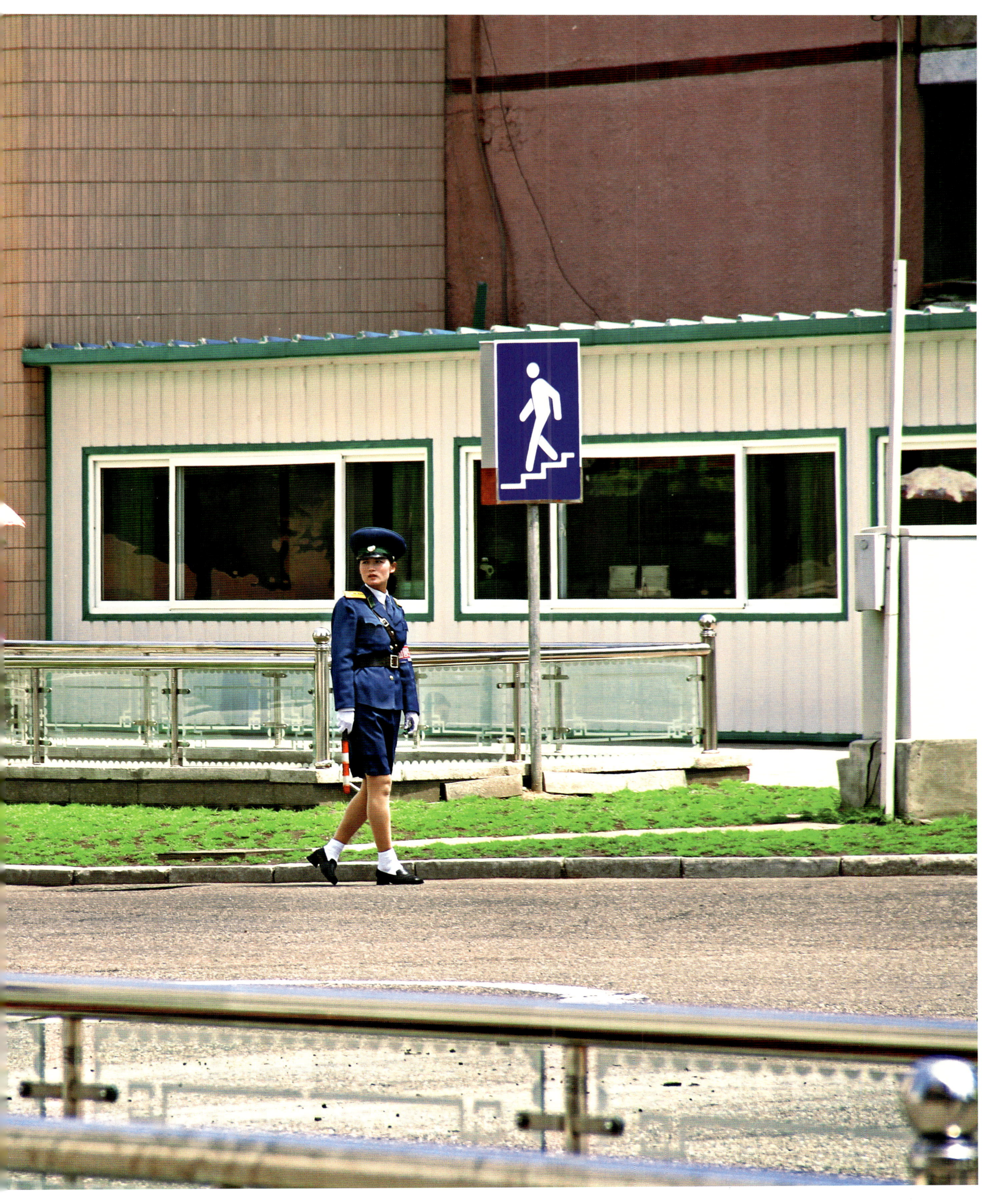

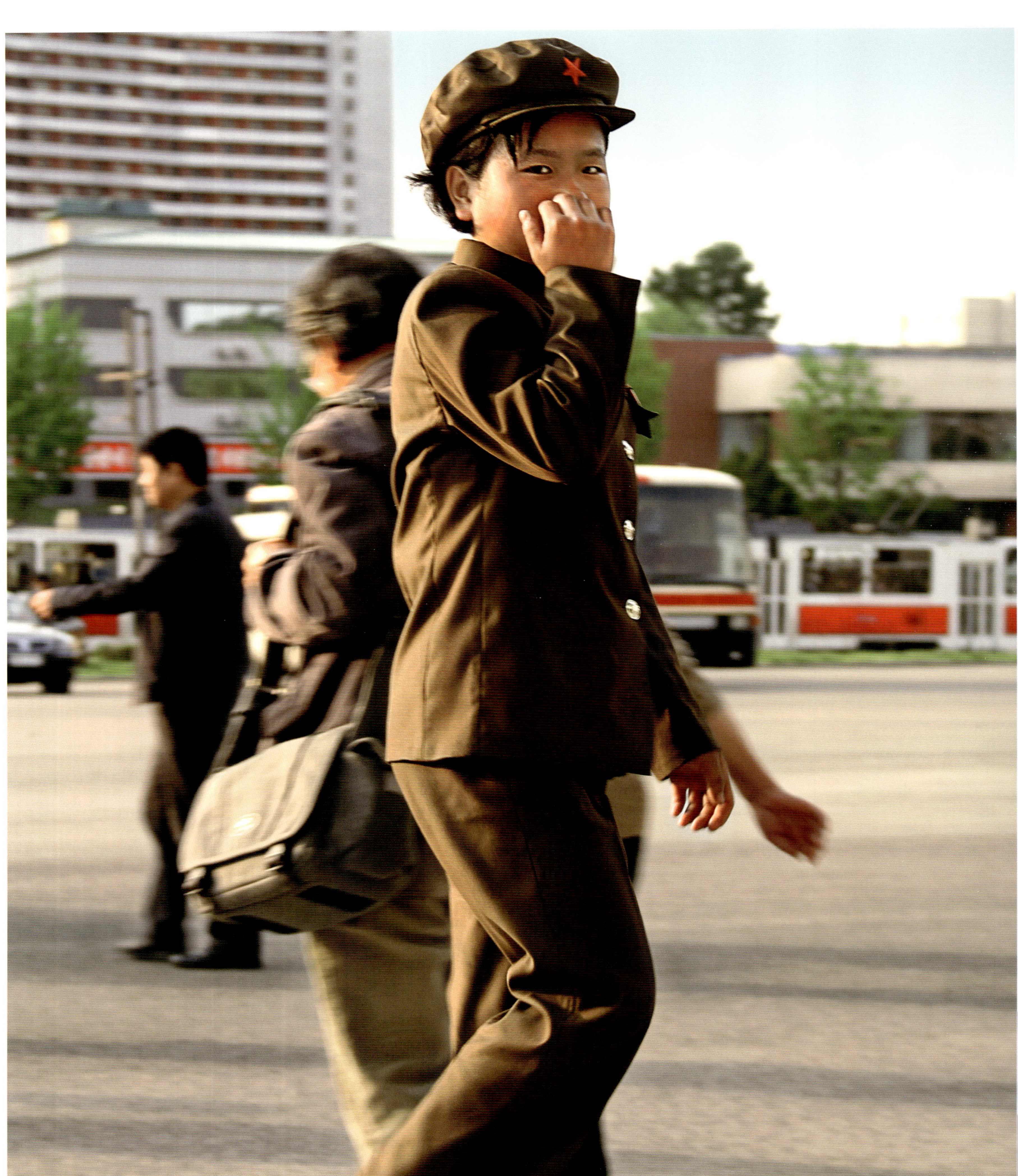

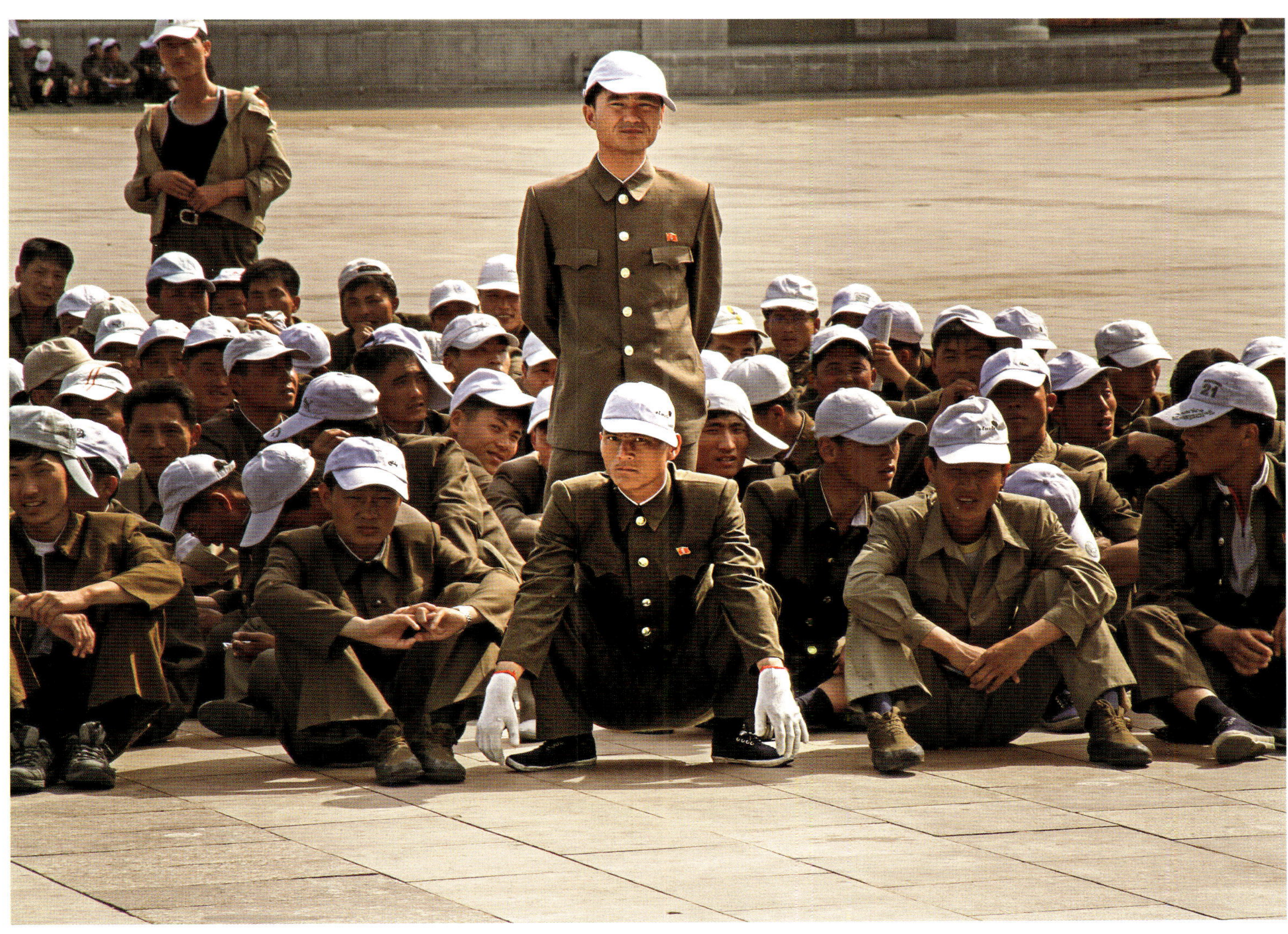

Left: Young construction worker
Right: Taking a break during a military exercise
Links: Junge Bauarbeiterin
Rechts: Pause während einer Militärübung
À gauche : Jeune ouvrière du bâtiment
À droite : Pause au cours d'un entraînement militaire

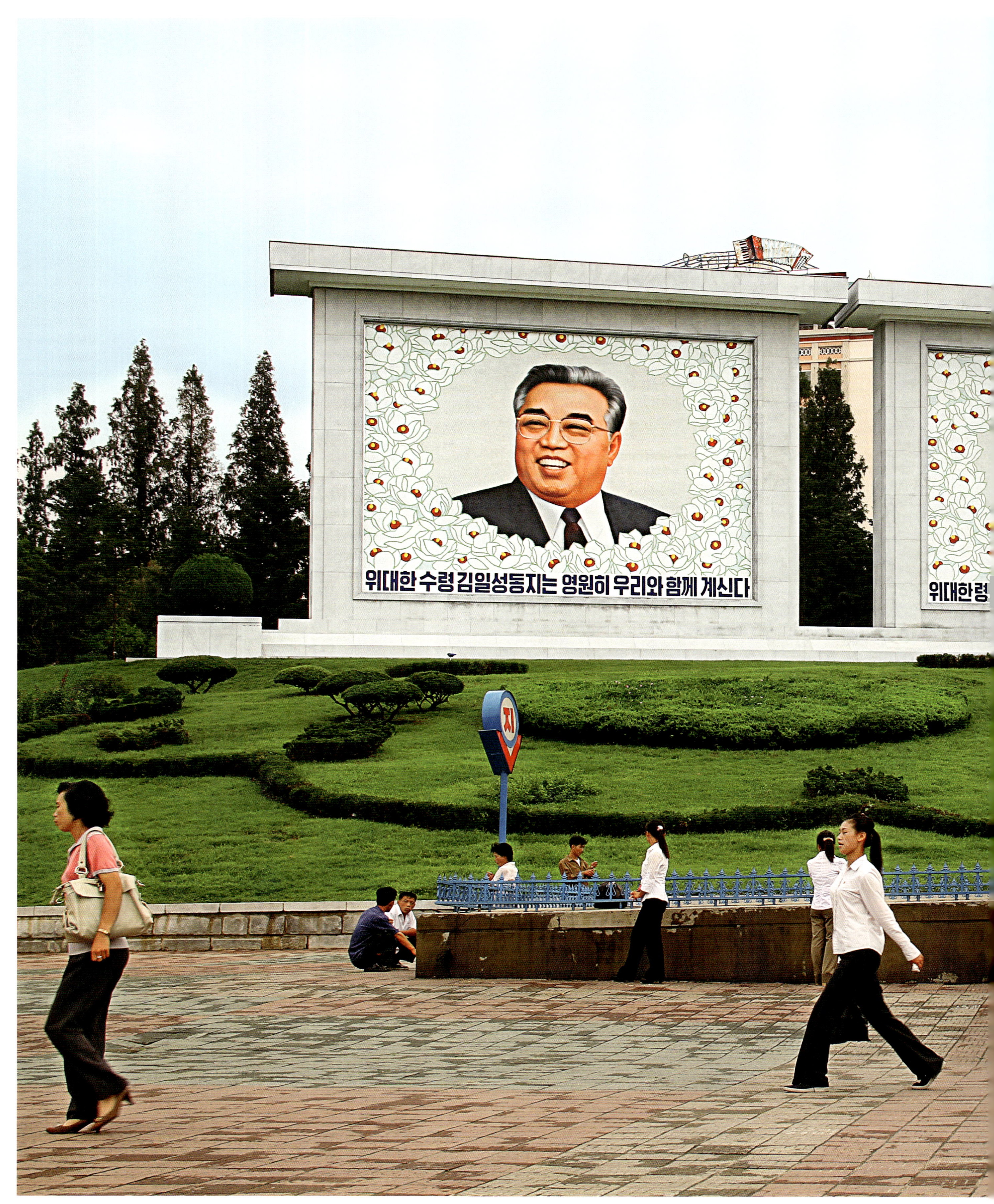
위대한 수령 김일성동지는 영원히 우리와 함께 계신다
지

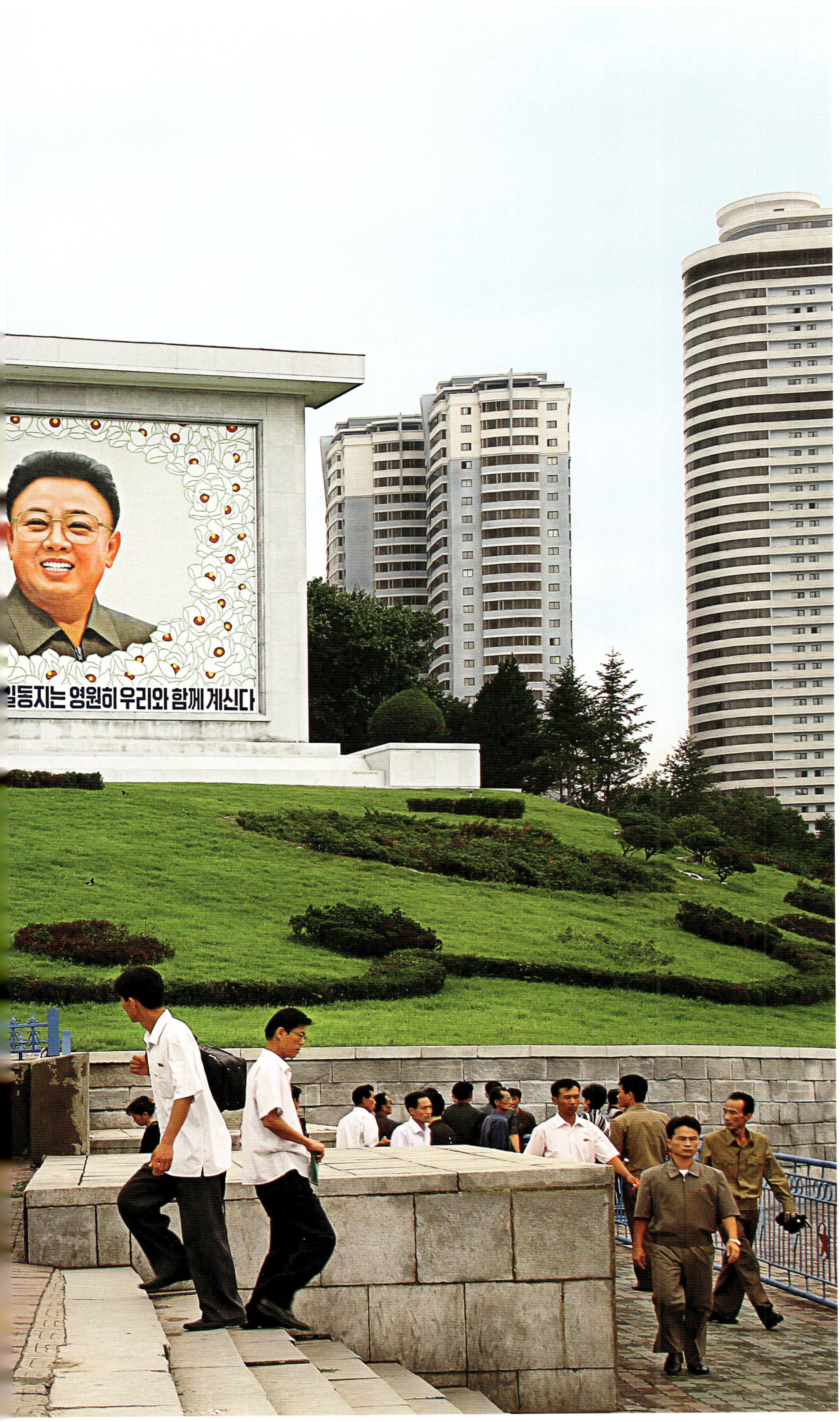

The first communist dynasty takes its course.
Die erste kommunistische Dynastie nimmt ihren Lauf.
La première dynastie communiste suit son cours.

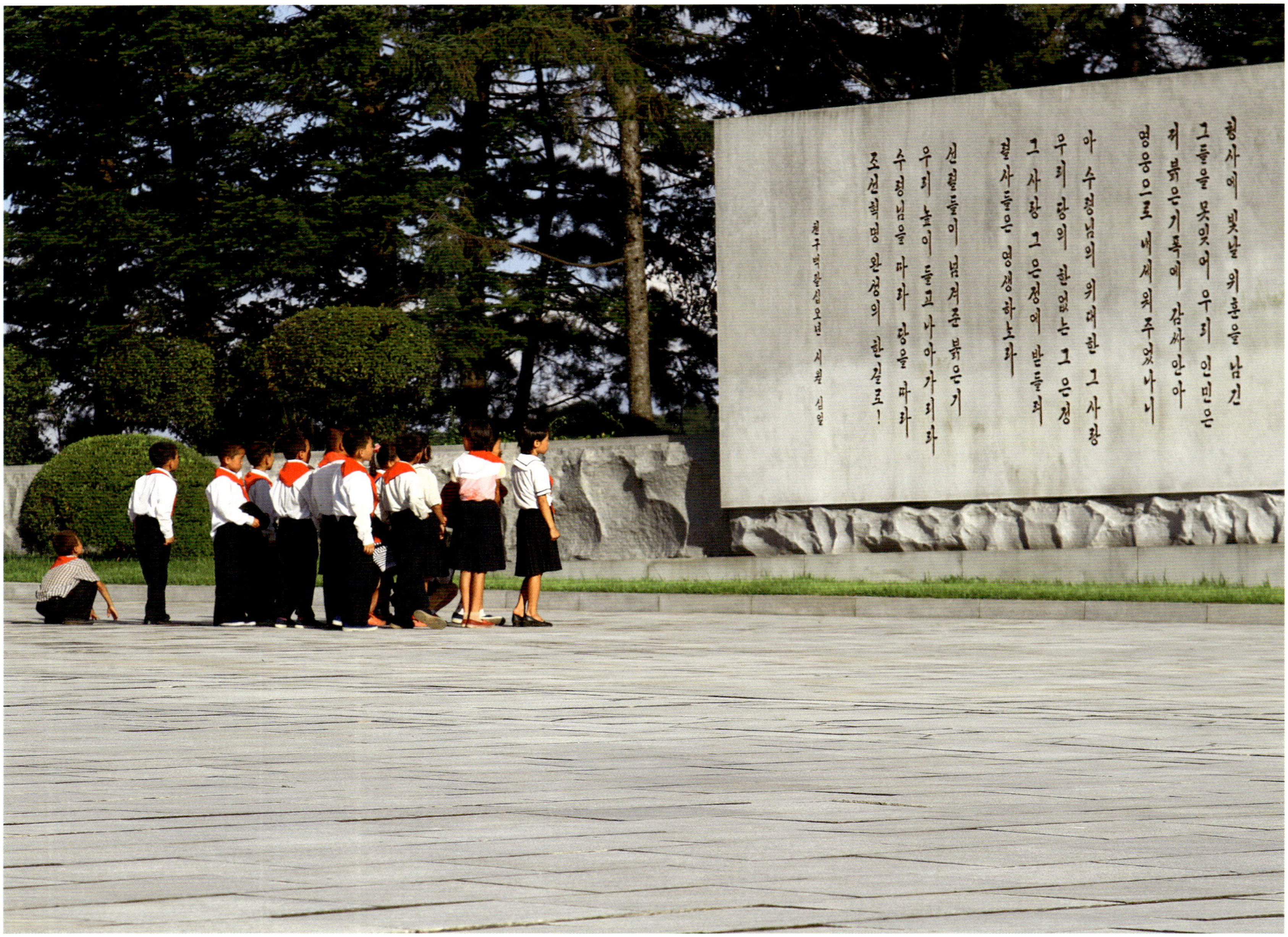

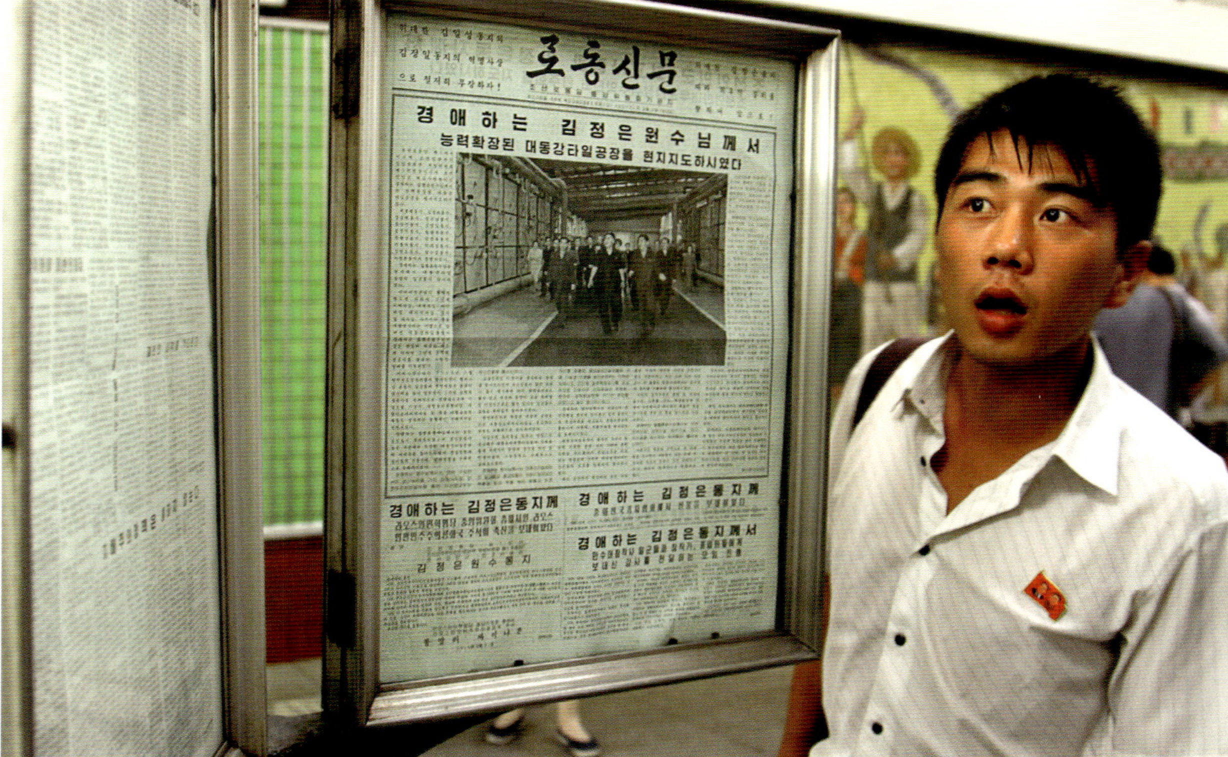

School trip: History chiseled in stone.
Many people have no access to the media other than public newspapers in the metro station.
Schulausflug: Geschichte in Stein gemeißelt.
Öffentliche Zeitungen in der Metrostation sind für viele der einzige Medienzugang.
Écoliers en excursion : l'Histoire gravée dans la pierre.
Les journaux mis à la disposition de tous dans les stations de métro sont pour beaucoup de personnes le seul moyen de s'informer.

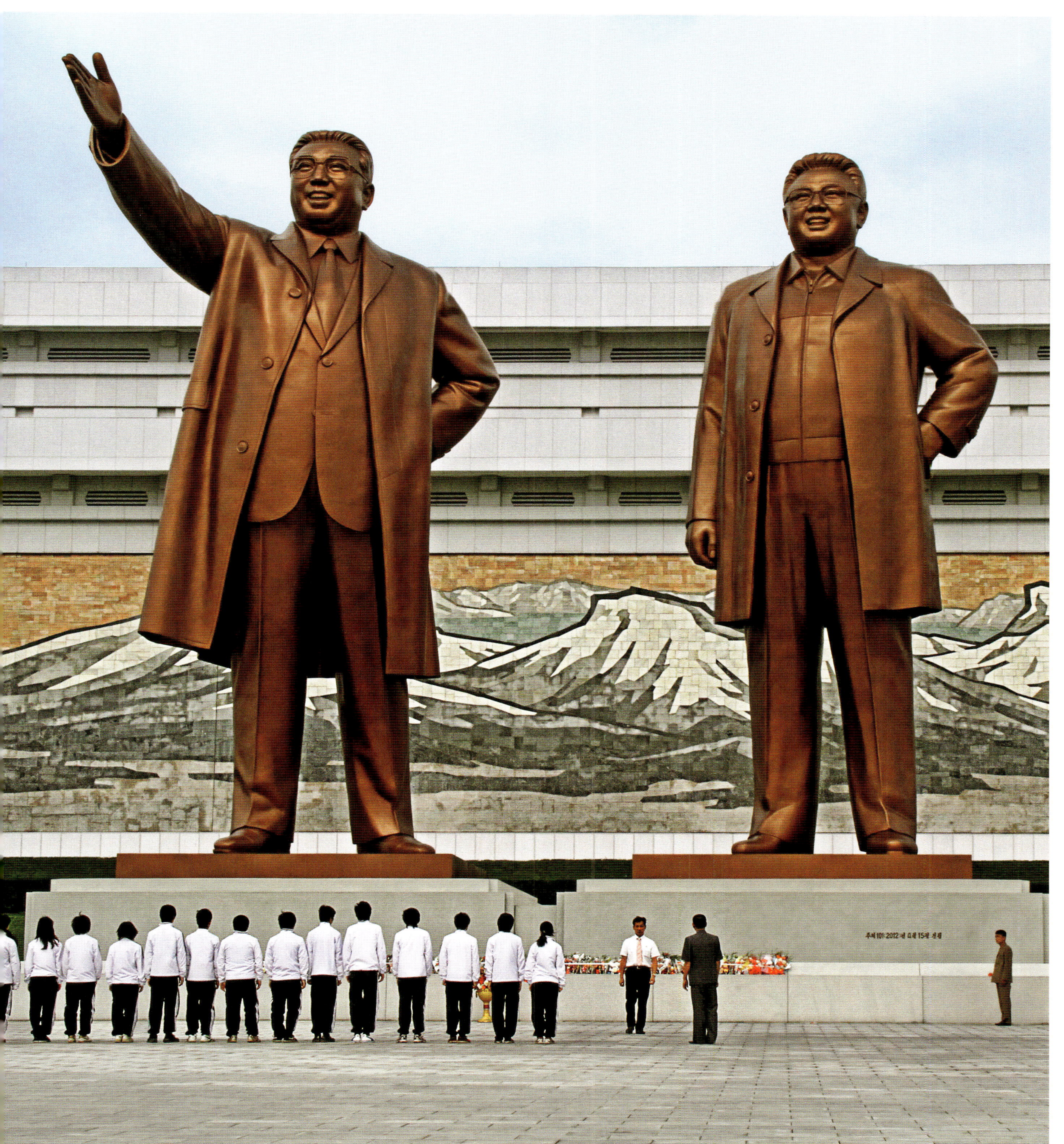

A ruler cult with religious overtones. You can take pictures of the statues, but only the entire figure and only from the front.
Herrscherkult mit religiösen Zügen. Die Statuen dürfen nur von vorne und nur im Ganzen fotografiert werden.
Culte de la personnalité mâtiné de religion. On ne peut photographier les statues autrement que de face et en pied.

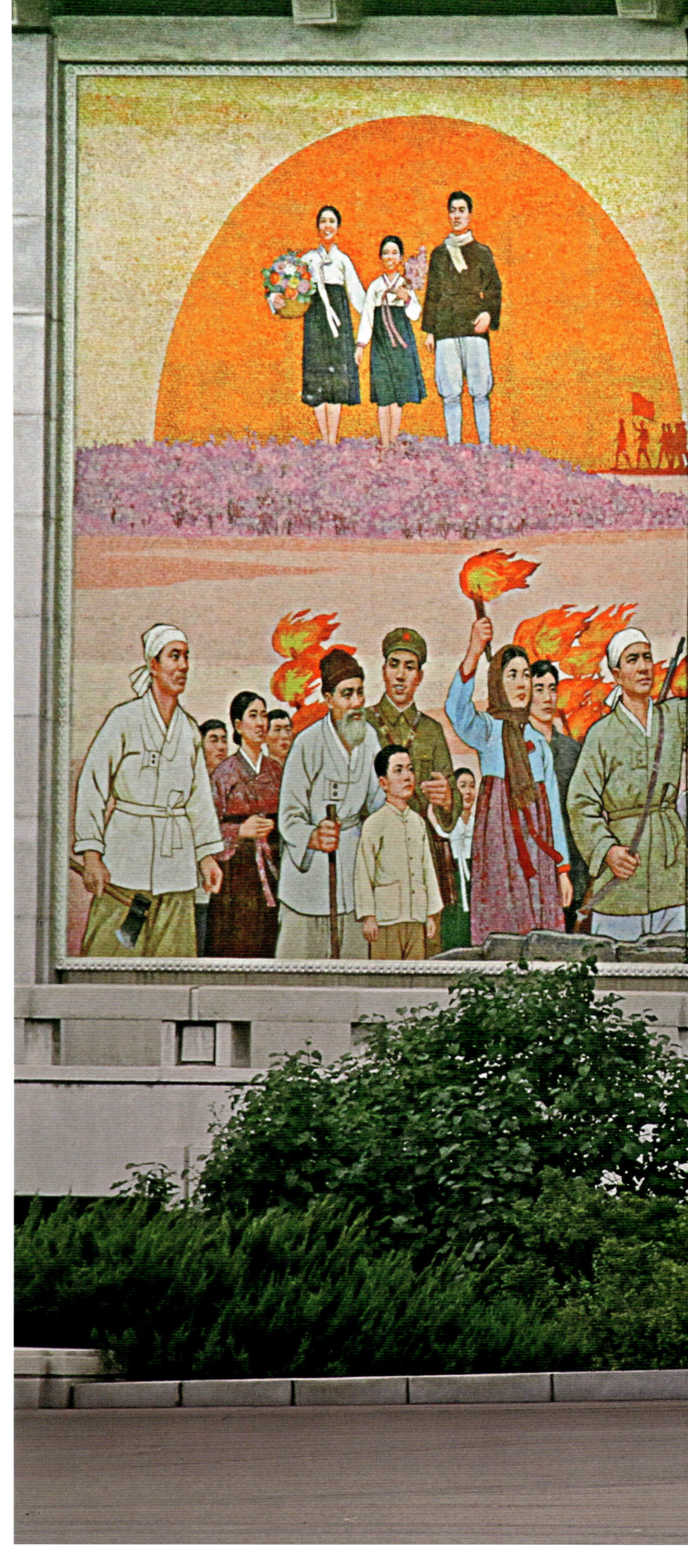

For flag and country: One of the numerous giant mosaics depicts North Korea's "Marianne," a female freedom fighter in the valiant struggle for brotherhood and equality.

Frau, Flinte, Fahne: Auf einem der unzähligen Riesenmosaike kämpft die „nordkoreanische Marianne" keusch für Brüderlichkeit und Gleichheit.

Femme, fusil et drapeau : sur l'une des innombrables mosaïques murales géantes, la chaste « Marianne nord-coréenne » lutte pour l'égalité et la fraternité.

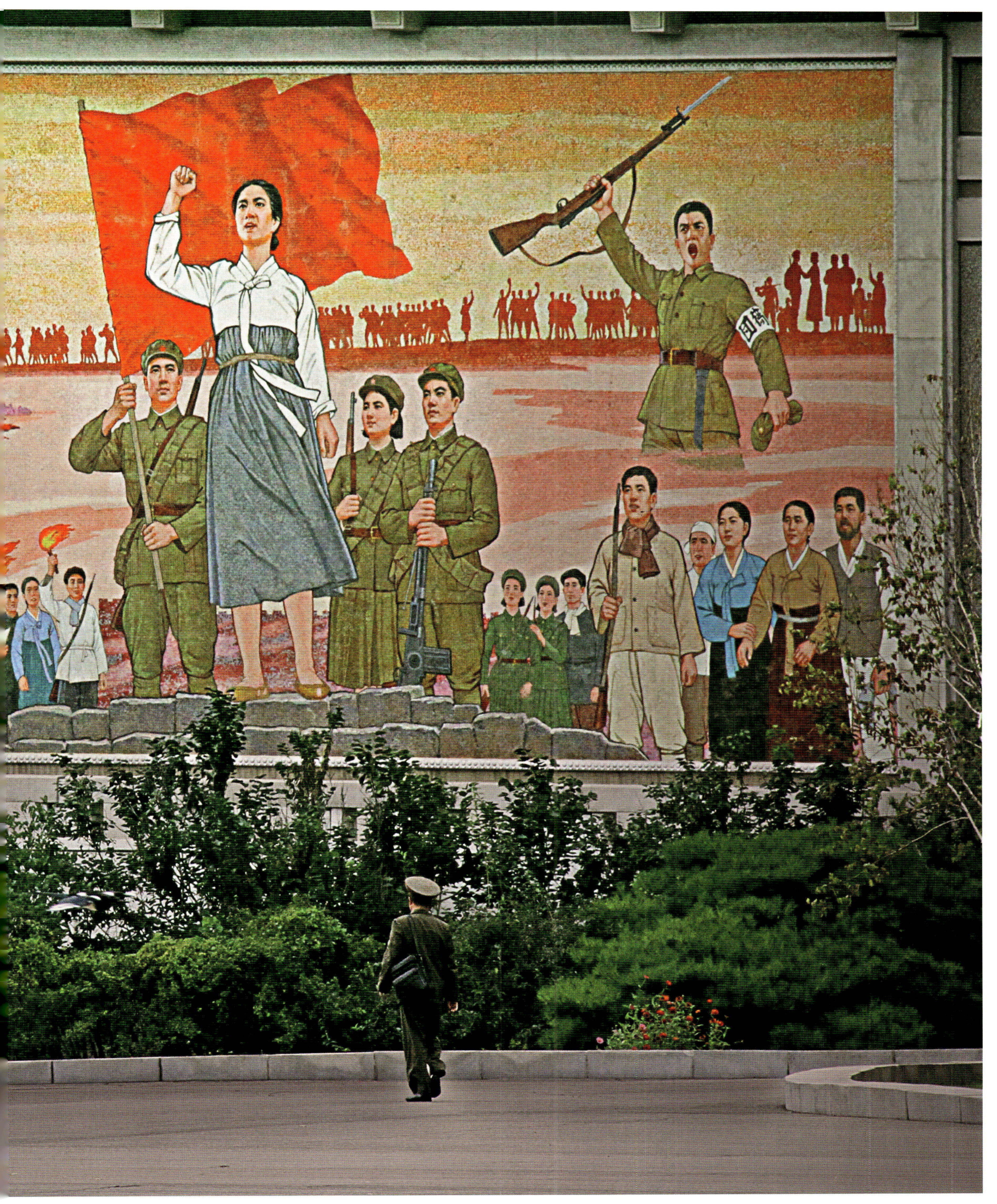

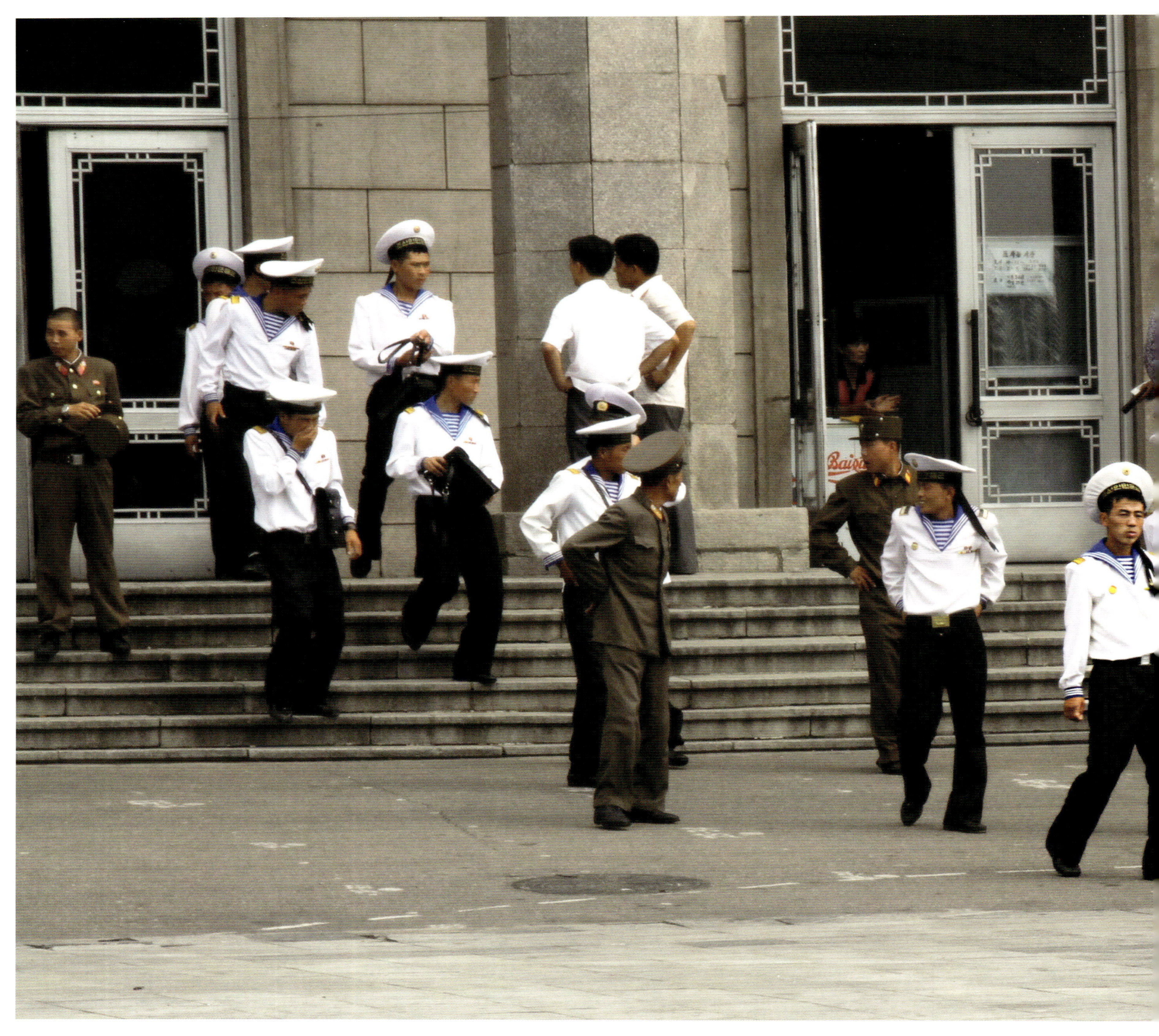

A successful gamble: It is forbidden to take pictures of soldiers. These troops are waiting to take up position in a military parade following a long march.
Hoch gepokert: Soldaten zu fotografieren ist verboten. Nach langem Fußmarsch warten sie auf ihren Einsatz in einer Militärparade.
On a risqué gros en photographiant ces soldats. Après une longue marche, ils attendent de participer à une parade militaire.

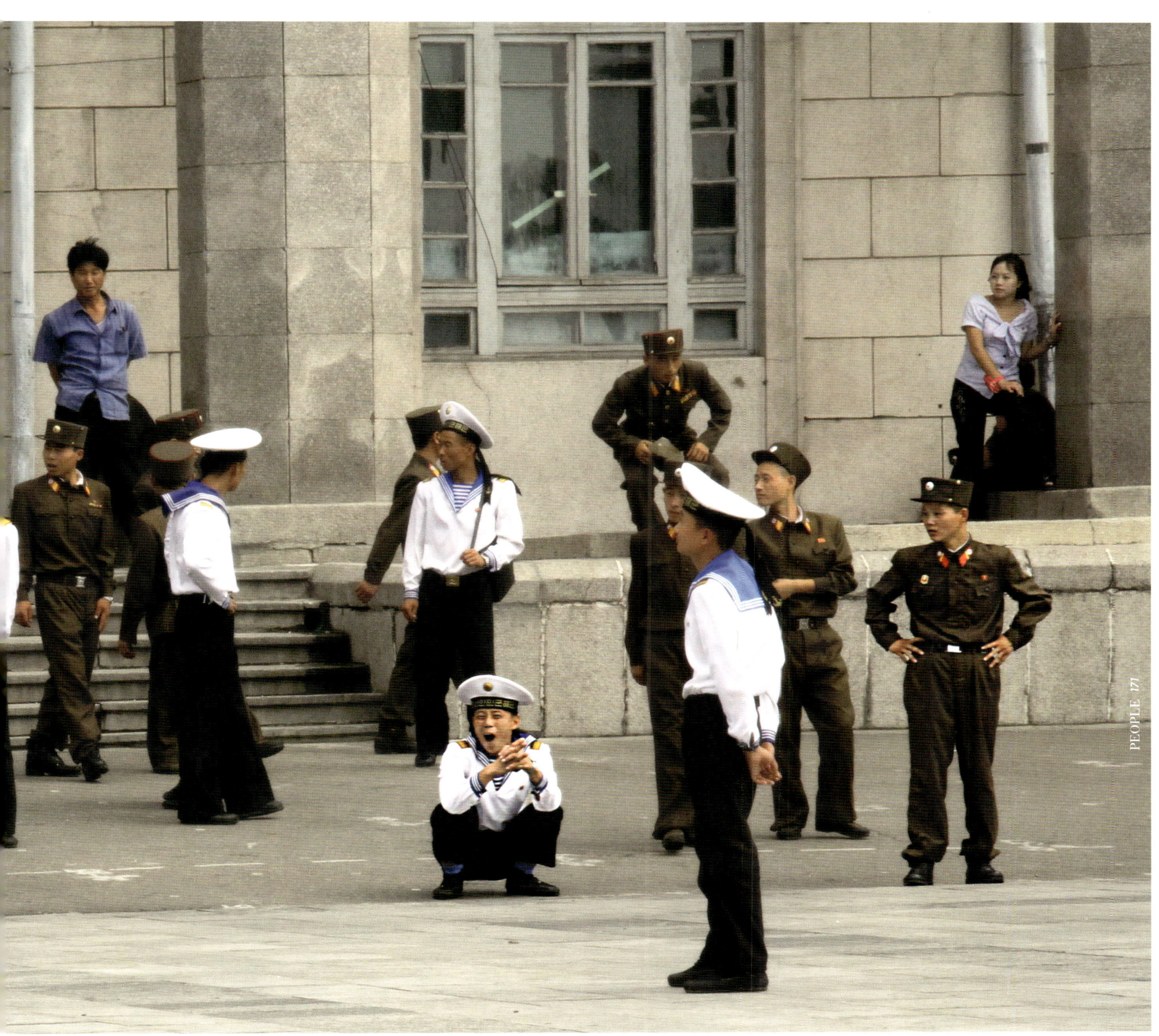

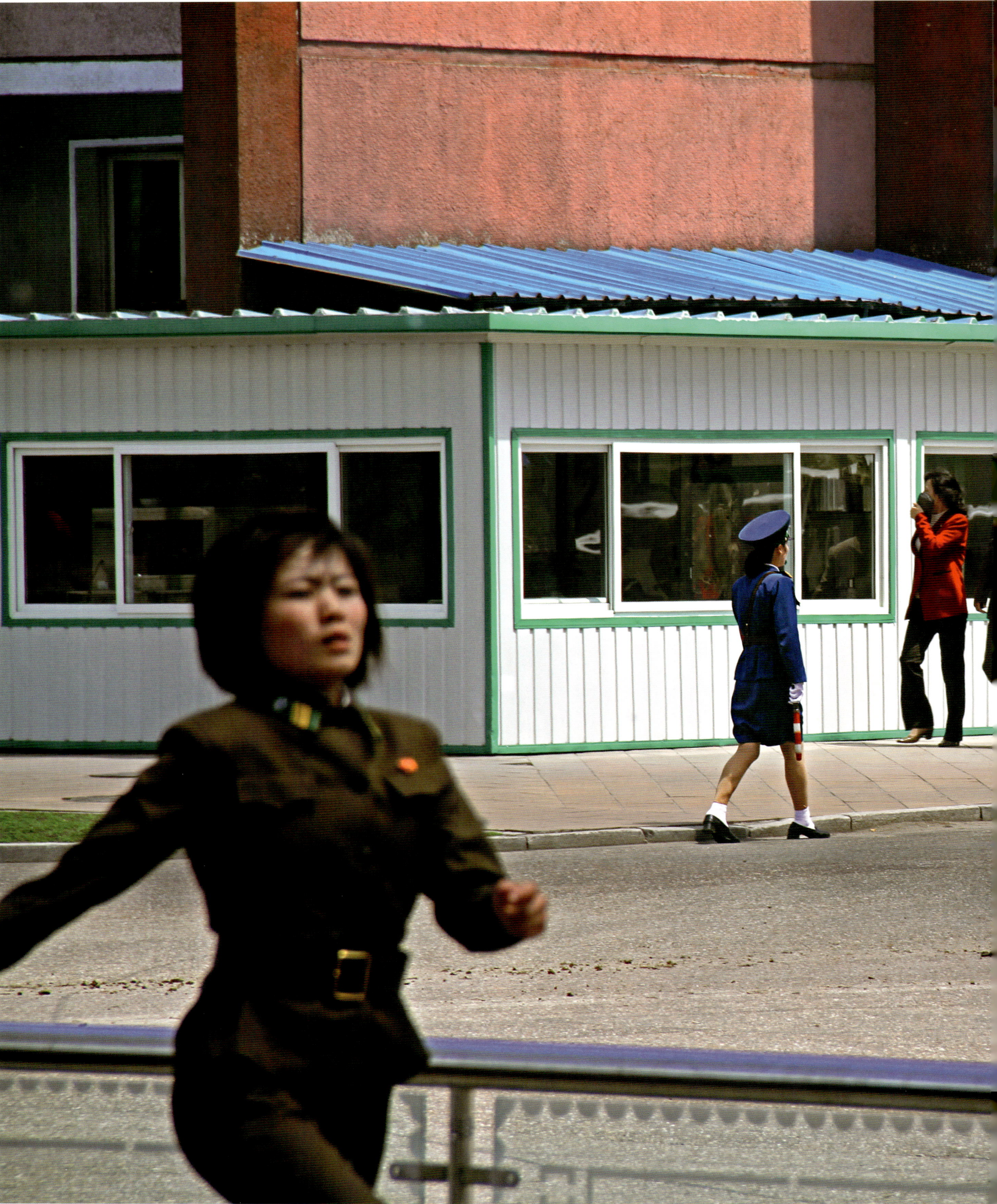

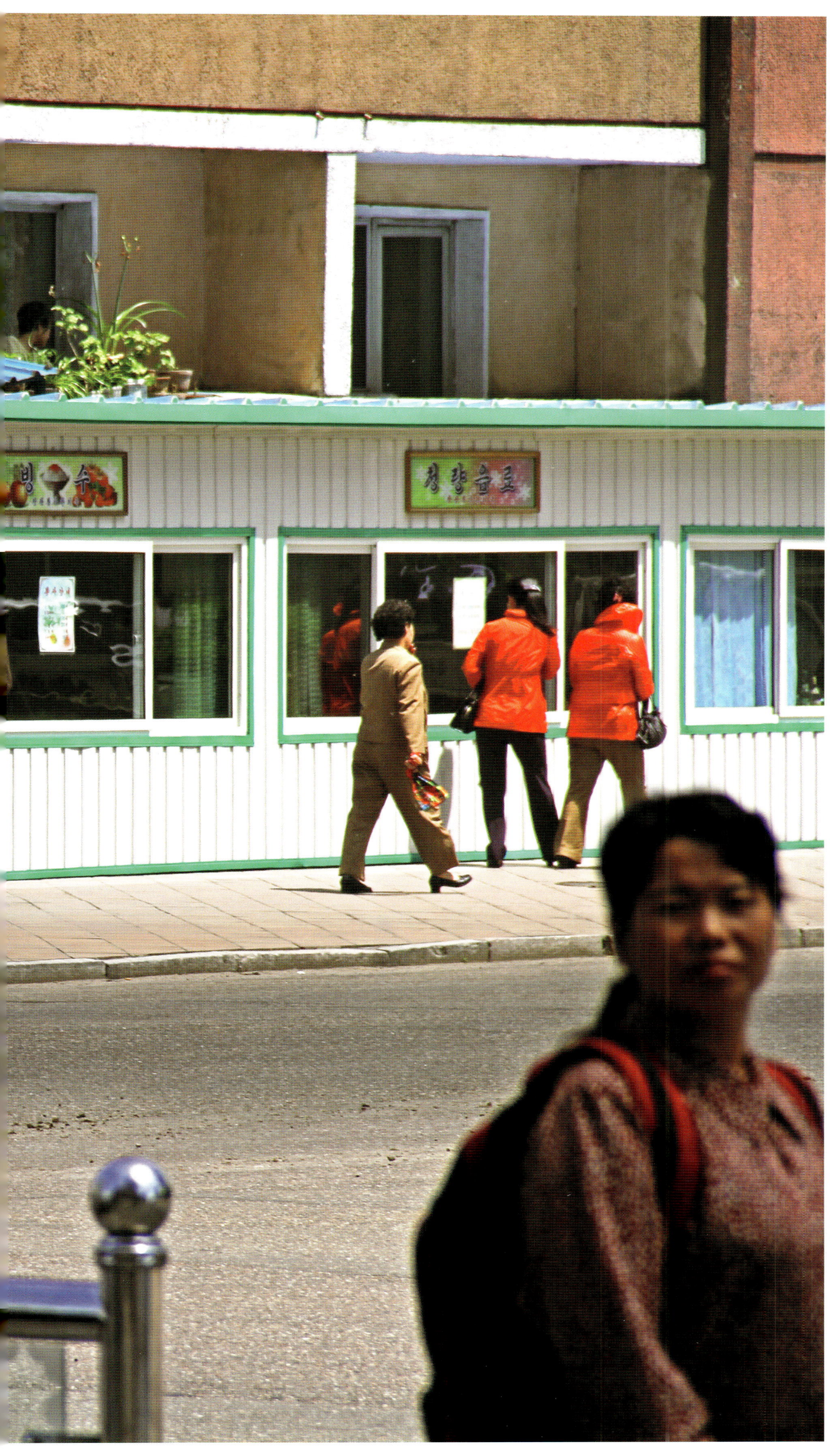

Window shopping in Pyongyang
Schaufensterbummel in Pjöngjang
Lèche-vitrines à Pyongyang

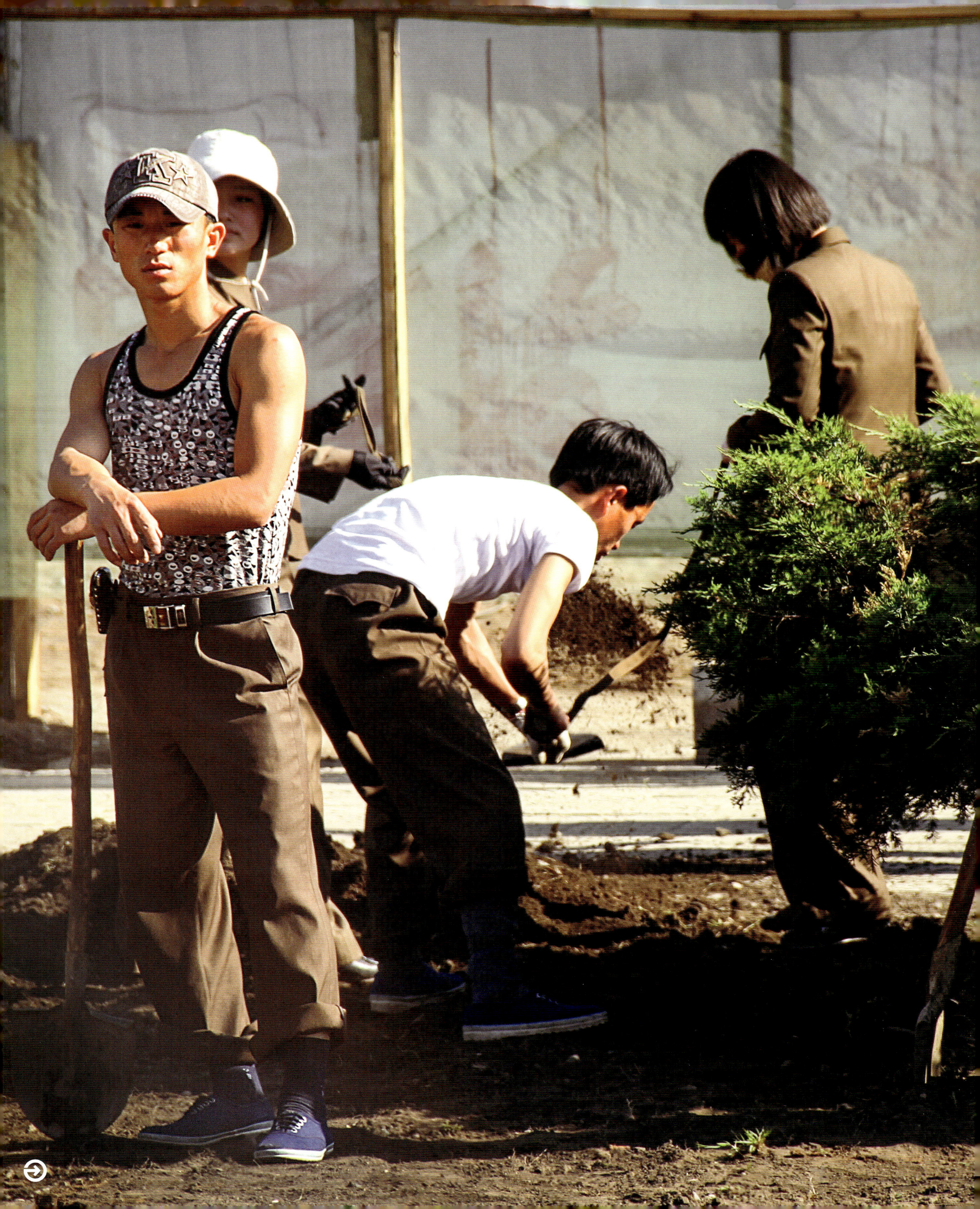

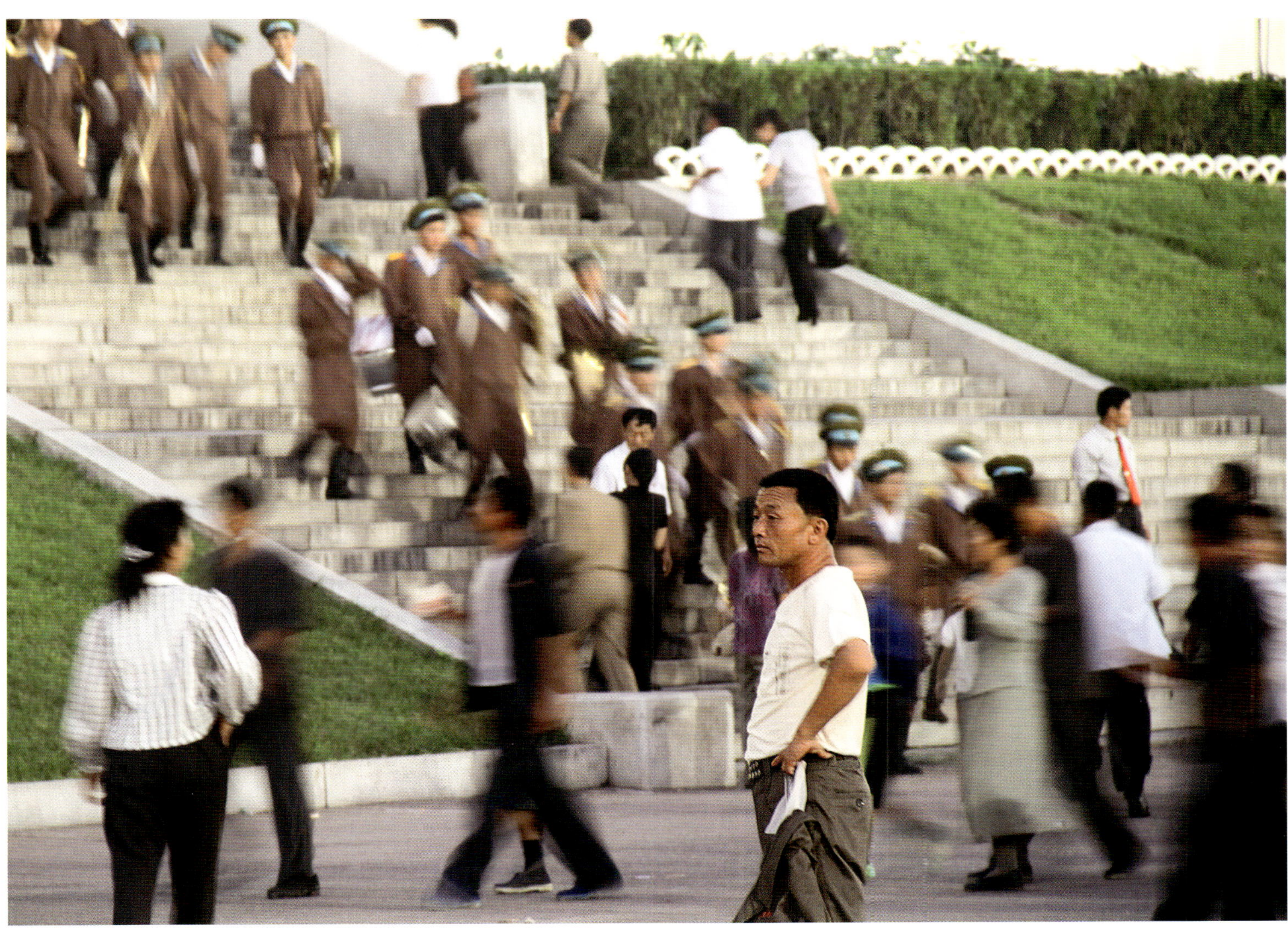

Gardeners cultivate the city's manicured look.
Gärtner sorgen für ein gepflegtes Stadtbild.
Des jardiniers veillent à donner une image soignée de la ville.

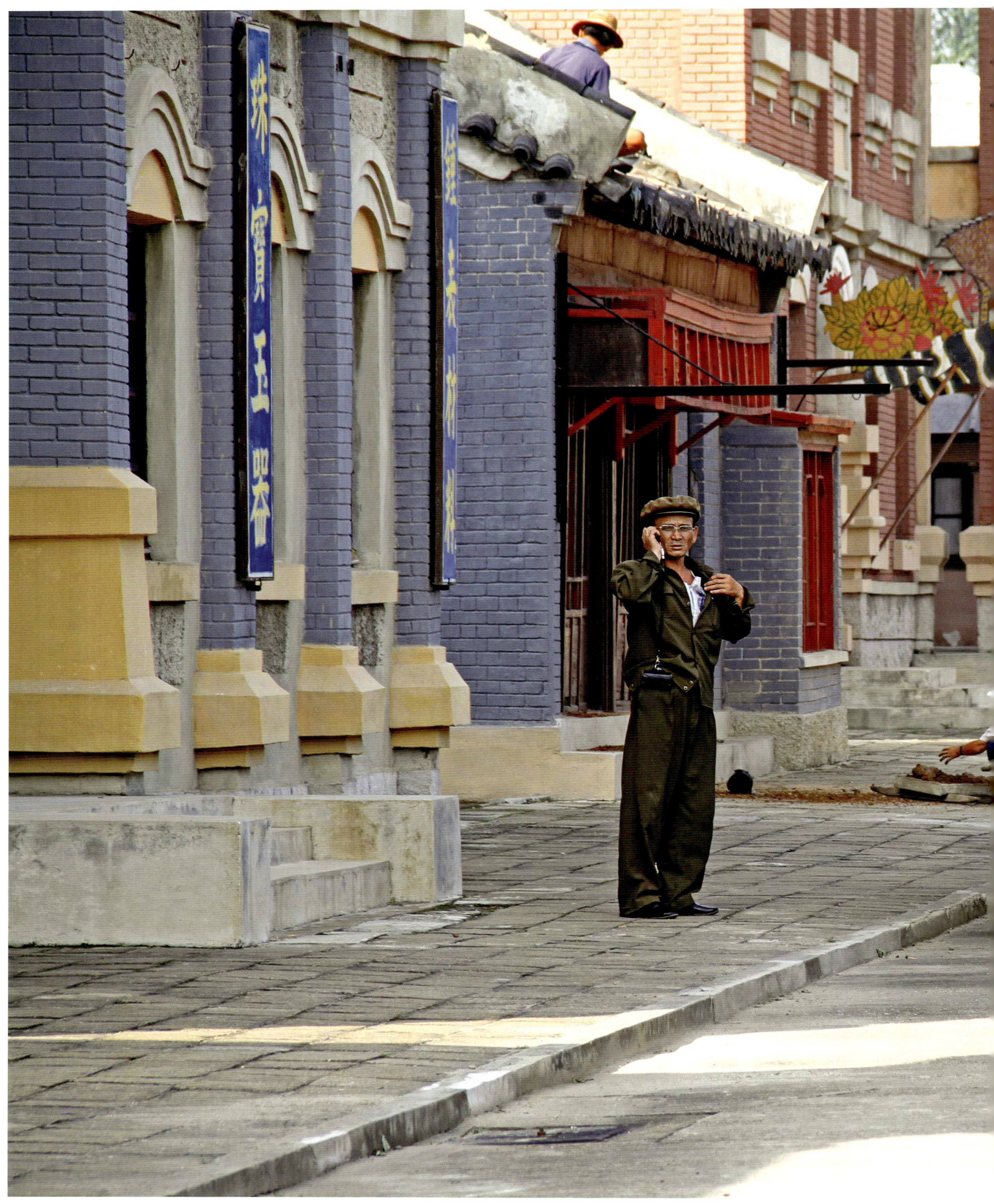
珠寶玉器

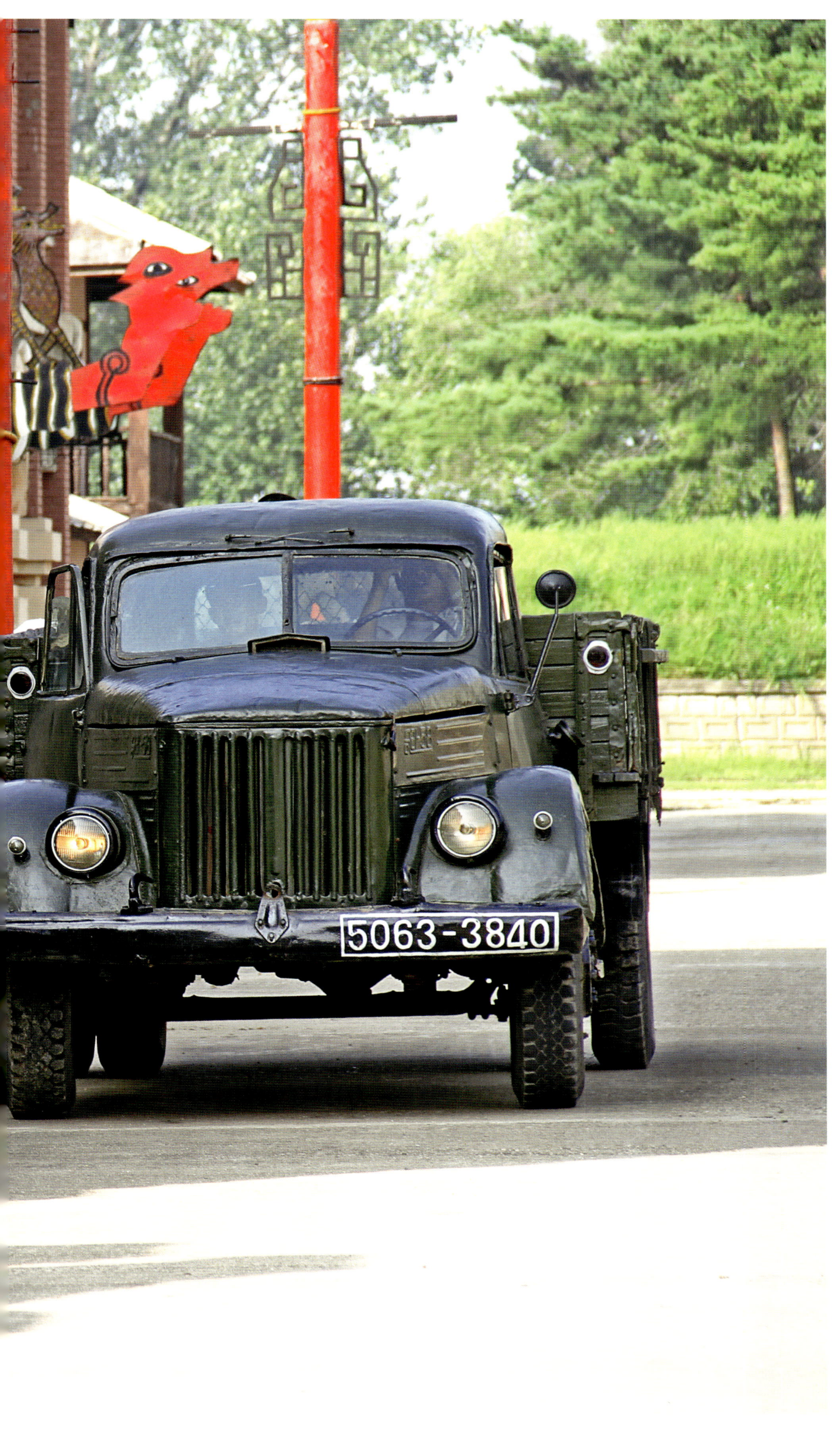

Hollywood in North Korea: Kim Jong-il was a movie buff who is said to have toured Pyongyang's film studios 10,000 times. He loved the cinema so much that he had a South Korean director abducted and forced him to shoot films in the North Korean capital. The director shot six movies here before he managed to escape.

Nordkoreas Hollywood: Der Cineast Kim Jong-il war angeblich 10 000 Mal zu Besuch in den Studios von Pjöngjang. Seine Liebe zum Film ging so weit, dass er einen südkoreanischen Regisseur entführen ließ, damit dieser Filme in der nordkoreanischen Hauptstadt dreht. Nach sechs Filmen gelang ihm schließlich die Flucht.

Hollywood à la mode nord-coréenne : le cinéphile Kim Jong-il aurait visité 10 000 fois les studios de Pyongyang. Son amour du cinéma était si fort qu'il a fait enlever un réalisateur sud-coréen pour le contraindre à tourner des films dans la capitale nord-coréenne. Au bout de six films, celui-ci a enfin réussi à s'enfuir.

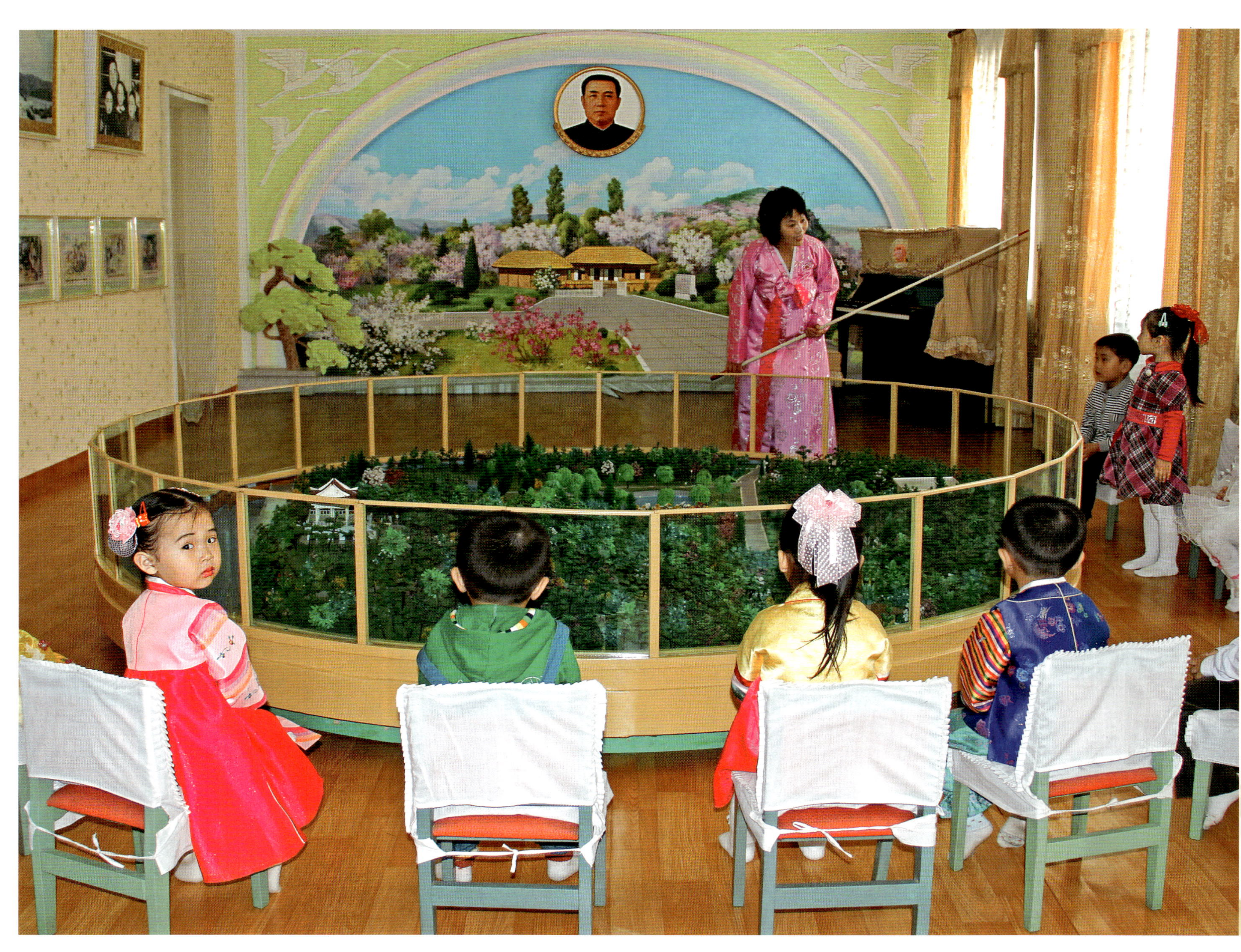

Kindergarten and elementary school in Pyongyang
Kindergarten und Grundschule in Pjöngjang
Écoles maternelle et primaire à Pyongyang

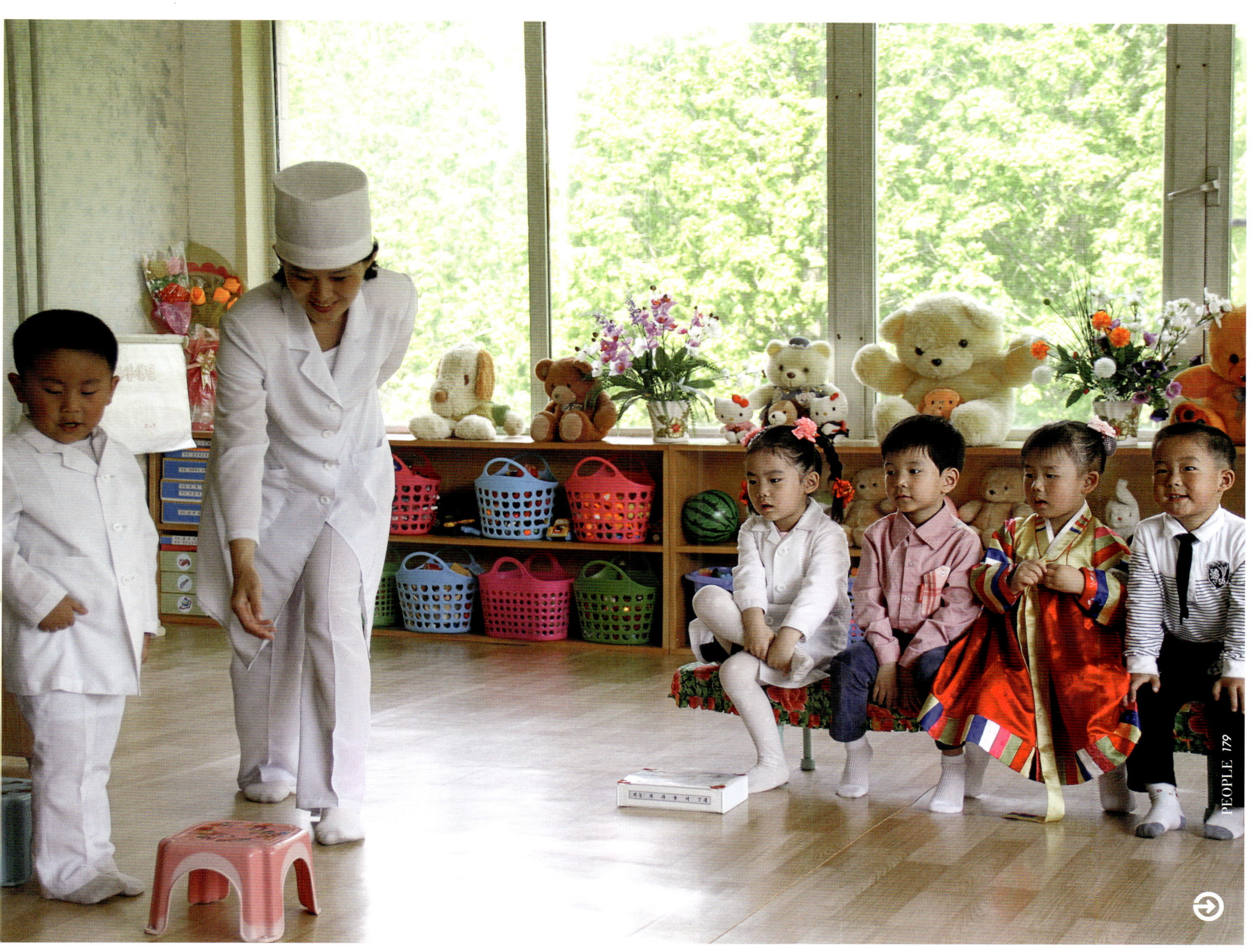

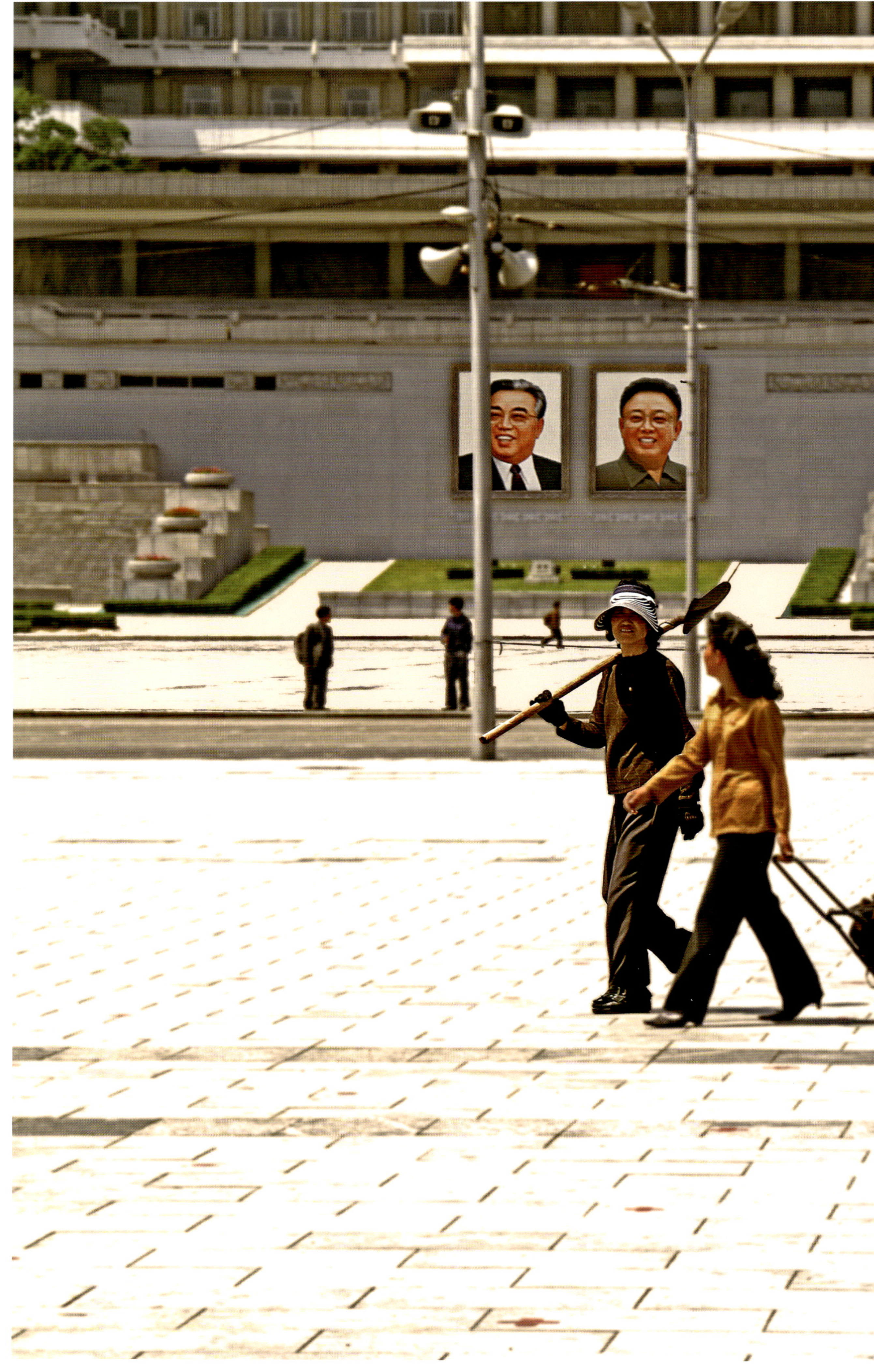

Sun umbrellas and spades. Strolling across Kim Il-sung Square in Pyongyang under the watchful gaze of the "Beloved Leaders."
Spaten und Sonnenschirm: Flanieren unter den Augen der „Geliebten Führer" auf dem Kim-Il-sung-Platz in der Hauptstadt.
Quand les personnages à la bêche et à l'ombrelle flânent sous les yeux des « chers dirigeants » sur la place Kim Il-sung, à Pyongyang.

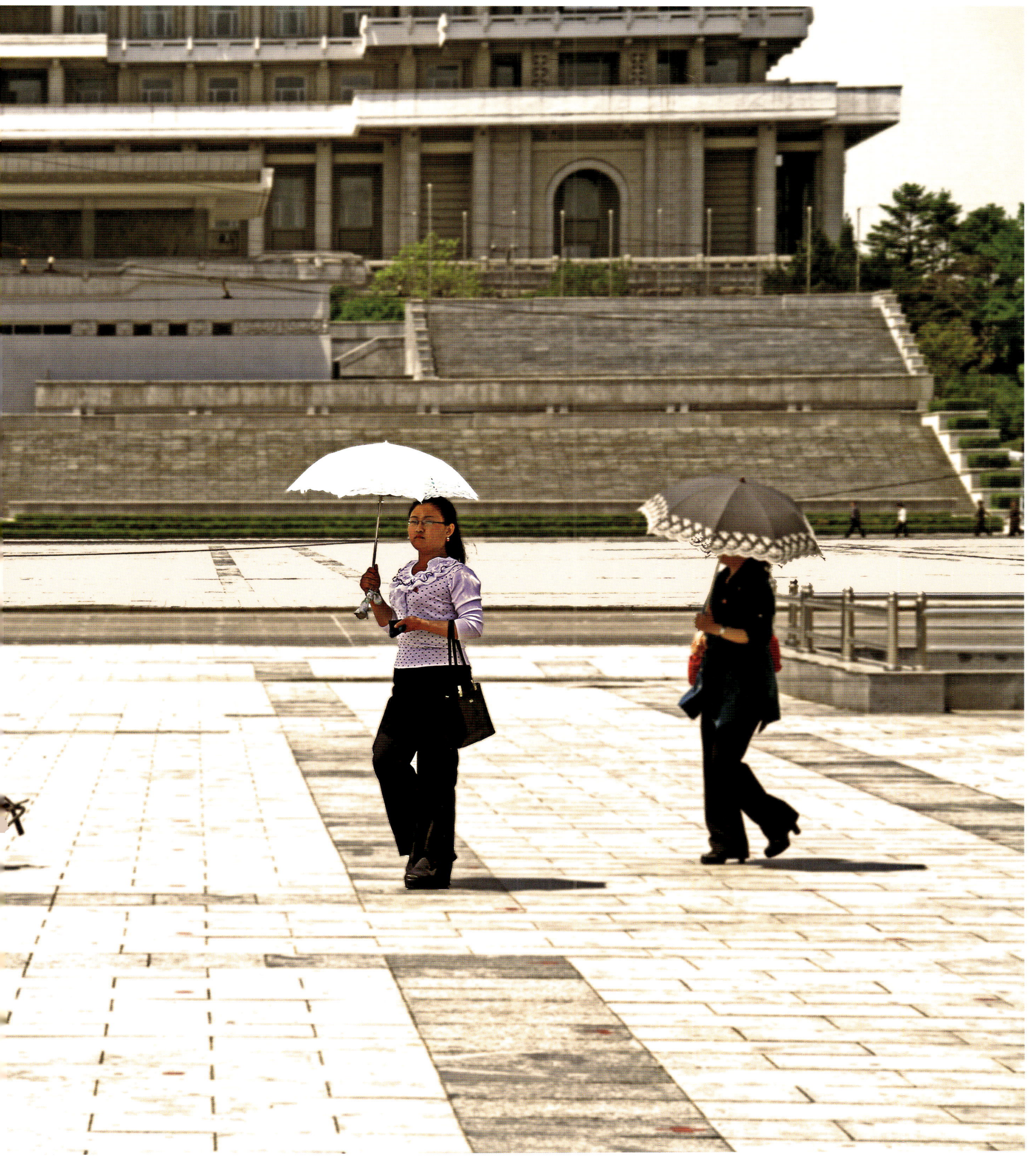

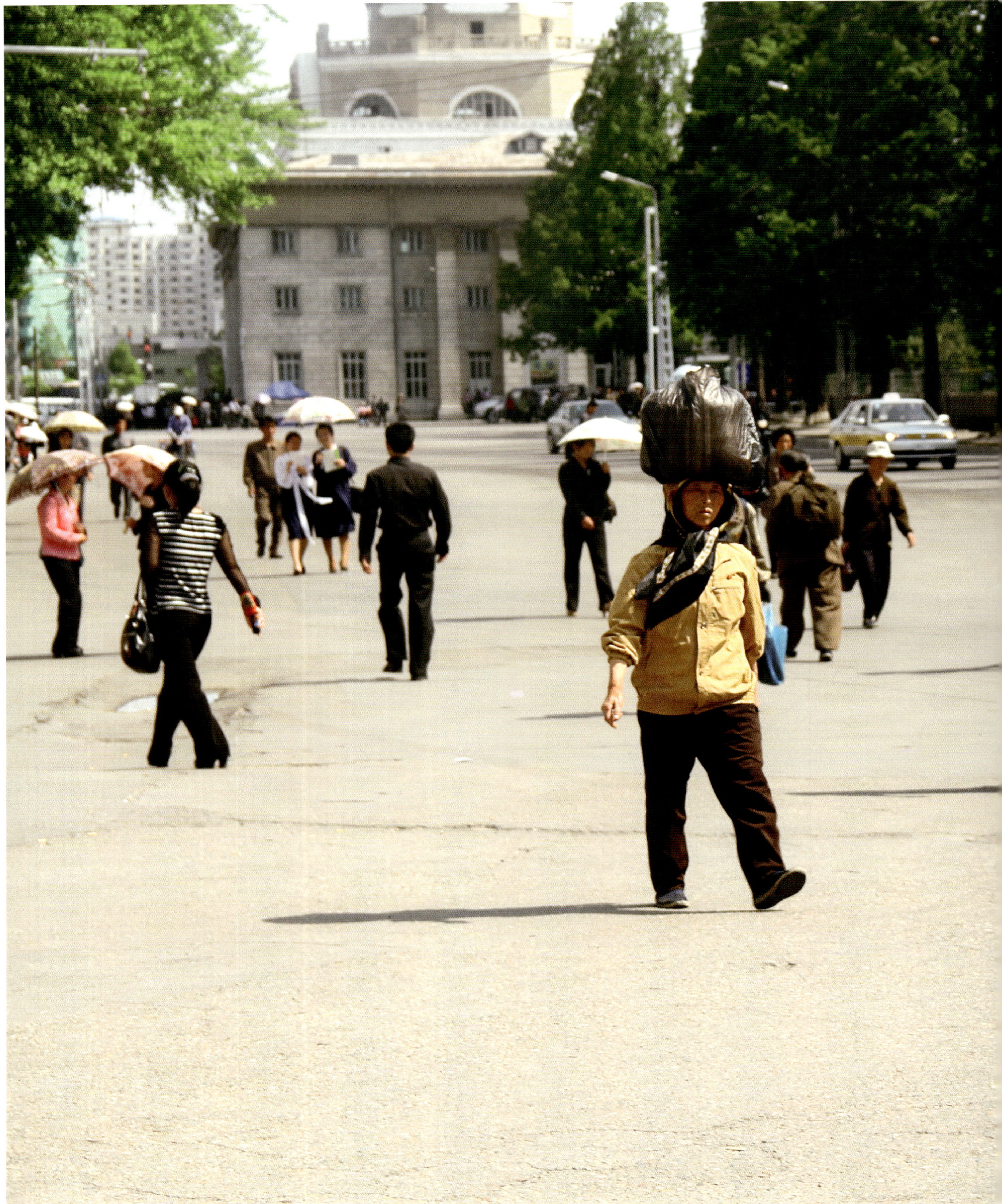

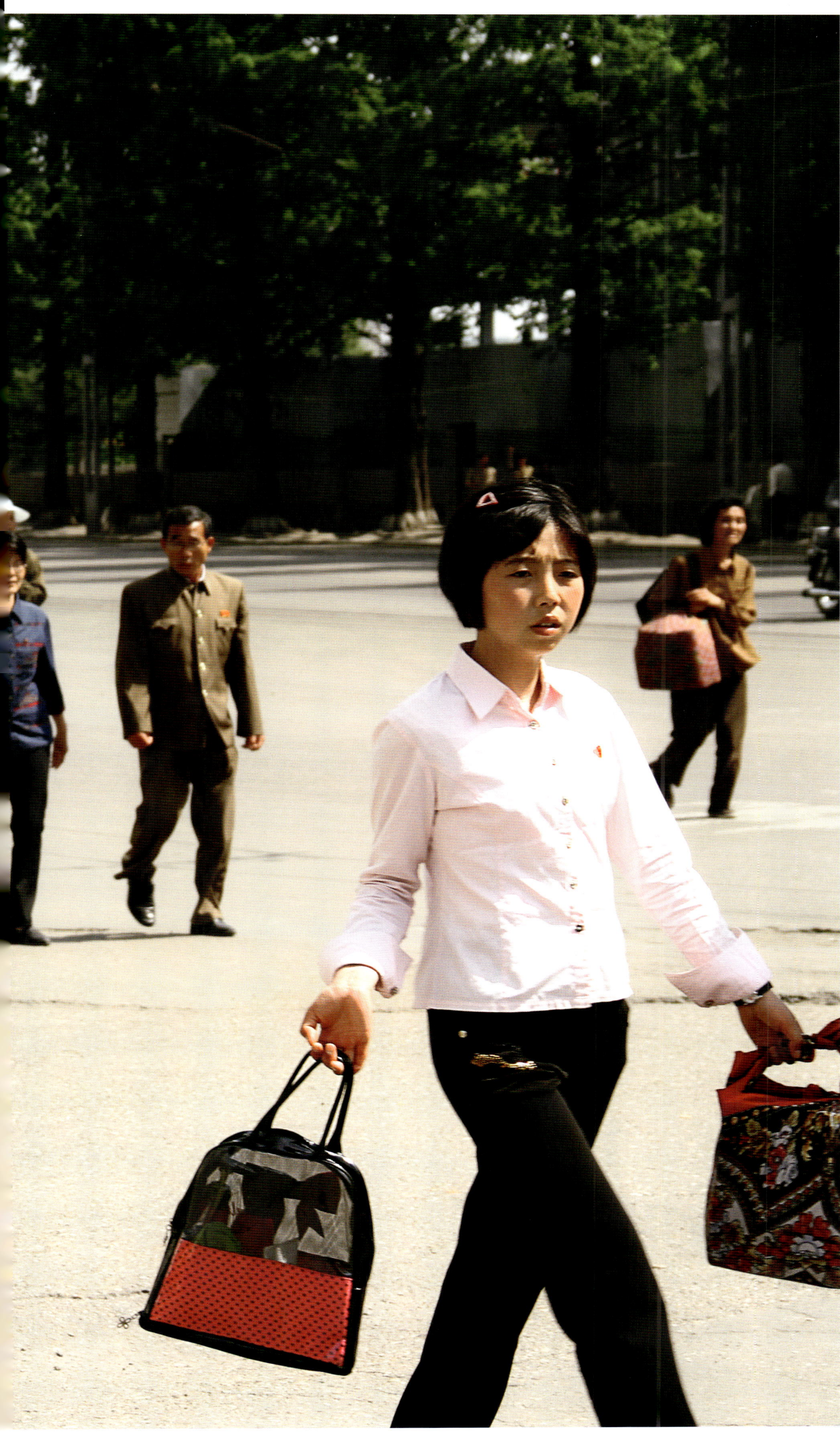

Going to work in Pyongyang
Auf dem Weg zur Arbeit in Pjöngjang
Habitants se rendant à leur travail à Pyongyang

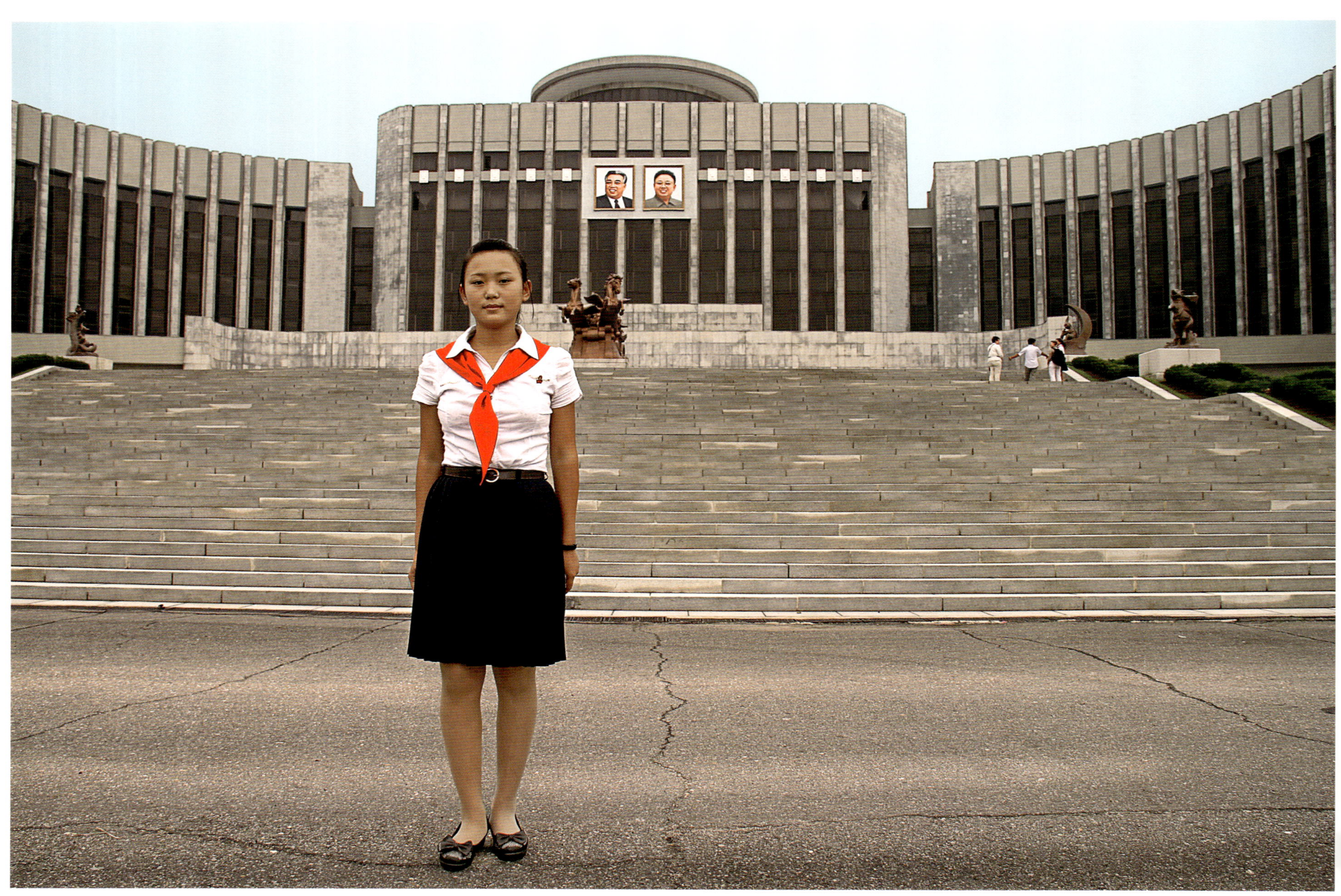

Girl in front of the Children's Palace in Pyongyang
Mädchen vor dem Kinderpalast in Pjöngjang
Jeune fille devant le Palais des enfants, à Pyongyang

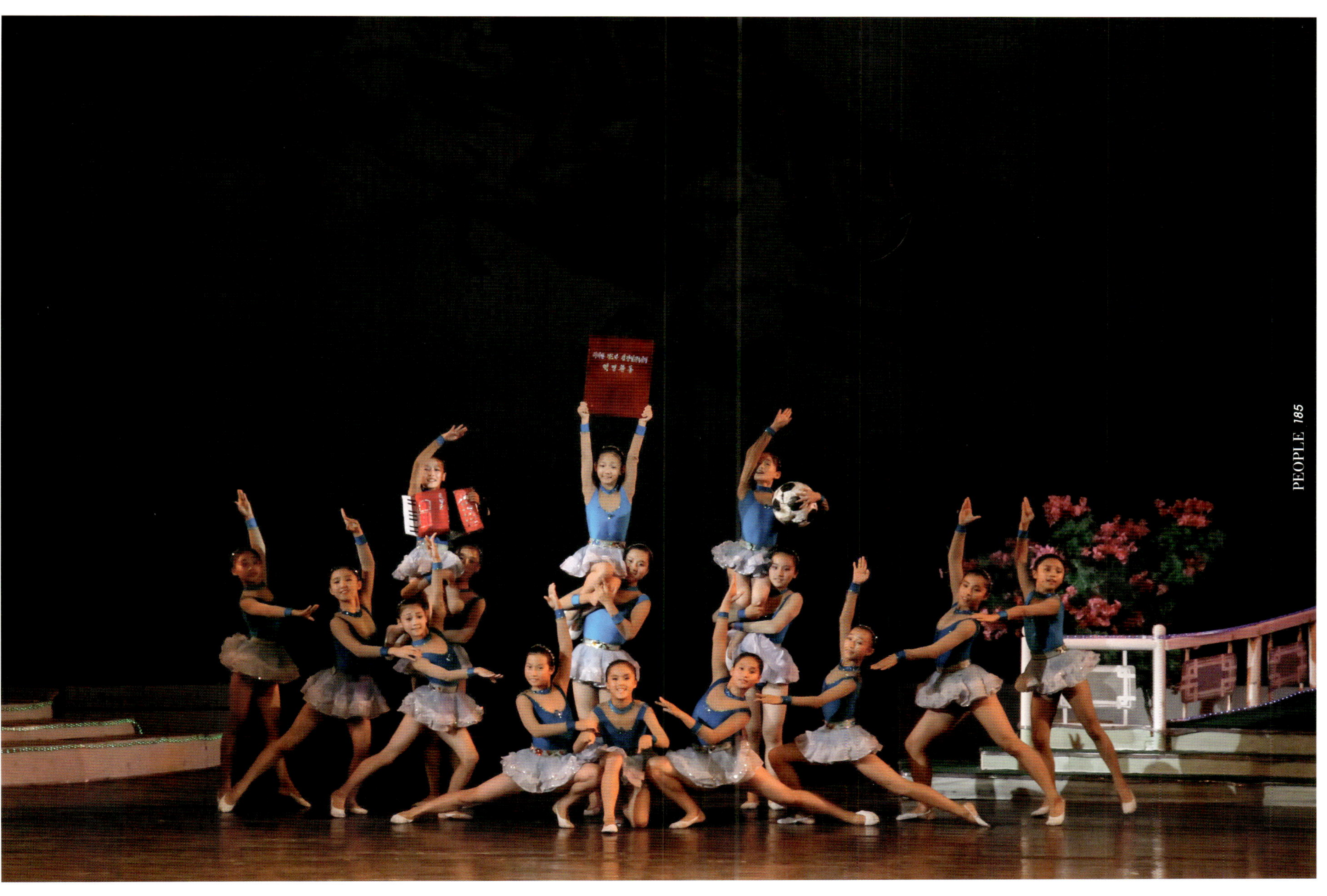

After school, ten thousand children come here to take classes in dancing, singing, calligraphy, embroidery, and similar subjects.
Nach Schulschluss werden hier 10 000 Kinder unter anderem in Tanz, Gesang, Kalligrafie und Sticken unterrichtet.
Après l'école, 10 000 enfants viennent y apprendre notamment la danse, le chant, la calligraphie et la broderie.

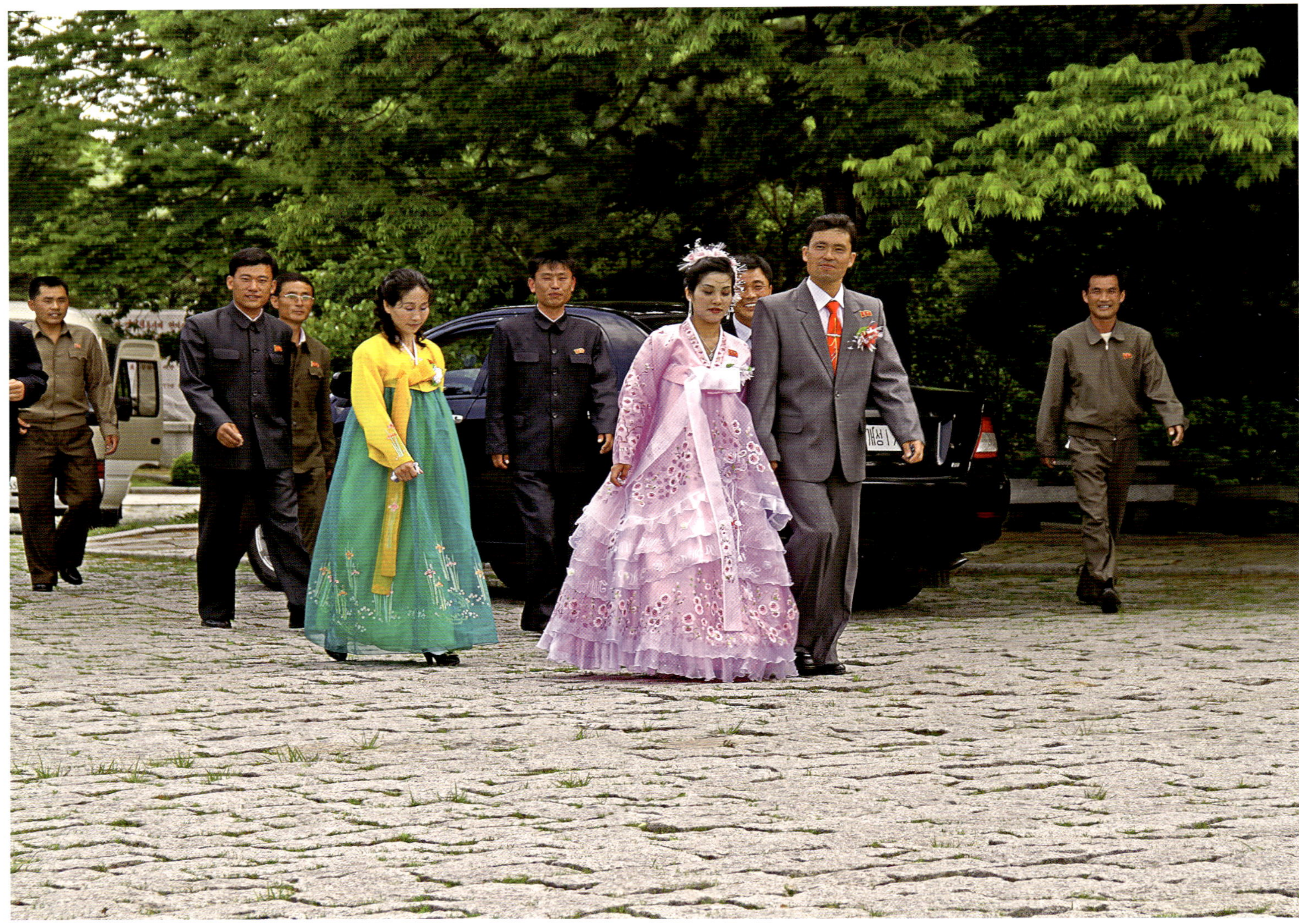

Left: A rare sight: a bride wearing a traditional dress in the seaport of Nampho
Right: View from the enormous West Sea Barrage, a symbol of progress
Links: Seltene Begegnung: Braut in typischer Tracht in der Hafenstadt Nampho
Rechts: Großer Fortschritt: Aussicht vom enormen Westmeerstaudamm
À gauche : Scène rare, une mariée en costume traditionnel dans la ville portuaire de Nampho
À droite : Vue depuis le colossal barrage de la mer Jaune, symbole du progrès technique

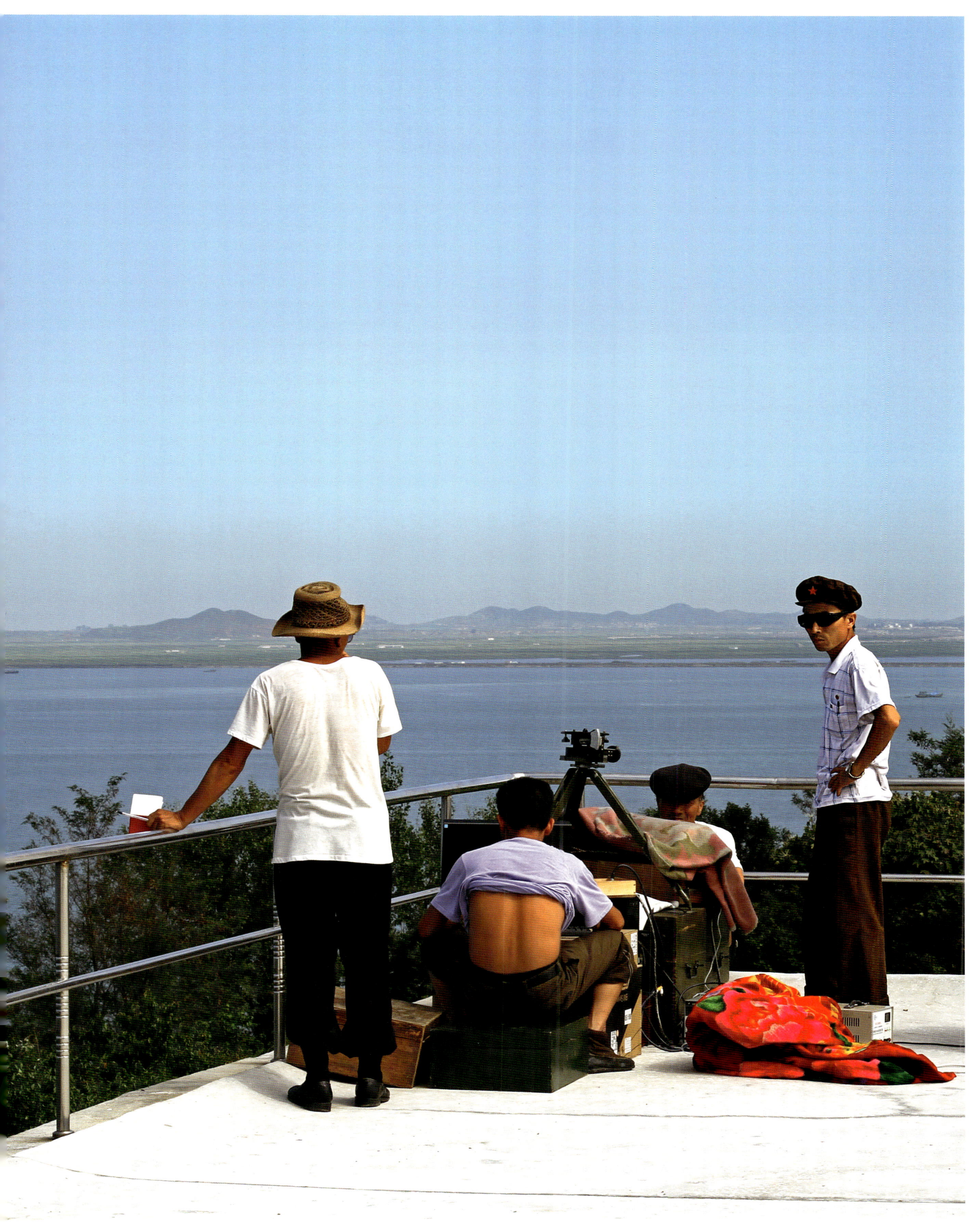

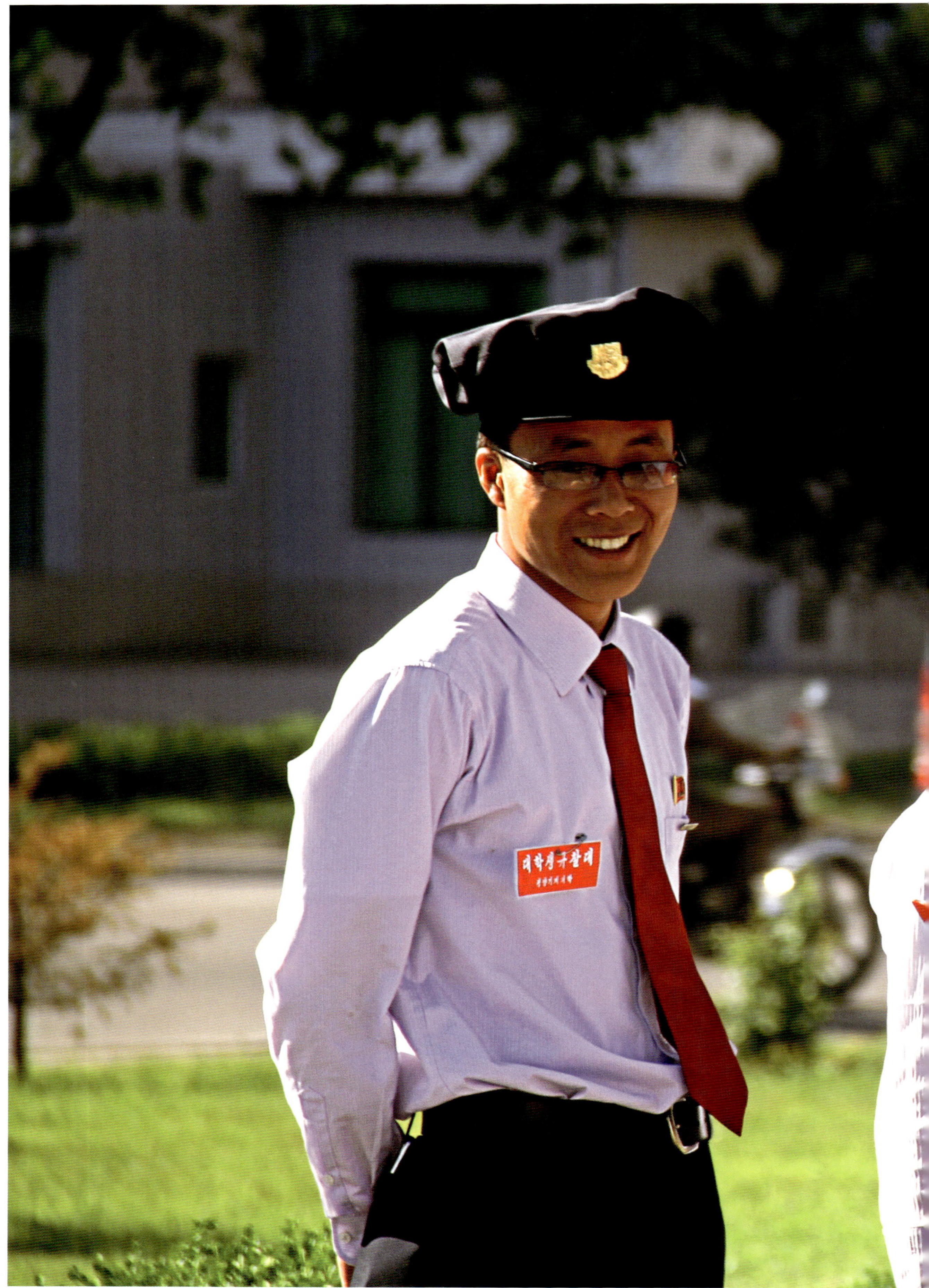

Neckties, bow ties, and other Western accessories are rare commodities.
Seltenheitswert: Schlips, Fliege und ähnliche Accessoires westlicher Kultur sieht man kaum.
Cravates, nœuds papillon et autres accessoires de la culture occidentale ne courent pas les rues.

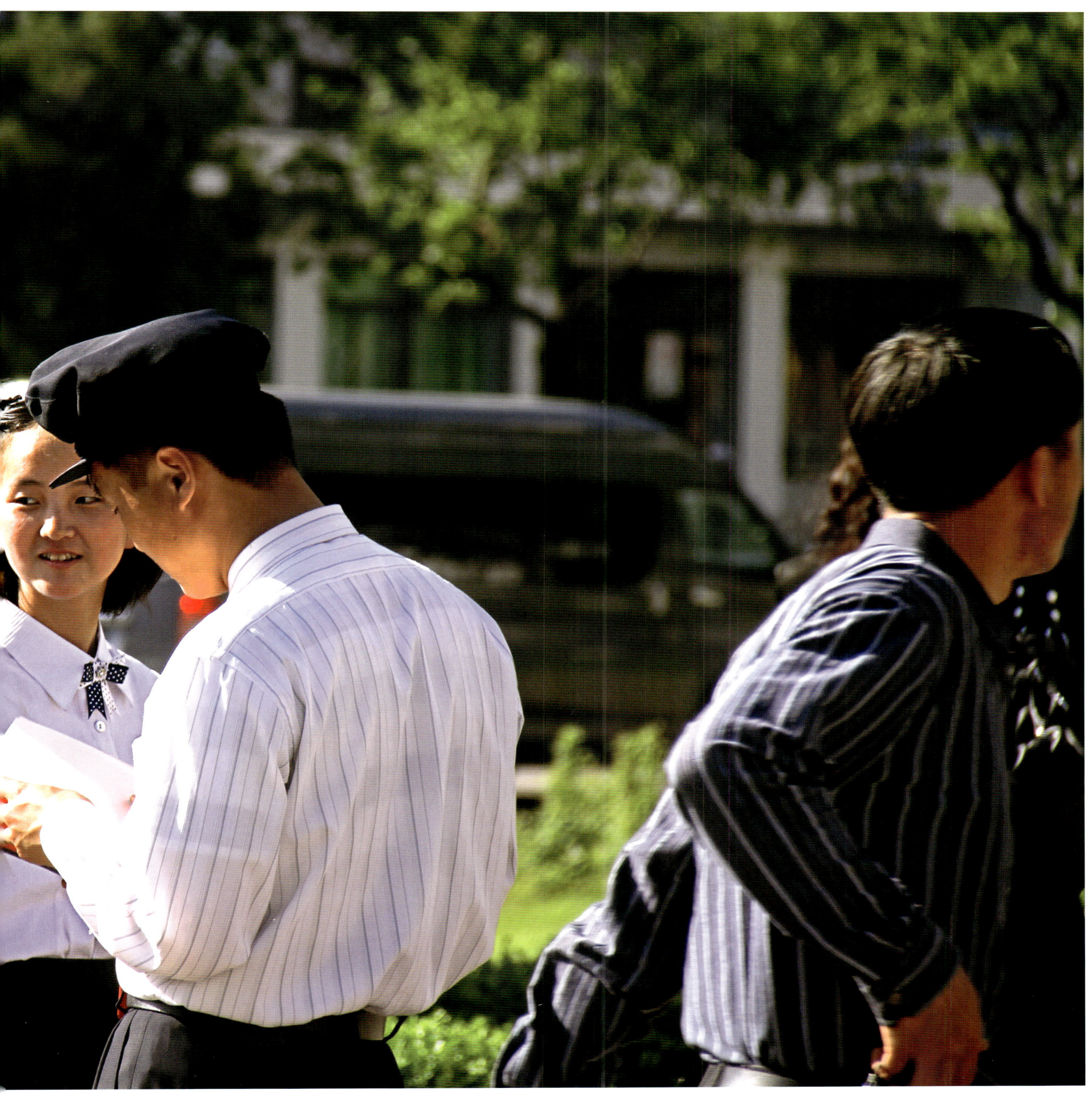

PROVINCES

PROVINZ
PROVINCE

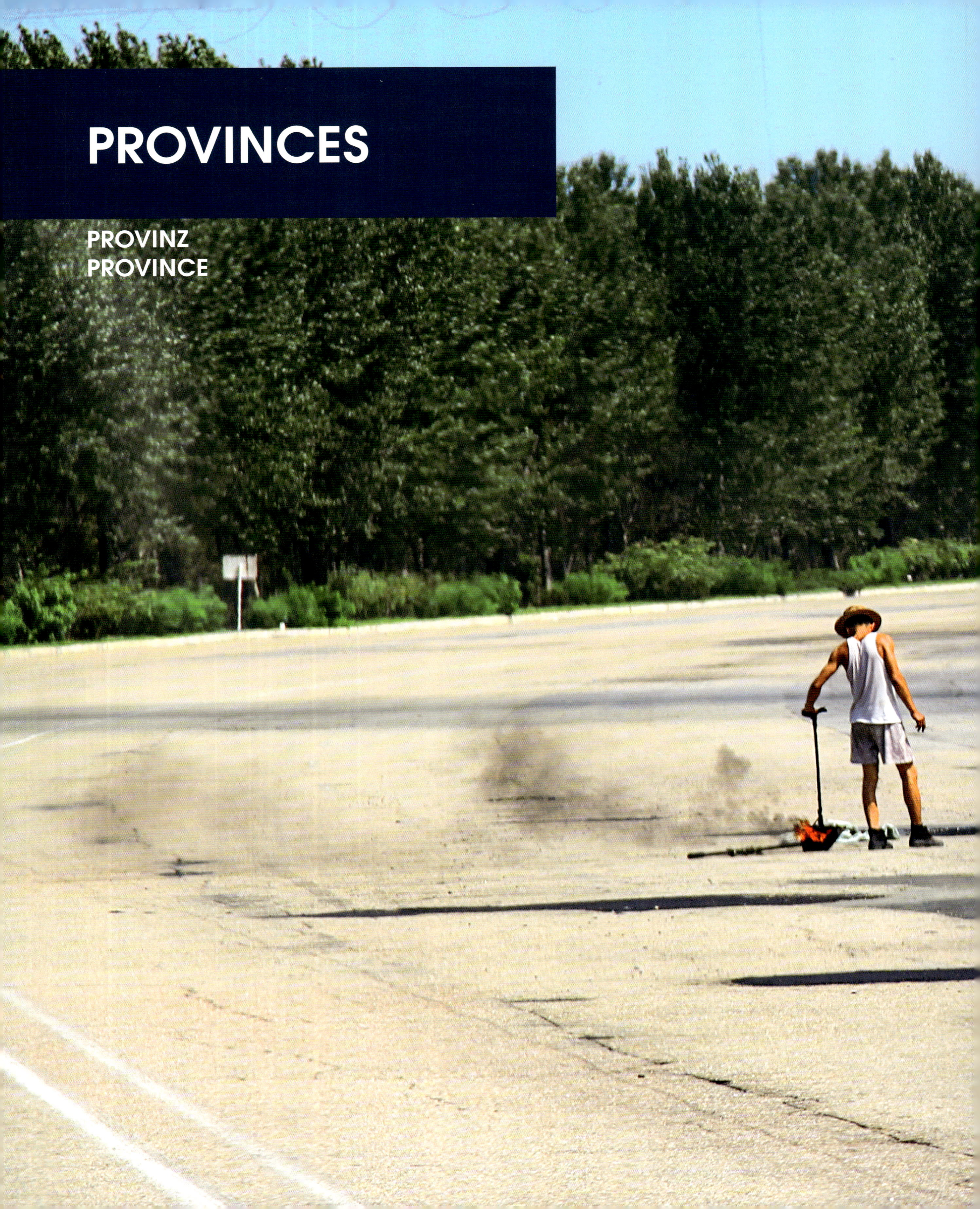

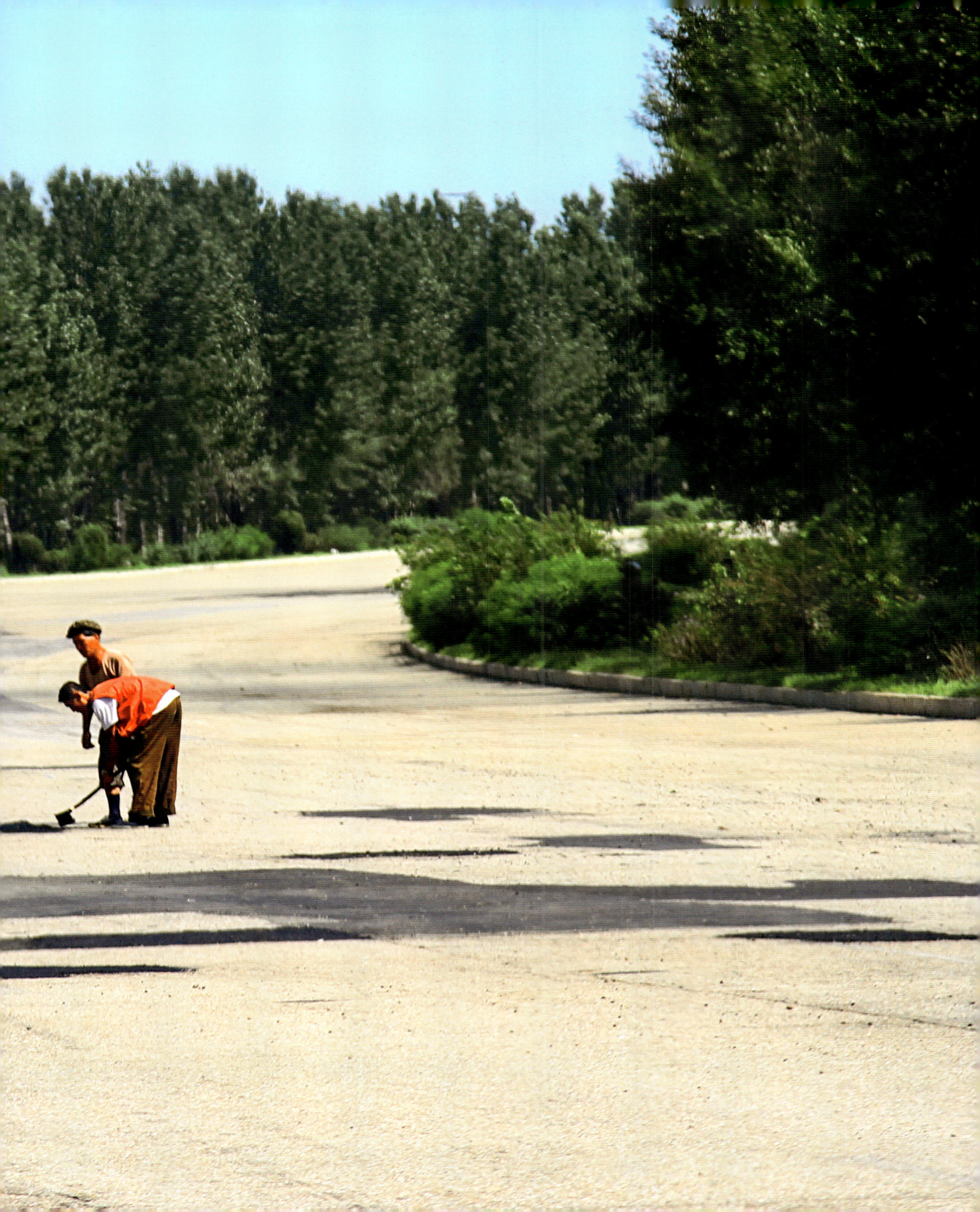

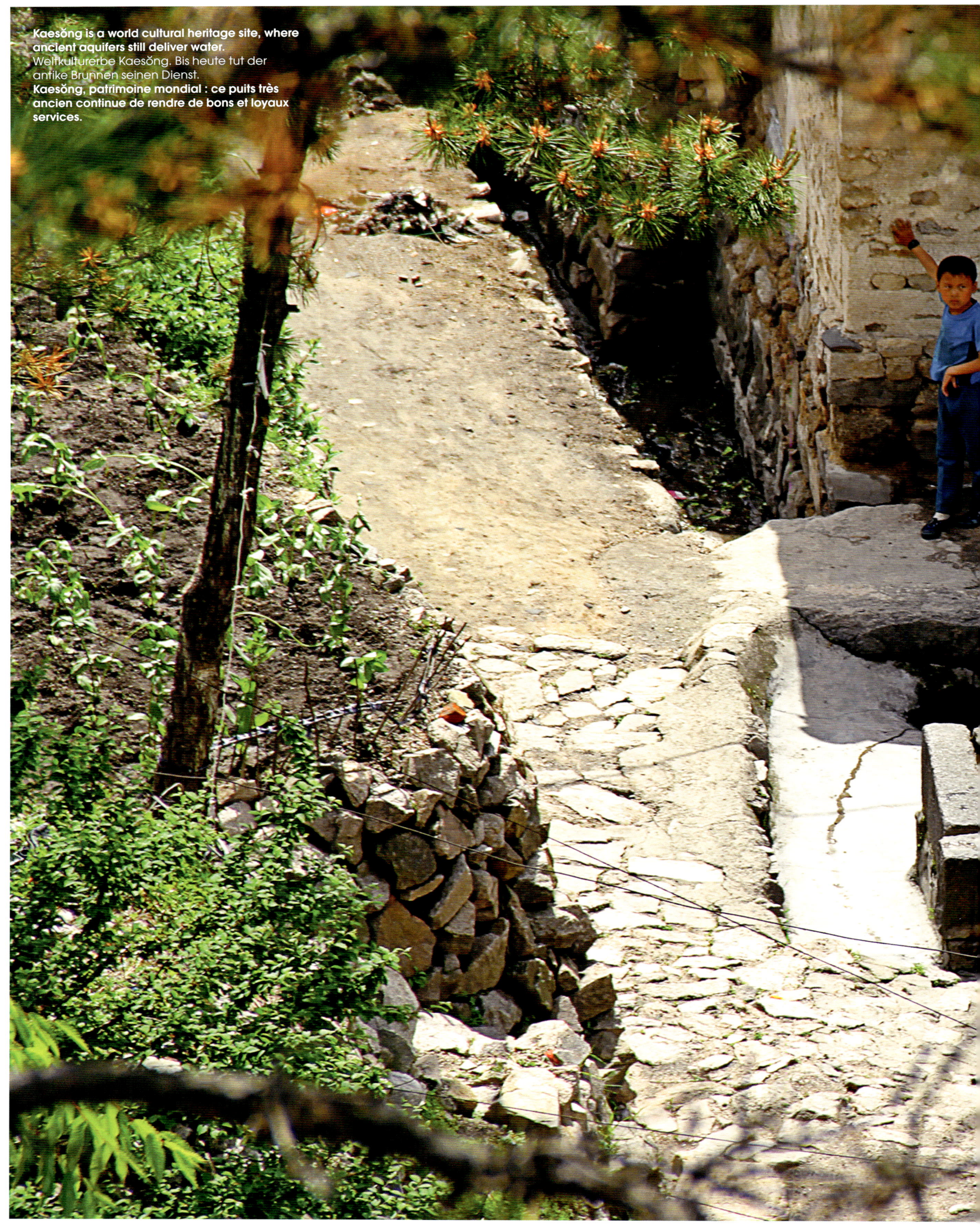

Kaesŏng is a world cultural heritage site, where ancient aquifers still deliver water.
Weltkulturerbe Kaesŏng. Bis heute tut der antike Brunnen seinen Dienst.
Kaesŏng, patrimoine mondial : ce puits très ancien continue de rendre de bons et loyaux services.

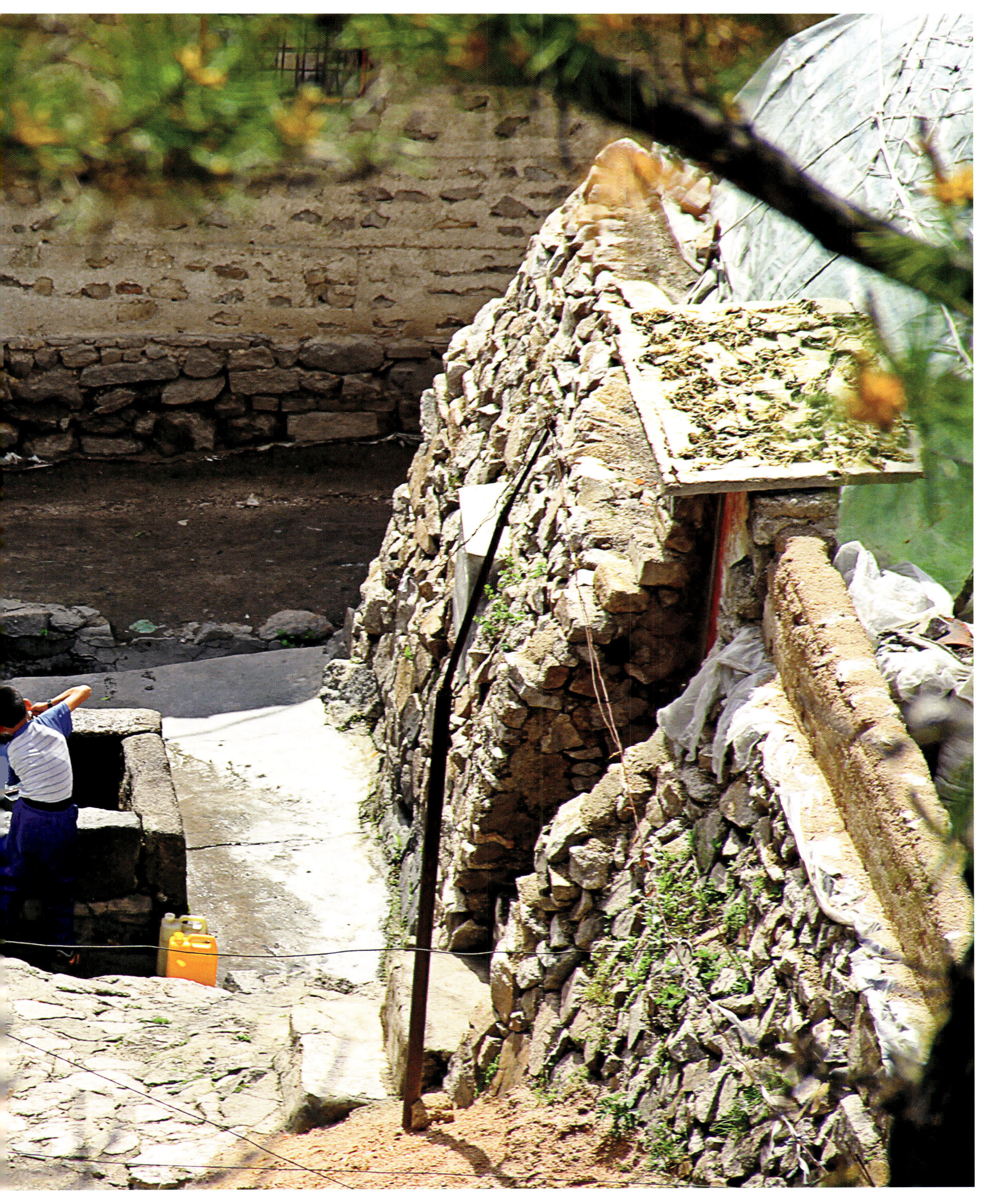

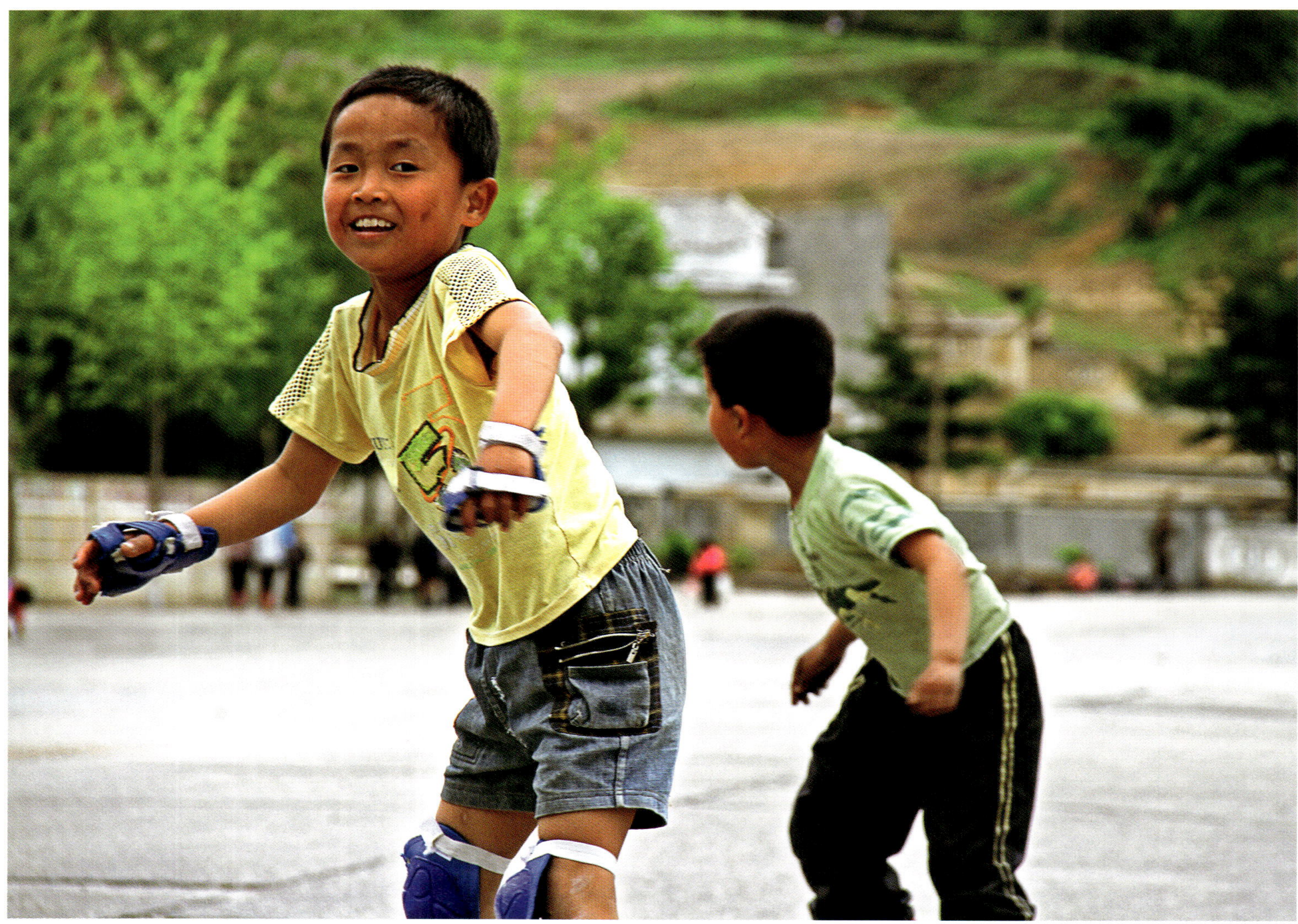

North Hwanghae Province: Inline skating is North Korea's latest trend.
Hwanghae-pukto-Provinz: Inlineskating ist der neueste Trend in Nordkorea.
Province du Hwanghae du Nord : les rollers font fureur en Corée du Nord.

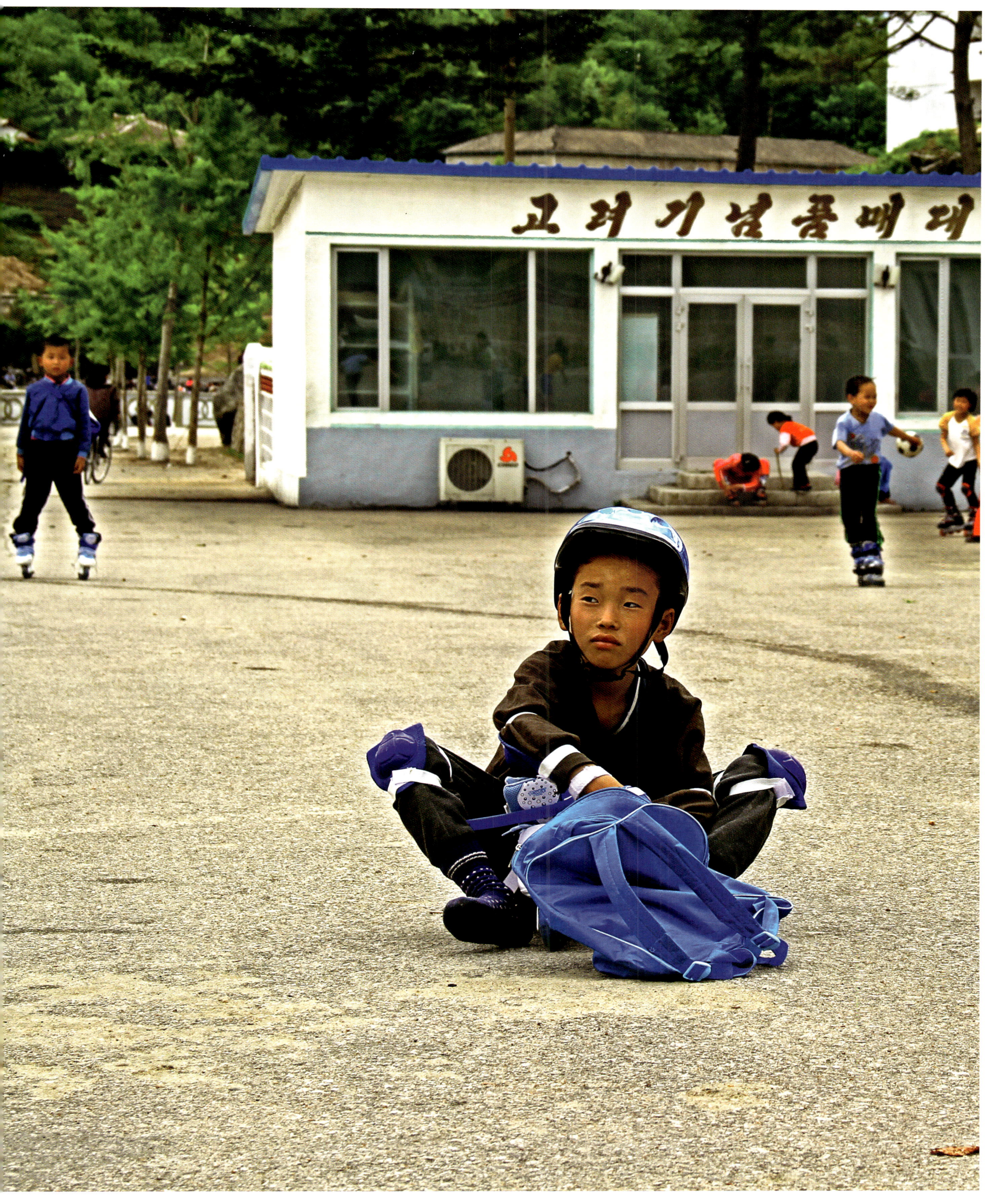
고려기념품매대

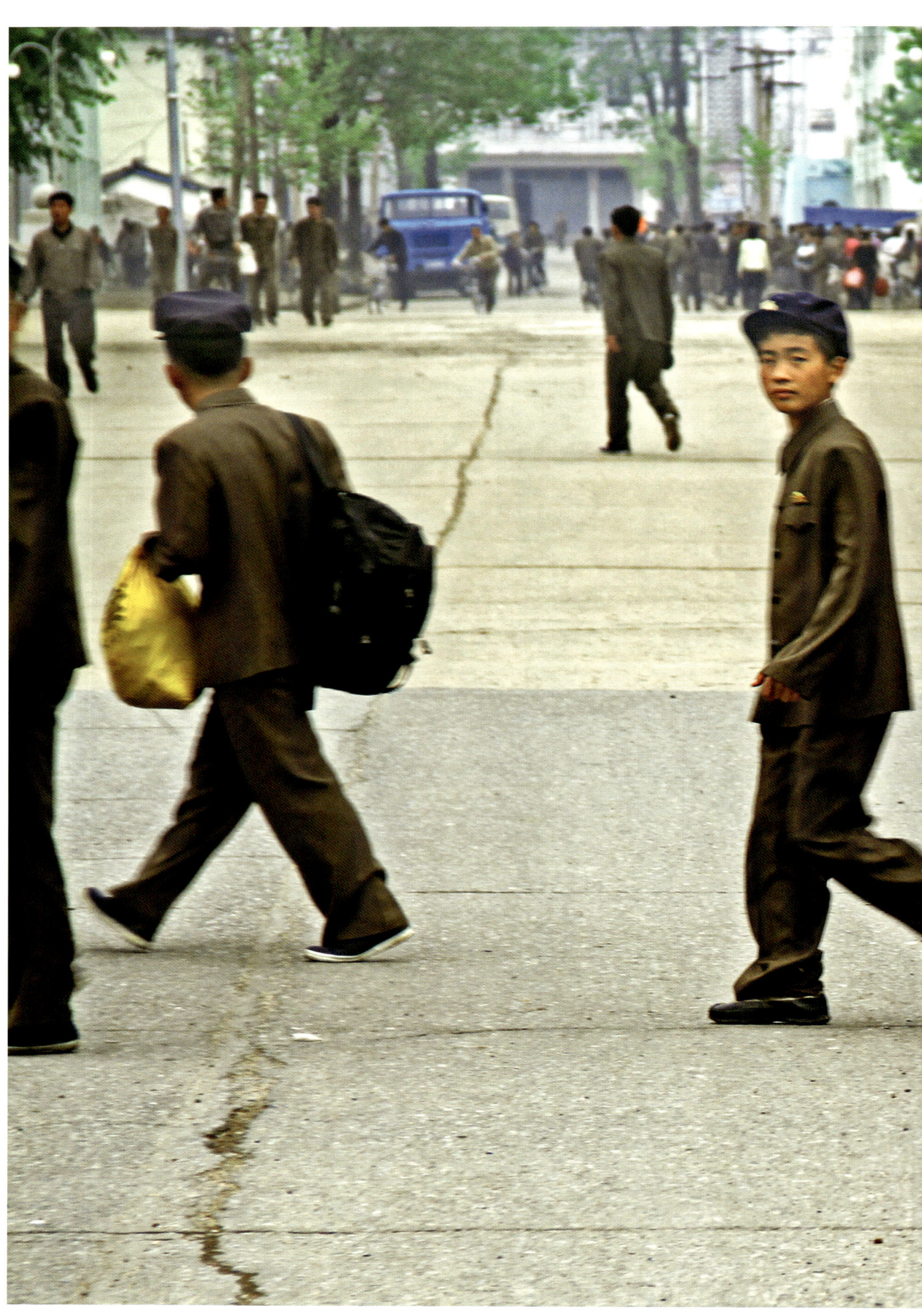

Workers early in the morning, Sariwŏn
Arbeiter frühmorgens in Sariwŏn
Ouvriers au petit matin à Sariwŏn

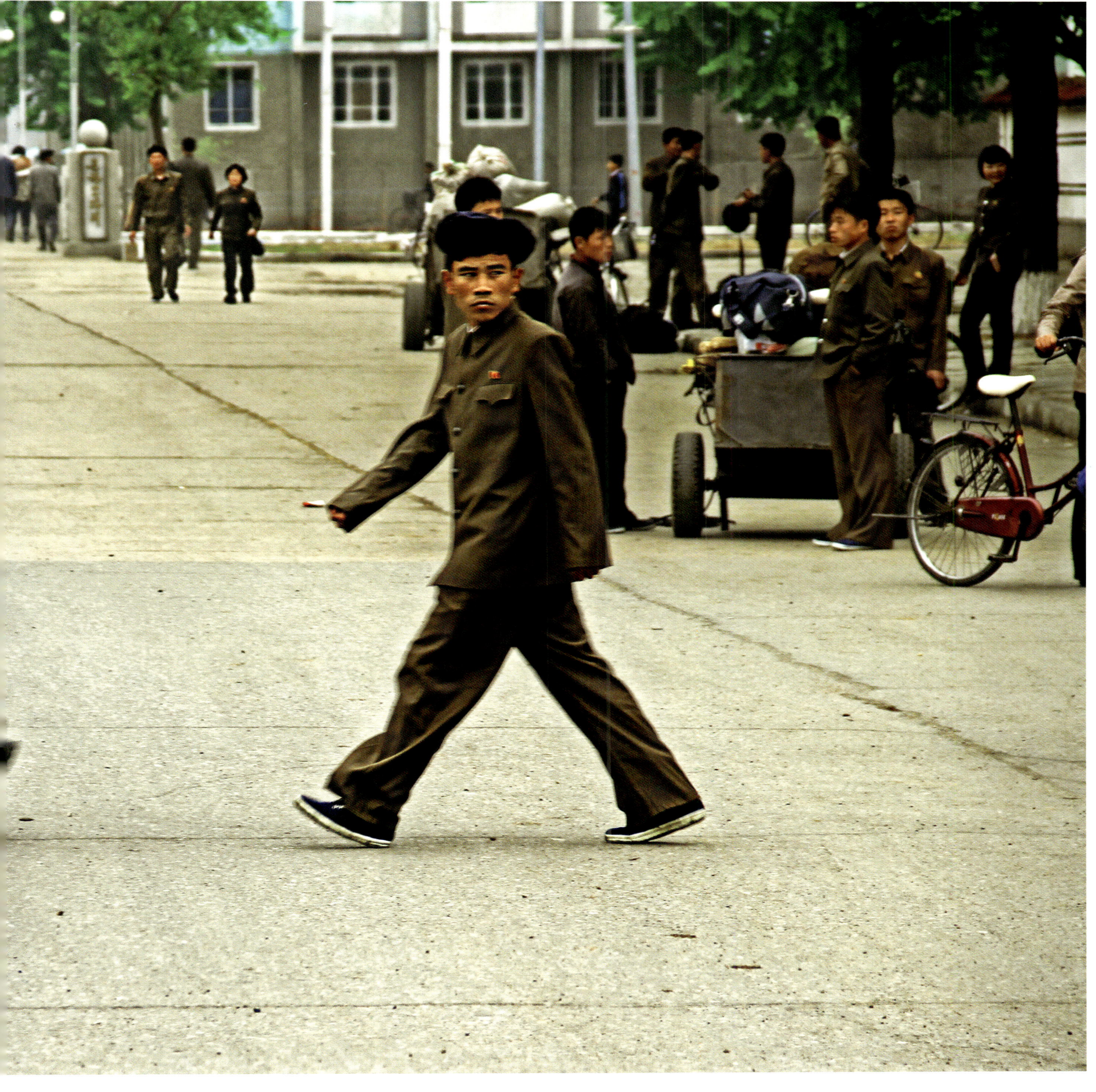

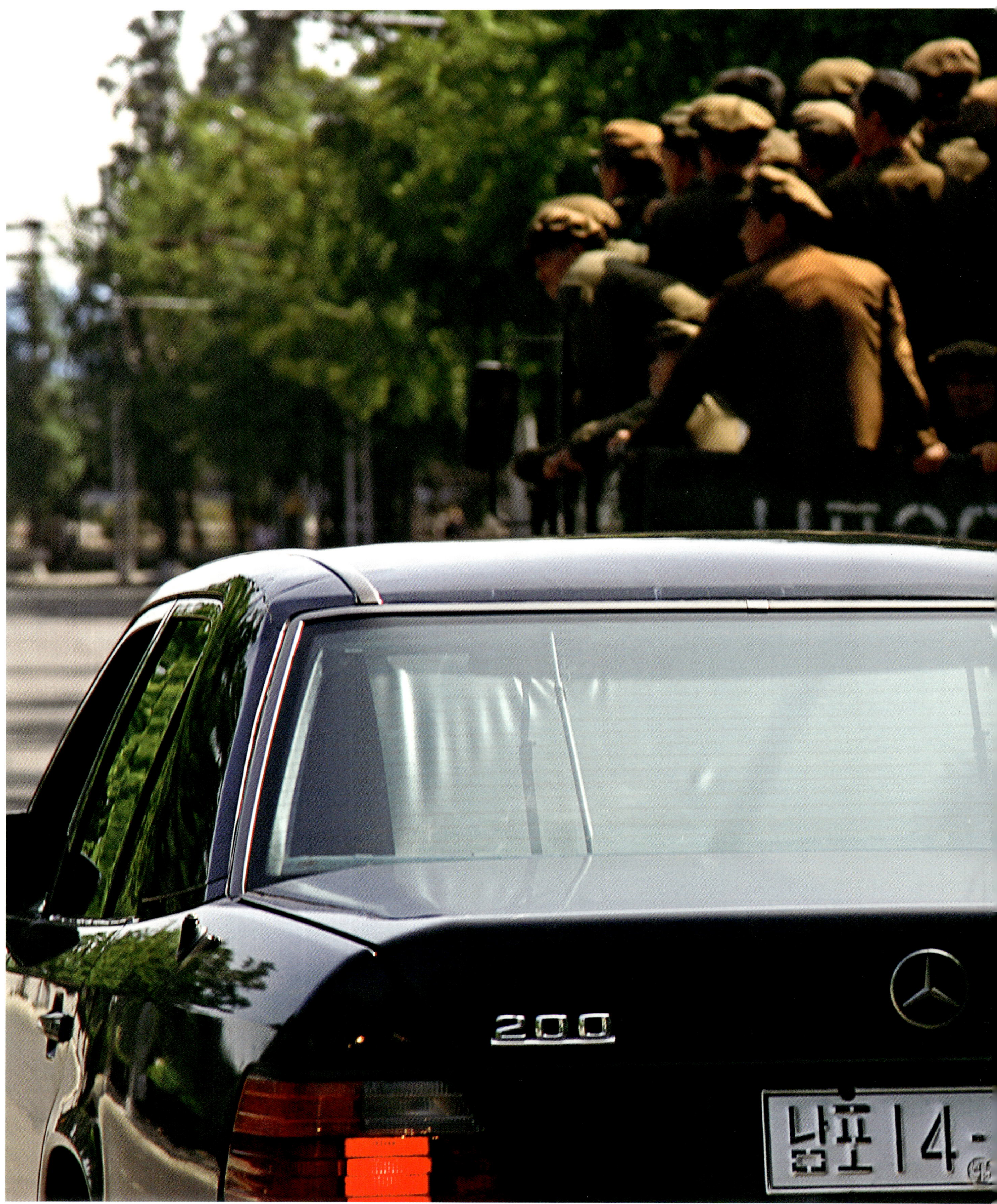
200
남포 14-

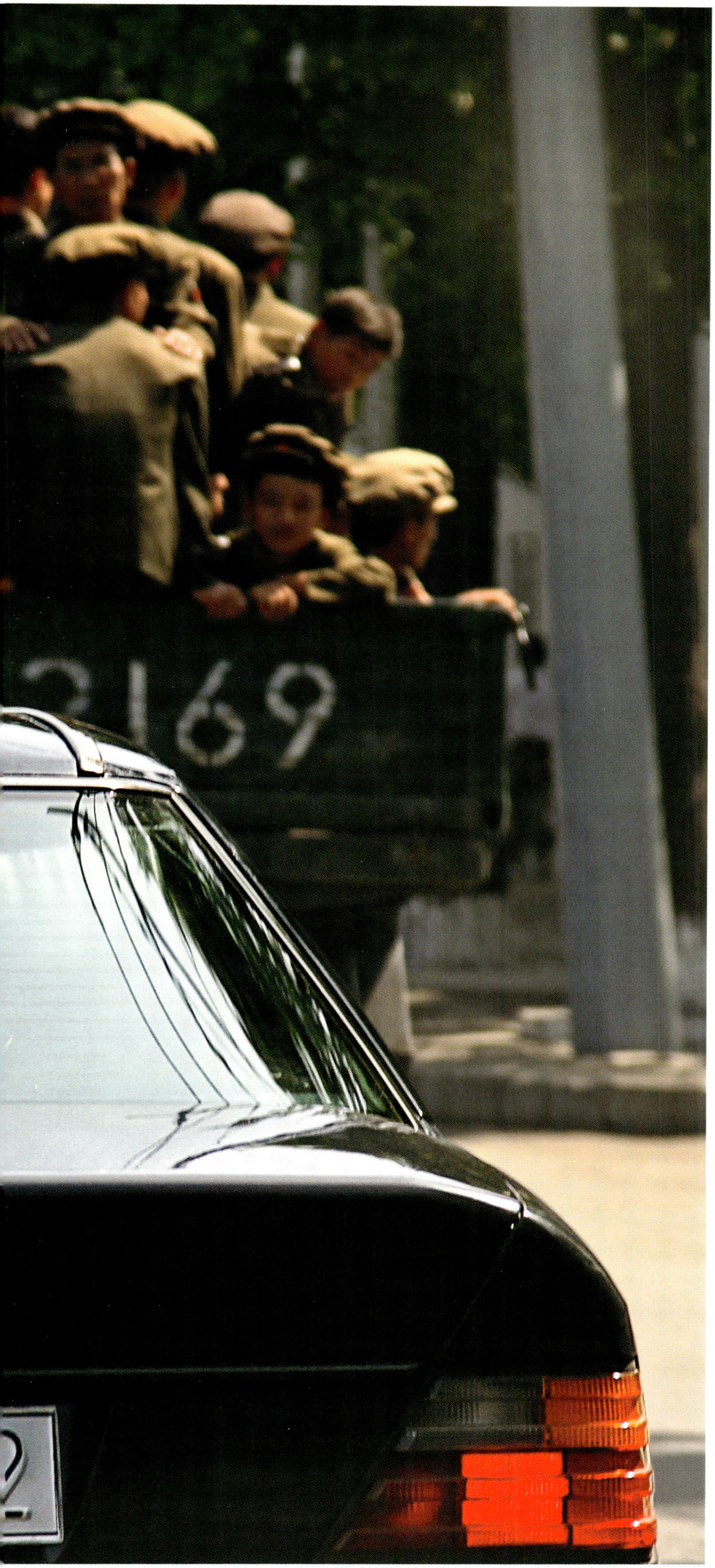

Different means of transportation
Unterschiedliche Fortbewegungsmittel
Différents moyens de locomotion

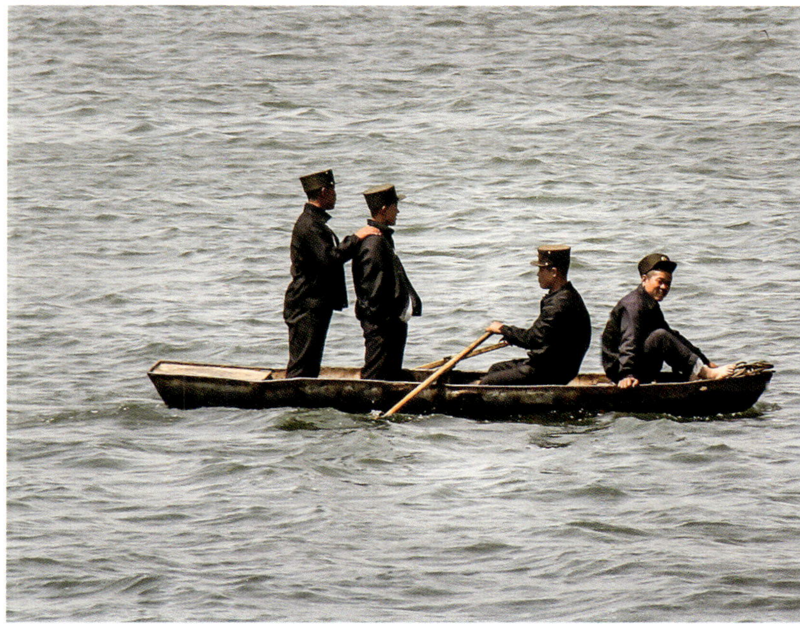

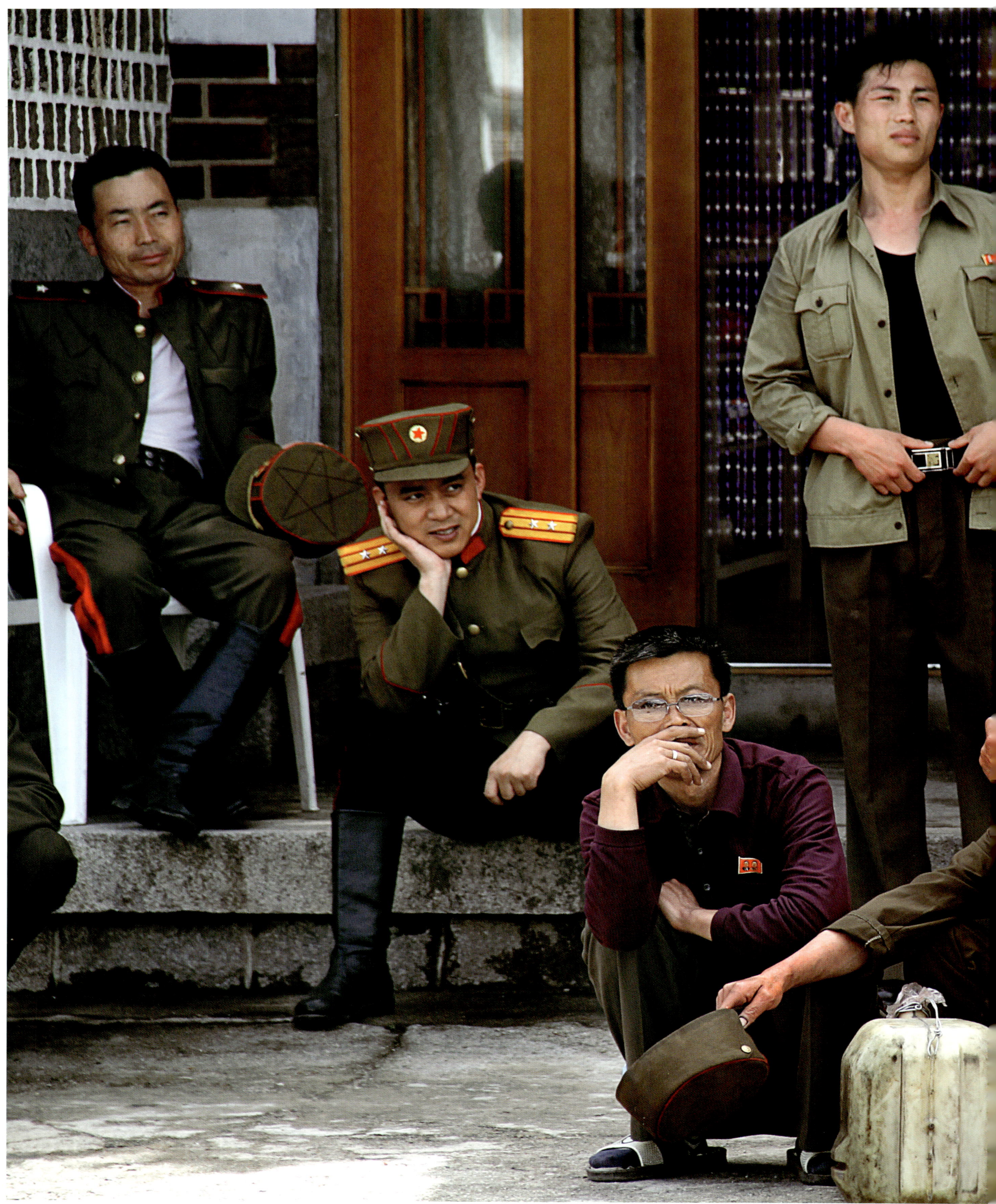

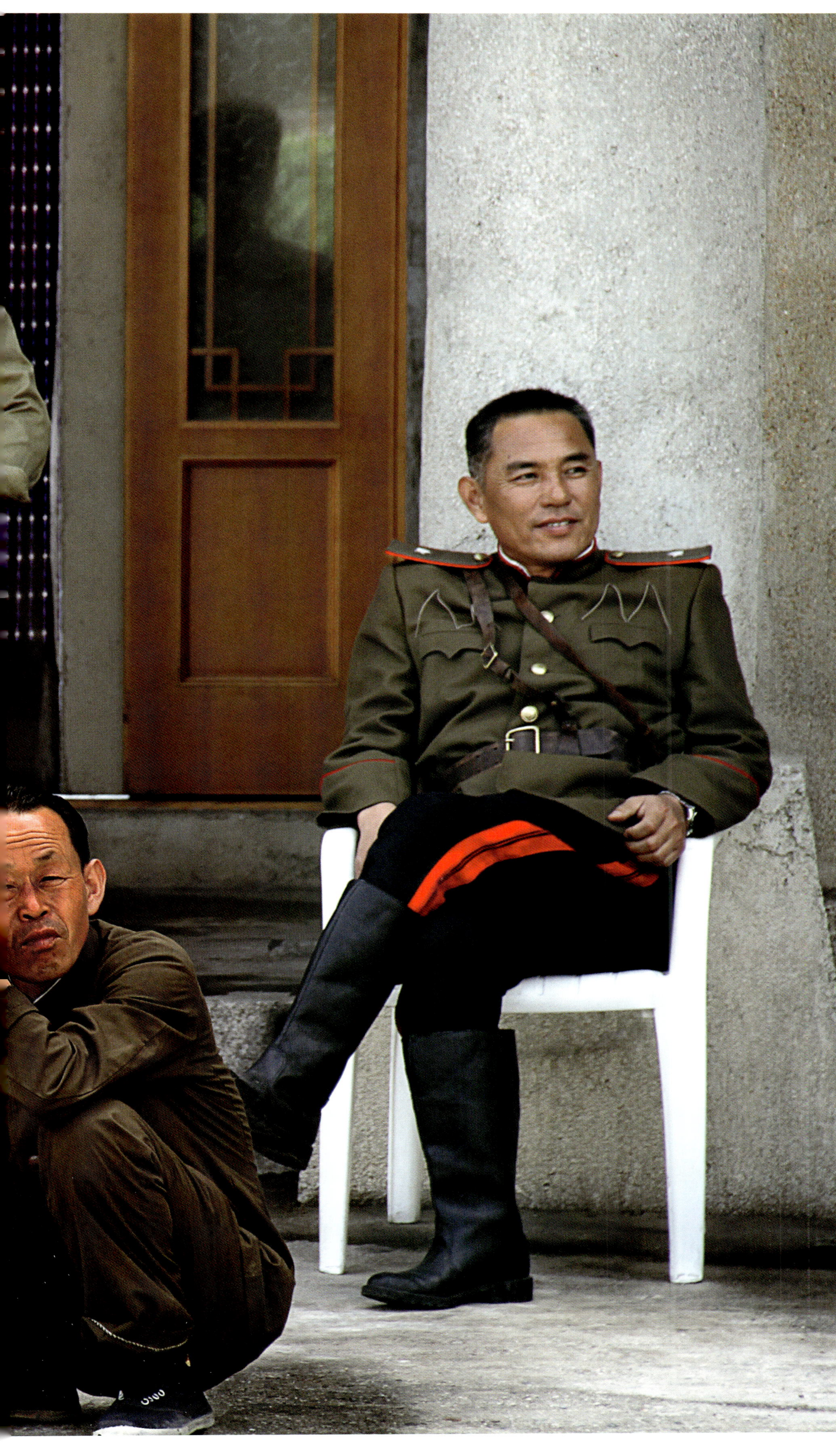

In front of the Minsok
Folk Hotel in Kaesŏng
Vor dem Minsok
Folk Hotel in Kaesŏng
Devant l'hôtel Minsok,
établissement typiquement
coréen de Kaesŏng

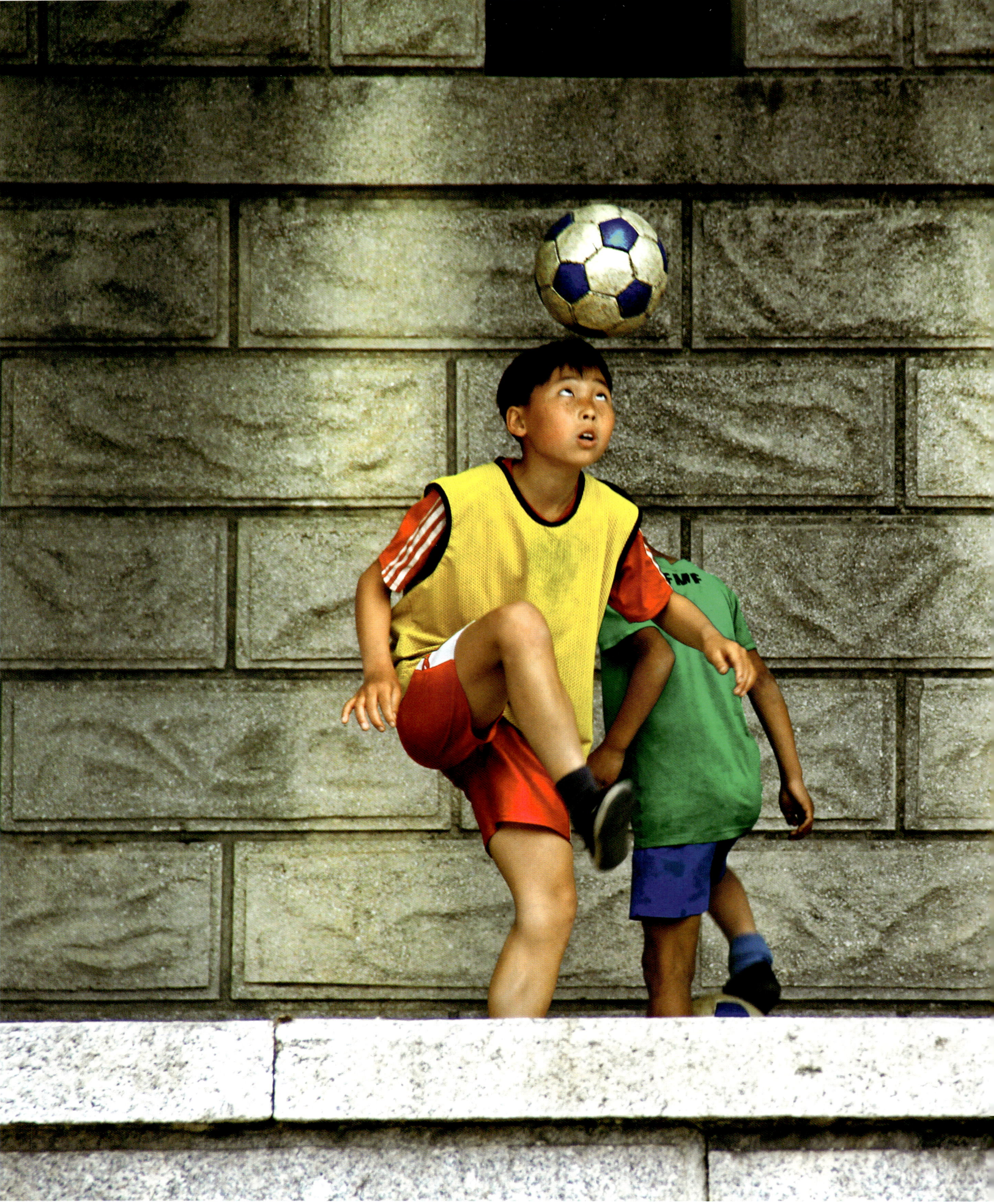

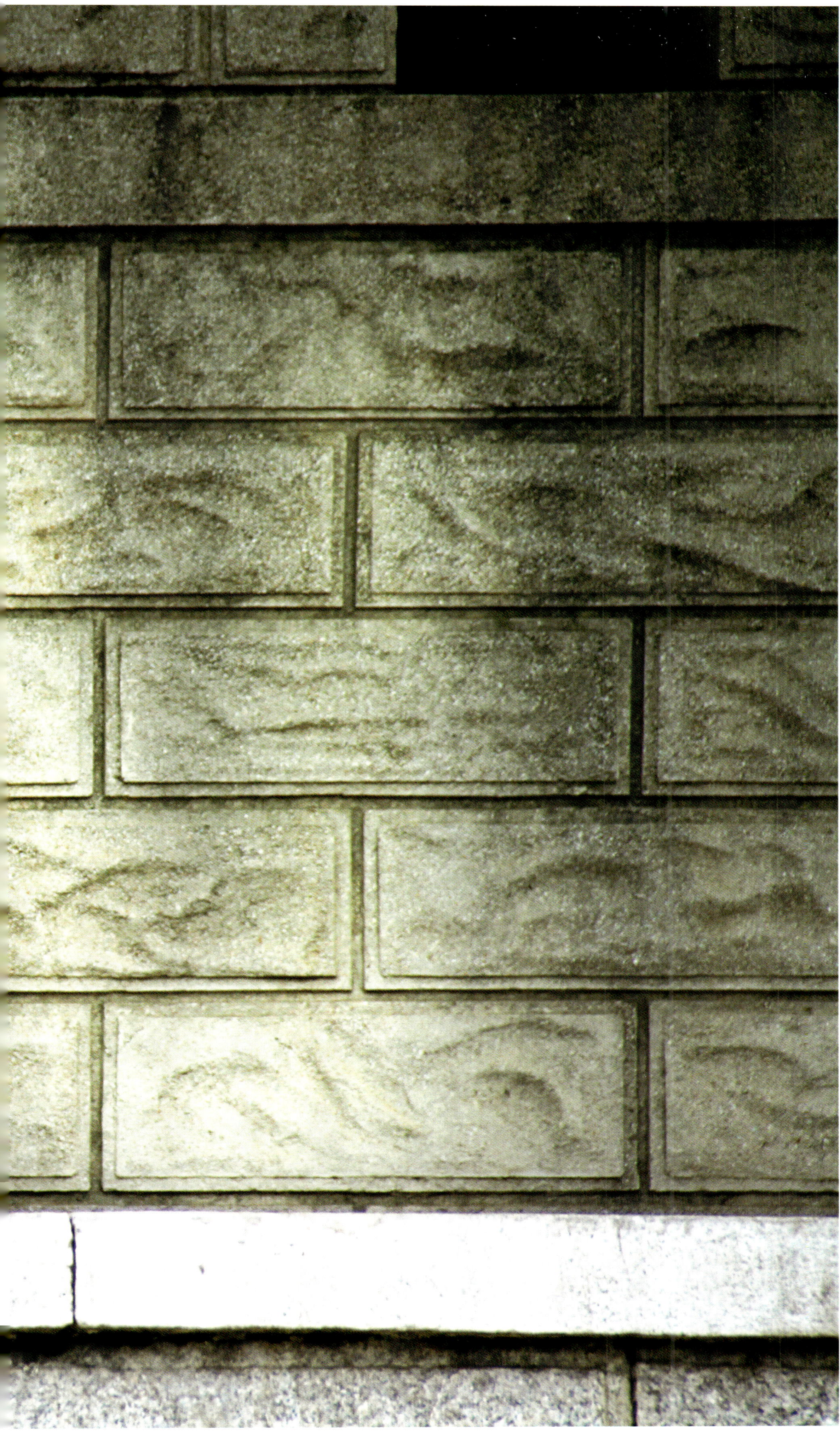

Like people everywhere,
North Koreans love to play soccer.
Wie überall auf der Welt: Auch in Nordkorea gibt es begeisterte Fußballspieler.
Comme tous les autres pays du monde, la Corée du Nord a ses passionnés de foot

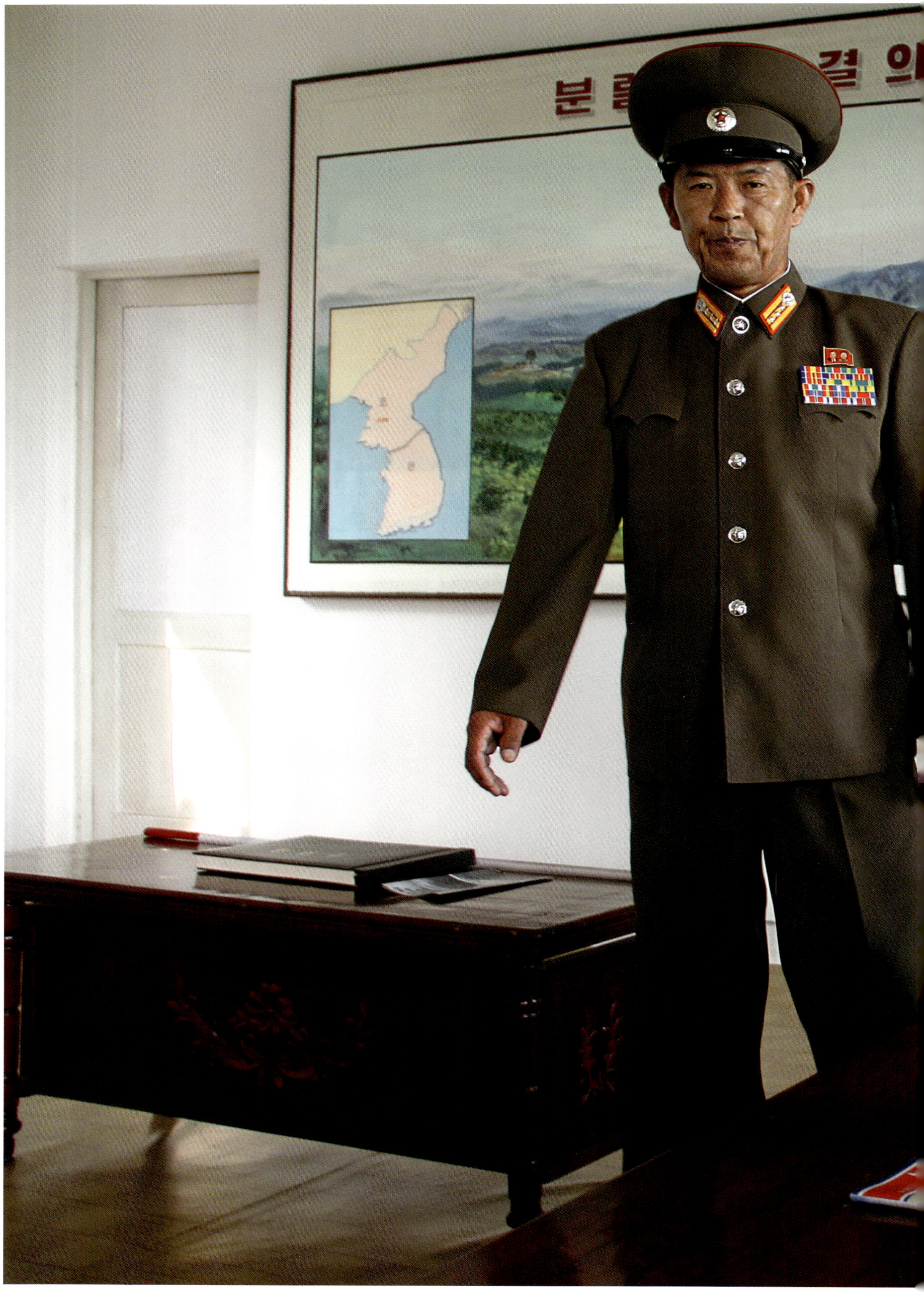

Major Hwang shows us the wall that South Korea refused to acknowledge for many years. One look through the telescope is all the proof you need that it exists.
Major Hwang zeigt uns die Mauer, deren Existenz Südkorea lange leugnete. Ein Blick durch das Fernrohr lässt keinen Zweifel.
Le chef d'escadron Hwang nous montre le mur dont la Corée du Sud a longtemps nié l'existence. Un coup d'œil dans une longue vue balaie tous les doutes.

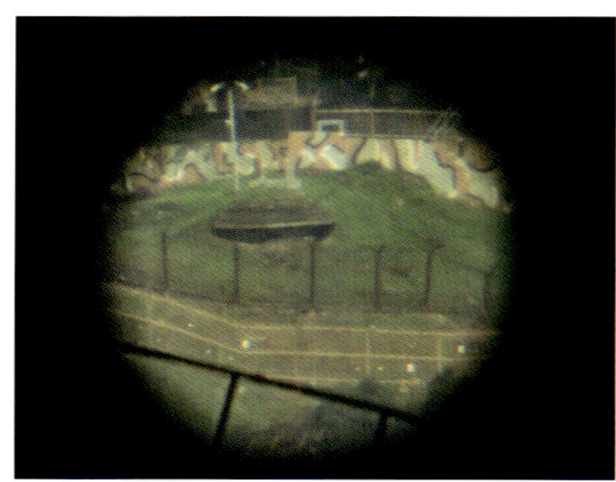

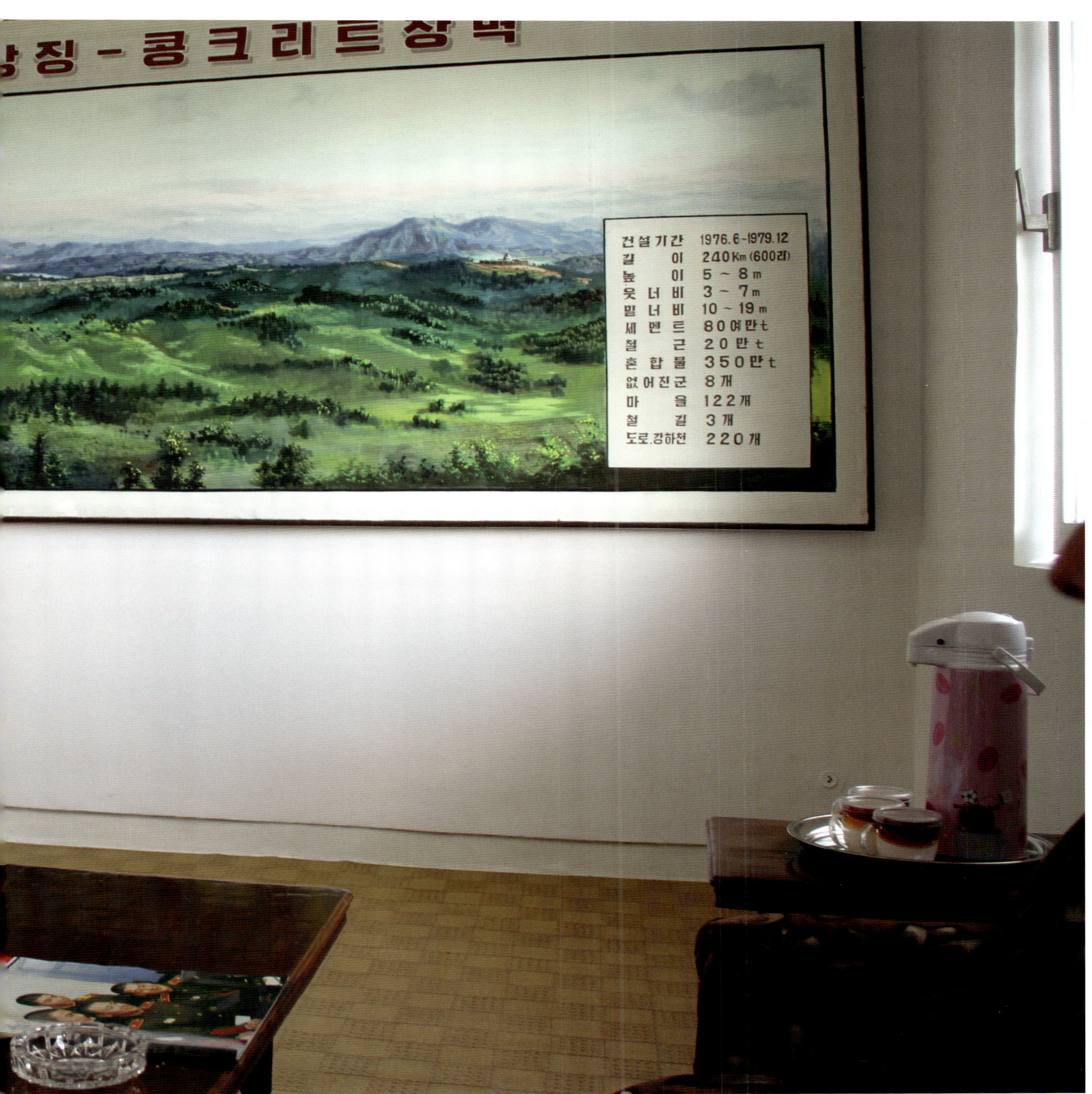
징-콩크리트장벽
건설기간 1976.6-1979.12
길이 240Km (600리)
높이 5 ~ 8m
웃너비 3 ~ 7m
밑너비 10 ~ 19m
세멘트 80여만t
철근 20만t
혼합물 350만t
없어진군 8개
마을 122개
철길 3개
도로.강하천 220개

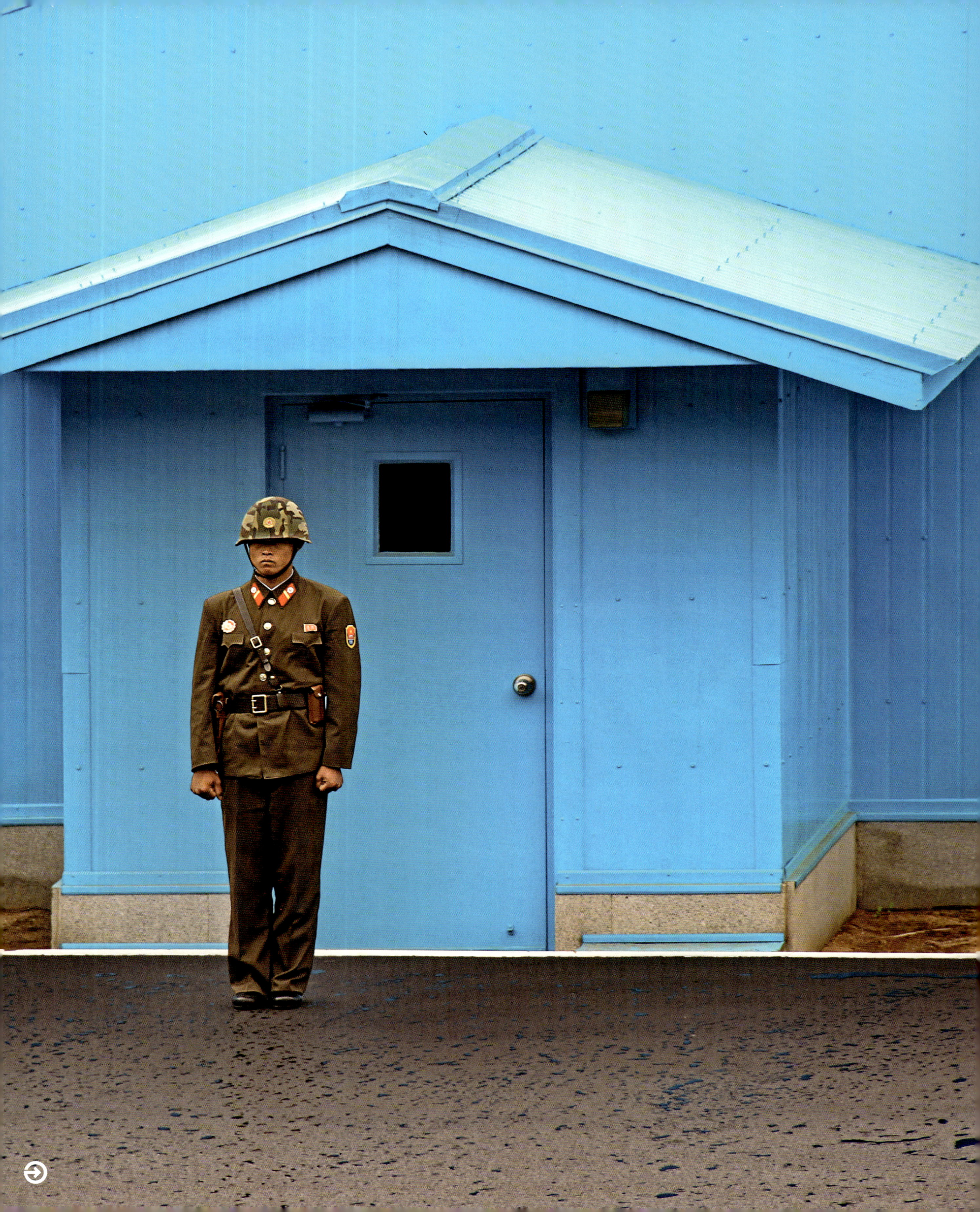

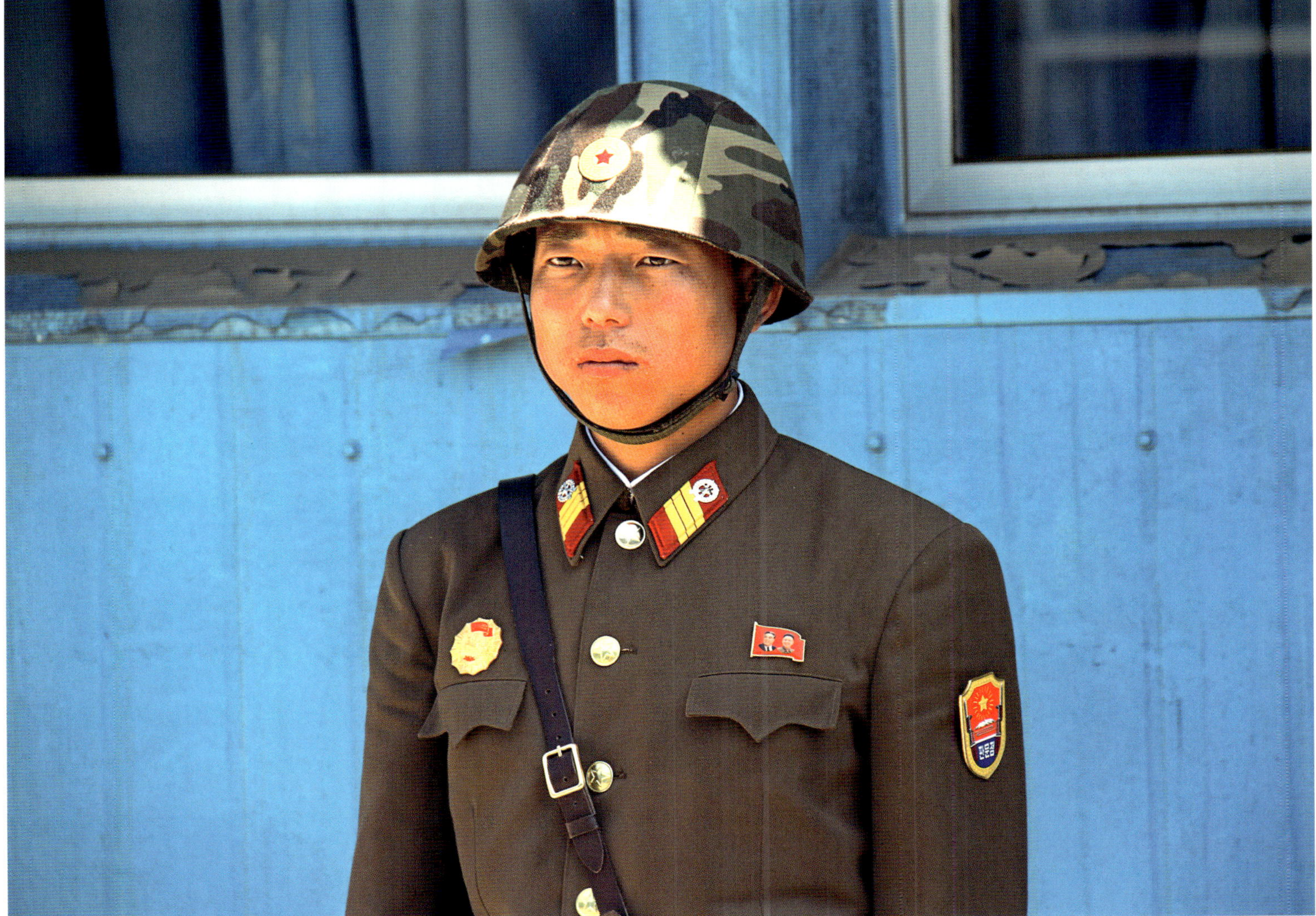

North Korean soldiers in the Demilitarized Zone along the world's most dangerous border, just a stone's throw from South Korea
Nur einen Steinwurf von Südkorea entfernt: nordkoreanische Soldaten in der demilitarisierten Zone an der gefährlichsten Grenze der Welt
À deux pas de la Corée du Sud : Des soldats nord-coréens dans la zone démilitarisée longeant la frontière la plus dangereuse au monde

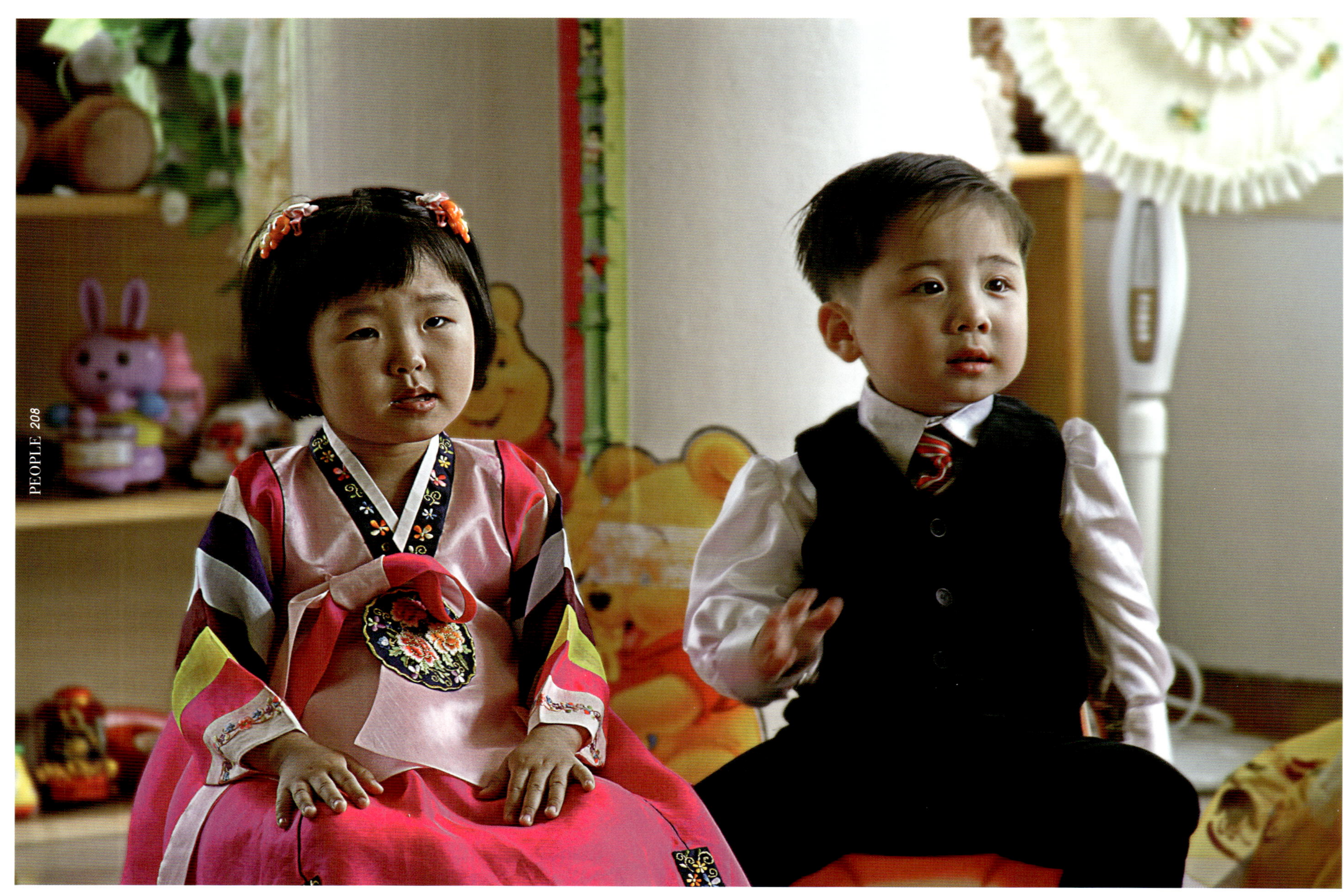

Kindergarten kids in Pyongyang, decked out in their very best
Kinder in festlicher Tracht im Kindergarten, Pjöngjang
Enfants en habits de fête dans une école maternelle de Pyongyang

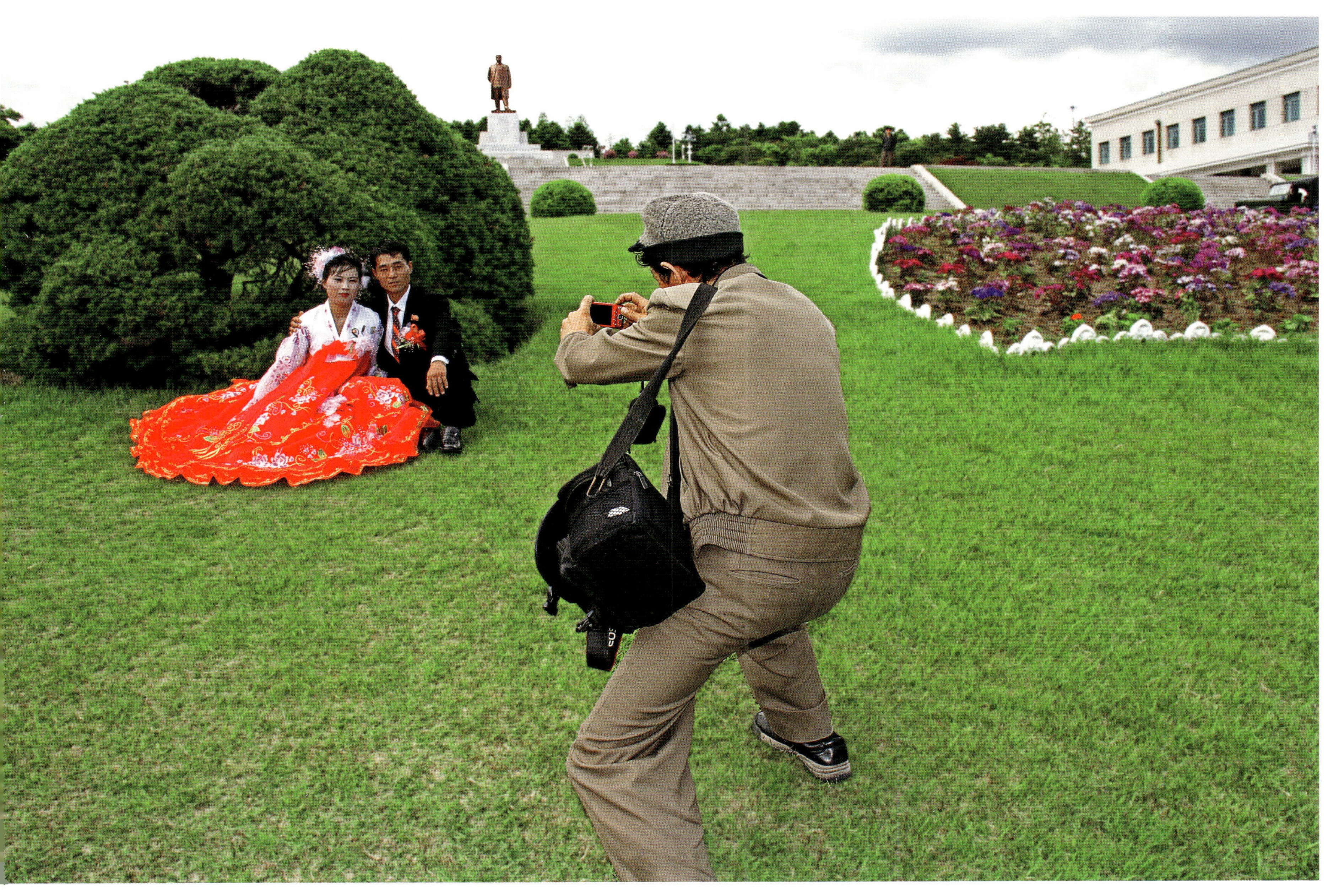

A bride and groom in Kaesŏng pose for a wedding photo.
Fototermin für ein Brautpaar in Kaesŏng
Séance photo pour des jeunes mariés à Kaesŏng

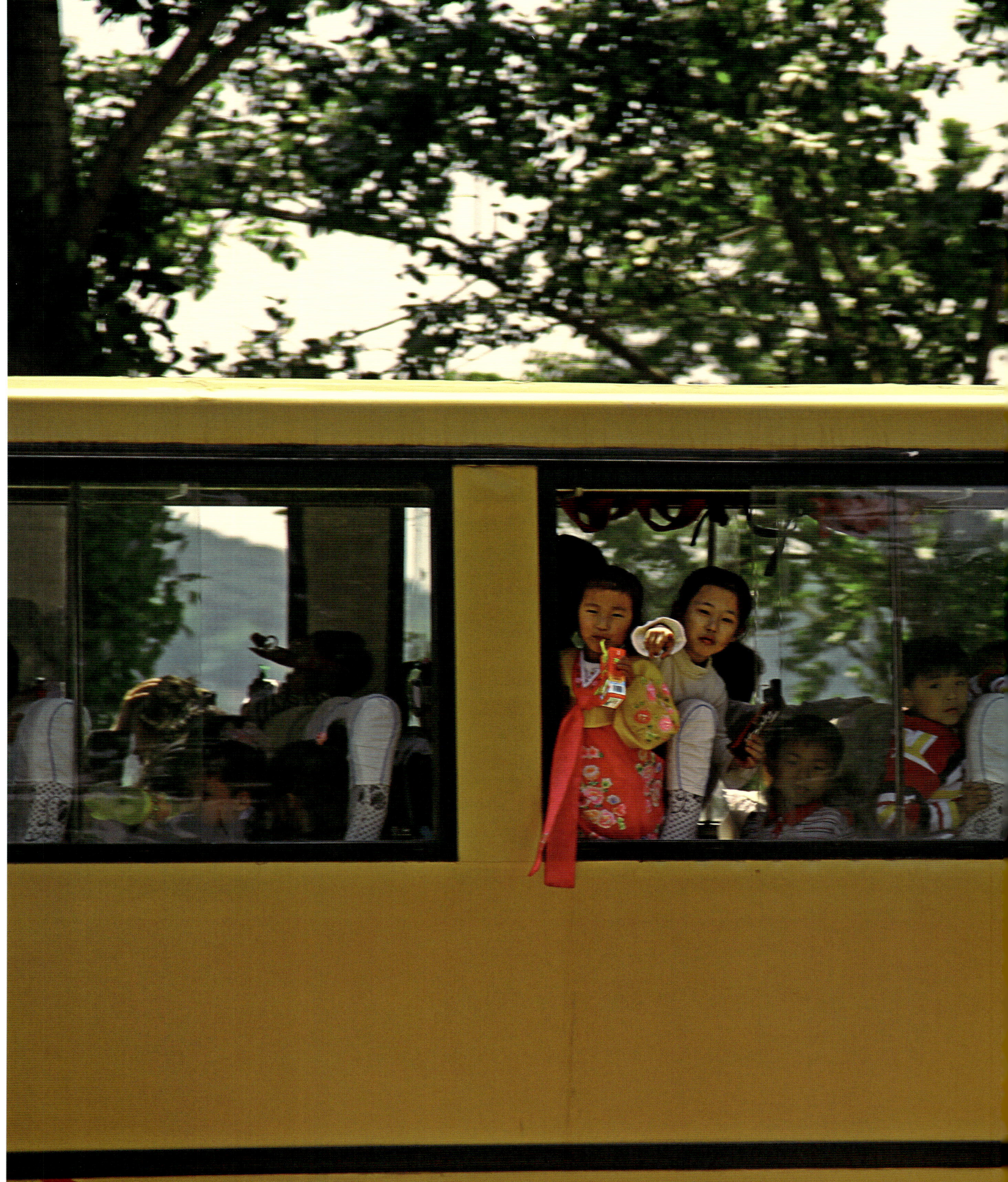

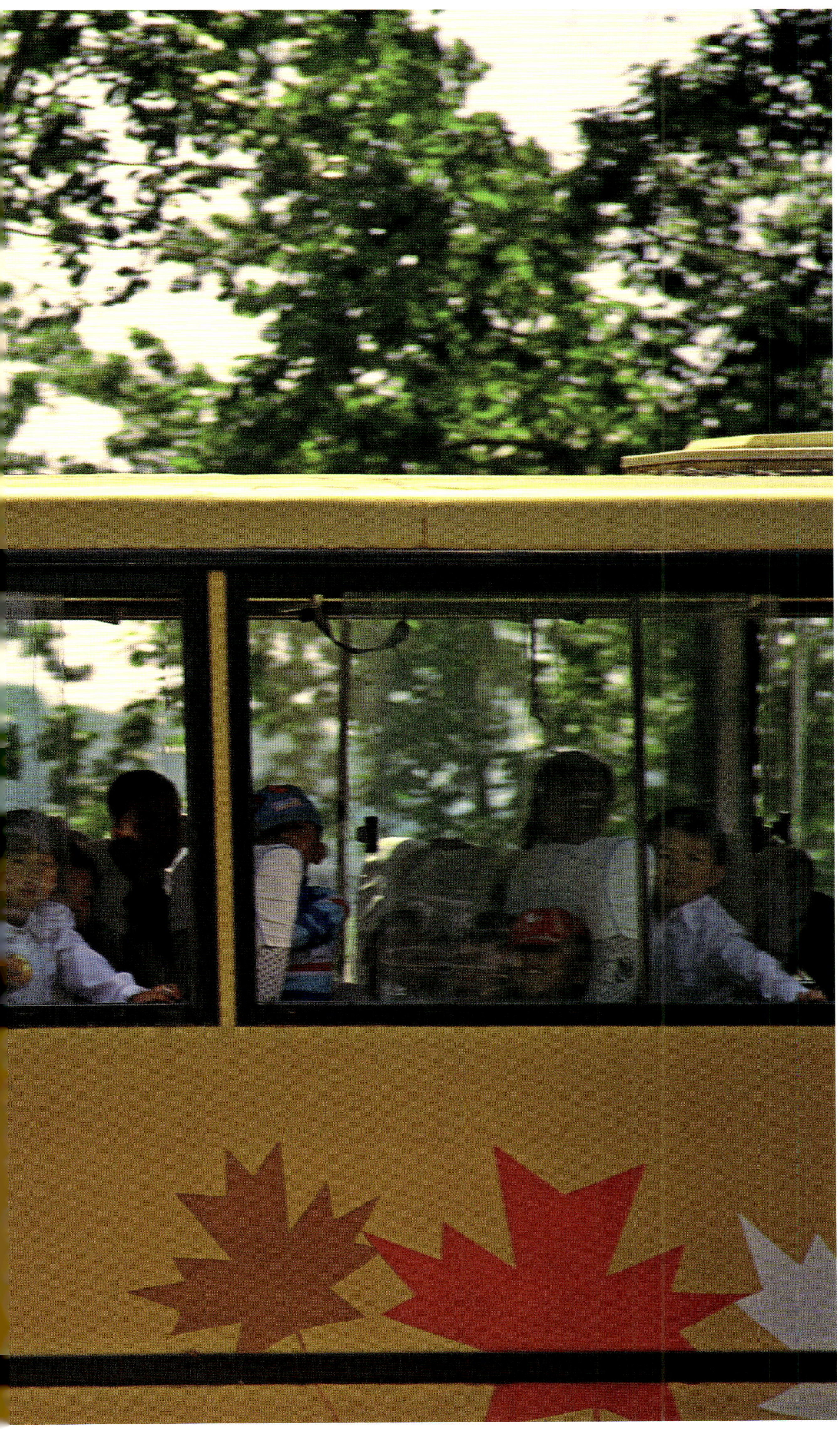

Both sides express enormous curiosity.
Die gegenseitige Neugier ist groß.
La curiosité est grande des deux côtés.

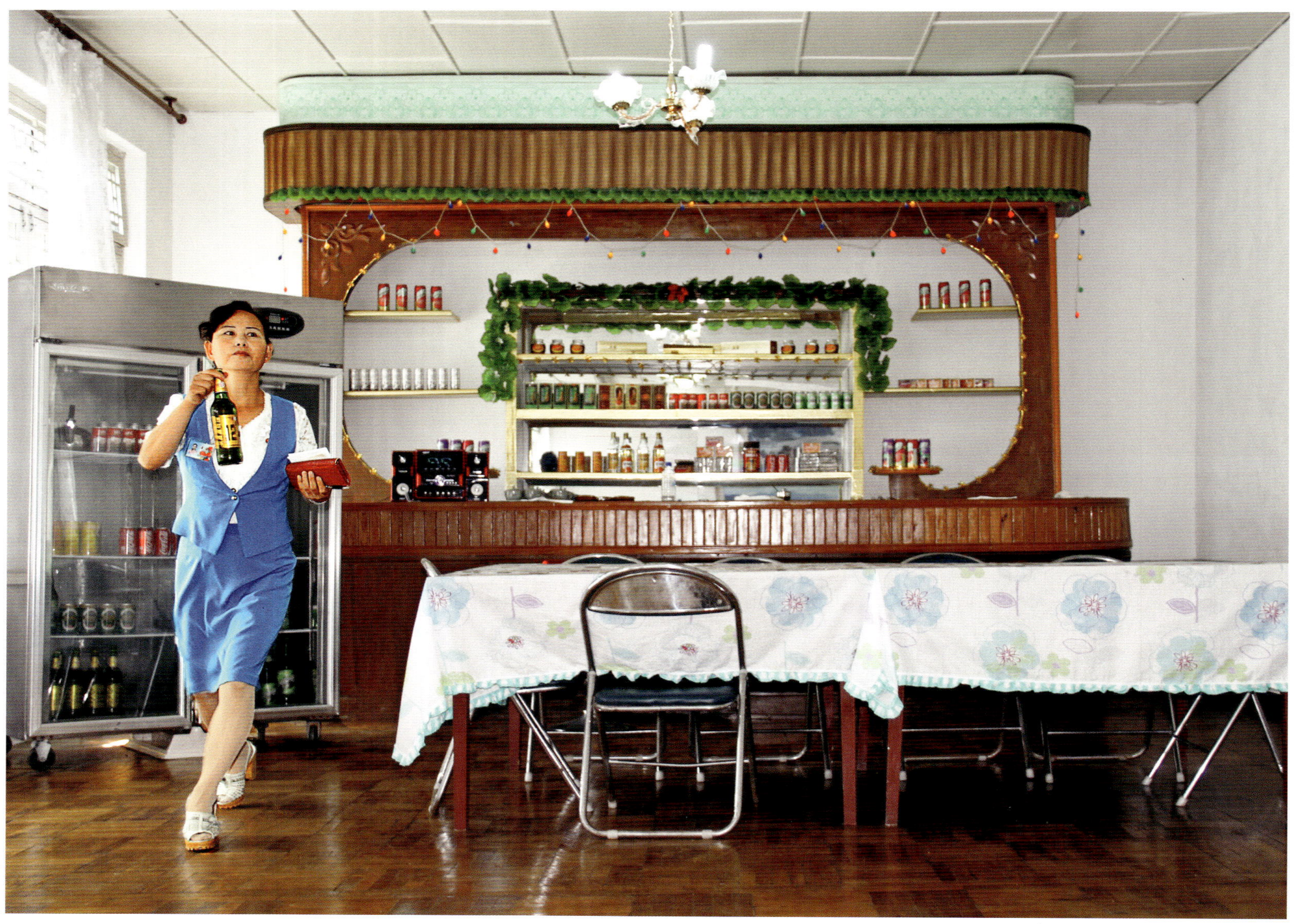

A waitress at a roadside restaurant serves excellent beer made in North Korea.
Raststätte: Die Kellnerin serviert nordkoreanisches Bier der Spitzenqualität.
Sur une aire de repos, une serveuse apporte de l'excellente bière nord-coréenne.

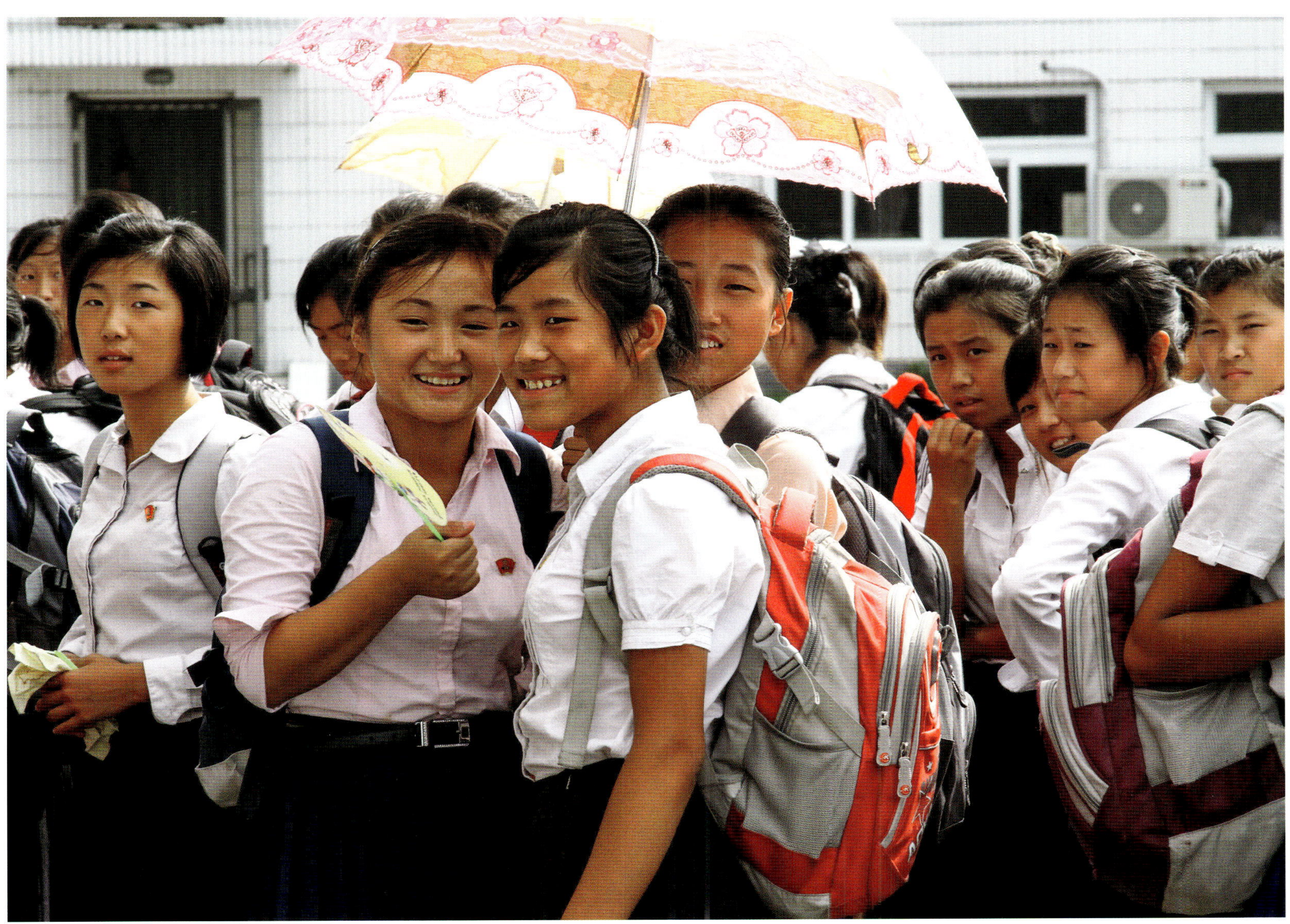

Schoolgirl with the insignia of the "Beloved Leader"
Schulmädchen mit Abzeichen des „Geliebten Führers"
Écolières arborant l'insigne à l'effigie du « cher dirigeant »

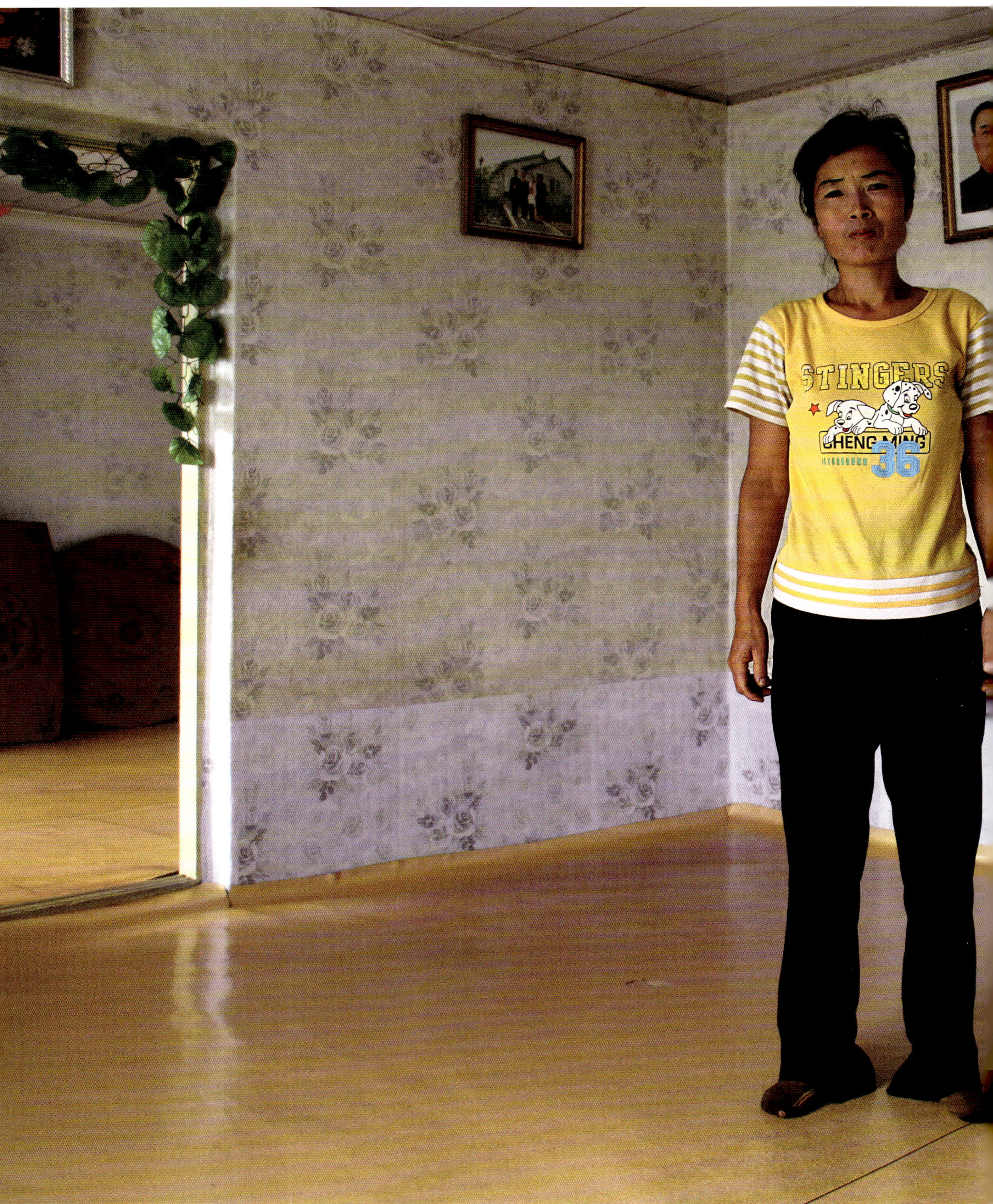
STINGERS
36

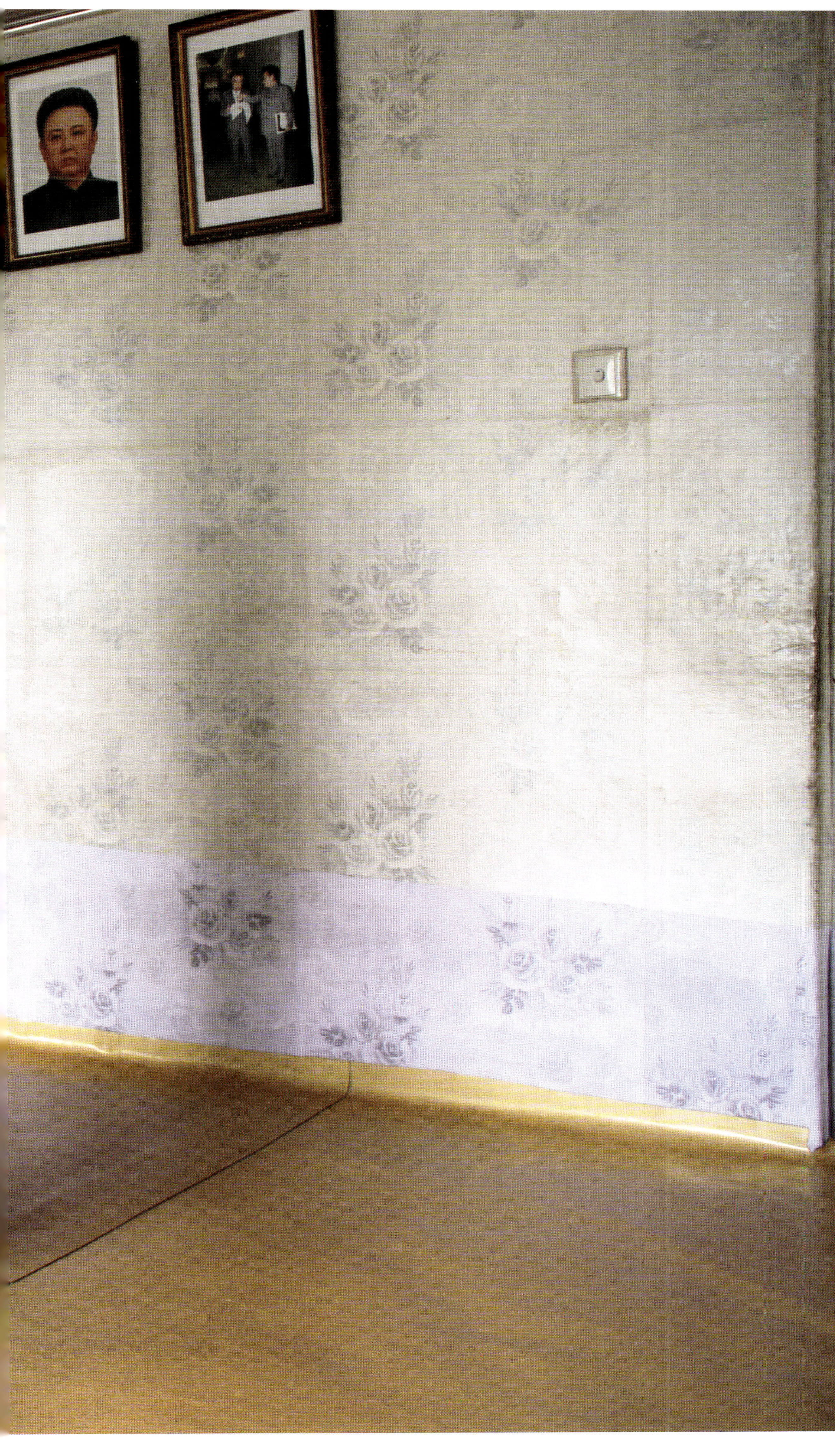

Farmworker O Yong-ae at home. The room lacks furniture, as is customary in North Korea.
Bäuerin O Yong-ae in ihrem Haus. Wie hier üblich stehen im Raum keinerlei Möbel.
L'agricultrice O Yong-ae chez elle. Comme le veut la coutume, la pièce ne contient aucun meuble.

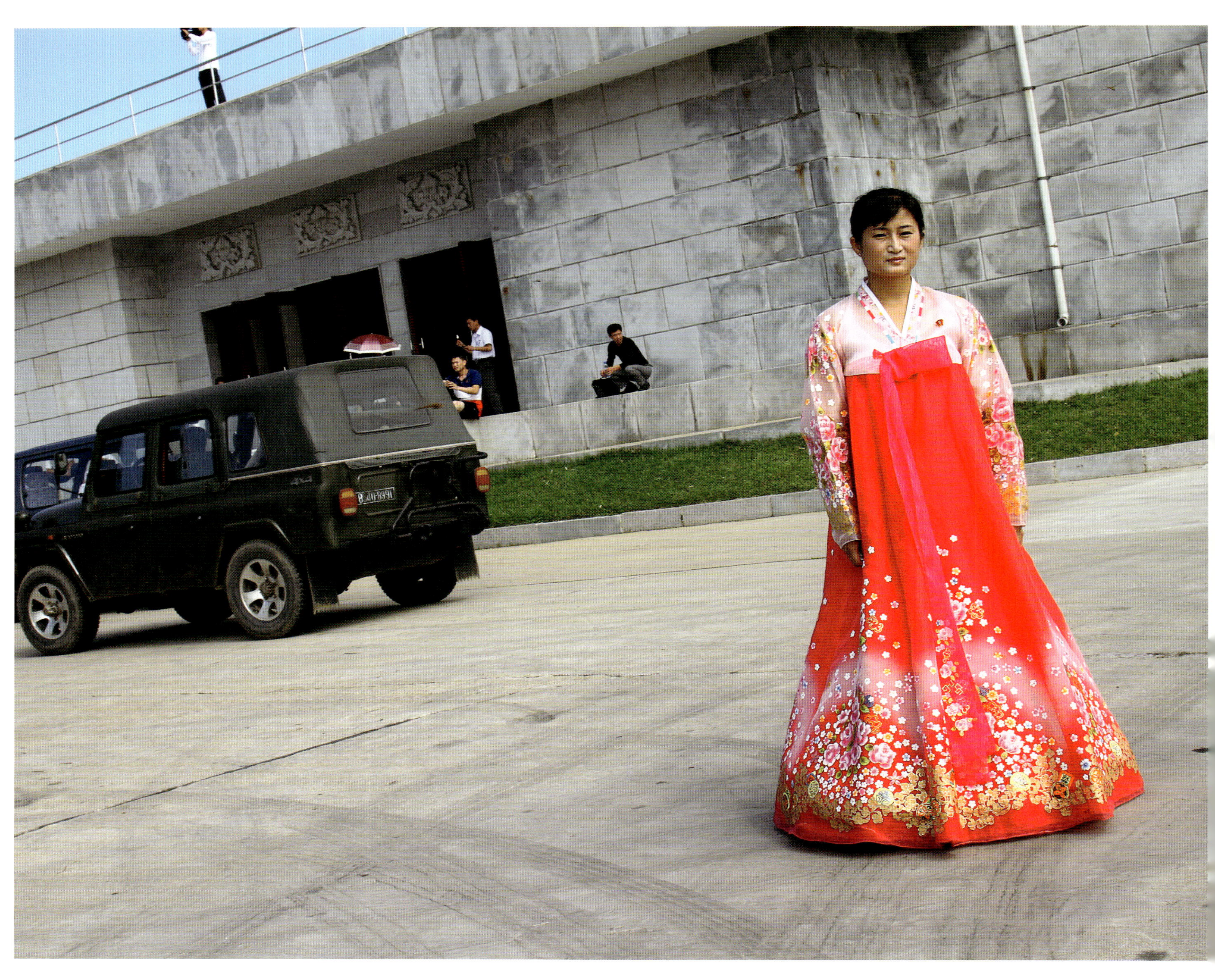

Lady in Nampho wearing Chosŏn-ot, the traditional costume of North Korea
Dame in der landestypischen Tracht Chosŏn-ot, Nampho
Dame en costume traditionnel Chosŏn-ot, à Nampho

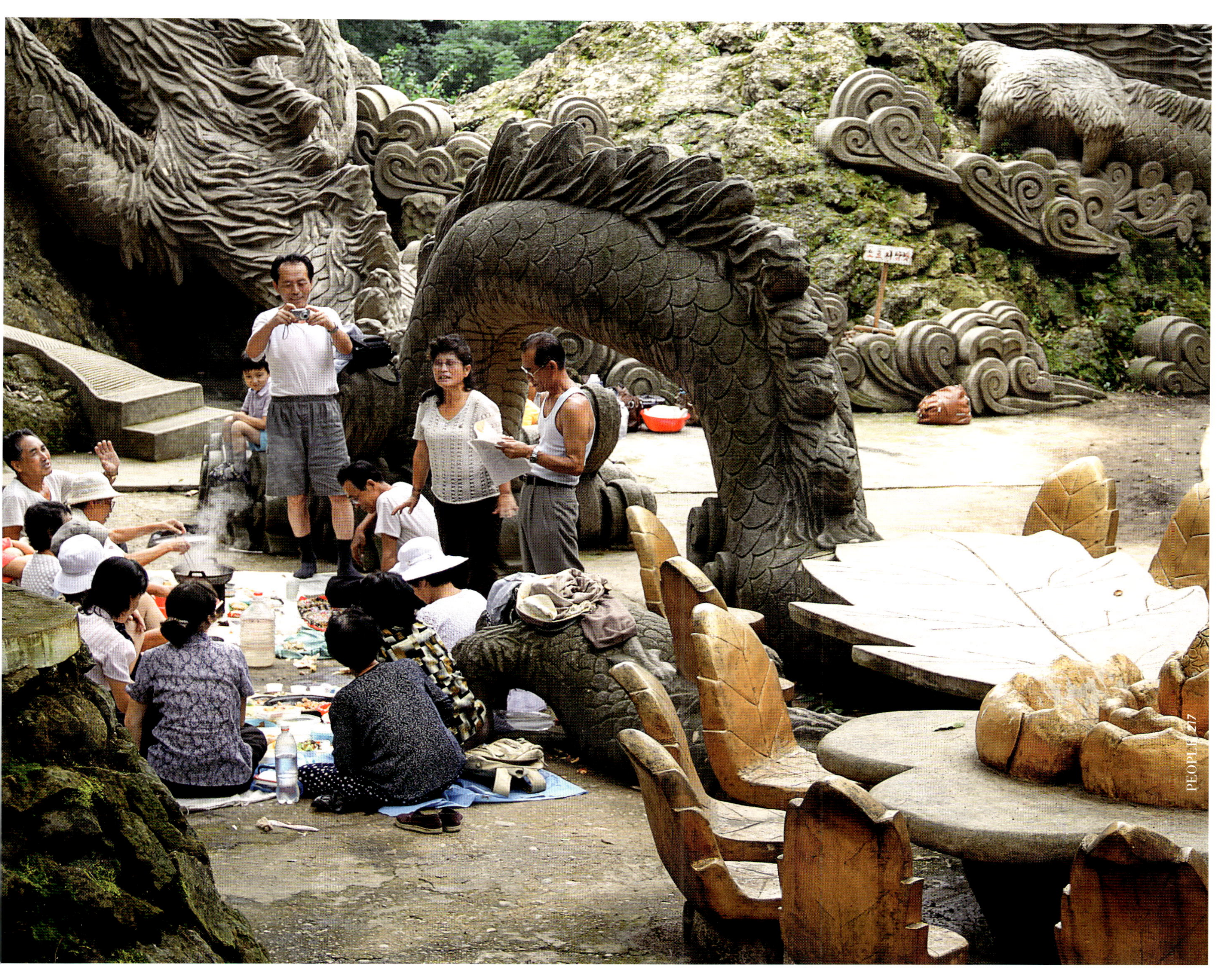

Picnic in the Myohyang Mountains: Even leisure activities take place in groups.

Picknick im Myohyang-Gebirge: Auch die Freizeit wird im Kollektiv verbracht.

Pique-nique dans les monts Myohyang : pendant ses loisirs, on n'échappe pas non plus à la collectivité.

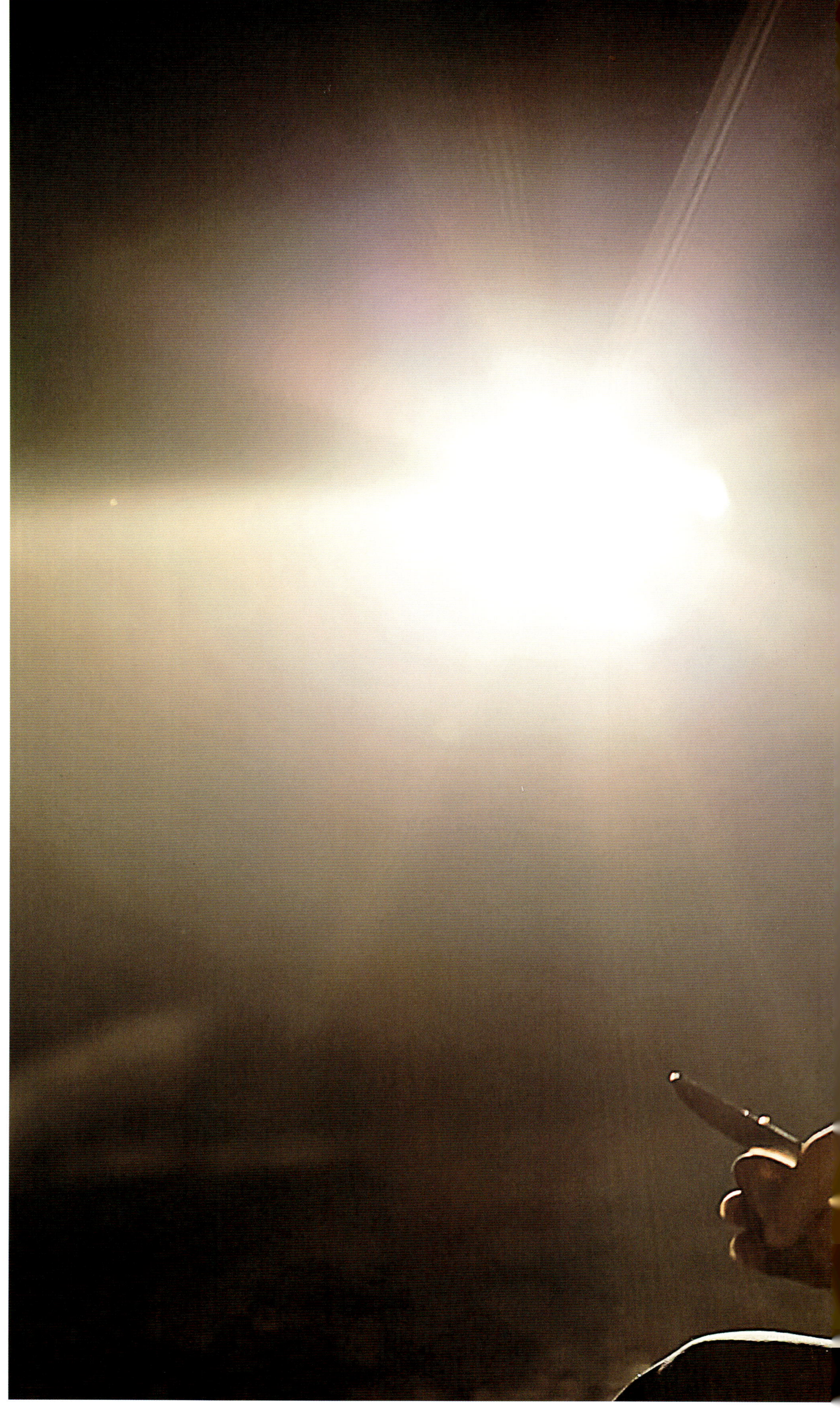

Feasting on mussels, a local delicacy, in the beam of headlights, Yonggang
Delikatesse: Muschelessen im Licht der Autoscheinwerfer, Yonggang
Mets de choix : dîner de moules à la lumière de phares de voiture, à Yonggang

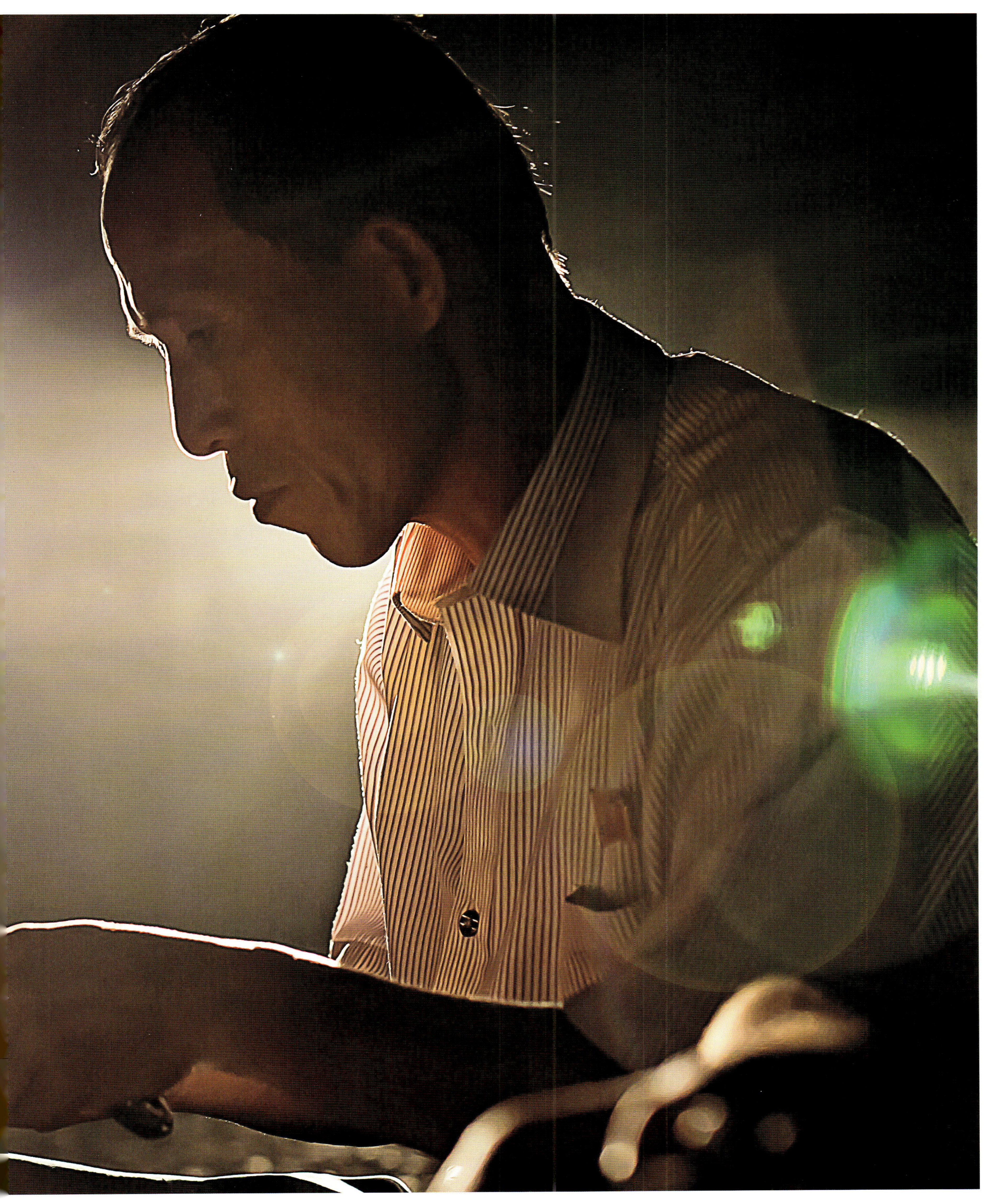

INDEX

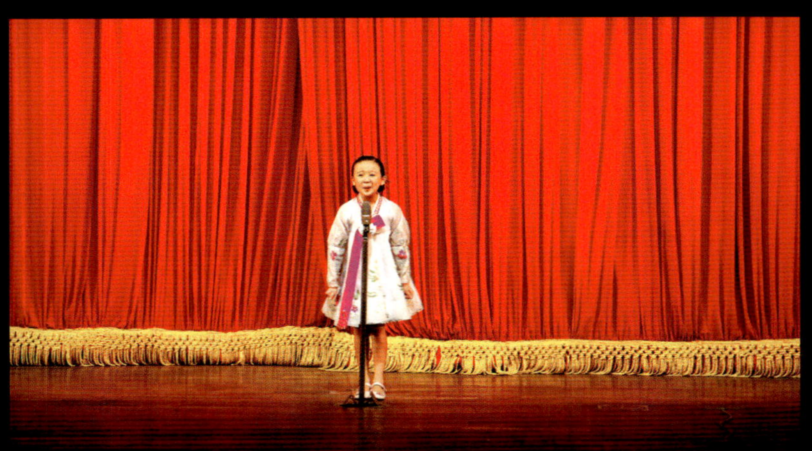

A performance at the Mangyongdae Children's Palace in Pyongyang. Classes end at noon, after which the children come to this educational establishment to study weaving, embroidery, painting, dancing, music, and similar subjects.
Aufführung im Kinderpalast Mangyongdae, Pjöngjang. Wenn die Schule am Nachmittag zu Ende ist, lernen Kinder in der Bildungseinrichtung unter anderem Weben, Sticken, Malen, Tanzen und Musizieren.
Spectacle au Palais des enfants de Mangyongdae, à Pyongyang. Les enfants fréquentent cette institution éducative après la classe pour y apprendre, entre autres, le tissage, la broderie, la peinture, la danse et la musique.

002

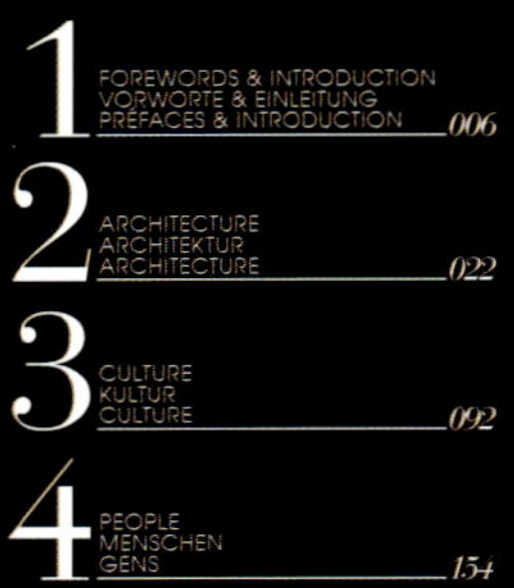

INDEX 220

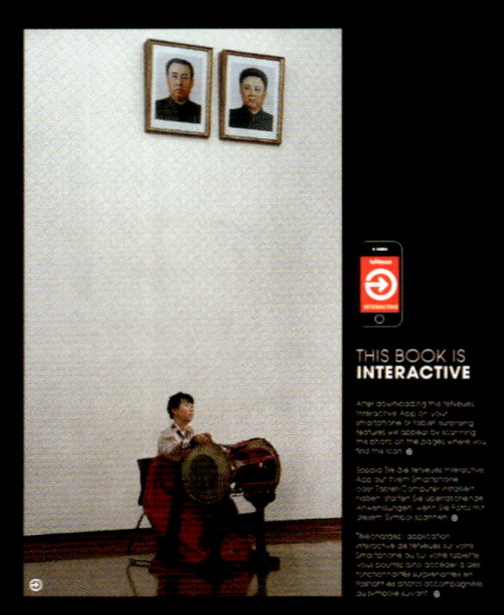

A music teacher playing the janggu. This traditional instrument was first documented in 1076.
Eine Musiklehrerin spielt Janggu. Schon 1076 wurde das Volksmusikinstrument erstmals erwähnt.
La professeure joue du janggu, instrument de la musique populaire coréenne attesté dès 1076.

004

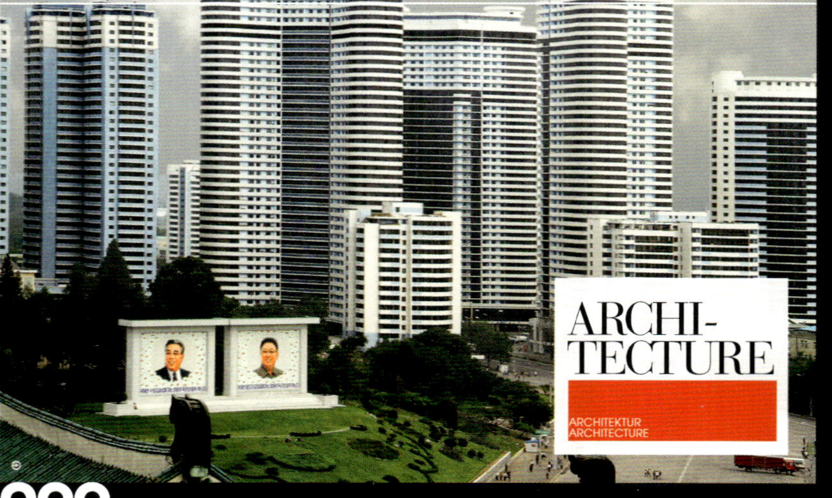

Mansudae Apartments in Pyongyang: This model apartment complex symbolizes modern-day North Korea under the leadership of the new Supreme Commander Kim Jong-un. "The nearly completed high-rise apartment is standing tall, boasting to the world of the greatness of our everlasting socialism under the respected Comrade Kim Jong-un." (Quote published in Rodong Sinmun, the North Korean Workers' Newspaper)
Mansudae-Apartments, Pjöngjang: Der Vorzeigekomplex steht für das moderne Nordkorea unter dem neuen Marschall Kim Jong-un. „Das bald fertiggestellte Wohnhochhaus präsentiert sich aufrecht der Welt und zeugt von der Größe unseres immerwährenden Sozialismus unter dem verehrten Genossen Kim Jong-un.“ (Zitat aus Rodong Sinmun, der nordkoreanischen Arbeiterzeitung)
Les logements de Mansudae, à Pyongyang : ce complexe vitrine symbolise la Corée du Nord moderne sous le nouveau maréchal Kim Jong-un. « Cette tour de logements bientôt achevée laisse le monde ébloui par la grandeur de notre socialisme éternel sous le vénéré camarade Kim Jong-un. » (Extrait du Rodong Sinmun, le journal ouvrier nord-coréen)

022

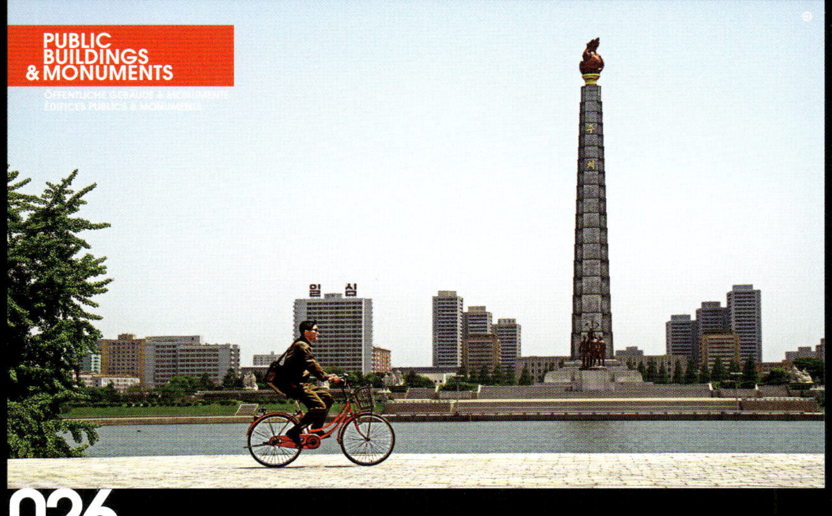

026

A torch that lights up at night crowns the Juche Tower. Often it is one of only a few light sources in the capital.

Das Juche-Wahrzeichen wird von einer Fackel gekrönt, die nachts leuchtet. Dann ist sie oft eine der wenigen Lichtquellen in der Hauptstadt.

L'emblème du Juche est coiffé d'une torche illuminée la nuit. C'est alors souvent l'une des rares sources de lumière dans la capitale.

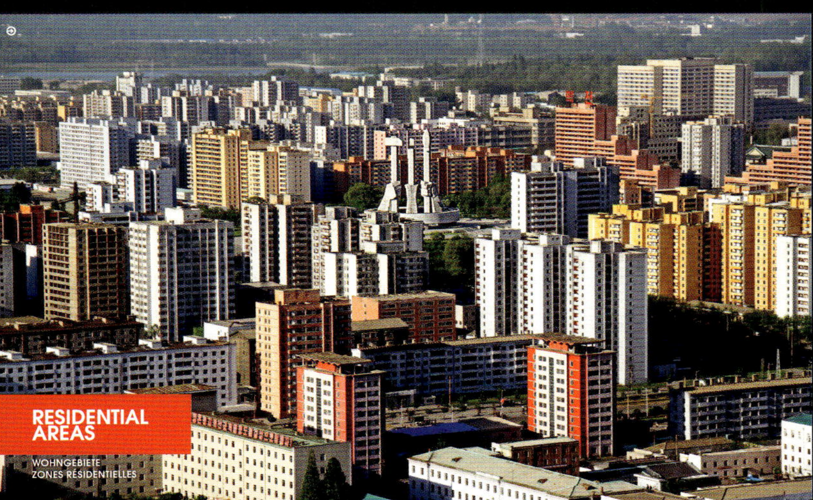

Although Pyongyang has a population of three million people, this metropolis is cut off from the rest of the world. Not even the international intelligence organizations know what goes on here.

Etwa drei Millionen Menschen leben in Pjöngjang. Doch die Metropole ist vom Rest der Welt abgeschottet. Was hier vor sich geht, wissen noch nicht einmal die Geheimdienste.

Pyongyang, métropole d'environ trois millions d'habitants, est coupée du reste du monde. Même les services secrets étrangers ignorent ce qu'il s'y passe.

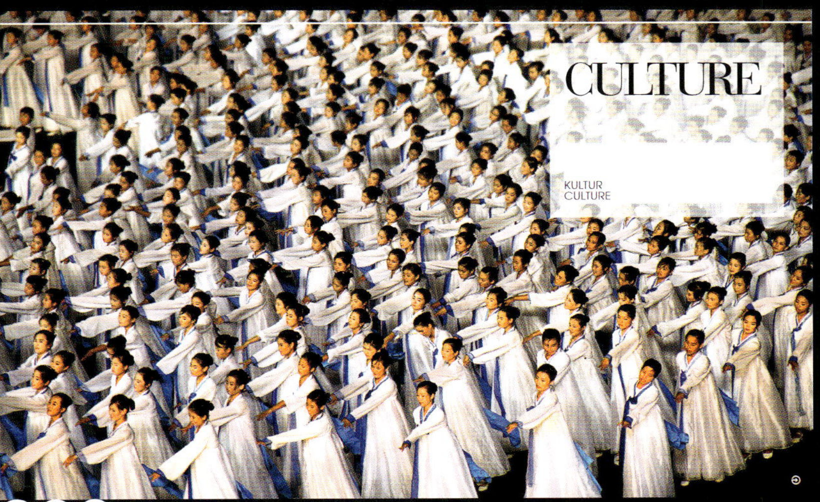

092

Arirang

Arirang

Arirang

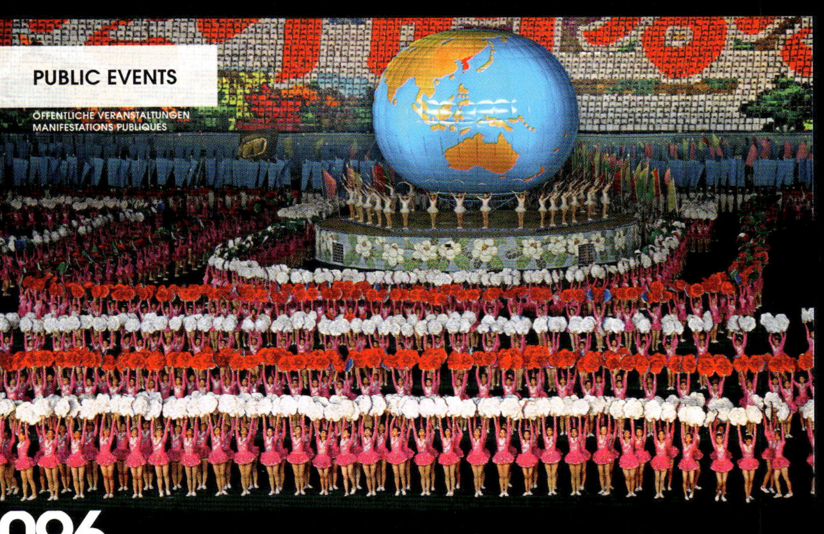

096

The Arirang Festival portrays North and South Korea as a single country at the center of the world, expressing North Korean yearning for reunification.

Der Wunsch nach Wiedervereinigung wird beim Arirang-Festival verbildlicht: Im Mittelpunkt der Welt sind Nord- und Südkorea wieder eins.

Le désir de réunification s'exprime en images au festival Arirang : la Corée réunifiée est représentée au centre du monde.

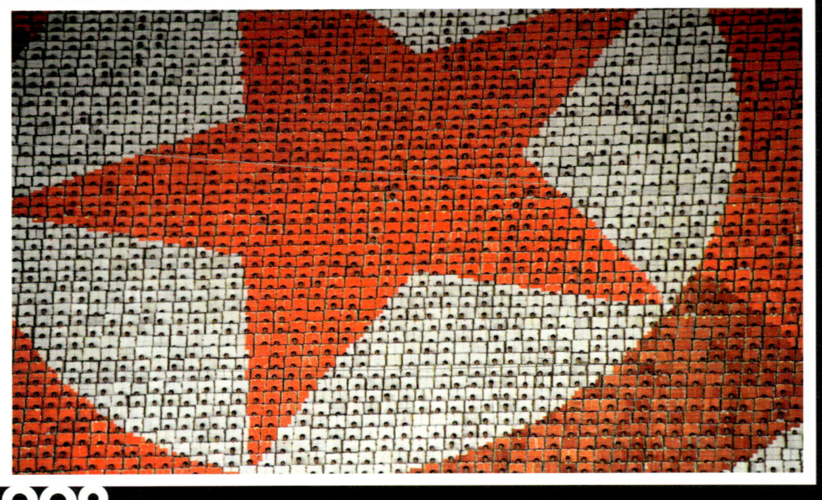

098

The five-point star symbolizes revolutionary traditions, and the white circle represents the Korean symbols of yin and yang, also known as taeguk.
Der fünfzackige Stern steht für die revolutionären Traditionen. Auf die ur-koreanischen Symbole Yin und Yang bzw. Taeguk verweist der weiße Kreis.
L'étoile à cinq branches renvoie aux traditions révolutionnaires, et le cercle blanc au taeguk, le yin et yang coréen.

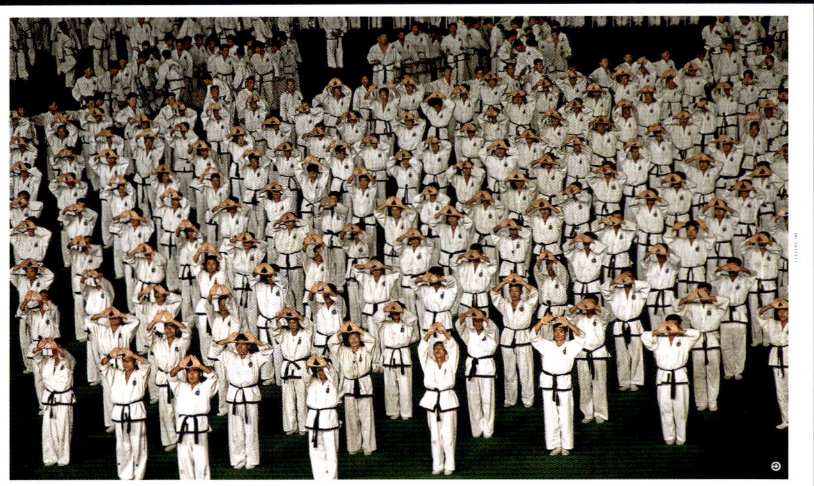

102

Taekwondo is a Korean martial art. It was banned during the Japanese occupation.
Taekwondo ist ein koreanischer Kampfsport. Unter der japanischen Besetzung wurde er im Land verboten.
Le taekwondo est un sport de combat d'origine coréenne. Sous l'occupation japonaise, sa pratique a été interdite.

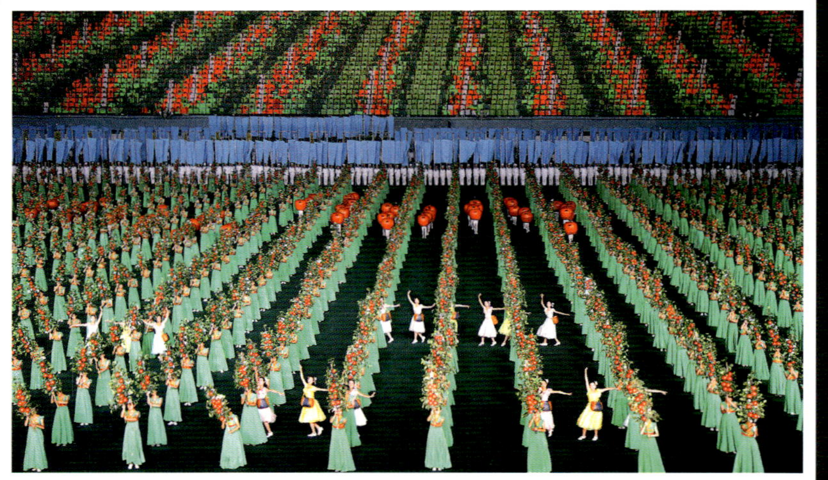

116

Both Korean governments petitioned UNESCO to add the Arirang folksong to its list of Intangible Cultural Heritage of Humanity.
Beide koreanischen Regierungen plädieren dafür, das Lied Arirang in die UNESCO-Liste des immateriellen Kulturerbes der Menschheit aufzunehmen.
Les gouvernements des deux Corées plaident en faveur de l'inscription du chant Arirang sur la liste du patrimoine culturel immatériel de l'humanité de l'UNESCO.

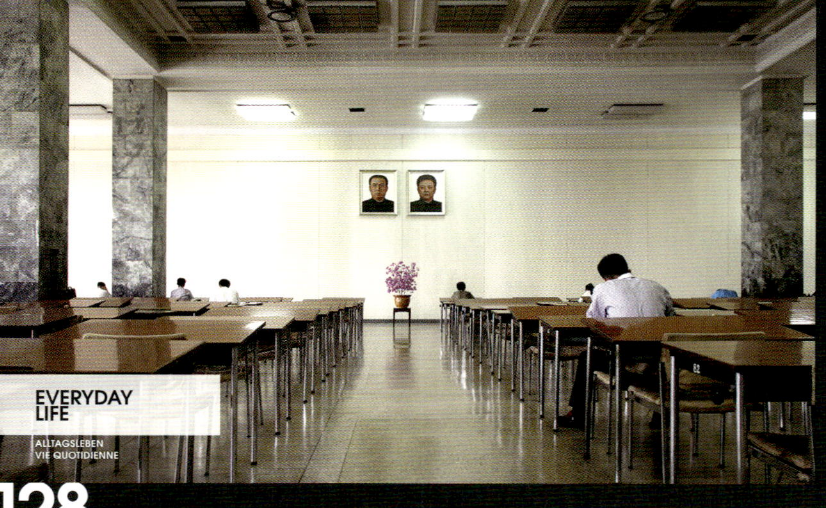

EVERYDAY LIFE
ALLTAGSLEBEN
VIE QUOTIDIENNE

128

Kim Il-sung received the title of "Eternal President" after his death, while his son and successor, Kim Jong-il, was promoted posthumously to "Eternal General Secretary." Under the law, North Korea is governed by two dead statesmen and one living leader, Kim Jong-un.
Kim Il-sung erhielt nach seinem Tod den Titel „Ewiger Präsident". Sein Sohn und Nachfolger Kim Jong-il wurde posthum zum „Ewigen Generalsekretär" ernannt. De jure wird das Land von zwei Toten und einem lebendigen Staatsmann, Kim Jong-un, regiert.
À titre posthume, Kim Il-sung a été proclamé « président éternel », et son fils et successeur Kim Jong-il « secrétaire général éternel » du parti du Travail. D'un point de vue juridique, la Corée du Nord est gouvernée par trois chefs d'État, deux défunts et un vivant, Kim Jong-un.

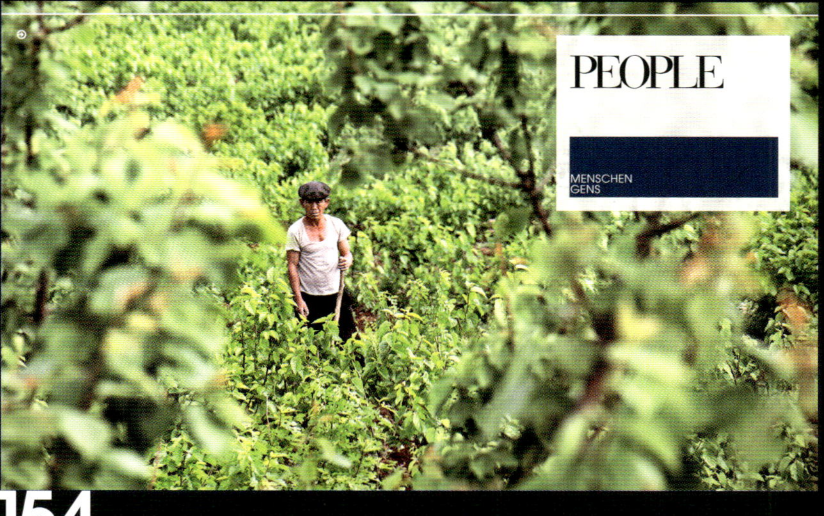

154

Laborer on an agricultural production cooperative. The 2,000 farmers who work the Migok Cooperative supposedly grow enough food to supply the entire region.
Arbeiter in einer landwirtschaftlichen Produktionsgenossenschaft. Angeblich versorgen die 2 000 Bauern der Kooperative Migok die gesamte Region.
Ouvrier agricole dans une coopérative de production. Les 2 000 paysans de la coopérative de Migok couvriraient les besoins de toute la région.

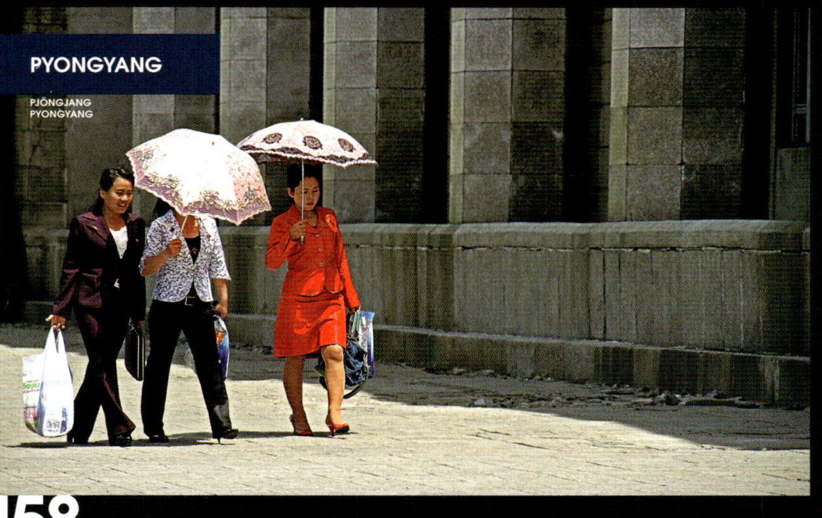

158

North Korea is relaxing its dress code. More and more women wear pants.
Gelockerte Kleidungsvorschriften. Immer mehr Frauen tragen auch Hosen.
Assouplissement du code vestimentaire : de plus en plus de femmes portent des pantalons.

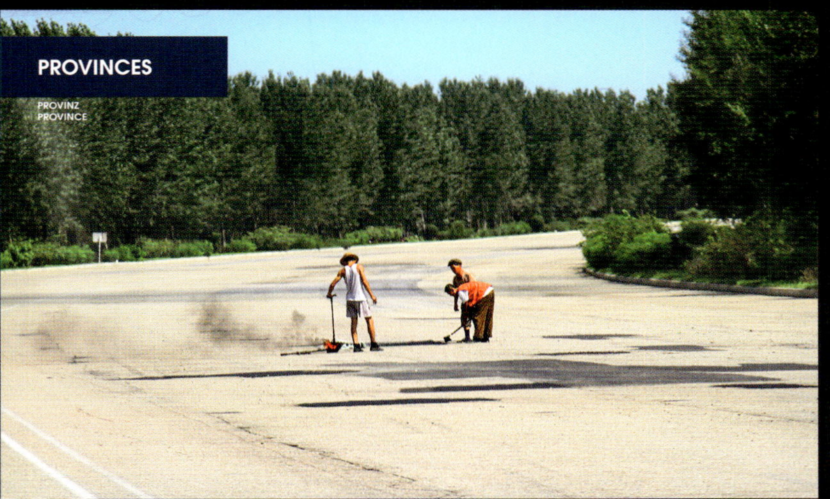

190

Building roads with manual labor. These workers seem to have missed the Industrial Revolution entirely.
Straßenbau ist Handarbeit. An den Arbeitern zog die Industrialisierung unbemerkt vorbei.
L’entretien des routes reste artisanal. L’industrialisation a oublié les ouvriers en chemin.

IMPRINT

ALL PHOTOGRAPHS BY JULIA LEEB, EXCEPT
P. 8 BY MARC AZOULAY; P. 84, P. 132 BY SIXTINA MACULAN;
PP. 218/219 BY GREGOR NICOLAI
PHOTO ASSISTANCE BY XENIA MACULAN

TEXTS JULIA LEEB, NIKO KARASEK, JR
COPY EDITING NICHOLAS THOMPSON (ENGLISH);
SIMONE NÖRLING, DERSCHÖNSTESATZ, KÖLN;
DR. SIMONE BISCHOFF; NADINE WEINHOLD (GERMAN);
CLAUDE CHECCONI (FRENCH)
TRANSLATIONS WESWITCH LANGUAGES,
HEIDI HOLZER (ENGLISH); CHRISTÈLE JANY (FRENCH);
WESWITCH LANGUAGES, ROMINA RUSSO LAIS (GERMAN)
EDITORIAL MANAGEMENT NADINE WEINHOLD
DESIGN & PREPRESS CHRISTIN STEIRAT
PHOTO EDITING XENIA MACULAN
COLOR SEPARATION ORT MEDIENVERBUND,
KREFELD, GERMANY
PRODUCTION DIETER HABERZETTL

FSC
www.fsc.org
MIX
Papier aus verantwortungsvollen Quellen
Paper from responsible sources
FSC® C005833